"POWERFUL AND ELEGANT . . .
A complicated story brilliantly told."
—*Kirkus Reviews*

"Elegantly written, revealingly detailed, and effortlessly narrated . . . Splendid work . . . Among her gifts, Weir has the two strengths essential to the historian: She writes with equal command about people as individuals and about the nature of power. Throughout, she is a canny and engaging guide to the unspeakably tangled workings of late-medieval political power. Military might, bloodlines, family alliances, regional loyalties, charisma, theatrics and image, revenge, greed, ruthlessness, and expediency all operated in tortuous formations and are here meticulously opened to scrutiny."

—Boston Globe

"[A] perfectly focused and beautifully unfolded account."

—Booklist (starred review)

"Stimulating . . . A well-written, entertaining narrative."

—Library Journal

by the same author

BRITAIN'S ROYAL FAMILIES:
THE COMPLETE GENEALOGY

THE SIX WIVES OF HENRY VIII

THE PRINCES IN THE TOWER

THE CHILDREN OF HENRY VIII

THE LIFE OF ELIZABETH I

ELEANOR OF AQUITAINE

The Wars of the Roses

Alison Weir

Ballantine Books • New York

Originally published as *Lancaster & York* in Great Britain in 1995 by Jonathan Cape, Random House, UK Ltd., London.

www.randomhouse.com/BB/

Library of Congress Catalog Card Number: 96-96058

ISBN 0-345-40433-5

Manufactured in the United States of America

First American Trade Paperback Edition: July 1996

20   19   18   17   16   15   14   13   12   11

This book is dedicated to
a much-loved uncle,
Rankin Lorimer Weir,
in commemoration of his ninetieth birthday.

It is also dedicated
in loving memory of
his beloved wife
Dorothy Weir.

And also to
my godson
David Jonathan Marston
on the occasion of his twenty-first birthday.

These matters be kings' games, as it were stage plays, and for the
more part played upon scaffolds.

Sir Thomas More

What about the getting of the garland, keeping it, losing and winning
it again, it hath cost more English blood than twice the winning of
France.

William Shakespeare, *King Richard III*

Contents

Illustrations

MAPS

Acknowledgements

I am indebted, as usual, to my editor, Jill Black, for her invaluable assistance and support, and also to Pascal Cariss of Jonathan Cape for all his hard work on a difficult manuscript. Thanks are also due to Cathie Arrington for her excellent picture research, and to my literary agent, Julian Alexander, for his constant encouragement.

I would also like to acknowledge, with grateful thanks, the help given me by my brother-in-law, Dr Ronald Weir of the University of York, in estimating monetary values in the fifteenth century. Lastly, I must once again thank my husband, Rankin, my children, John and Kate, and my parents, Doreen and James Cullen, for their forbearance, help and enthusiasm over the last two years.

Introduction

When I was working on my last book, *The Princes in the Tower*, I was aware that in some respects I was telling only half a story. I was writing about the final phase of that conflict so picturesquely named the Wars of the Roses, a conflict that lasted for more than thirty years, from 1455 to 1487. There were, in fact, two Wars of the Roses; the first, lasting from 1455 to 1471, was between the royal houses of Lancaster and York, and the second, from 1483 to 1487, was between the royal houses of York and Tudor. Having touched only briefly on the former in *The Princes in the Tower*, which describes in some detail the second phase of the wars, I felt that a prequel might be an interesting book with which to follow it. This present book, then, is the story of Lancaster and York and the first of the Wars of the Roses.

During the course of my research, I have studied many sources, both ancient and modern, and of the modern ones nearly all focus primarily upon the practical and military aspects of my subject. This book will naturally touch upon those matters, and in some detail in parts, but my main intention has been to portray the human side of history – the people and personalities involved, the chief protagonists in one of the most fascinating and long-drawn-out feuds in English history.

At the centre of this bloody faction fight was the pathetic figure of the mentally unstable Henry VI, whose ineptitude in government and mental incapacity gave rise to political instability, public discontent, and dissensions between the great landed magnates that in turn led ultimately to war and a bitter battle over the throne itself. Henry's chief rival was Richard Plantagenet, Duke of York, the man who should have been king, according to the law of primogeniture as it was then understood. After York's death, his claim to the throne was inherited by his son, who became King Edward IV, a ruthless charmer who would in the end bring about the ruin of the House of Lancaster.

This book is also the story of a woman's bitter and tenacious fight for her son's rights. Henry's queen, Margaret of Anjou – who was accused by her enemies of having planted a bastard in the royal nursery – took up arms in the cause of Lancaster and battled over many years and against seemingly insurmountable odds for the rights of her husband and child. This was remarkable in itself, for she was a woman in a violent man's world, in which most members of her sex were regarded as movable goods, chattels and political nonentities.

There are many other human faces in the unfolding pageant of treason and conflict. Margaret's son, Edward of Lancaster, inured to violence at an early age, shocked his contemporaries by his callous precocity. Richard Neville, Earl of Warwick – 'Warwick the Kingmaker' – was the archetypal over-mighty subject of the late Middle Ages, who raised and deposed kings, yet whose loyalty, in the final analysis, was only to himself. The Wars of the Roses would not only bring about the fall of a royal dynasty but also that of magnates such as Warwick.

I have tried to present the members of the royal houses of Lancaster and York as real people, identifiable by their personal characteristics and foibles, and not just names on a tangled family tree. The Beauforts, bastard descendants of John of Gaunt, lorded it as princes at court and, some said, in the Queen's bed. The Tudors were also royal issue of dubious lineage, and – like the Beauforts – were staunchly loyal to the House of Lancaster, whose heirs they later claimed to be. There are the kings – neurotic and extravagant Richard II, the usurper Henry IV, whose reign was marred by rebellions and crippling ill-health, and that cold warrior, Henry V, the people's hero, whose misjudged foreign policy led to disaster for his son, Henry VI. Then there are the queens: the chic, amoral Katherine of Valois, who found love with a Welsh squire after the death of her husband, Henry V; and Elizabeth Wydville, whose glacial beauty masked greed and ruthlessness. Besides these, our story is peopled with colourful, mysterious or tragic figures, from the notorious Jack Cade, who led a revolt, to the sadistic John Tiptoft, Earl of Worcester; and from a host of mighty lords to Warwick's fragile and ill-fated daughters, Isabel and Anne Neville. All were involved in one way or another in the conflict. This is indeed a history of factions, yet it was the people who made up those factions that make it a tale of absorbing interest.

The history of the Wars of the Roses has been told many times and by many historians, yet today it is unfashionable to follow the Tudor view that the origins of these wars lay in the deposition of Richard II, which took place more than fifty years before their outbreak. However, it is indeed possible to trace the roots of the conflict to that time, and in order to understand the causes of the Wars of the Roses and the dynastic heritage of the chief protagonists, we need to go back even further, to the founding of a race of magnates of royal blood by that most prolific of Plantagenet kings, Edward III. Thus this book tells not just the story of the Wars of the Roses but also that of the houses of Lancaster and York up to the year 1471.

Sources for this period are meagre and often ambiguous, yet much research has been done over the last hundred years to illuminate a little for us what is often described as the twilight world of the fifteenth century. Many misconceptions have been swept away, yet even so the dynastic conflict still confuses many. My aim has been throughout to eliminate that confusion and try to present the story in chronological sequence, clarifying the problems of the royal succession in an age in which no certain rules of inheritance applied. I have also tried to bring the world of the fifteenth century to life by introducing as much contemporary detail as space permits, in order to make the subject relevant to any reader, academic or otherwise. Chiefly, however, I have tried to re-tell an astonishing and often grim story of power struggles in high places that involved some of the most charismatic figures in English history.

This story begins in 1400 with the murder of one king, and ends in 1471 with the murder of another. One murder could be said to have been a direct result of the other. The story of what happened between 1400 and 1471, which is the story told in this book, answers the question: how?

Alison Weir
Surrey
February 1995

I

The Riches of England

In 1466 a Bohemian nobleman, Gabriel Tetzel, visited England and described it as 'a little, sea-girt garden'. The Italian scholar Polydore Vergil, writing at the end of the fifteenth century, was impressed by the country's

> delectable valleys, pleasant, undulating hills, agreeable woods, extensive meadows, lands in cultivation, and the great plenty of water springing everywhere. It is truly a beautiful thing to behold one or two thousand tame swans upon the River Thames. The riches of England are greater than those of any other country in Europe. There is no small innkeeper, however poor and humble he may be, who does not serve his table with silver dishes and drinking cups.

England, wrote Piero da Monte, papel envoy to the court of Henry VI, was 'a very wealthy region, abounding in gold and silver and many precious things, full of pleasures and delights'.

Much of the land was then covered by forest and woodland. Flocks of sheep were to be seen everywhere, for the prestigious wool trade was the life-blood of the kingdom. Cattle, too, were much in evidence, as were herds of deer. Arable land was often still divided into the open strips typical of feudal farming, but in many places there were abandoned villages, fallen into decay around ruined churches. The Warwickshire antiquarian John Rous speaks of 'the modern destruction of villages' being 'a national danger'. Many villages had disappeared after a large proportion of their inhabitants had died in the great epidemic of plague known as the Black Death of 1348-9. This depopulated some villages, and left others with too few inhabitants to cultivate the land. Those who remained were often able to negotiate cash wages in return for their labour and sometimes to exploit the social mobility that this new development gave them by moving elsewhere. Other villages had been swallowed up by farmers and landowners enclosing land that had formerly been common with hedges and fences, so as to provide grazing for wool-producing sheep.

There were 10,000 townships in England, but nearly all were the size of many modern villages. London was by far the largest city: around 60–75,000 people lived there. York, the second most important city, had 15,000 inhabitants, lesser towns perhaps 6,000 at most. Most towns and cities were bounded by the confines of their walls, and nestled in a rural environment. Trade centred on them and it was controlled by merchant guilds.

There was a network of roads linking towns and villages, but few minor roads. The upkeep of roads was generally the responsibility of local landowners, but they were often less than conscientious. In many parts of England travellers were obliged to hire local guides to see them to their destination, and roads were often rendered impassable by rain and mud. Contemporary records indicate that the climate was colder and wetter than it is now.

By 1485, England had a population of between 750,000 and 3,000,000. Estimates vary because the only available sources are the Poll Tax returns of 1381 and parliamentary records dated 1523-4. What is certain, however, is that England's population was shrinking during the fifteenth century, and also that many people moved to the great wool-cloth producing areas in Yorkshire, East Anglia and the West Country. About nine-tenths of the population worked on the land; Venetian visitors noted how few people inhabited the countryside, and commented that the population of the realm did 'not appear to bear any proportion to her fertility and riches'.

The Venetians saw the English as 'great lovers of themselves. They think that there is no other world than England.' Englishmen were deeply conservative: 'If the King should propose to change any old established rule, it would seem to every Englishman as if his life were taken away from him.' Foreigners, or 'strangers', as the insular English called them, were resented, and tended to live in tight communities, mainly in London, which was more cosmopolitan, or in East Anglia, where many Flemish weavers settled.

The Burgundian chronicler Philippe de Commines thought the English a choleric, earthy and volatile people, who nevertheless made good, brave soldiers. In fact he regarded their warlike inclinations as one of the chief causes of the Wars of the Roses. If they could not fight the French, he believed, they fought each other.

Many foreigners were impressed with English standards of living. One Venetian remarked that everyone wore very fine clothes, ate huge meals and drank vast amounts of beer, ale and wine. The roast beef, commented Vergil, 'is peerless'. The Venetian ambassador was guest of honour at a banquet given by the Lord Mayor of London which lasted ten hours and was attended by a thousand people. What impressed him most, though, was the absolute silence in which the proceedings were conducted. This reflected the current English preoccupation with manners and etiquette. His retinue were moved to comment upon the extreme politeness of the islanders.

Northerners and southerners were seen as two distinct peoples – southerners were perceived as sophisticated, better educated, civilised, treacherous, even cowardly, being said to resemble Homer's character Paris rather than the martial Hector. Northerners were regarded as brash, proud, fierce, warlike, violent, rapacious and uncouth. Their reputation for plundering was notorious, due no doubt to the primitive conditions in which they lived, for while southerners enjoyed luxuries, northerners subsisted on the breadline. As a result southerners feared northerners as much as northerners resented them.

As today, there were local variations in dialect, but in the fifteenth century these differed so much that even Kentishmen and Londoners had trouble understanding each other. Society was insular and localised and people referred to the county or shire in which they lived as their 'country'; people in other 'countries' were regarded as foreigners.

Most travellers from abroad commented on the alabaster beauty and charm of Englishwomen, and many were amazed by their forwardness. One Bohemian visitor, Nicholas von Poppelau, discovered that they were 'like devils once their desires were aroused'. He and others were enchanted, however, with the English custom of kissing on the mouth on greeting: 'To take a kiss in England is the equivalent of shaking hands elsewhere.'

In the fifteenth century Western Europe regarded itself as a united entity bonded by a universal Catholic Church and the philosophy of a divinely ordered universe. Late mediaeval man held a deep-rooted belief that society was also ordered by God for the good of humanity, and this concept of order expressed itself in a pyramidical hierarchy that had God enthroned at the summit, kings immediately beneath Him, then – in descending order – the nobility and princes of the Church, the knights and gentry, the legal and professional classes, merchants and yeomen, and at the bottom the great mass of peasants. Each man was born to his degree, and a happy man was one who did not question his place in life.

God's law was the natural law of the universe, as revealed in the Scriptures and in the divinely inspired canon and civil law of Church and State. Authority derived from God was sacrosanct. Peace and order could only be achieved when all classes of society were in harmony with each other. Disorder – such as heresy, rebellion, or trying to get above one's station in life – was regarded as the work of the Devil and therefore as mortal sin. It was held that one of the chief duties of a king was to ensure that each of his liege men lived in the degree to which he was born. Sumptuary laws passed during the period regulating dress and behaviour were intended to preserve order in society; that they were necessary is evidence that already some traditional ideals were being challenged.

By the late fourteenth century the structure of English feudal society was showing signs of crumbling as a result of the social revolution engendered by the Black Death. In the fifteenth century the unity of Christendom was undermined by a decline in respect for the papacy and the Church and by a burgeoning nationalism in the countries of Western Europe. Men were also questioning the old concept of order in society. In 1381, the leaders of the Peasants' Revolt had asked: 'When Adam delved and Eve span, who was then the gentleman?' In the following century a new materialism fostered by trade and private enterprise gave birth to the beginnings of capitalism, just as the old land-based economy was changing in response to economic demands.

Change did not take place overnight. The order imposed upon society by Church and State was still a potent force in the fifteenth century. The English Church was then part of the 'Christian Republic' of Catholic Europe, and was subject to papal laws and taxes. However, the princes of the Church enjoyed less power than in former centuries, and were gradually giving place to the magnates as a result of the increasing secularisation of government. The power of the bishops was more of a judicial than a spiritual nature, and many enjoyed a luxurious existence which was increasingly perceived as being at variance with the example set by Jesus Christ.

The fifteenth century was a time of stark contrasts within the English Church. On the one hand there was an escalating interest in sermons, homilies, pious moralising and mysticism, while on the other the heretic Lollards, inspired by the teachings of John Wycliffe, were attacking abuses in the Church and even questioning its authority in spiritual matters. Lollardy appealed to the poorer classes of society, but was so ruthlessly suppressed by successive kings that in most areas its influence became negligible.

Growing anti-clerical sentiment meant that the clergy were not immune to the general lawlessness of the age, and many cases of violence against men in holy orders were brought before the courts.

Religious faith was still as lively and deep-seated as ever. England boasted thousands of parish churches and was not for nothing known as 'the ringing isle'. There was a steady rise in the number of inmates of the monasteries and convents throughout the period, although there were few new foundations. However, chantries grew steadily in number. Pious folk would leave money in their wills to found chantry chapels in which priests would say masses in perpetuity for the salvation of the soul of the departed and his family. Some of these foundations were very large and comprised whole colleges of priests serving collegiate churches which housed several chantry endowments. Many parish churches were converted into such colleges and beautified accordingly.

The transitory nature of life on earth was an ever-recurring religious theme. Given the high rate of infant mortality and relatively low life expectancy, death was an accepted part of life. Men lived to an average of around fifty, with about one fifth surviving to their sixties. Women, as a result of the perils of childbearing, could only expect to live to an average of thirty, while it is possible that up to half of all children did not reach twenty. It was held that those who suffered in this world would receive their reward in Heaven. Death was the great leveller and all, kings and popes together with merchants and peasants, must one day be called to account before the seat of Judgement. The general preoccupation with death manifested itself in the pictures, literature and tomb sculpture of the time: the rich were sometimes buried in tombs with two effigies, the upper one showing the person as in life, nobly attired, while the lower one portrayed a rotting corpse, eaten by life-like worms.

Heaven was perceived as a magnificent and incorrupt royal court, to which the devout and godly would be admitted. Hell – as revealed in vivid Doom paintings on church walls – was an ever-present and very real deterrent to sinners.

People believed that the hand of God directed and guided the affairs of princes. There was also a firm conviction that God bestowed victory in battle to vindicate the right of the victor. A king was the Lord's anointed, hallowed at his coronation with holy oil. His chief functions were to protect his people by defending them against their enemies, to govern with justice and mercy, and to preserve and enforce the law of the land. 'To fight and to judge are the office of a king,' wrote Lord Chief Justice Sir John Fortescue in the 1460s. The qualities required were courage, wisdom and integrity, and the character of the sovereign was therefore all-important and on it depended the security and well-being of his subjects. Late mediaeval monarchy was a highly personal system of government: in this period kings ruled as well as reigned, and they wielded vast power.

Over the centuries, however, the administration of government had become increasingly cumbersome, and kings had delegated more and more of it to the growing number of departments of state within the royal household. These all carried out their particular functions in the king's name while the monarch retained direct responsibility for foreign policy, the exercise of the royal prerogative and patronage, and control of the nobility. Kings were in theory at liberty to do as they pleased, but it was widely recognised that this 'liberty' was bound by the constraints of law and justice. The king's 'grace' enabled him to adopt new ideas while preserving the ancient customs and traditions of the realm. The kingdom of England was regarded as the property of the monarch but, as Fortescue pointed out, although the royal power was supreme, kings could not make laws or impose taxes without the consent of Parliament.

A king was not only expected to protect and defend his realm but also had to be seen as a competent warrior. A king who inclined towards peace courted adverse public opinion, for most people placed great value on success in arms and the glorification of the nation's reputation.

English kings of the fifteenth century did not maintain a standing army but relied on their nobility to provide them with troops when necessary. Hence it was important for a monarch to maintain good relations with the aristocracy and gentry, who might, if sufficiently provoked, use the armed strength at their disposal against him. It was also the duty of the sovereign to prevent power struggles between magnates, especially where these affected the stability of the realm. As we shall see, failure to do this could lead to dire consequences.

The people and 'common weal' of the realm were dependent on the monarchy producing heirs who were fit and able to rule and who could command the respect and loyalty of their subjects. Above all, a king's title to the throne had to be beyond dispute, for this could and did lead to civil war, with all its attendant horrors. Thanks to the Wars of the Roses, by the end of the period covered by this book a king's title to the throne had come not to matter as much as his ability to hold on to that throne and to govern effectively.

In the late mediaeval period the law of succession to the throne was ill-defined. Generally, primogeniture – the succession of the eldest son and his heirs – was the rule, but there were other important elements involved, such as recognition by the lords spiritual and temporal and, later, the ability to provide stable government.

Since the twelfth century, when Matilda, daughter of Henry I, had made a disastrous attempt to wrest the crown from her cousin, King Stephen, the English had been averse to the idea of a female ruler, believing that the concept was against nature and that women were incapable of good government. However, the law of the Salic Franks, which barred succession through a female, did not apply in England, where there was no statutory bar to a woman succeeding to the throne or transmitting a claim to her descendants. In fact, the issue had never been put to the test because, until the fifteenth century, the House of Plantagenet had produced a sufficiency of male heirs.

Apart from their distrust of female rulers, the English also feared the political instability of minorities, which occurred on the thankfully rare occasions when a child succeeded to the throne. Prior to the accession of Richard II in 1377 there had been only two minorities since the Norman Conquest of 1066; both had witnessed political turmoil.

From 1399 to 1499 the crown became the object of feuds, wars and conspiracies, not because of a dearth of heirs, but because there were too many powerful magnates with a claim to the throne. During this period a new and disturbing element became involved in determining the royal succession: the prevalence of might over right. This brought a new awareness of the lack of statute law governing the succession and a debate as to whether the rights of a senior heir general, with a claim transmitted through a female, could take precedence over the rights of a junior heir male. But in the final analysis strength and success were what counted: an effective ruler was more likely to remain on the throne, however dubious his title. Weak or tyrannical rulers met with disaster.

During the fifteenth century some attempts were made to regulate the laws of succession, but the highest legal authorities in the land, fearful of reprisals from interested magnates, repeatedly refused to pronounce conclusively on so weighty a matter, saying that the issue could not be determined by reference to common law.

The Wars of the Roses were primarily wars between the great magnates. The magnate class consisted of a small number of dukes – usually related to the royal house – marquesses and earls, and a great number of barons, knights and gentry. These were the men who owned most of the landed wealth of the kingdom and who exercised the greatest influence in their own territories, where they were respected and often feared.

John Russell, Bishop of Lincoln and Lord Chancellor in the 1480s, looked upon the English nobility as the rock and firm ground in a storm-tossed sea. Upon their shoulders lay the responsibility for the government of England. The nobility looked to the crown for promotion and rewards in return for services rendered in politics, in the field of battle, in the administrative departments of the royal household, in the diplomatic service, or in local government.

Rank was everything. During the Wars of the Roses, experienced commanders deferred to teenage boys simply because the latter were of the blood royal. The higher the rank, the richer the lord. A great magnate such as the Duke of York enjoyed an annual income of above £3000.* A baron could expect around £700 per annum, a knight anything between £40 and £200. The cost of building a defensive castle, such as Caister in Norfolk, was in the region of £6000.

From the fourteenth century onwards, the number of magnates had diminished. Wars, plagues, feuds and tournaments had led to many male lines dying out. Titles were frequently transferred via the marriages of heiresses, and inheritances grew consequently larger. By the fifteenth century the magnates, though fewer in number, had wider lands, greater wealth, and more power than ever before. Very few of the old Anglo-Norman families were left, but prominent families of the period – the Montacutes of Salisbury, the Courtenays of Devon, the Percies of Northumberland, the Nevilles, FitzAlans, Beauchamps, Staffords and Mortimers – were descendants of barons and knights, and were almost indistinguishable from this group, from which they frequently chose marriage partners. Many knightly

---

* 1450 values may be roughly related to 1995 values by multiplying by 234. Thus the Duke of York's income would be equivalent to approximately £702,000 in 1995 prices. The multiplier of 234 is derived from the following calculation:

1 The price of a quarter of wheat in 1450 compared to 1914, which gives a multiplier of 4.68.

2 The change in the price level between 1914 and 1995, which gives a multiplier of 50. After 1914 wheat is not a very useful indicator of prices (food expenditure dropped with rising incomes and the 1930s tariffs on wheat distort prices). Reference may therefore be made to the retail price index for 1914 to 1995, which rises 50 fold: 4.68 x 50 = 234. For this calculation I am indebted to Dr R. B. Weir, Provost of Derwent College at the University of York and lecturer in economic history.

families such as the Tiptofts and Bonvilles enjoyed substantial lands and influence, and would in the fifteenth century be elevated to the peerage. They would also look to increase their wealth by inter-marrying with rich, mercantile families.

By the mid-century many of the great magnates were creating considerable wealth for themselves by investing in trade, while judicial marriage alliances were calculated to extend still further their lands and influence. Thus evolved what Lord Chief Justice Fortescue referred to as the 'over-mighty subject', who could command the loyalty and support of a huge army of tenants and retainers. Indeed, the prestige of a nobleman during the period came to be measured by the size of his private army and his 'affinity', those who were bound by contract to serve him.

By the reign of Henry VI (1422–61), feudalism had given way to what is often now described as 'bastard feudalism'. Men of all classes had profited financially from the Hundred Years War with France, and when they returned home some used their profits to establish landed families. However, survival depended upon earning sufficient income to support such a lifestyle, and many men placed themselves under the protection of a powerful magnate, not as feudal vassals who swore allegiance to the lord and in return for his protection performed knight service when required, but as liveried retainers under contract. These contracts, or indentures, would bind both parties for a set period, often for life. The retainer became a member of the lord's affinity, would wear his livery – a uniform and badge – and accompany him on military campaigns. In return, the magnate would assure the retainer of 'good lordship', which meant protection from his enemies and payment of an income known as a pension. The retainer could also expect rewards for services rendered, and these were often substantial, such as land or lucrative offices.

By means of this system, the wealthy magnates were able to gather around themselves affinities that could be used as formidable fighting forces. Without the existence of such private armies the Wars of the Roses could not have taken place.

Personal loyalty played little part in the new relationship between lord and retainer. A lord could only command a large following if he was rich, successful and influential. Self-interest, greed and the prospects of advancement were determining factors, 'for the people', wrote Fortescue, 'will go with him that best may sustain and reward them'.

Bastard feudalism had its origins in the thirteenth century, but its growth had been facilitated by the decline of feudalism, the Hundred

Years War, and the economic and social effects of the Black Death. By the end of the fourteenth century the government was already concerned about the effect this trend was having on the administration of justice at local level, and legislation was passed restricting the wearing of liveries. Up until the reign of Henry VI, however, the nobility were more preoccupied with the wars with France than with building up power bases at home. But by 1450 it was becoming alarmingly apparent that bastard feudalism was a threat, not only to local society, but also to the stability of central government itself. The private armies of noblemen were holding the countryside to ransom by bribery, extortion and violence, and subverting law and order by intimidation and threats, often with the backing of the great lords who employed them, whose duty it was to maintain the King's peace. This led to a lessening of confidence in the judicial system. Justice, it seemed, was available only to those who could pay enough to secure a 'right verdict'.

Fortescue warned of 'the perils that may come to the King by over-mighty subjects. Certainly there may be no greater peril than to have a subject equivalent to himself.' Some magnates were 'of livelihood and power like a king' already, and this did not augur well for the peace of the realm.

Some magnates were well-educated, cultivated men who carried out their duties conscientiously. Like all their caste, they were committed to the ideal of the triangular power structure presided over by the monarchy and to their time-honoured right to act as the king's chief advisers. The fourteenth-century French chronicler Jean Froissart had praised the English nobility for being 'extremely courteous, friendly and approachable', but in the fifteenth century this was not always the case. Some were rough, violent men, whose brutish instincts were barely concealed by the trappings of chivalry. A few, like John Tiptoft, Earl of Worcester, were notorious sadists.

Many aristocrats lacked a sense of political responsibility. They were often at loggerheads with each other, or deeply divided by factional interests. Those in positions of the greatest power were frequently corrupt, avaricious and partisan, ruthlessly competing for royal patronage, jealously guarding their own interests and sparing little concern for those weaker than themselves. 'The officers of the realm peeled the poor people and did many wrongs,' wrote a chronicler in the 1450s.

The chief magnates rarely scrupled to exploit the generosity of a weak king, such as Henry VI, snatching as many Crown lands, honours and lucrative appointments as they could, and growing ever richer while the Crown sank into a morass of debt. Without a firm hand to curb their behaviour, these magnates were virtually out of control, and that posed another threat to the security of government.

The fifteenth century was an age of escalating change in society. The middle classes were growing more prosperous and influential, and some were even defying established custom by intermarrying with the gentry and knightly classes, while others were using the profits from mercantile enterprise to buy themselves a standard of living hitherto permitted only to those of noble birth. At the same time, the nobility were dabbling in trade – the dukes of Suffolk were actually descended from a Hull merchant. The lower classes, fuelled by the teachings of the Lollards, were increasingly questioning the established order. With these challenges came a degree of social anarchy and a lessening of respect for authority and the law.

From the beginning of Henry VI's reign complaints about corruption, public disorder, riots and the maladministration of justice grew ever more vociferous. By the 1450s the situation had deteriorated so badly that there were urgent demands from all strata of society that something be done by the government to halt the decay. Law and order were in a state of collapse and crime was on the increase. Many soldiers returning from the wars in France found little to welcome them at home. Destitute, inured to violence and freed from military discipline, they frequently took to a life of brigandage and law-breaking. Some were employed by rich lords to intimidate, assault and even murder their enemies, who were often men of the gentry class and unable to defend themselves from armed thugs employed by their social superiors.

The blame for the endemic disorder may be laid squarely at the door of Henry VI, whose responsibility it was to control his magnates and enforce law and order. But the King, far from trying to right the wrongs suffered by his subjects, did nothing. The justices of the peace, who administered justice in his name, continued to be intimidated or bribed, and while the English were justly proud of their legal system and flourishing legal profession, they were by no means blind to its abuse by the great, recognising that the perversion of justice was the greatest evil of the age.

The chronicler John Hardyng wrote:

> In every shire, with jacks and sallets clean,
> Misrule doth rise and maketh neighbours war.

Most criminals appear to have got away with their crimes. They might be hauled before the justices, if they were caught at all, but many were acquitted, and even if they were not, the Lancastrian kings, especially Henry VI, issued thousands of pardons.

Capital punishment was the penalty for treason – reckoned by far the most heinous crime – murder and theft of items worth more than a shilling (5p). The prescribed punishment for traitors was hanging, drawing and quartering, a barbaric procedure in use since the thirteenth century. Traitors of noble birth usually escaped the full horrors of this method of execution and were dispatched by decapitation, but the lowlier-born were not so fortunate. Some traitors did not stand trial, but were condemned to forfeiture of life, titles and property by Acts of Attainder passed in Parliament. A large proportion of these attainders were later reversed, enabling the accused or his heirs to be restored 'in blood', or to their inheritance .

An Italian visitor observed, 'It is the easiest thing to get a person thrown into prison in this country.' Prisons were occupied mainly by debtors and common felons, while those who had committed crimes against the state were usually lodged in the Tower of London or other fortresses. There was no police force. The maintenance of law and order was the responsibility of the sheriffs and their local constables, who were often either corrupt or ineffectual.

The prevailing disorder of the period did not stem the creation of wealth by the merchant class. After 1450 the wool trade slowly declined in importance, but at the same time there was increasing demand abroad for other English products, such as woollen cloth, tin, lead, leather and alabaster carvings from Nottinghamshire.

The English-owned port of Calais in north-west France was the chief market-place for England's wool. A monopoly was enforced by the Merchants of the Staple, who sold the wool exported there to merchants from all over Europe. The stability of Calais was all-important to the merchant classes, but it was undermined during the Wars of the Roses when feuding magnates regarded it as a refuge in exile or, more alarmingly, as a springboard for invasion of England.

Many merchants, especially those in London, grew rich by importing luxury goods from the Mediterranean, which was a centre for commodities from even further afield – spices, medicines, paper, oriental silks, manuscripts, armour, wines, cotton, sugar, velvets and precious stones. For centuries the English had imported wine from Bordeaux and Gascony, and mercifully, with the cessation of the Hundred Years War and the victory of the French, the trade did not cease or suffer unduly.

Fortescue was of the opinion that 'the common people of this land are the best fed and the best clad of any nation'. Serfdom had declined after the Black Death, and a shortage of labour had resulted in magnates and other landowners being willing to pay men to work on their land. Government efforts to impose wage controls had not succeeded, and hired labour was much in demand. Many lords had vacant tenancies for lease, since leaseholds were rapidly replacing feudal service, and rents were attractively low.

With the disappearance of serfdom the peasants enjoyed greater freedom and mobility, but their lot was often a gruelling one, especially in winter when food was scarce and there was little protection from the cold. Many peasants lived in tiny cottages with one or two rooms, earthen floors, a small window and basic items of furniture. Their livestock lived with them. Many existed in grinding poverty and relied on the charity dispensed by the Church or rich lay persons.

Few peasants suffered hardship, however, as a result of the agricultural depression that lasted from the late fourteenth century to around 1460, during which much land was converted into pasture for sheep. The depression led to falls in rents and prices, which meant that the peasant class, whose labour was so much in demand, had never before been so prosperous. Many farms fell into ruin, especially in the north, and land could be had cheaply. A phenomenon of the age was the self-made peasant who had managed to buy his own land and become prosperous. One such man from Wiltshire gained rich profits from making woollen cloth and left £2000 in his will, an enormous sum for the time.

The average peasant earned between £5 and £10 a year; in 1450 labourers were paid 4d a day, while skilled craftsmen earned between 5d and 8d. It cost around £3.4s.0d. (£3.20) to build a cottage. Food, however, was half the price it had been in the fourteenth century, with eggs at 5d for a hundred, milk or beer 1d a gallon, and luxuries such as red wine 10d a gallon, sugar 1s.6d. (7½p) per pound, and pepper 2s (10p) per pound.

The government of the country was carried out by the king's Council, which sat almost continuously and was made up of lords both temporal and spiritual as well as able men of lesser rank. The king sometimes presided over the Council but his presence was not always necessary to its smooth functioning; however, all its business was carried out in his name.

The Council's chief functions were to assist the king in the formulation of policy and to carry out the day-to-day business of government. The long minority of Henry VI strengthened the prestige and authority of the Council as well as that of the magnates, giving both a prolonged taste of sovereign power that would not easily be relinquished.

It was the Council that governed the realm, not Parliament. Parliament was not as important, although its power was increasing throughout the fifteenth century. It comprised the three estates of the realm: the lords spiritual and temporal and the commons, who were represented by knights from the shires and burgesses from the boroughs. Parliament's chief functions were the granting of taxation and the consideration of petitions. It was also the supreme court of justice.

The king could summon and dismiss Parliament at will, but there were occasions when he could not function without it. Making war was something 'the King cannot undertake without assembling his Parliament', wrote Commines. 'It is a very just and laudable institution and therefore the kings are stronger and better served. The King declares his intentions and asks for aid from his subjects; he cannot raise any tax in England except for an expedition to France or Scotland or some other comparable cause. They will grant them very willingly, especially for going to France!' Nor could new laws be passed without the consent of Parliament. Elections, however, were frequently rigged, and the magnates did not shrink from packing Parliament with men of their affinity when their own interests might be at stake.

Parliament could be summoned to meet anywhere in the kingdom, but it usually assembled in Henry III's wonderful Painted Chamber in the Palace of Westminster. Sometimes the Lords would gather in the White Chamber or the Marculf Room in the palace, while the Commons would meet in the refectory of Westminster Abbey.

The administration of government was centred on the enormously influential royal household, which consisted of the court and various departments of state, chiefly the Chancery, the Exchequer, the Chamber and the Wardrobe. These were responsible for the legal, financial and administrative aspects of government, as well as providing for the court and the ceremonial and personal requirements of the king and his family, even to the provision of horses, clothing and food. The royal household was therefore the political nerve-centre of the kingdom and its officers enjoyed a tremendous degree of influence simply by being in close proximity to the monarch.

The capital city and chief seat of government was, of course, London, which then extended to approximately one square mile to the north of the River Thames, and was bounded by a wall with seven gates, all of which were locked at night. The city's main defences were centred on the Tower of London – fortress, palace and state prison – which had not yet acquired its later sinister reputation.

London had a single bridge, built of white stone across nineteen arches and lined with houses, shops and a chapel. The Thames was London's main thoroughfare, and travel through the city was quickest by barge or wherry, since the narrow, malodorous streets were frequently congested by carts, crowds and livestock. There were therefore many landing stages along the banks of the river, and hundreds of boatmen plied their trade in waters already crowded with merchant ships and private barges. The average fare paid by travellers was 1d. Along the river were quays, docks, warehouses, wharfs and cranes, and further along, by the Strand, gardens swept down from the mansions of the nobility to the river, each with its own private jetty.

Visitors were struck by the noble buildings – the perpendicular splendour of old St Paul's Cathedral, the Guildhall, the fine houses of the great, the Palace of Westminster, the nearby abbey, and no less than eighty city churches. Suburbs were already growing outside the walls, but they were small developments, and in 1483 the Italian observer Dominic Mancini was struck by the pastoral peace and fertile green fields that surrounded the capital.

London was governed by its elected Lord Mayor, aldermen and Court of Common Council, all drawn from the ranks of wealthy merchants, men who were jealous of the city's privileges and exerted considerable political influence. 'It all belongs to craftsmen and merchants,' observed Mancini. The city of London was to play a decisive part in the Wars of the Roses, and its support – or the lack of it – for the various contenders for the throne would be crucial.

London was described by one foreign visitor as the busiest of cities, while a Milanese envoy believed it was 'the wealthiest city in Christendom'. However, it was a Scotsman, William Dunbar, who most aptly summed up the spirit of London, in a poem written in the 1490s:

> Strong be thy walls that about thee stand,
> Wise be the people that within thee dwell,
> Fresh be thy river with his lusty strands,
> Blithe be thy churches, well-sounding be thy bells;
> Rich be thy merchants, in substance that excels,
> Fair be their wives, right lovesome, white and small,
> Clear be thy virgins, lusty under kirtles:
> London, thou art the flower of cities all!

The fifteenth century was a period in which people's standards of living rose considerably. Surviving churches, castles and manor houses, as well as inventories of furnishings and property, bear witness to this.

In spite of the unsettled times few heavily fortified castles were built, and existing castles were modernised by the addition of great halls, large windows and luxurious domestic accommodation. The rich built themselves country mansions and manor houses that satisfied their need for comfort and aesthetic pleasure. These houses were not built with defence in mind, although many sported defensive features such as moats, crenellations and gatehouses as features of decoration. This trend in building shows a certain confidence in the long-term stability of the country, and it continued even throughout the Wars of the Roses, serving as proof that those wars had less effect on the social and cultural life of the nation at large than might have been imagined from a reading of the works of contemporary chroniclers.

In addition to a great hall, most houses were now built with a number of smaller chambers for family use, reflecting a new taste for privacy. The fireplace replaced the open hearth in the centre of a room, windows became larger, letting in more light, and often had carved frames of wood or stone; glass was less of a luxury than it had been, and wealthy families would commission stained-glass windows, often depicting coats of arms, for their new homes. Furnishings, such as tester beds, settles, tables, stools, chests and cupboards, were few but of good quality and fashioned from solid wood. Elaborately carved beds with rich hangings, woven tapestries or painted hangings, and utensils of gold and silver plate were often bequeathed in wills.

This was the great age of church building and adornment. English craftsmen were particularly skilled in carving wood and alabaster, making decorative grilles and producing jewel-coloured glass. It was also a growth period for English music. The Yorkist court was famed for its musicians and for its patronage of composers. The carol, originally a piece of music composed in honour of any great occasion in the calendar, which could be sung and danced to, was particularly fashionable. Many of today's most popular Christmas carols date from this period.

English was by this time the language of all classes, and many books were written in the vernacular. The nobility were mostly able to speak French, which had been the language of the court and the legal profession until the late fourteenth century, and most educated people were taught Latin, which was still the international language of the Church and of Christendom. There was a steady growth in public literacy throughout the period. Books, although luxury items because they were hand-produced, were more readily available and no longer confined to the libraries of the Church or the universities. Many nobles, knights and merchants now collected books, and some amassed quite large libraries. The fifteenth century produced no great literary figures of the stature of Chaucer, whose works were still widely read. The foremost writers of the period were John Gower, Thomas Hoccleve and John Lydgate.

Many schools were founded, most administered by the Church, although some lay persons were founding secular grammar schools in towns and cities. The régime in all schools was strict and followed the precept 'Spare the rod and spoil the child'. Whereas the sons of the nobility had long received an education in both military and academic skills, the rising middle classes now also wanted their sons reared 'to cunning learning and erudition', because they knew it was possible to secure worldly advancement with a sound education. Many went on to university and thence into the Church. There was a planned expansion in the universities, mainly to provide sufficient academics to meet the needs of the Church, but also to provide more secular opportunities for ambitious young men.

Formal education was provided for boys only. Women were seen as the inferior sex and regarded as the chattels of men. The author of *The Goodman of Paris* (c. 1393) advised wives to behave like faithful dogs in order to please their husbands, and Margaret Paston of Norfolk referred to John Paston as 'right worshipful husband' in her letters. The husband was lord of his family as God reigned supreme over the universe. The chief duty of a wife, therefore, was to be submissive. If there was discord in a marriage, or infertility, people automatically assumed it was the wife's fault. Women had virtually no freedom beyond that which their fathers or husbands allowed them. Within these confines, however, many managed businesses, shops, farms or noble estates, and proved themselves the equal to men.

Marriages were arranged for social, financial or territorial advantage. The concept of marrying for love was an alien one, hence the outrage in 1464 when King Edward IV impulsively married a commoner who refused to be his mistress.

A wife was expected to manage her husband's household, and his estates in his absence, set a good example to her children and servants, and – above all – bear sons to ensure that her lord's estates remained within the family. Daughters were useful for securing marriage alliances, but every man of property wanted a son to inherit it. The price women paid for this was high. Many died in childbirth or worn out by repeated pregnancies by the time they were thirty, the average life expectancy of women at this time.

Marriage was regarded by the Church as a necessary evil, following the dictum of St Paul, who said it was better to marry than to burn. Most people married, unless they were apprentices or in holy orders, and child marriages were not uncommon. One heiress, Grace de Saleby, had been thrice married by the age of eleven; John Rigmardin was a bridegroom at three years old, and thirteen-year-old John Bridge, after being put to bed with his bride on their wedding night, bawled to go home to his father.

Fifteenth-century children were by no means spoiled. Their elders enforced strict codes of behaviour and manners. and demonstrations of affection were rare. Parental love expressed itself in worldly expectations. Children were expected to be wholly obedient to their parents, and the slightest fault was punished by a beating, in the child's own interests. One Venetian ambassador commented, 'The want of affection in the English is strongly manifested toward their children.' When he asked some parents why they were so harsh, 'they answered that they did it in order that their children might learn better manners'.

Upper-class children, even the heirs to estates, were rarely brought up at home but were sent at an early age to be educated and reared in the household of some noble and influential lord, who would hopefully secure future preferment for them. Few of these children then returned home. 'The girls are settled in marriage by their patrons and the boys make the best marriages they can.' Childhood ended early. Most children were married, apprenticed or in the cloister or university by their early teens.

The fifteenth century was a turbulent age, and that turbulence manifested itself in England in the civil wars known as the Wars of the Roses, a conflict that was by no means continuous but which dragged on intermittently for a period of thirty years and more. This book tells the story of the struggle between Lancaster and York.

Part I

The Origins of the Conflict

2

A Race of Magnates

Since 1154 England had been ruled by the House of Plantagenet and the succession to the crown had passed fairly peaceably from father to son or brother to brother. The Plantagenet kings, who were reputed by legend to have descended from the Devil, were mostly dynamic men and outstanding leaders, energetic, warlike, courageous, just and wise. They were distinguished by aquiline features, red hair and a ferocious temper truly terrible to behold.

Edward III (1327–77) was the archetypal Plantagenet king – tall, proud, majestic and handsome, with chiselled features and long hair and beard. Born in 1312, he was only fourteen when his father, Edward II, was deposed and murdered, and eighteen when he assumed personal control of the government of England.

In 1328 Edward married Philippa of Hainault, who bore him thirteen children. His occasional infidelities did not affect this happy and successful marriage, which lasted forty years. Edward had inherited the notorious Plantagenet temper, but the Queen exerted a restraining influence on him; in a famous incident in 1347, she successfully interceded with him for the lives of the doomed burghers of Calais, which Edward had captured after a long siege.

Edward lived in great splendour in the royal residences which he enlarged and beautified, and his court was a renowned centre of chivalry. He had a special reverence for St George, the patron saint of England, and did much to promote his cult. In 1348, he founded the Order of the Garter, which was dedicated to the saint.

Above all, Edward desired to win glory by great deeds. In 1338, concerned by French incursions into his duchy of Aquitaine, in which was centred England's prosperous wine trade, he laid claim to the throne of France, asserting that he was the true heir by virtue of descent from his mother, who was sister of the last Capetian king.

However, the Salic Law, which barred women from succeeding or transmitting a claim to the throne, obtained in France, and the French had already crowned Edward's cousin, Philip of Valois, who was the male heir of the Capets.

Edward's quartering of the lilies of France with the leopards of England on his coat of arms led to the conflict that later became known as the Hundred Years War because it dragged on intermittently for more than a century. Under Edward's leadership, the English at first scored several victories: Sluys in 1340, Crécy in 1346 and Poitiers in 1356. These were the first important battles in which the English longbowmen demonstrated their supremacy over the heavily armoured French cavalry. However, the early successes of the English were not sustained, and in 1360 Edward was forced to return some of the lands he had conquered under the terms of the Treaty of Brétigny, which brought the first phase of the war to a close. When Edward died, apart from the duchy of Aquitaine, all that remained of his French territories were five towns and the land around Calais known as the Pale.

Edward III's reign saw many changes. Parliament, now divided into Lords and Commons, began to meet regularly and to assert its authority through financial controls. Parliament's principal function at this date was to vote taxation, and in this respect it did not always co-operate with the King's wishes. In 1345 the law courts became permanently established in London and no longer followed the King's person on progress around the kingdom. In 1352 treason was defined by statute for the first time. In 1361 the office of Justice of the Peace was created – gentlemen of good standing in their locality were appointed magistrates – and the following year English replaced French as the official language of the law courts. Edward's reign also witnessed the rise to prosperity of the merchant classes and the beginning of the spread of education among laymen.

The King was a great patron of artists, authors and architects. The origins of the English Perpendicular style in architecture may be traced to his reign. This was also the period of the first great names in English literature: the poets Richard Rolle, Geoffrey Chaucer, John Gower and William Langland. The latter's epic poem *Piers Plowman* is an indictment of the oppression suffered by the poor after the Black Death, and of Alice Perrers, the rapacious mistress whose sway over Edward in his declining years was notorious.

Edward died in 1377. The face of the wooden effigy carried at his funeral, which is still preserved in Westminster Abbey, is a death mask, and the effects of the stroke which killed the King may be seen in the drawn-down corner of the mouth.

Edward III had thirteen children, including five sons who grew to maturity. He provided for them by marrying them to English heiresses and then creating the first ever English dukedoms for them. Thus he brought into being a race of powerful magnates related by blood to the royal line, whose descendants would ultimately challenge each other for the throne itself.

It is tempting to criticise Edward for bestowing upon his sons so much landed power, but it was then expected of him to provide for his sons to the best of his ability and make sufficient provision to enable his children to maintain establishments and retinues befitting their royal rank. In Edward's own lifetime the way in which he married his children into the upper echelons of the nobility and thereby secured for them substantial inheritances, while at the same time extending royal influence, was seen as a very successful undertaking. In 1377, the Chancellor spoke at Edward's last Parliament of the love and trust within the royal family, saying that 'no Christian king had such sons as the King has had. By him and his sons the realm has been reformed, honoured and enriched as never before.'

The eldest son, Edward of Woodstock, Prince of Wales, was known from the sixteenth century as the 'Black Prince'. While only sixteen years old, the Prince won his knightly spurs at Crécy, and by his exploits during the next decade earned the reputation of being the finest knight in Christendom. The nickname given him may have been inspired by the colour of his armour or, more probably, the ferocity of his temper. In later years, dogged by ill-health, he tarnished his fame by ordering the notorious massacre of innocent citizens at Limoges. He predeceased his father in 1376, leaving one heir, nine-year-old Richard of Bordeaux, who succeeded his grandfather in 1377 as Richard II. It is one of the ironies of history that the successor of the fertile Edward III should produce no children at all, a circumstance which indirectly brought about the Wars of the Roses half a century later.

Edward III's second son, Lionel of Antwerp, Duke of Clarence (1338–68), made a highly advantageous marriage to Elizabeth de Burgh, sole heiress of the Anglo-Irish Earl of Ulster and a descendant, through her mother, of King Henry III (1207–72). Elizabeth died in 1363, having produced only one daughter, Philippa of Clarence (1355–81). After his wife's death, Lionel, in a bid to establish some kind of Italian principality for himself, married Violante Visconti, daughter of the Duke of Milan, but he died in

Italy in mysterious circumstances, possibly of poison, only six months afterwards.

Lionel's marriage to Elizabeth de Burgh brought him an Irish earldom and the ancestral lands of the de Burgh family in Ulster, although Ireland was in such chaos that he was never able to exercise more than nominal control over his inheritance. Nevertheless, this was the beginning of the long association between his family and the land and people of Ireland.

Lionel's daughter Philippa became the wife of Edmund Mortimer, 3rd Earl of March (1352–81). In 1363, on the death of her mother, Philippa became Countess of Ulster in her own right. The House of York would one day base its claim to the throne on its descent from Edward III through Philippa of Clarence, and certainly by the law of primogeniture, after the Black Prince's line failed, the crown should have passed to the heirs of his next brother, Lionel. But it did not, and this was one of the crucial issues raised during the Wars of the Roses.

The Mortimers were a family of great barons whose chief sphere of influence was along the Welsh border – the Marches. Their principal seats were Wigmore Castle – now a ruin – and Ludlow Castle. Through marriage, they had absorbed the estates of other Marcher barons, the Lacys and the Genvilles. At the peak of their power, in the late fourteenth century, they were the richest of all the magnates and the most powerful family on the Welsh Marches. They owned extensive estates, not only there, but also in Ireland, Wales, Dorset, Somerset and East Anglia. They extended and improved Ludlow Castle, building a magnificent range of domestic apartments which are considered to be the best surviving examples of the domestic quarters of a late mediaeval aristocrat.

Edmund Mortimer had become 3rd Earl of March at the age of eight on his father's death; he was also Earl of Ulster in right of his wife. In 1379 he was appointed Lieutenant of Ireland, a post held by several of his descendants. His tour of duty there lasted less than three years, but he achieved a great deal in that time. He drowned whilst crossing a ford in Cork in December 1381, leaving his son Roger (1373–98) as his heir.

Edward III's third surviving son was John of Gaunt (1340–99), who became Duke of Lancaster by right of his marriage to his distant cousin Blanche, the heiress of the House of Lancaster, which had been founded by Edmund Crouchback, Earl of Lancaster, second son of Henry III, in the thirteenth century. The Duchy of Lancaster was a palatinate, which meant that it was virtually an independent state in which the king's writ counted for very little.

Gaunt, a tall, lean man of military bearing, was a fabulously wealthy prince. Proud and ambitious, he maintained an impressive establishment organised along the lines of the royal household and staffed by a retinue of 500 persons. He owned vast estates, scattered throughout England and France, thirty castles and numerous manors, and could summon a formidable army of tenants at will. Gaunt's favourite residences were his London palace of the Savoy, which rivalled Westminster in magnificence but was burned down in the Peasants' Revolt of 1381, and Kenilworth Castle in Warwickshire, a place much beloved by his Lancastrian descendants. It is now a ruin, but Gaunt's magnificent banqueting hall with its huge windows remains.

He loved ceremony and, like most of his class, held to the laws of chivalry as if they were a second religion. He was a cultivated man who loved books, patronised Chaucer, and enjoyed jousting. Dignified, reserved in manner and guarded in conversation, he was also peaceable, rarely exacting revenge for wrongs done to him and looking after his tenants. He was merciful to the humble and compassionate to villeins, or bondsmen, who wanted their freedom and even to lepers, the outcasts of mediaeval society. When dealing with rebellious peasants after the revolt, he acted with fairness.

Although he fought many campaigns, Gaunt never achieved any significant military success, and thus remained very much in the shadow of his father and elder brother, never enjoying, as they did, the status of public hero. Indeed, by the 1370s he had become very unpopular with the people of England. Edward III was sick and enfeebled, given over to the wiles of his rapacious mistress, Alice Perrers; the Black Prince was wasting away with a crippling disease. England's victories in the Hundred Years War were long past, while her government, lacking cohesive leadership, blundered from one crisis to another. Gaunt, as the senior active member of the royal house, was blamed for its failings and the loss of some of England's conquests in France. His wealth and influence were also resented, and after the Black Prince died there were rumours that he meant to seize the throne for himself. Other rumours had it that Gaunt was a Flemish changeling, smuggled into his mother's bedchamber to replace a stillborn daughter. None of the rumours was true, but when his nephew Richard II succeeded, Gaunt made a great show of loyalty and avoided being identified with any opposition to the minority government. Thereafter he saw his life's work as maintaining the honour and integrity of the English Crown. He remained faithful to Richard, during whose minority he was virtual ruler of England, but he nevertheless made bitter enemies, especially among the clergy, who attacked him for supporting John Wycliffe, who caused a furore by attacking abuses within the Church. Many magnates suspected him of harbouring designs on the throne, but in fact the only throne Gaunt coveted was that of Castile, which he claimed through its heiress, his second wife Constance, though he failed in his attempt to establish himself as king there.

Until the 1390s, Richard II respected, trusted and relied upon Gaunt. The latter's status as a politician had so improved by that time that even his avowed enemy, the chronicler Thomas Walsingham, was moved to describe him as a man of worth and loyalty. Chaucer, whose sister-in-law became Gaunt's third wife, called his patron 'treatable, right wonder skilful, and reasonable', while Froissart described him as 'sage and imaginative'.

According to Chaucer, who dedicated his work *The Book of the Duchess* to Gaunt's first wife, Blanche of Lancaster was beautiful, golden-haired, tall and shapely. She could read and write, which was unusual in an age when female literacy was discouraged because it would give women the means to write love letters. But so pure was Blanche's reputation that she was regarded as a chaste patroness of men of letters. She bore Gaunt eight children, of whom only three grew to maturity: Philippa, who married John I, King of Portugal; Elizabeth, who married John Holland, 1st Duke of Exeter; and Henry of Bolingbroke, Gaunt's heir. Blanche died during the third outbreak of the Black Death in 1369, and was buried in Old St Paul's Cathedral.

Gaunt's second marriage to Constance of Castile was made for political reasons. They had two children, John, who died as a baby, and Katherine, who married Henry III, King of Castile. Constance died in 1394.

On 13 January 1396, at Lincoln Cathedral, Gaunt married for the third time, this time for love. The bride was the lady who had been his mistress for a quarter of a century. Her name was Katherine Swynford, and she was the daughter of a herald of Guienne and the widow of Sir Hugh Swynford, who died fighting the French in 1372. At the time of her marriage to Gaunt she was about forty-six. She is thought to have been the sister of Philippa le Picard, a lady-in-waiting to Edward III's queen and pantrywoman to Blanche, Duchess of Lancaster, and probably also the wife of the poet Geoffrey Chaucer.

Katherine first came to Gaunt's attention when she was employed as 'gouvernante' to his daughters by Blanche. Froissart alleges their affair began the year before Blanche's death. It was certainly going on when Gaunt married Constance, but did not become notorious until 1378, when, according to Walsingham, the couple began openly living in sin. Three years later the liaison had become common knowledge. Gaunt's accounts record gifts given to Katherine between 1372 and 1381, but in that year, interpreting his losses during the Peasants' Revolt as evidence of God's displeasure, he renounced Katherine, and in 1382 she resigned her post and retired to the estates given her by her lover in Lincolnshire and Nottinghamshire.

Katherine bore Gaunt four children, all surnamed Beaufort after a lordship and castle once owned by him in the Champagne region of France, but lost in 1369, before they were born. These children and their descendants were to dominate English politics for the next century and more, and it has been said with truth that the history of the Beauforts is the history of England during that period. Their dates of birth are not recorded, but the eldest, John Beaufort, must have been born in the early 1370s because in 1390 he rode in triumph at the celebrated jousts held before the French court at St Inglevert in France. From John would be descended the Beaufort dukes of Somerset and ultimately the royal House of Tudor. The second son, Henry, was educated in law at Aachen, in Germany, and then at Cambridge and Oxford, before entering the Church, within which he would rise to the rank of cardinal and become one of the most influential men in the kingdom. The third son, Thomas, was too young to be knighted in 1397, when the Beauforts were legitimised, but went on to become Duke of Exeter and play a prominent part in the French wars, while Joan, the only daughter, would marry the powerful Ralph Neville, 1st Earl of Westmorland, and become matriarch of the widespread Neville family.

In 1388, in recognition of the esteem in which she was held by Gaunt, Richard II made Katherine Swynford a Lady of the Garter, and we should perhaps assume that she and Gaunt again became lovers at that time. Hostile chroniclers compared Katherine to Alice Perrers, calling her an adventuress and worse: it was said she had none of Alice's charm but far more influence. Priests delivered sermons on her vices and the common people spat at her when she appeared in public. But in Gaunt's magnificent residences, as well as at court, the great deferred to Katherine, and were not too proud to present petitions to her, hoping she would exert her influence on their behalf. After her marriage, she ranked as first lady in the land until Richard II married Isabella of France, though her lowly birth and scandalous past made her the butt of much gossip on the part of the great ladies of the court, who protested that they would not come into any place where she would be present. Froissart says they thought it a 'great shame that such a duchess should have the pre-eminence before them'. But Katherine continued to behave with a decorum and dignity that would silence them in the end.

Edward III's fourth surviving son was Edmund of Langley, Duke of York (1341–1402), an ineffectual ditherer of little ability, whose achievements were few, for he lacked the ambition and energy of his brothers. His remains, exhumed during the reign of Queen Victoria, showed him to have been a stocky man of about 5'8" tall. Although his contemporaries described him as handsome, he had an abnormally sloping forehead and a prominent, thrusting jaw. On his body there was evidence of several wounds, none of them in the back, which suggests that if Edmund was somewhat lacking in brain power, he was no coward in the field. His long military career began when he was eighteen, when he fought the French, but in the years that followed, despite the odd moment of glory, he was dogged by one misfortune after another and was rarely given an independent command.

During the reign of Richard II Edmund was a political lightweight; his views were deferred to because of his rank, but he enjoyed little real influence. The greatest passion in his life was hawking, which he preferred to any political duty. The chronicler John Hardyng described Edmund as a cheerful and well-meaning man who 'lived without wrong', but whose abilities did not match the role his birth dictated.

Edmund was staunchly loyal to his brother, Gaunt. In 1372 he married Isabella, the younger sister of Gaunt's second wife Constance. Her corpse was also examined by Victorian experts, who discovered she was only 4'8" tall and had strange, forked teeth. In life she was said to be beautiful and notorious, with a number of lovers, the most famous being John Holland, later Duke of Exeter. Chaucer satirised their affair in a poem entitled 'The Complaint of Mars', while monastic chroniclers referred to Isabella as a 'soft and lascivious woman, devoted to lust and worldliness'. She loved beautiful things: in her will are listed items of exquisite jewellery, such as a heart set with pearls, and illuminated manuscripts of romances. In later years she became faithful to her husband and turned to religion, dying in 1392 'pious and repentant'. Isabella left three children: Edward (born c.1373), his father's heir; Richard (born c.1375–6); and Constance, who married Thomas le Despenser, who later became Earl of Gloucester.

Edmund was the founder of the House of York and received his dukedom from Richard II on 6 August 1385. In July, Edmund had helped to command an army on an abortive expedition to Scotland, and had camped at York on the way there. Although he had no special connection with the city, Richard II may have intended the creation to signify his gratitude to York for its recent hospitality and also his intention to make it the capital of England instead of London, where Richard was at that time very unpopular.

The fifth son of Edward III was Thomas of Woodstock, Duke of Gloucester, whose fifteenth-century descendants were the Dukes of Buckingham.

Richard II's reign was one of the most disastrous in English history. It laid the foundations for a power struggle that would last well into the next century and lead ultimately to the Wars of the Roses. Richard had been raised to the throne at too early an age. Impressed very young with a strong sense of his unique importance, he came in later life to bear grudges against any who dared criticise him. The praise he earned, at fourteen, for his courageous behaviour during the Peasants' Revolt convinced him that he was a born leader of men.

He was six feet tall, slim and very fair-skinned, with dark blond hair which he wore at shoulder length. He cut an impressive figure, but he was no soldier and never took part in a joust. Yet he could be brave, and a passionately loyal friend. He was also at times unstable, extravagant, headstrong, suspicious, temperamental, irresponsible, untrustworthy, and cruel. Politically inept, he was often abrupt in conversation, and capable of insulting behaviour, on occasions bawling out his detractors in Parliament. Once, in a violent temper, he tried to take a sword to the Archbishop of Canterbury, and had to be forcibly restrained from doing so.

Richard was a highly cultivated man and a great patron of the arts and literature. He was impressed by French culture and customs, and installed French cooks in his kitchens, something his subjects viewed as fraternising with the enemy, against whom they would have preferred to be scoring military victories. But Richard was no seeker of martial glory and considered that peace with France was preferable to war, a highly unpopular view at that time.

The King had pronounced aesthetic sensibilities and raised the cult and mystique of monarchy to an art form, giving much thought to the ceremony and pageantry attached to it. He dressed ostentatiously – one coat cost 30,000 marks – and was very fastidious: he is credited with inventing the handkerchief – 'little pieces [of cloth] for the lord King to wipe and clean his nose'. He had exquisite taste and his elegant court reflected his passion for the arts, its fame adding lustre to his crown.

Richard was a great builder and improver of the royal palaces, to the extent of installing bathrooms with hot and cold running water, stained-glass windows, vivid murals depicting heraldic symbols, and colourful floor tiles. He lived in the greatest luxury, and Westminster Hall, which he rebuilt, remains today as testimony to the splendours of his reign.

His household was sumptuous and extravagant. Walsingham describes the courtiers as rapacious and 'more valiant in bed than in battle', accusing them of corrupting the young King. Many chroniclers strongly criticised the outlandish fashions of the court, targeting the men's built-up shoulders and collars, pointed-toed shoes and tight hose that prevented their wearers from kneeling in Church. Long sleeves that swept the floor were reviled as 'full of slashes and devils'.

In 1384, after an uneasy minority, Richard had assumed personal rule. However, his incompetence in government and his reliance on favourites such as Michael de la Pole, Earl of Suffolk, and Robert de Vere, Earl of Oxford, provoked bitter opposition among his nobles. Richard's first queen, Anne of Bohemia, exercised some restraint over him during her lifetime, but not enough, and although he loved her deeply, they were childless.

Richard's infatuation for Robert de Vere was a political disaster. De Vere was a courageous, ambitious and resourceful young man, and as a magnate he had a legitimate role to play in government, but many believed his influence over the King to be pernicious and unnatural and his abilities mediocre. Married to the King's cousin, Philippa de Coucy, he embarked upon a notorious affair with one of Queen Anne's Czech ladies, Agnes de Launcekrona, whom he abducted and made his mistress. He then produced fraudulent evidence to secure an annulment of his marriage in order to marry her. As if this were not scandal enough, there were strong indications that his relationship with Richard was of a homosexual nature. Walsingham refers to 'the depths of King Richard's affection for this man, whom he cultivated and loved, not without a degree of improper intimacy, or so it was rumoured. It provoked discontent among the other lords and barons, for he was no superior to the rest of them.' Elsewhere, Walsingham describes the relationship between the King and de Vere as 'obscene'.

De Vere compounded his offences by continually urging Richard to ignore the advice of his nobles and the decrees of Parliament, and Richard, completely besotted, complied; some said bitterly that if de

Vere said black was white, the King would not contradict him. He lavished land, honours and wealth on the favourite, and turned a blind eye to his adultery and the slighting of his royal wife, which aroused the anger of many of Richard's family.

One nobleman who was particularly dismayed by the King's behaviour was his cousin Henry of Bolingbroke, Gaunt's heir, who had hitherto been as loyal to the King as Gaunt himself.

Henry of Bolingbroke had been born in 1367 at Bolingbroke Castle in Lincolnshire. For much of his youth he was styled Earl of Derby, one of Gaunt's lesser titles. Around 1380–1 he married Mary, co-heiress of Humphrey de Bohun, Earl of Hereford, Essex and Northampton, and a descendant of Henry III. The Bohuns were of ancient Norman stock, one of England's greatest noble families, and Mary's sister Eleanor was the wife of Bolingbroke's uncle, Thomas of Woodstock, later Duke of Gloucester.

Mary, born around 1369–70, had hardly reached puberty by the time of her marriage. She had been reared for the cloister but Gaunt wanted her half of the Bohun inheritance for his son. Unwisely, the young couple were allowed to cohabit immediately, with the result that Mary's first son died at birth in 1382. Five years later she bore her next child, Henry of Monmouth, and then five others in quick succession: Thomas in 1388, John in 1389, Humphrey in 1390, Blanche in 1392 and Philippa in 1394. Mary did not survive this last birth. Henry's faithfulness to his wife was commented on throughout the courts of Europe, and he sincerely mourned her death.

Henry of Bolingbroke was of medium height, good looking, strongly built and muscular. Examination of his corpse in 1831 showed his teeth to have been good and his hair to have been a deep russet colour. In life, he had a curling moustache and a short, forked beard. He was a man of great ability, energetic, tenacious, courageous and strong. He had a charismatic personality, being humorous, courteous, even-tempered and somewhat reserved and dignified. However, he could be stubborn and impulsive, and occasionally lacked foresight.

He was well-educated, and proficient in Latin, French and English. For preference, he spoke Norman-French, the traditional language of the English court. A skilful jouster, he loved tournaments and feats of arms, and his reputation as a knight was widespread. He adored music, and a consort of drummers, trumpeters and pipers accompanied him wherever he went, while he himself was a musician of note. Like his father he maintained great state and kept a large retinue.

Bolingbroke was devout and markedly orthodox in his religious views, and his charities were lavish. He went twice on crusade, first in 1390 with the German Order of Teutonic Knights against Lithuanian pagans in Poland, and secondly in 1392 to Jerusalem. He was popular and respected, and thus was a potentially formidable opponent to Richard II.

To counteract the threat posed by de Vere, Bolingbroke allied himself in opposition to the King's favourites with his uncle, Thomas of Woodstock, Richard FitzAlan, Earl of Arundel, a leading magnate, Thomas Mowbray, Earl of Nottingham, and the Earl of Warwick. Because they were appealing to Richard to restore good government, they called themselves the 'Lords Appellant'. In 1387, Bolingbroke and his allies scored a victory over de Vere at Radcot Bridge in Oxfordshire, which led to the Earl of Oxford's enforced banishment. After the battle Richard had no choice but to submit to the demands of the victors, and in 1388, in the 'Merciless' Parliament, the Lords Appellant asked for other royal favourites to be executed and de Vere's property confiscated. After that, it was only a matter of time before Richard, compliant for the present, took his revenge.

In 1389 Richard wrested the reins of government from the Lords Appellant, and for the next eight years ruled England himself, governing fairly wisely and achieving some success in establishing his authority in Ireland. Anne of Bohemia's death in 1394 removed a moderating influence from the King. Thereafter he refused to listen to advice and began to govern with increasing autocracy.

In 1392 de Vere had died in abject poverty at Louvain, after being savaged during a hunt by a wild boar, but in 1395 the King had his embalmed body brought back to England for burial. Most magnates refused to attend the funeral, and those who did were scandalised to see Richard order the coffin opened so that he could once more see de Vere's face and kiss his friend's hand.

In 1396 he signed a 28-year truce with France and sealed it by marrying Isabella, the six-year-old daughter of Charles VI. Both the peace and the marriage were unpopular with the English people, who would have preferred to see England's claim to France reasserted, but, with the advantage of historical hindsight, we can now appreciate that the truce was a wise move on the part of a king who knew that England's resources could not support another prolonged war.

At this time, in the face of so much opposition from his other magnates, Richard was anxious to retain Gaunt's loyalty, and that same year he persuaded Pope Boniface XI to issue a bull confirming

Gaunt's marriage to Katherine Swynford and the legitimacy of the Beauforts. On 9 February 1397, as Gaunt and his family stood in the House of Lords beneath a canopy known as a 'care cloth', which was used in a ceremony for the legitimising of those of noble birth, the King issued letters patent and a royal edict declaring the Beauforts to be legitimate under English law, and this was afterwards confirmed by Act of Parliament. Shortly afterwards he created John Beaufort, the eldest, Earl and then Marquess of Somerset and a knight of the Garter, while in 1398 the ageing Bishop of Lincoln was forced out of his diocese so that the King could bestow the bishopric on Henry Beaufort.

The Kirkstall Chronicle says that in 1397 the King emerged like the sun from the clouds, but in fact it was at about this time that he began to display pronounced megalomanic, even psychopathic tendencies. His growing paranoia and detachment from reality, and the obvious concern of his friends, all argue some kind of mental breakdown, and it has been suggested he was perhaps suffering from schizophrenia.

From 1397, Richard was determined to be an absolute monarch and rule without Parliament. That year by fair or foul means he took steps to see that Parliament was packed with enough supporters to vote him sufficient funds to ensure that he never needed to summon it again. He then dismissed it. This heralded his reckless slide into disaster: he now ruled as a tyrant, banishing any magnate who opposed him and declaring that the laws of England were within his own mouth and breast and that the lives and property of his subjects were at his mercy, to be disposed of at his pleasure.

He doctored the Rolls of Parliament so that his enemies could be attainted without judicial process; he gathered a formidable private army to intimidate his enemies and protect himself; he imposed illegal taxes; he failed to keep order at a local level in the realm; he tried unsuccessfully to secure his election as Holy Roman Emperor; he became irascible, unpredictable, and broke countless promises. Petitioners, even the Archbishop of Canterbury, were made to grovel before him on their knees, and he would sit on his throne for hours at a time in silence, with the whole court gathered around him; if his gaze rested upon anyone, that person had to make obeisance to him.

That same year Richard felt strong enough to move against his youngest uncle, Thomas of Woodstock, whom he had never forgiven for Radcot Bridge and the banishment of de Vere. He instructed his cousin Edward, Earl of Rutland, son of the Duke of York, to arrange Gloucester's murder. Rutland, it was rumoured, sent two servants to the inn where his uncle was lodged in Calais, and here they smothered him beneath a mattress.

Rutland had by this time replaced de Vere in the King's affections, and he too may have been a homosexual, since his marriage to Philippa de Mohun produced no children. In appearance and character, Rutland took after his Castilian mother: he was intelligent and good looking, but later became very overweight. His chief role was that of courtier, but he was also a cultivated man who wrote a popular treatise on hunting. Richard 'loved him exceedingly, more than any other man in the kingdom', according to the French chronicler Jean Creton, and Rutland quickly became the most influential man at court.

Richard was now ready to deal with the other former Lords Appellant. Thomas Mowbray secretly warned Bolingbroke that the King intended to destroy them all, and that his malice was directed chiefly towards the House of Lancaster. Bolingbroke confided this to Gaunt, who nevertheless went at once to the King and repeated what Mowbray had said. Bolingbroke, who was with him, pointed at Mowbray and accused him of speaking treason, which Mowbray hotly denied, flinging the same charge at Bolingbroke. The King decreed that the dispute should be referred to a panel of lords. In April 1398 these lords decided that the issue should be settled 'according to the laws of chivalry' – by trial by combat, an ancient European custom whereby God was invited to intervene by granting a victory to the righteous party.

On 16 September, at Coventry, the two Dukes faced each other before a tense crowd in the presence of the King and the whole court. Bolingbroke cut a dashing figure in full armour and mounted on a white destrier caparisoned in blue and green velvet embroidered with antelopes and gold swans, the swan being the Duke's personal badge. Mowbray was resplendent in crimson velvet.

Just as the combat was about to begin, the King threw down his baton from the dais to call a halt to the proceedings. He then deliberated for two hours while the dukes sat waiting on their restive mounts. Then Richard returned and, without preamble, sentenced both men to exile, Bolingbroke for ten years, Mowbray for life. Walsingham commented that the sentence was based on 'no legal grounds whatsoever' and was 'contrary to justice', being merely an excuse to rid himself of two former opponents. Nor would the remaining Lords Appellant escape the King's wrath: Arundel was executed the same year and Warwick was exiled for life.

As soon as the sentence was passed, the King summoned Bolingbroke's ten-year-old heir, Henry of Monmouth, to court as a hostage for his father's good behaviour. Bolingbroke sought refuge in Paris, where he was lent a mansion by a French nobleman. Mowbray never saw England again: he went on pilgrimage to Jerusalem, but died of the Black Death on the way home.

The King's childlessness was a matter of concern to most of his subjects, for Queen Isabella would be unable to produce children for several years. Richard's heir was Roger Mortimer, 4th Earl of March, grandson of Lionel of Antwerp, Edward III's second son. In 1398 Roger was twenty-four; like his father, he served the Crown as Lord Lieutenant of Ireland, though he could not bring the wild Irish tribal factions under control. In June that year, March made an attempt to impose his authority on the lands to which he held title in Ireland, but was ambushed and killed by the Irish at Kenlis in Leinster. He left a son, Edmund, aged only seven – heir not only to his father's earldoms, but also to the throne itself.

Richard II and Gaunt were now virtually estranged. Saddened by the exile of his son, Gaunt fell ill. He died in 1399 at Leicester Castle and was buried beside Blanche of Lancaster in St Paul's Cathedral.* Gaunt had loved Katherine Swynford to the end, referring to her in his will as 'my very dear companion'. She survived him by four years and was buried in Lincoln Cathedral.

Gaunt's death was fatal to Richard. Despite their differences, Gaunt had been a loyal supporter of the monarchy, and now that he was gone there was nothing to prevent a confrontation between the King and Bolingbroke.

Tidings of his father's passing reached Bolingbroke in Paris. Although the King's sentence of exile prevented him from returning to England for another nine years, he was comforted by the knowledge that he was now Duke of Lancaster, premier peer of the realm and enormously wealthy, for the Lancastrian inheritance was by far the richest in England. Prior to his leaving England, the King had assured him that his possessions were safe and had issued letters patent to that effect.

But then came shattering news: Richard had revoked the letters patent and sequestered all Bolingbroke's lands, distributing them among his own supporters. Worse than that, Bolingbroke's exile was to be for life. This act of betrayal made Bolingbroke decide to return to England and to deal with the problem of Richard once and for all.

* Their tomb was lost in the Great Fire of London.

In May 1399 Richard II sailed to Ireland in what was to prove an unsuccessful attempt to defuse the ugly situation that had developed there after March's death. Prior to his departure he had March's young son proclaimed heir presumptive, and appointed York regent during his absence. Rutland went with the King to Ireland. Richard was not to know it, but his absence from England would prove crucial.

Bolingbroke landed in Yorkshire around 4 July at Ravenspur, a port that has long since disappeared due to coastal erosion. On disembarking, the Duke knelt down and kissed the soil of his native land. He had come in rebellion against his lawfully crowned and anointed sovereign, although he initially claimed that it was only to safeguard his Lancastrian inheritance and reform the government. Indeed, he acknowledged Richard's title as king and the right of the Earl of March to succeed him.

At the time of the invasion there was a huge tide of popular feeling against Richard, especially in London, where Bolingbroke was well liked, and York was not the man to rally the few supporters Richard had left. Bolingbroke's arrival placed York in a dilemma, for he had to choose between loyalty to his royal nephew and loyalty to the son of his best-loved brother, Gaunt. Typically, he remained undecided for three weeks.

As he progressed south Bolingbroke was gratified to find so many people ready to support him. Nobles and commons flocked to his banner and he quickly collected a large army, meeting little resistance anywhere. The princes of the Church offered their support and the Archbishop of Canterbury assured all who joined Bolingbroke of the remission of their sins and 'a sure place in Paradise'. In Bristol, the Duke found some of Richard's most hated advisers and summarily ordered their heads cut off, which greatly pleased the citizens.

Bad weather meant that news of Bolingbroke's invasion took some time to reach the King in Ireland, and as soon as he knew the worst, Richard sailed home, determined to raise an army and meet his cousin in the field. Late in July he landed in South Wales, but was unable to rouse much support; indeed many of his followers were deserting him, including Rutland, who dismissed the King's remaining soldiers and rode off to join Bolingbroke, whom York had now finally decided to support. Abandoned and panic-stricken, Richard disguised himself as a friar and fled to Conway Castle, where he surrendered to a deputation sent by Bolingbroke. At Lichfield, on the way to London, he tried to escape by climbing out of a tower window, but was caught leaving the garden below. After that he was never alone, being guarded by ten or twelve armed men.

On 2 September Bolingbroke entered London to a tumultuous reception. King Richard, a prisoner in his train, was greeted with jeers and pelted from the rooftops with rubbish, and later that day he was confined in the Tower of London. There was no doubt in anyone's mind as to who was now ruling England. Nevertheless, Henry had sworn at Conway that Richard should 'keep his royal power and dominion'.

Throughout September the King made repeated demands to be publicly heard in Parliament. Even the pro-Lancastrian chronicler, Adam of Usk, who saw him in prison at this time, felt compassion and noted 'the trouble of his mind, hearing him talk on the fate of kings in England'. Doubtless he was haunted by the fate of Edward II, murdered after his deposition in 1327.

Meanwhile, Bolingbroke, forgetting his promise, had appointed a commission to consider who should be king. Many of the magnates were unhappy at the prospect of his taking the throne; several committees of lords, having examined his claim to rule by right of descent, declared it flawed. Yet Adam of Usk says that the magnates found reasons enough for setting Richard aside: 'perjuries, sacrileges, unnatural crimes, exactions from his subjects, reduction of his people to slavery, cowardice and weakness of rule'. Henry, it seemed, was the only realistic alternative, for the legitimate heir, March, was just a child. Usk claimed that Richard was 'ready to yield up the crown', but this was a Lancastrian fiction. Ready or not, 'for better security it was determined that he should be deposed by the authority of clergy and people, for which purpose they were summoned hastily, in the King's name, on Michaelmas Day'.

In fact, Richard was by no means willing to give up the throne, and Bolingbroke knew it. His first impulse was to make Richard stand trial by his peers in the high court of Parliament, but there was no precedent for this and, such was the mystique of kingship, it might not produce the desired result. He therefore used every means in his power to force Richard to abdicate, for he was anxious that the removal of his cousin from the throne and his own subsequent accession should have some basis in law. Knowing that his own title was precarious, the official line was to be that Richard's misgovernment justified his deposition. The laws of succession were best left out of it.

Although Richard at first had had no intention of abdicating, he soon realised he had little choice. For a month, systematic coercion and threats were used to persuade him to co-operate, and at the end of that time, a shattered and broken man, he gave in. According to one of his supporters, a Franciscan friar called Richard Frisby, he agreed to abdicate 'under compulsion, while in prison, which is not a valid abdication. He would never have resigned had he been at liberty.'

On the morning of 29 September 1399, some of the lords assembled for Parliament, accompanied by a committee of lawyers, waited upon Richard in the Tower. They returned in the afternoon, when the King, with a smiling face, signed an instrument of abdication, in which he requested that he be succeeded by his cousin of Bolingbroke. As a token of goodwill he sent Henry his signet ring.

The next morning, Parliament assembled in Westminster Hall. Richard had asked that he should not come before it 'in horrible fashion' as a prisoner, which was agreed to. When he entered the hall, he stood before the empty throne, removed his crown and, placing it on the ground, 'resigned his right to God'. He then made a short speech expressing his hope that Bolingbroke would be a good lord to him and ensure that he was comfortably provided for. Although thirty-three accusations against him were read aloud, he was not allowed to say anything more, even in his defence.

In the official record of the proceedings, written in the Parliament Roll, Richard is described as looking cheerful as he read out the transcript of his instrument of abdication, but this is at odds with the evidence of Adam of Usk and the chronicler monk of Evesham, who describe his demeanour as anything but happy. Later that day the Bishop of Carlisle protested that Richard should have had a chance to answer the charges against him, but his was a lone voice.

Yet even though it had been summoned in the King's name, this 'Parliament' was not a strictly legal or normal assembly. There was no Speaker, and a crowd of hostile Londoners had been admitted, probably to intimidate the former king.

After Richard had been taken back to the Tower, the assembled lords declared him deposed. His removal from the throne was the catalyst for the dynastic and political instability that characterised the century that followed it. Shortly after, Bolingbroke entered Westminster Hall, preceded by his four sons and the archbishops of Canterbury and York. In the hushed throng Sir Thomas Percy's voice rang out, 'Long live Henry of Lancaster, King of England!' This was the cue for the whole assembly to respond with the words, 'Yes! Yes! We want Henry to be king, nobody else!'

Bolingbroke acknowledged their acclaim, then placed himself in Gaunt's former seat, occupying it as Duke of Lancaster. But the two archbishops took him by the hand and led him to the empty throne. Silence fell as he rose to speak, saying, 'In the name of the Father,

Son and Holy Ghost, I, Henry of Lancaster, challenge this realm of England and the crown, as I that am descended by right line of the blood coming from the good lord Henry the Third, and through him that right that God of His grace hath sent me with help of my kin and of my friends to recover it, the which was in point to be undone for default of governance and undoing of the good laws.'

After he had finished speaking, he showed the assembly Richard's signet ring, as proof that the former king had designated him his successor. There was rapturous applause, and both lords and commons enthusiastically acknowledged him as king of England and of France. At the close of proceedings, proclamation was made that Richard had abdicated and that Bolingbroke had succeeded him as King Henry IV. Some voices were publicly raised in protest. They were to be the first of many.

3

The Usurping Dynasty

Certainly Henry IV and the Lancastrian kings who succeeded him were usurpers. Henry had achieved the royal dignity by deposing England's lawful sovereign, and the legitimacy of his title to the throne would remain a sensitive issue. The basis of his claim to rule by right of blood was an ingenious lie which, says Adam of Usk, had already been rejected by a committee of lords and clergy. Henry had asserted that Edmund Crouchback, 1st Earl of Lancaster, from whom he was descended through his mother, Blanche of Lancaster, had in fact been the eldest son of Henry III, not the second son, and had been overlooked because of bodily deformity in favour of his 'younger' brother, Edward I, an ancestor of his own father, John of Gaunt. This claim had serious implications because, if accepted, all the kings since Edward I's time must be deemed usurpers. It also ensured that the children of Gaunt's later wives, especially the Beauforts, were excluded from the succession, and made Henry's claim through his mother far superior to that which he inherited from his father.

Even though the committee had rejected this preposterous claim, Henry clung to it, preferring to stress his descent through his mother rather than basing his title solely on his descent from Edward III through John of Gaunt, which of necessity involved overlooking the prior claim of the Mortimers. This falsified descent was fraught with contradictions, since, to counteract any legitimist sympathisers, he also took his stand on the Salic Law, which prevented claims to the throne by or through a female. In France the Salic Law did apply to the royal succession, and it was because of it that the French had denied Edward III's claim through his mother to the throne of France. The English, Henry among them, had repeatedly disputed the existence of the Salic Law, even in France, though he now used it to nullify the claim of the legitimate heir to England.

Henry's blatant attempts to justify his succession by massaging the facts about the royal descent deceived no one. Although it was vital to present himself as a lawful king, his title was really derived from his already being *de facto* king of England. His birth, wealth, abilities, and the fact that he had four strapping sons all convinced his subjects that he had been the only viable candidate for the empty throne. He was also the only man capable of restoring law and order and firm government to the country. Henry also claimed to rule by divine appointment: God, by granting him the victory, had thereby called him to the throne. He certainly did not believe he held his crown by right of parliamentary election; Parliament had merely recognised him as king. He and his successors of the House of Lancaster were similarly acknowledged by every great institution of Church and State, were hallowed and anointed at their coronations and acclaimed by the magnates, who swore fealty to them. Nevertheless, Henry had set a dangerous precedent. Although he had no right to it, he had taken the throne by force. In time, others, with a better or worse right, might do the same. It remained to be seen whether Henry IV could successfully hold on to the throne which he had taken.

During all these proceedings, no one had thought to support the superior claim of the legitimate heir-general, the seven-year-old Earl of March. Henry was a renowned and popular figure, a man of authority and power, whereas March was an unknown and untried child. Indeed, Archbishop Arundel took it upon himself to preach a sermon justifying the setting aside of the boy. England, said the Archbishop, would from now on be ruled by men, not boys. As a result of the decision to overlook March, the claim of the rightful heirs to the throne would remain dormant for sixty years after Henry IV's accession, although its existence remained an ever-present threat to the House of Lancaster because it provided a focus for rebels and malcontents. Henry IV himself regarded young March as a dangerous rival, and with good reason, as we shall shortly see.

On 13 October, Henry was crowned in Westminster Abbey with oil said to have been given by the Virgin Mary to St Thomas à Becket for the sanctifying of a king who would regain the realm lost by his ancestors. Unfortunately, as the sacred moment of the anointing arrived, the Archbishop discovered that the King's head was alive with lice; and at the offertory, Henry dropped his gold coin, which rolled away and could not be found. The superstitious took these to be evil omens.

Henry marked his coronation by instituting a new order of chivalry, the Order of the Bath, and his four sons were its first members. Two days after the coronation, the King's eldest son, Henry of Monmouth, aged twelve, was proclaimed heir apparent to the throne and created Prince of Wales, Duke of Cornwall and Earl of Chester, titles borne by the Black Prince and conferred ever since then on the eldest son of the reigning monarch.

After the coronation, York, now in poor health, retired to his beloved manor at Langley. Henry appointed him Master of the Royal Mews and Falcons, giving him the opportunity during his retirement to indulge his passion for falconry. The Yorkist badge of the 'falcon and fetterlock' is thought to have its origins in this appointment. York died in 1402, and was succeeded as 2nd Duke by his son, Rutland.

Rutland had suffered for his support of Henry IV. Twenty courtiers whose sympathies lay with the deposed Richard had thrown their hoods at his feet in challenge. Treated with contempt and hatred, Rutland was subject to verbal abuse or angry silences when he showed his face at court. Nevertheless, he now enjoyed the King's favour, and Henry protected him from his enemies, although he kept a watchful eye on one who had been so close to Richard II.

Henry IV soon discovered that it was less easy to hold on to the crown than to usurp it. He had promised to provide good and just government but, because of his dubious title to the throne, the first decade of his reign was troubled by conspiracies to overthrow him. He dared not emulate Richard II's reliance on the advice of favourites, and took steps to ensure that he was seen to be ruling with the advice and support of Parliament. In order to woo Parliament, Henry sanctioned laws giving it unprecedented powers, and established the custom of free debate and the immunity of members from arrest, leaving them free to criticise the King as they pleased.

Henry had the delicate task of restoring prestige to a throne he had weakened by usurping it and at the same time retaining the loyalty of those who had supported him. Yet the charisma which had attracted them to his cause and the heady burst of popularity that greeted his accession were not so much in evidence after it, especially when people realised that the evils of Richard's misgovernment could not be put right overnight. Henry was an industrious man of business and could be ruthless when it came to dealing with rebels, but a permanent shortage of money, exacerbated by the cost of putting down rebellions, and the distrust of some magnates, were problems he could not surmount, and consequently his reign was a time of continual tension. He did secure the support of the Church, having authorised the passing of the statute *De Heretico Comburendo*, which condemned heretics to be burned to death. This was aimed chiefly at the Lollards, whom Henry believed were a threat to his throne, not so much because of their religious beliefs, but because many supported Richard II.

Although Henry IV brought the vast wealth of the duchy of Lancaster to the Crown, as well as much of the wealth of the de Bohuns, it proved insufficient. He had therefore to make a virtue of the necessity to consult Parliament because he needed to obtain grants of money. It could truly be said that the bankruptcy of the Lancastrian kings did more to undermine the stability of the monarchy than their usurpation of the throne.

From 1399 onwards, the government of Charles VI of France steadfastly refused to recognise Henry IV as king of England, denouncing him as a traitor to his lawful sovereign and referring to him, when addressing English envoys, as 'the lord who sent you'. This led in 1401 to the reopening of the Hundred Years War. The Valois court was at that time divided into opposing factions led by Charles VI's powerful relatives, the dukes of Burgundy and Orléans. Henry IV became adept at playing these two nobles off against each other, but despite England's declaration of war, little action was seen in France during his reign.

Meanwhile, the former King Richard was still a prisoner in the Tower in the care of Sir Thomas Rempson. Thomas Walsingham heaps praises on Henry IV for his courteous treatment of Richard at this time, but it would not be long before Adam of Usk was referring to his being held in chains.

On 21 October 1399, the Commons petitioned in Parliament that Richard be called upon to answer the charges laid against him. One magnate suggested he be put to death to ensure the security of Henry's throne, but Henry strongly objected. On 23 October Parliament sat in secret session and debated what to do, concluding that it would be dangerous to let Richard be seen by the public because he would be a natural focus for rebellion. It was therefore decided, on a majority vote, that the ex-king should be condemned to perpetual imprisonment in a secret place from which no one could rescue him, and this sentence was read out in Parliament four days later. Denied any opportunity of speaking out in his own defence, Richard was made to disguise himself as a forester and on 28 October conveyed secretly by river from the Tower to Gravesend, and thence to Leeds Castle in Kent, a luxurious dower palace of the queens of

England. But he was not to remain so comfortably lodged for long, for within a few days he was moved north, first to Pickering Castle in Yorkshire, then to Knaresborough Castle, and finally to Pontefract Castle, where he was placed in the custody of Sir Thomas Swynford, son of the Duchess of Lancaster by her first husband, and a staunch Lancastrian.

Richard still had friends in high places who were determined to restore him to the throne and so regain their former influence. They wore his badge of the 'white hart', called themselves 'Richard's nurselings', and even had someone to impersonate him, a priest called Richard Maudelyn. After Christmas, four of these lords, the earls of Salisbury, Gloucester, Exeter and Surrey, made an attempt to assassinate Henry IV and his sons. But Rutland, who had become involved, betrayed their plans to the King, who wasted no time in gathering a great army and tracking down the traitors. Three of the rebel lords were lynched and decapitated by hostile mobs, and twenty-six other persons, including Maudelyn, were executed by process of law. The King returned to Westminster with the heads of the traitors, which were publicly displayed in London as a deterrent to other would-be rebels. Henry had been badly shaken by the rebellion, and was beginning to realise that he would not sit safely on his throne while Richard still lived.

The order for Richard's murder probably went to Pontefract soon after the executions of his friends in January 1400. Adam of Usk says that death came miserably to the former king as 'he lay in chains in the castle of Pontefract, tormented by Sir Thomas Swynford with starving fare'. A French source described in graphic detail how, in the agony of starvation, Richard used his teeth to tear strips of flesh from his arms and hands and devoured them. Most of his contemporaries believed he had been deliberately starved to death, although the government claimed that, having learned of the abortive plot to restore him, he was so distraught that he killed himself by voluntary starvation. When it had become too late, he had tried to break his fast, but his throat was too constricted to swallow: thus he could not have been guilty of the mortal sin of suicide. In the seventeenth century, a panel of distinguished antiquarians examined Richard's skull, which showed no marks of a blow or wound, thus giving the lie to other contemporary tales that he had been bludgeoned to death.

Predictably, there is very little official evidence as to his fate. Even the date of his death is not known. The Council's minutes for 9 February 1400 state that, if Richard still lived, he should remain in close confinement; if he was dead, his body should be shown to the people. The wording of this implies that he was actually dead or dying a long-drawn-out death. He had certainly died by 17 February, because on that date the Exchequer issued funds to cover the cost of bringing his body to Westminster.

It was important to Henry IV not only that Richard should be dead, but also that he should be seen to be dead. Only then would his supporters be deterred from rising on his behalf. On 27 February, his corpse was therefore conveyed to London at a cost of £80, being shown to the people at the more populous places that lay along the route. At length it was put on view for two days at St Paul's Cathedral. Only the face, from the forehead to the throat, was exposed; the rest of the body was encased in lead. While the corpse lay in state, King Henry attended a solemn requiem mass in the cathedral and laid a rich pall on the coffin. He also commanded chantry priests to say one thousand masses for the repose of Richard's soul. On 12 March, the former king was buried in the church of the Dominican Friars at King's Langley. A richly decorated tomb adorned with heraldic shields, which may have once held Richard's body, may still be seen there today.

In the spring of 1400, Henry IV may have felt rather more secure on his throne, but he was shortly to be disabused of that comfortable illusion.

When the news of Richard's death was broken to his ten-year-old widow, she was stunned with grief and lay prostrate for a fortnight. Young as she was, she guessed who had been responsible for depriving her of the husband who had been so kind to her, and when she returned to France the following year, she went 'clad in mourning weeds, giving King Henry angry and malignant looks, and scarcely opening her lips', according to Adam of Usk. Eight years later, having married the poet Duke of Orléans, who adored her, she died in childbirth.

Richard II was more popular in death than he had ever been in life. Rumours that he was alive persisted for nearly two decades after his murder, and were so strongly believed that people were willing to incite rebellions and risk a traitor's death in order to restore him to the throne. Some were prepared to impersonate Richard in the belief that he was alive somewhere and would materialise once the Lancastrian usurper was out of the way. Others tried to assassinate Henry IV: in September 1401 a caltrap with three poisoned spikes was found in his bed. Soon after this, Jean Creton, having been asked by the French government to ascertain the truth about Richard, sent his masters evidence obtained from certain persons in high places which proved to their satisfaction that the former king was dead. But there were many who believed otherwise.

In 1402, Friar Richard Frisby was tried for plotting to restore Richard II in order to make Henry 'the Duke of Lancaster, which is what he ought to be'. Frisby and his associates had been caught before they had a chance to do anything. Asked what he would do if he learned that King Richard were still alive, Frisby retorted that he would fight anyone to the death on his behalf. The friar told Henry IV to his face:

> I do not say that he is alive, but if he is alive he is the true King of England. You usurped his crown. If he is dead, you killed him. And if you are the cause of his death you forfeit all title and any right you may have to the kingdom.

These words sealed Frisby's fate, and he was hanged, drawn and quartered wearing the habit of his order.

In 1407, according to Walsingham,

> documents circulated in many parts of London which claimed that King Richard was still alive and would return in glory and splendour to recover his kingdom. But shortly afterwards the lying fool who had committed such a rash act was captured and punished. This tempered the joy he had aroused in many people by his lies.

At the same time, a man was going about London pretending to be Richard. The Lord Mayor, Sir Richard Whittington, had him arrested, and thereafter the rumours ceased for a time. But although it was now a capital crime to spread false rumours of Richard's continued existence, nothing could prevent continued speculation on his survival, especially in the north. For years, the belief persisted that Richard was living in Scotland, a conviction fuelled by the fact that the Scots had coached a lunatic, known as the 'Mummet', to impersonate him. Although Henry IV was not deceived, others were, and the Mummet was retained by the Scots until 1419.

Impersonations of his dead rival were not all that Henry IV had to contend with. Shakespeare calls the first decade of his reign 'a scrambling and unquiet time' because it witnessed a series of rebellions against the King.

Henry believed that young March would be an obvious focus for malcontents, and because of this he ordered that the boy be kindly treated but kept under house arrest in the care of a governess. To this post the King appointed his cousin Constance of York, Countess of Gloucester, whose husband had been executed in 1400 for plotting Henry's death. As we shall see, she was an unwise choice.

A far greater threat came at this time from Wales. Owen Glendower was an obscure Welshman, a descendant of the princes of Powys, who had studied law in London before serving Bolingbroke as a squire, in which capacity he demonstrated extraordinary martial abilities. By 1400 he was living in a moated wooden manor house at Sycarth in Wales with his wife and a brood of children, but in that year he quarrelled over possession of a minor Marcher property with one of the King's councillors, Lord Grey de Ruthin, and this led to a serious rift with Henry IV. Glendower appealed to the Welsh to support him and began calling himself Prince of Wales, at which the King had him proclaimed an outlaw. Thereafter, Glendower inspired the Welsh people to revolt against English rule, and made efforts to drive the invaders out of Wales. The English hated and feared him, and his guerrilla warfare and devious but deadly strategies earned him the reputation of being a wizard.

Owen was a man of great ability and charisma, and by 1404 his power in Wales was such that he was able to summon a Welsh parliament. In that same year he made a treaty with France and secured French aid against the English.

In June 1402, Glendower scored a great victory over the English at Pilleth in Radnorshire, and had the good fortune to capture Sir Edmund Mortimer, March's uncle. Mortimer, an important Marcher baron, was a considerable prize and a potential bargaining counter, and he was treated with great courtesy by his captor. He soon came under Glendower's spell and, already resentful of his nephew's claim having been passed over, abandoned his allegiance to Henry IV, entered into an alliance with Glendower and was given the hand of his daughter Katherine in marriage.

Henry IV was by no means anxious to ransom Mortimer, much to the chagrin of the elderly but formidable Henry Percy, Earl of Northumberland, and the Earl's son, the brave and volatile Harry Percy, nicknamed 'Hotspur', who was married to March's aunt, Elizabeth Mortimer. The Percies, powerful lords in the north, were a constant thorn in Henry's side and he feared they would form a coalition with the disaffected Mortimer, which is exactly what did happen when Glendower made much of Henry's failure to ransom his kinsman, fanning the flames of Mortimer's disaffection.

In December 1402, from his base in Radnorshire, Mortimer informed his tenants and supporters that he and Glendower intended to rescue Richard II, restore him to the throne, and secure for

Glendower his rights in Wales. If Richard was indeed dead, then March, 'my honoured nephew, who is rightful heir to the crown', would be made king. Mortimer then appealed to Hotspur for support, which was readily given, and very soon the northerners were rising in revolt against Henry IV.

This led to open warfare between the King and the Percies. Hotspur sent a formal defiance to the 'Duke of Lancaster', accusing him of breaking his promises not to harm Richard, levy high taxes or break the laws, and of forcing Parliament to proclaim him king to the detriment of March, the rightful claimant. Henry regarded this as treason, and took to the field against Hotspur. At the Battle of Shrewsbury on 23 July, Hotspur was killed and the conspiracy shattered. The King had his mangled corpse exhumed, salted and cut into quarters, which were then put on display in various cities. Northumberland fled from Henry's wrath, and sought to ally himself with Glendower and Mortimer, who were planning to invade England.

Unknown to the King, the Countess of Gloucester, March's governess, had secretly remained loyal to her husband's belief that the crown belonged of right to the late king or his true heir, March. She had concealed her antipathy to the House of Lancaster well, because Henry IV had entrusted her, not only with the care of March, but also with that of his younger brother. Late in 1404, the Countess learned that Glendower was in control of Glamorgan, and decided that, if she could somehow get them there, her charges would be in safe hands and at liberty among men who would fight for their cause. In February 1405, she managed to remove the boys from Windsor and travelled west with them as far as Cheltenham, where they arrived a week later. Here, however, the King and his men caught up with them and placed them under arrest. After this, young March and his brother were kept under a much stricter guard.

After her arrest, the Countess had her revenge on her brother, the new Duke of York, for his abandonment of Richard II. She accused him of conspiring to assassinate Henry IV in order to place March on the throne, alleging he meant to murder Henry in his bed. The King had York arrested and kept in strict confinement in the Tower, where he occupied his time by writing a treatise on hunting called *The Master of Game*, which he prudently dedicated to the Prince of Wales. Nothing could be proved against him, and he was released after nine months. By 1406 he was once again the King's 'dear and loyal cousin'.

After his return to favour York devoted his attention to building a spacious choir and other buildings in and around the church at Fotheringhay, one of his principal residences. The foundation of a collegiate chantry dedicated to the Virgin Mary and All Souls at Fotheringhay had been the brainchild of York's father, but he had died before it could become reality. York founded a college of priests there in 1411 and endowed it with six acres of land between the castle and the newly built rectory house, and Henry IV further endowed the college with an annual grant of £67.6s.8d (£67.33). During the fifteenth century the House of York would beautify and enrich this magnificent foundation, intending it to be their mausoleum. Eventually, there were twelve chaplains, eight clerks and thirteen choristers, all under the rule of a Master, and their chief duty was to pray for the good estate in life and the souls after death of the King and Queen, Prince Henry, the Duke of York, and all the royal family.

In Wales, Glendower, Mortimer and Northumberland still plotted the overthrow of Henry IV. When this had been accomplished, they proposed to divide the realm of England between them: Northumberland would rule the north, Mortimer the south, and Glendower Wales. This was enshrined in an agreement known as the Tripartite Indenture, and it was signed in February 1405 at Bangor. The conspirators reckoned, however, without the martial Prince of Wales, who vengefully descended on them with a great host, crushed the incipient rebellion, and began the gradual task of clawing back the lands that had been lost to Glendower.

In May 1405, at the Battle of Shipton Moor, the victorious Prince captured one of the rebels' chief supporters, Richard Scrope, Archbishop of York, a connection of the Percies who had given the rising the Church's blessing. The King considered this the ultimate treachery and, despite an appeal from Archbishop Arundel for clemency, insisted on Scrope's execution. Scrope paid the extreme penalty in a field of barley belonging to the nuns of Clementhorpe, having ridden there 'ignominiously facing the tail of his mare'. Most people regarded the beheading of Scrope as an outrage, and this single act turned the tide of public feeling against Henry IV. He would almost certainly have been excommunicated for executing a prince of the Church but for the fact that the Church was then riven by schism, with rival popes battling for pre-eminence. However, there were many who claimed that miracles were taking place at the dead archbishop's tomb, and it was said that the King had murdered a saint.

After the rebellion had been suppressed, Northumberland fled abroad, while Glendower and Mortimer, realising that their power was in decline, entrenched themselves in the seemingly impregnable castle at Harlech. In 1408, Northumberland, who had returned to take up arms against the King, was killed at the Battle of Bramham Moor, and the following year, after a six-month siege, Harlech Castle fell to the Prince of Wales, When he breached the walls, the Prince found that Mortimer had 'brought his days of sorrow to an end' by dying during the siege. His three infant daughters, and Glendower's two adult daughters, were still in the castle. These the Prince sent to the Tower where they shortly afterwards died.

Of Glendower there was no trace. He had disappeared into the Welsh hills whence he had come and thence into legend. Such records as we have are mostly silent as to his activities or existence after this time, although he was probably dead by 1417, when his son received a royal pardon.

Henry IV's title to the crown was enshrined in an Act of Parliament passed in 1406. In 1407 the King took further steps to ensure the future security of his dynasty by excluding his Beaufort half-siblings from their rightful place in the succession. As the only surviving legitimately born son of Gaunt, Henry may well have resented the promotion of the Beauforts, and although he confirmed Richard II's statute legitimising them, he added an amendment by his own letters patent, inserting the words '*excepta dignitate regali*', which effectively barred the Beauforts and their descendants from inheriting the throne of England.

However, this amendment was of dubious legality and caused some controversy because it was never incorporated into an Act of Parliament, nor was it approved by Parliament. Nevertheless, it had the effect of debasing the status of the Beauforts, and it was not until much later in the fifteenth century that lawyers acting on their behalf would assert that letters patent could not supersede an Act of Parliament and that consequently the Beauforts should not have been excluded from the succession. That Henry's bar was not very highly regarded was proved in 1485, when the son of a Beaufort became king of England.

All the Beauforts were competent, vigorous and ambitious people. Lacking an inheritance from Gaunt, whose lands and titles descended to Henry IV, they acquired land and wealth from the Lancastrian kings in return for faithful service and sheer hard work. Both John and Thomas Beaufort were good friends and advisers to Henry IV, serving him in the council chamber and in the field of battle. John's estates were located mainly in the west of England, and his chief residences were at Corfe Castle in Dorset and Woking in Surrey. He became Great Chamberlain of England and Captain of Calais before dying in 1410 at the Hospital of St Katherine-by-the-Tower in London. He was buried in Canterbury Cathedral and succeeded as Earl of Somerset by his son, who died childless in 1418. He in turn was succeeded by his younger brother, another John Beaufort.

Henry Beaufort had turned out to be a clever and gifted lawyer, and had acquired a substantial number of church appointments. While still in his twenties he had become Chancellor of Oxford and Bishop of Lincoln, and in 1399 he had abandoned Richard II in Ireland and hastened to join Henry of Lancaster. Bishop Beaufort now enjoyed substantial wealth and a luxurious lifestyle. In every sense he was a prince of the Church, and his vow of celibacy did not preclude him from keeping a mistress.

In 1402, the Bishop was made a member of the King's Council, and in 1404 he was translated to the influential and richest – at around £4000 per annum – of English bishoprics, that of Winchester, where he succeeded William of Wykeham. Despite his youth, he was now a central figure in English politics, entrusted with important matters of diplomacy. His fortune grew steadily from ecclesiastical revenues, the export of wool and manorial rents, and it was at this time that he began to operate as chief financier to the House of Lancaster, to whom he made a steady series of substantial loans and gifts.

Beaufort was proud, volatile and provocative, and had already incurred the enmity of Archbishop Arundel, who was instrumental in persuading Henry IV to exclude the Beauforts from the succession. This enmity may well have been the result of Beaufort making the Archbishop's niece pregnant.

The youngest of the Beaufort brothers, Thomas, had matured into a man of integrity and wisdom. Less grasping than Henry, he carried out his duties with diligence. Henry IV entrusted him at various times with the offices of Admiral of the North West of Ireland, Aquitaine and Picardy, Commander of Calais, and Chancellor of England. He proved an able strategist and perceived the crucial importance of defending England's possessions in France. Thomas married a kinswoman of his brother-in-law, the influential Ralph Neville, Earl of Westmorland, and thereby gained a firm friend in the Earl and the backing of the powerful Neville affinity.

Henry IV could count himself fortunate in having the support of his Beaufort half-brothers, whose descendants would remain loyal to the House of Lancaster for the next sixty years.

By 1409 the rebels who had dominated Henry's first decade as king had been eliminated. He was now on better terms with the French and the Scots, and also with his own magnates, and therefore in a much stronger position. However, he was still short of money, and there had been a noticeable degeneration in law and order. But this was not all that the King had to contend with: from 1405 onwards he suffered extreme ill-health.

The Brut chronicle says that immediately after Archbishop Scrope's execution Henry was smitten with leprosy, while Giles's Chronicle claims that the leprosy broke out during the same hour as Scrope's death. Most people, including the King himself, regarded this visitation as evidence of God's wrath. The first attack of the disease was terrible indeed, and caused Henry to scream with pain and cry out that he was on fire. Worse still, with pain came disfigurement. John Capgrave says that from 1405 'the King lost the beauty of his face. He was a leper, and ever fouler and fouler.' His face and hands were covered with large pustules 'like teats' and his nose became misshapen. The swellings and rashes on his skin grew so vile that few people could bring themselves to look at him. Later on, a tumour grew beneath his nose, and his flesh began to rot. The doctors could do nothing for him. Rumours about his condition were manifold: the French believed his toes and fingers had fallen off, the Scots that he had shrunk to the size of a child.

What was this terrible disease? It was certainly not leprosy. Modern medical opinion is that it could have been syphilis, or tubercular gangrene, combined with erysipelas, which produces a burning sensation. The condition of Henry's well-preserved face, seen upon his exhumation in 1831, proved that contemporary descriptions of his skin disease were somewhat exaggerated. But in 1408 the King also suffered a mild stroke and thereafter his general health deteriorated. He suffered fainting fits and some form of heart complaint, and was essentially an invalid, unable even to walk on occasions.

As the King's health declined, the Beauforts successfully increased their influence at court. The Prince of Wales, impatient to wear the crown, sought to gain control of the kingdom and allied himself with his Beaufort uncles in an attempt to seize power. This led to exceedingly strained relations, and eventually total estrangement, between father and son. Despite his illness, the King refused to abdicate. He was determined to govern England himself right to the end, even though he was becoming increasingly enfeebled. When, at times, the burden of sovereignty became too much he relied on Archbishop Arundel, his Chancellor, who tried unsuccessfully to ensure that the Prince of Wales and the Beauforts did not gain control of the government. In 1409 Arundel was forced through young Henry's machinations to resign as Chancellor, and the Prince and his faction became the dominant power on the Council.

In 1412, Henry IV declared war on France, a war he could not hope to prosecute, although he was planning to lead an army into Aquitaine. Walsingham wrote: 'I believe that he could have taken France if the strength of his body had equalled the strength of his spirit.'

On 20 March 1413, the King walked painfully to the shrine of St Edward the Confessor in Westminster Abbey, where he knelt to pray. Suddenly, he collapsed in agony with a seizure. His attendants carried him into the nearby Jerusalem Chamber, so called because of the tapestries depicting the history of Jerusalem which hung there. When he could speak, Henry recalled that he had once expressed a desire to go on a final crusade and die in Jerusalem.

They laid him on a pallet by the fire, but in spite of the warmth he complained that his arms and legs felt cold. Guilt seems to have weighed heavily on him, for he was heard to whisper, 'Only God knows by what right I took the crown.' The King's confessor arrived and begged Henry to repent of the murder of Archbishop Scrope and his usurpation of the throne. Henry replied that he had already received absolution for the killing of Scrope: as for usurping the crown, his son would never let him abjure it.

He was obviously dying. Custom decreed that the crown be placed by his side on a cushion of cloth of gold, and it was brought at once. By then the King appeared to be dead and a napkin was laid over his face. The Prince of Wales had been summoned; he entered the chamber and picked up the crown, about to place it on his head. At that moment the King stirred. He talked for a while with the Prince and was heard to say that he repented of ever having charged himself with the crown of England, for it had proved too heavy a burden for him. At the last he made his peace with his son, and died blessing him.

Henry IV was buried behind the high altar of Canterbury Cathedral, near to the tomb of the Black Prince and the shrine of St Thomas à Becket. Later a fine tomb was erected to his memory, on which were placed marble effigies of Henry and his second wife, Joanna of Navarre, who outlived him by twenty-four years.

Henry left England more prosperous and in a more settled state than he had found it: while he had achieved nothing that brought glory upon himself, he had successfully vanquished his enemies and driven baronial opposition underground, and, although there were still those who regarded him as an upstart whose right to the crown was dubious, his son succeeded unchallenged to the throne.

4

The Flower of Christian Chivalry

On Passion Sunday, 9 April 1413, Henry of Monmouth was crowned as King Henry V at Westminster Abbey. Becoming king had a profound effect on him: Walsingham states that 'as soon as he was made king he changed suddenly into another man, zealous for honesty, modesty and gravity, there being no sort of virtue that he was not anxious to display'. His biographer, Titus Livius, says that he reformed and amended his life. Elevated to kingship, he abandoned his dissolute young friends and paid heed to the experienced men of affairs on his Council. His main objective at the beginning of his reign was to distance himself from his father's style of government and thereby earn fresh popularity and support for Lancaster.

In youth Henry had led a debauched life. The evidence for this cannot be discounted, although it may have been exaggerated in later years. Thomas Elmham, the chronicler, wrote that 'passing the bounds of modesty, he was the servant of Venus' and 'found leisure for the excesses common to ungoverned age'. Having fought his first battle at fifteen, he had gained an early and wholly justified reputation as a brilliant soldier and military strategist. He also had a passion for singing, and was an accomplished musician.

According to Thomas Elmham, Henry V had 'an oval, handsome face with a broad, open forehead, a straight nose, ruddy cheeks and lips, a deeply indented chin, small, well-formed ears, hair brown and thick, bright hazel eyes, and stature above the average'. In youth he was clean-shaven and wore his hair cut short and straight in the Norman military fashion. He was of lean and muscular build, agile and very strong. French envoys once described him as 'a prince of distinguished appearance and commanding stature. His expression seemed to hint at pride.' However, a French priest, Jean Fusoris, thought he looked more like a priest than a soldier.

Besides having a love of music, Henry V was an enthusiastic sportsman who enjoyed hawking, fishing, wrestling, leaping and running, in which 'he excelled commonly all men', being faster, it was said, than a dog or even an arrow. Surprisingly, he had little interest in jousting.

Books were his greatest treasure. He had an extensive library and was literate in English, French, Latin and Welsh. He enjoyed books on history, theology and hunting, as well as the works of Chaucer, Hoccleve and Lydgate. He was also a connoisseur of the arts and architecture, although not on the same scale as Richard II.

English chroniclers are unanimous in their praise of Henry V, excelling themselves in superlatives. Walsingham describes him as 'prudent, far-seeing, magnanimous, firm, persistent, war-like and distinguished'. However, those who knew him found him a cold man who inspired respect rather than love. Taciturn in speech, a man of few words who could be a good listener and was gifted with a rather dry wit, he was highly self-disciplined and expected others to be too. He had a formidable presence, a lordly and severe manner, and was somewhat melancholy in temperament, tending to look serious at moments of triumph. However, he usually reacted positively to setbacks.

Henry had a good deal of common sense, being a perceptive man who was a wise judge of character, and he could also be persuasive and often aggressive when it came to asserting his rights. He was discreet, even secretive, but made it a point of honour to treat everyone with the utmost affability. 'He went straight to the point,' wrote a French envoy. On occasion he could appear sanctimonious and pedantic, parading his virtues, and making no secret of the fact that for seven years after his accession he remained chaste. His worst fault would prove to be a ruthless brutality that was only unleashed when his authority was challenged. Once, during a siege, a man danced on the wall of the fortress, mocking the King and blowing a trumpet so as to imitate a fart; when the town was captured Henry made a point of having him executed.

Henry V inherited the same insecurities his father had faced. Many regarded the House of Lancaster as a usurping dynasty and looked upon March as the rightful king; some even believed Richard II was still alive. However, in fourteen years of Lancastrian rule, people had generally grown used to the new dynasty and it had gained a considerable degree of acceptance, something that the new King was able to reinforce.

Henry V was fortunate in that he possessed all the attributes required of a successful mediaeval ruler. He was deeply pious in an unquestionably orthodox way, spending hours at prayer each day and making many pilgrimages to the shrines of saints. One of his ambitions was to wrest Jerusalem back from the Turks. He was severe with heretics and virtually stamped out Lollardy.

He was also a brilliant general, a courageous leader who took a personal interest in his men and in the routine practicalities of warfare, but who was also a stern disciplinarian prepared summarily to execute anyone who disobeyed him. His contemporaries saw him as the embodiment of the 'parfait, gentil knight' described by Chaucer, a Christian hero-king to whose name legends swiftly attached themselves. He embodied as such all the ideals of chivalry, and his magnificent reputation made a powerful impression on his contemporaries, and indeed on English history. Not for nothing was he called the flower of Christian chivalry.

He had 'a great will to keep justice, wherefore the poor folk loved him above all others, for he was careful to protect them from the violence and wrong that most of the nobles had done them'. To the poor, he was approachable and generous: his justice was strictly impartial, meted out to friend and foe, high and low alike. He was not a merciful king and his enemies feared his vengeance, which made his conquests easier since his reputation rode before him.

Henry V was a born leader who ascended the throne with astonishing confidence, determined to provide England with 'good governance'. Dedicated to his task, he proved an adept administrator and a superb politician, believing that the prosperity of the realm depended on the integrity and orthodoxy of its ruler and that any threat to the monarchy was a threat to a divinely ordered society. Even his enemies praised him as a wise ruler. He was careful in his spending, avoided borrowing money, and planned well ahead, all of which resulted in a significant recovery of the royal finances. Henry closely supervised the royal administrators who worked under him, and sacked any corrupt officials.

He made consistent efforts to win the support and co-operation of his magnates. His aggressive war policy united them behind him and also brought England to the forefront of European politics. The resultant concord between the King and his nobility made for a greater degree of success in his enterprises. He replaced Arundel as chancellor with Henry Beaufort, Bishop of Winchester, his 'oldest uncle and closest councillor', but relations between them were not always smooth. In 1417 the ambitious Beaufort accepted a cardinal's hat and the office of papal legate from the Pope without first bothering to obtain Henry's permission, as law and custom demanded. The King was furious and made him surrender both hat and appointment, which put paid to Beaufort's ambition to occupy a position centre-stage in the European Church.

Shakespeare would later portray Henry V as the vindicator of the House of Lancaster, whose deeds and reputation removed the taint of usurpation that adhered to his dynasty. Certainly, England had not been so well governed since the time of Edward III.

Henry embarked upon a general policy of conciliation. As soon as he became king he demonstrated his confidence as a ruler by releasing the Earl of March, now twenty-one, from house arrest, and he also restored Hotspur's son to the earldom of Northumberland. On the day before his coronation, Henry made March and his brother Roger Mortimer Knights of the Bath in a ceremony at the Tower of London. Clearly he did not regard March as a rival; nor did he acknowledge his superior claim to the throne, for he named his own brother Thomas, Duke of Clarence, as heir presumptive to the crown. March was a political unknown, unlikely to command significant support from the magnates, and a stranger to the populace at large, even if there were still those in high places who felt that he was rightful King of England and had been shabbily treated. Henry V took steps to rectify this: he made the Earl a member of his household and admitted him to his inner circle of advisers.

Fortunately for Henry, March was not particularly ambitious. His early experiences had perhaps crushed his self-confidence, and he lacked the qualities required of a king. He was a pleasant man, friendly and kind, entirely lacking the dynamism that drove Henry V. He found it hard to trust anyone, and went in fear of his awesome sovereign.

March was also, however, an impulsive and headstrong young man. Shortly after his release he secretly married his cousin, Anne Stafford, a great-granddaughter of Edward III, without first obtaining the requisite permission from the King. Henry was extremely displeased and fined the Earl £6666.13s.4d. (£6666.67). It has been conjectured that the forfeiture of such a vast sum made March resentful towards his sovereign, but since there is no record of his ever having paid the fine, it may well be that the King, knowing March's loyalty was crucial, exercised his prerogative of mercy, having shown his cousin how easily he could ruin him.

March lived in great splendour in his London residence, Baynard's Castle, on the banks of the Thames. His personal accounts survive and show him to have been an inveterate gambler. In the winter of 1413–14 he lost £157 at cards, backgammon, dice and cock-fighting. He kept a mistress called Alice at a house in Poplar, east of London, and spent large sums on her. He also frequented taverns and was not averse to the company of low-born folk.

By 1415, March had gained a degree of fame, and Jean Fusoris, who visited the English court from France that year, reported that many people would have preferred him to Henry for their king. However, their opinions were shortly to undergo a rapid change.

Not two months after Henry's accession a poster had been nailed to the door of Westminster Abbey proclaiming that Richard II was still alive in Scotland. The monks of Westminster Abbey had continued to support those who wished to restore Richard, even to the extent of backing an earlier Lollard conspiracy against Henry IV, which was suppressed with shocking brutality: seven proven culprits were roasted in chains over a slow-burning fire and another twenty-four were hanged.

In 1413, therefore, Henry V arranged for the body of Richard II to be moved from Langley to Westminster Abbey by night in a ceremony conducted with great pomp. The reinterment took place by the light of 120 torches in the presence of the King and many mourners, who watched as the coffin was laid to rest in the tomb occupied by Anne of Bohemia. Henry had not ordered Richard's reburial as an act of atonement, but to emphasise to the public that he was really dead. Nevertheless, claims by rebels that he was still alive were made twice in 1417 and even as late as 1419. Only then was the ludicrous pretence of the deposed king's survival finally abandoned.

Having established himself firmly on the throne and taken steps to neutralise potential enemies, Henry V turned his attention to the fulfilment of an ambition he had cherished since he was Prince of Wales: the prosecution of his ancestral claim to the kingdom of France and the conquest of that kingdom. In this enterprise, Henry firmly believed that God was on his side, that his cause was just, and that he was undertaking a sacred duty. He also knew that the accomplishment of his desire would immeasurably strengthen his position and thereby ensure the future of his dynasty. By unifying his people, high and low, in such a cause, he would channel their energies and interests into a profitable enterprise and so avert any threat of rebellion.

The magnates, and the people at large, greeted Henry's declared war policy with enthusiasm, as did Parliament, which did not hesitate to vote funds for an invasion force. This seemed the ideal moment to strike: the mad King Charles VI reigned in France and the country was divided by the aristocratic quarrels of the Burgundian and Armagnac factions.

Henry, blinded by zeal for his cause, cannot have imagined the enormity of the task he was about to undertake, nor did he foresee that England's resources would never be sufficient to carry his plans through to their conclusion. It did not occur to anyone that the successful prosecution of Henry's war policy depended on him alone.

One day, in the summer of 1415, as preparations for war were advancing steadily, Sir Thomas Grey of Heton was summoned to attend the Earl of Cambridge at Conisburgh Castle in Yorkshire. Grey held an important position on the King's Council and was constable of the castles of Bamburgh and Norham in his native Northumberland. He was connected by marriage to the Nevilles and the Percies, and was a prominent and respected figure in the north, having distinguished himself also in a military capacity. His son was betrothed to Isabella, the four-year-old daughter of the Earl of Cambridge.

Cambridge was the King's cousin, the younger son of Edmund, Duke of York, by Isabella of Castile. He had been born at Conisburgh in c.1375–6, and the twelfth-century stronghold, improved by his father, became his principal seat. Richard was named after his godfather, Richard II, and during the reign of Henry IV he had supported at least one impersonator of the late king. Some time after June 1408, when a dispensation was granted, he had married his distant cousin, Anne Mortimer, March's sister, who had been born in 1390 and spent her childhood at Wigmore Castle on the Welsh border. Anne's second child, born on 21 September 1411, was a son named Richard, who would grow up to be one of the central protagonists in the Wars of the Roses. Sadly, Anne died during or soon after his birth, and was buried beside her father-in-law in King's Langley Church. After her death Richard married Matilda, sister of John Clifford, Hotspur's brother-in-law, but there were no children of this union.

In May 1414, in Parliament, Henry V had confirmed York, Richard's elder brother, in his dukedom. At the same time, York had surrendered his father's earldom of Cambridge to the King, who bestowed it on Richard, who was indentured to supply Henry, on request, with two knights, fifty-seven esquires and 160 mounted archers. The new Earl of Cambridge was not a wealthy man and had not the resources to support his new status. Normally, the monarch granted some endowment when he raised a man to the peerage, but Henry V had omitted to do so in Cambridge's case. His title was an empty conceit and, being an ambitious man, he resented the fact.

The business that Cambridge wished to discuss with Grey at Conisburgh was treason: the assassination of Henry V and his brothers and the proclamation of Richard II – in the person of the Mummet in Scotland – as rightful king. If the Mummet proved to be an impostor then March would be raised to the throne. Cambridge was the most important of the plotters, but it is unlikely that he was the prime mover in the conspiracy. That honour probably belonged to Henry, 3rd Lord Scrope of Masham, a clever, gifted and attractive man who, like the other conspirators, the King should have been able to trust implicitly. Scrope was forty-two, well-born, well-connected and rich. Archbishop Scrope had been his kinsman but he had not been involved in his rebellion. He was a serious and pious man, given to reading mystical religious works, and owned eighty-three manuscripts, a sizeable library for the time. His private chapel was his pride and joy, and was stocked with ninety copes.

Scrope had been close to Henry V for some years, and on occasion they even shared a bed, a practice having no homosexual overtones in those days, when it was regarded as a sign of especial royal favour. Scrope had been Treasurer of England under Henry IV and was Treasurer of the Household to Henry V; Titus Livius called him 'an ornament of chivalry'. Scrope's second wife, Joan Holland, was the widow of Cambridge's father, York. There were thus strong family ties between the conspirators, and these proved greater than their loyalty to the Crown.

Why Scrope should have plotted to kill the King remains a mystery. Most of his contemporaries believed he had been offered financial inducements – some said as much as one million pounds, though this must have been an exaggeration – by the French government, who were anxious to prevent the English from invading France. The timing of the plot argues this, and the bribes could have been offered during a recent visit by French envoys to the court at Winchester. Scrope later denied being the instigator, as did Cambridge; both claimed they had been persuaded to join the conspiracy by the others.

The Earl of Northumberland was also involved, and it was probably he who suggested that Cambridge enlist the support of Grey. At Conisburgh, the Earl took Grey into his confidence and told him the details of the plot. Grey enthusiastically committed himself to joining the conspirators, and he and Cambridge rode south to meet the others. Cambridge had most to gain if the outcome was successful: his son Richard was March's heir, and March had so far remained childless. The Earl cherished dreams of his son wearing a crown.

As soon as Cambridge and Grey reached Southampton, Grey sought out Scrope, and several meetings of the conspirators took place. At this late stage, March was brought into the plot. It seems that the others persuaded his chaplain to urge him to claim the throne because it was his by rightful inheritance. March also owed Scrope large sums of money, and this may have been the price of his involvement, but he was a lukewarm conspirator, fearful of what would happen if the conspiracy failed, and not privy to all its details.

The conspirators were now meeting at March's manor of Cranbury, near Winchester, and at a house at the Itchen Ferry, beneath the walls of Southampton. Various suggestions as to how to kill the King were considered, such as setting fire to the invasion fleet, but most were rejected. Eventually a plan was formulated: Northumberland would raise the north, while March would raise his standard in the New Forest and advance into Wales, where he would be proclaimed king and Henry V branded a usurper. The Scots and Welsh would be asked to support the rebellion, and even the legendary Glendower would be called out of retirement if he could be found. The notorious Lollard rebel, Sir John Oldcastle, then in hiding on the Welsh Marches, would help to raise the West Country, and the King would be assassinated on 1 August, after which March would be crowned as King Edmund I. It was a masterplan involving every contentious element in Britain, one of the most dangerous conspiracies of the late Middle Ages, and it had a very good chance of success.

However, March had angered the religiously orthodox Scrope by bringing the Lollards and the taint of heresy into the plot. Scrope had soundly berated him for ruining everything, and at this March's courage – never very great at the best of times – failed him, and he tried to dissuade Scrope from going through with their plans. When this plea fell on deaf ears, he decided to confess everything to the King.

Henry had ordered the building of a fleet of ships for his invasion of France. On 1 August, the date set for his murder, he was at Porchester Castle inspecting his troops. That night, the Earl of March arrived, insisted on seeing the King urgently, and confessed all. Henry at once perceived that these were tidings 'most ominous as a presage for the future'. He was bitterly hurt by Scrope's betrayal, which was indeed incomprehensible to most people at the time.

Henry acted at once, summoning the chief magnates who were in his retinue to attend him. After urgent talks, they recommended that the King have the traitors arrested and tried. All were taken that same night, charged with high treason, and imprisoned in Southampton Castle, where they confessed their crimes.

Grey was tried on 2 August in the hall of what is now the Red Lion Inn in the Lower High Street of Southampton. He had made a written confession of his guilt and was condemned to a traitor's death. He made a pitiful plea for mercy but this was ignored, although the King graciously commuted his sentence to simple decapitation. He was then taken from the court to the Bargate, the northern entrance to the town, and beheaded outside it. His head was sent to Newcastle to be exhibited as a warning to the men of the north.

On that same day, Cambridge and Scrope, as lords of the realm, claimed trial by their peers. A committee of twenty lords, including March and Cambridge's brother York, was appointed to hear them. On 5 August they were brought to trial, found guilty, and sentenced to death. In Southampton Castle afterwards, Cambridge wrote to the King, begging for his life, but Henry was implacable, and later that day the Earl was beheaded outside the Bargate. His head and torso were buried in the chapel of God's House in Southampton, and all his honours, titles and estates were declared forfeit to the Crown that same day.

The sentences on Grey and Cambridge had been commuted but no such mercy was shown to the faithless Scrope, who was seen as the most wicked of the conspirators and who consequently suffered the full punishment reserved for traitors. He had asked in his will to be buried with his kinsfolk in York Minster, but the King ordered that his head be displayed in York above the Micklegate Bar,

Walsingham says that Henry wept over the fate of Cambridge and Scrope, but his ruthless treatment of the plotters ensured that there were no more serious rebellions against the House of Lancaster during his reign. March was pardoned and thereafter remained staunchly loyal to the King, serving under him in France and helping to guard England against any naval threat from her enemy. In November, Parliament confirmed the sentences of the Southampton court by passing retrospective Acts of Attainder upon the condemned men. The foiling of the conspiracy strengthened Henry's position, for people were inclined to see the hand of God in his preservation, Even Northumberland made his peace with the King, as did Oldcastle's son after his father's execution in 1417.

In 1421, March's kinsman, Sir John Mortimer, made a futile

attempt to place the Earl on the throne. He was arrested and imprisoned in an underground dungeon in the Tower, from which he managed to escape, only to be recaptured and held more securely. Mortimer had raised little support for his venture; in fact, few took him seriously, and in 1424, after a second attempted escape, he was convicted of treason and hanged, drawn and quartered at Tyburn.

In the late summer of 1415, Henry V crossed to France with an army of 10,000 men, laid siege to the port of Harfleur and took it. Many of his men died during the siege, not so much of wounds as of dysentery. The King then led his depleted force to Calais. Although he imposed strict discipline and banned prostitutes and alcohol, his men marked their progress through northern France by violence, murder, robbery, arson and rape; nor did Henry himself show any mercy to the French civilian population.

In October, the English scored an unexpected and spectacular victory over the flower of French chivalry at the Battle of Agincourt. Henry's force was heavily outnumbered and, had it not been for his brilliant generalship, the victory would surely have gone to the French. Once again, as at Crécy and Poitiers in the reign of Edward III, it was the skill of the English archers that proved the decisive factor. The arrows from their longbows were deadly against the heavily armoured French knights who, once unseated, were often unable to rise from the ground, and in any case found it almost impossible to fight effectively on foot. Henry had positioned his troops in such a way that the initial advance of the French was across marshy ground, and he kept his own armoured cavalry in reserve until the charge of the French cavalry had been thrown into confusion by his archers.

The King, says Walsingham, 'fought not as a king but as a knight, leading the way, the first to assail the enemy, giving and receiving cruel blows'. After the battle, however, he so far forgot his oath of knighthood as to order the slaughter of all disarmed prisoners, noble or otherwise, and his foot soldiers watched, deeply shocked, as two hundred archers stabbed, clubbed or burned the captives to death.

After returning to England, Henry was received in London with an outburst of rejoicing, and was fêted with nine hours of pageantry and processions culminating in a service of thanksgiving in St Paul's, as the bells of London pealed out. Not once, in all that celebration, was the austere King seen to smile, even though his people were wild with joy and shouting their acclaim.

The importance of Agincourt must not be underestimated. Apart from demoralising the French, it fired the imagination of every Englishman, made Henry V a popular hero, and bolstered the growing nationalism of his subjects. Few would now question the title of Lancaster to the throne, for both Henry and his people believed that God had vindicated his right by granting such a decisive victory. A grateful Parliament happily voted further subsidies to finance the continuation of the war, even though the cost of the campaign had been enormous and had placed some strain on an already overburdened treasury.

The English had suffered very few casualties at Agincourt. The only nobleman killed was Edward, Duke of York, who had commanded the right flank of the army during the battle. He was a big man and very overweight, and it was reported that he either suffocated to death in his armour or suffered a heart attack in the press of the fighting. His corpse was put in a huge cauldron of water and boiled all night, so that the flesh dissolved and the bones could be transported back to England, where they were buried in the collegiate church at Fotheringhay. A handsome monument to York's memory was later raised on the orders of Elizabeth I, and may still be seen today.

York left no children, and on his death his dukedom fell into abeyance. The attainting of his dead younger brother Cambridge meant that the latter's four-year-old son, Richard, could not inherit it, although he was able to inherit the entailed estates of the earldom of Cambridge, but not the title. Attainders, however, were often reversed, and there were those who foresaw that this little boy might one day inherit not only the dukedom of York, but also – through his mother – the vast wealth of the Mortimers, for he was also heir to the childless Earl of March, his maternal uncle. For the time being, however, the orphaned Richard, now a royal ward, was being brought up in Yorkshire, at Pontefract Castle and Methley Hall, under the guardianship of a royal retainer, Robert Waterton.

In 1417, Henry V began a well-planned campaign to conquer Normandy, the patrimony of his ancestors. Caen and Lisieux fell to him that year, Falaise, Domfront and Louviers in 1418. The Norman capital, Rouen, capitulated in 1419 after a long and bitter siege, occasioning great celebrations in London. Henry then went on to take Paris, the capital of the kingdom of France. In 1419 the Duke of Burgundy, England's ally, was murdered by supporters of the Dauphin Charles, heir to Charles VI. The murder drove his son, the new duke, Philip the Good, into an even stronger alliance with the English, which was highly advantageous to King Henry.

As the war dragged on, the King's reputation for cruelty grew. At the siege of Rouen, his harsh treatment of non-combatants – women, children and old men – resulted in 12,000 people dying from hunger and exposure. A French monk of the Abbey of St Denis accused Henry of abusing 'the right of kings to punish disobediences'. Anyone bearing arms who refused to surrender to him was put to death, and once Henry had a deserter buried alive before his horrified companions. When Caen fell, 2000 people were rounded up into the market place and slaughtered, their blood running in rivulets through the streets. Henry himself turned a deaf ear to the cries of the doomed citizens until he came upon the corpse of a decapitated woman with a dead baby at her breast. Only then did he call a halt to the killing, although he allowed his men to continue to plunder and rape. As he rode by on his charger, stern and implacable, hordes of terrified people fell on their knees, crying for mercy.

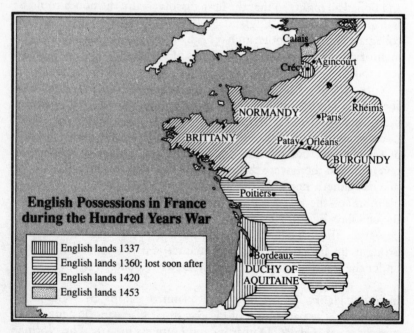

By 1420, Henry was master of Normandy, Brittany, Maine, Champagne and the Duchy of Aquitaine (or Guienne). But already there was in England a backlash of opinion against the war. The King was a hard taskmaster, and as the memory of Agincourt grew dimmer, Englishmen were becoming less enthusiastic about serving under him in France. Some of his soldiers were deserting and turning to a life of crime back in England.

Henry V ignored this, for the greatest prize of all was almost within his grasp. On 21 May 1420 a peace treaty was ratified at Troyes by the kings of England and France, by the terms of which Henry V and his heirs were designated the lawful successors to Charles VI. Normandy was formally ceded to Henry and he was appointed Regent of France until such time as he should succeed to his new inheritance. The Treaty of Troyes effectively disinherited the House of Valois and the Dauphin Charles, and marked the pinnacle of Henry V's achievement in France. However, it made little difference to the war, and hostilities continued as before, while the Dauphin, a penniless exile, set up a rival court at Bourges.

The Treaty of Troyes was sealed by the marriage of Henry V to Katherine of Valois, youngest daughter of Charles VI; their 'magnificent espousals' took place on 2 June at Troyes Cathedral. The marriage was supposed to lend dynastic credence to Henry's new status as heir to the French throne, and as he made his vows he appeared, according to one chronicler, 'as if he were at that moment king of all the world'.

The marriage had been under discussion since 1414, and according to Martin's Chronicle Katherine had 'passionately longed' for it; from the moment she set eyes on Henry, she 'constantly solicited her mother till the marriage took place'. She was undoubtedly handsome, if not beautiful, but Henry would probably not have cared if she were otherwise; to him, she represented France. He was never a doting husband, and Katherine seems to have been somewhat in awe of him. Theirs was essentially a dynastic match, and it is unlikely that love played much part in it.

Katherine had been born in 1401 in Paris of a demented father and a nymphomaniac mother, Isabeau of Bavaria. She had had a terrible childhood: she and her sister Michelle were neglected by their parents and nobody cared much about their welfare. They were filthy, often starving, and frequently abandoned by their unpaid attendants. The two princesses scavenged around for food or had to rely on the charity of their remaining servants.

Their father, a terrifying and sometimes violent figure, rarely saw them, but once, when he had one of his periods of lucidity, he demanded to know why his daughters were so unkempt and dirty. Their governess told him the truth, and he gave her a gold cup to sell so that necessities could be provided for the girls. Occasionally Queen Isabeau visited them, but she was too preoccupied with her many lovers and her political intrigues to spare much time for her vast brood of children, not all of whom were the King's. Eventually Katherine was packed off to be educated at the convent at Poissy, where she learned at least one language if little else. She seems not to have been a particularly bright girl, nor was she gifted with a vivacious personality, but she emerged from the convent with looks, her rank and her precocious sensuality to commend her, as well as the most engaging manners. The Burgundian chronicler, Jean de Waurin, called her 'a very handsome lady, of graceful figure and pleasing countenance', and her funeral effigy at Westminster Abbey shows her to have had a long neck, good bone structure, and the long Valois nose.

Henry and Katherine returned to England in December 1420, being carried ashore in triumph on the shoulders of the barons of the Cinque Ports. Katherine was crowned with due magnificence in February 1421, and in the summer of that year, the King left her pregnant when he returned to France for what was to be his last campaign. Before he went he is said to have forbidden her to go to Windsor for her confinement because of an old prophecy which foretold that 'Henry of Windsor shall long reign and lose all'.

Katherine disobeyed him. She went to Windsor in the autumn and there, at four o'clock in the afternoon of St Nicholas's Day, 6 December, after a painful labour, she bore a son, who was styled Duke of Cornwall from his birth. Henry V was besieging Meaux when he heard he had a male heir, and sent word that his son must be christened Henry and that his wife must without delay hear a mass of the Trinity and offer the child to God. Archbishop Chichele officiated at the baptism, while the King's next brother, John, Duke of Bedford, Bishop Beaufort, and Jacqueline, Duchess of Hainault stood sponsors. There was great public rejoicing. The little prince throve, and in January 1422 one Joan Astley was appointed his nurse.

Henry V never saw his son, and when the Prince was six months old Katherine left him behind in England in the care of his uncle, Humphrey, Duke of Gloucester, Henry V's youngest brother, and went to join her husband.

Henry V did not live to become King of France. The stresses of war and endless campaigning had prematurely aged him. In later life he grew a beard and let his curly hair grow long. A stone effigy of him in York Minster, executed around 1425 and recently identified as a true likeness, portrays him thus, as does the obverse of his great seal. He looks careworn and tired, and, indeed, he was intermittently ill from 1419 onwards.

In June 1422 Henry was at Senlis with the King and Queen of France when the Duke of Burgundy requested his aid in relieving a garrison on the Loire from attack by the Dauphin's men. Although he was unwell, having contracted a 'lengthy illness as a result of long and excessive labours' during the siege of Meaux, which had ended in May, Henry set off on yet another expedition, having said what was to prove a final farewell to his wife. He tried resolutely to ignore his illness, which took the form of high fever with violent dysentery, but at length he became so incapacitated that he could not sit astride a horse and had to be carried in a litter. Even this caused him terrible agony, and he had to be taken by boat along the Seine to the castle of Bois-de-Vincennes, near Paris, having resigned his command to his brother Bedford.

On arrival at Vincennes, he insisted on riding on horseback to the castle, but could endure no more than a few steps. His attendants lifted him, half fainting, into a litter, where he lay wild with pain. The illness had so consumed his strength that the doctors dared not give him any medicines, and it was clear that he was dying.

On 31 August the King demanded to know the truth about his condition. His physicians told him he had at best two hours to live. Bedford had come to say farewell, as had his other captains, Thomas Beaufort, Duke of Exeter, and Richard de Beauchamp, Earl of Warwick. Queen Katherine was still at Senlis with her parents. As the evening of 31 August wore on, the dying King's sufferings increased. His intestines, genitalia and lungs were already in a state of putrefaction. Shortly before two o'clock in the morning of 1 September 1422, Henry whispered that his constant desire had been to recapture Jerusalem from the Turks. Then, clutching a crucifix, he murmured, '*In manuas tuas, Domine, ipsum terminum redemisti,*' and died.

His death, says Walsingham, 'was deservedly mourned' for 'it left no one like him among Christian kings or princes. Thinking of his memorable deeds, people felt awe at his sudden and terrible removal,' which in years to come proved to have been a greater tragedy than anyone then living could have foreseen.

When Henry died his body was so skeletal that there was little flesh left to decompose, and his corpse was prepared for burial in the usual way, with even the intestines left inside. So that it should not stink during the journey back to England, it was embalmed with aromatic herbs, wrapped in waxed linen, lead and silken cloth, and placed in a coffin. This was laid on a black-draped bier surmounted by an effigy wearing royal robes and a crown, and escorted by a mighty host of mourners in doleful procession through France, across the sea, and home to its final resting place. The Queen was chief mourner, and it was she who commissioned the fine tomb of Purbeck marble which was raised to Henry's memory in a new chantry next to the shrine of St Edward the Confessor in Westminster Abbey. On this was placed an effigy of wood, painted in silver and gilt, with a solid silver head. During the Reformation of the 1530s, Henry VIII's commissioners stripped the tomb of its silver, leaving only a headless effigy. This remained for over four hundred years until a new head, based on contemporary portraits, was added in the 1970s.

As a king, Henry V had been extremely successful: he had kept the peace at home by governing with firmness, justice and mercy, and had united his people behind him in a common endeavour. His victories had added lustre to the name of Lancaster, and he had restored the prestige and authority of the Crown. In fact, his achievements were regarded by his contemporaries as little short of miraculous, and his early biographers wrote extravagantly flattering accounts of him, thus giving rise to the legend of a hero-king that found its greatest expression in Shakespeare's play and has influenced writers of English history to this day. Only now, in the twentieth century, are some of the less palatable truths about Henry V acknowledged.

His death was an unmitigated disaster for England. So much of France remained to be conquered and, even with a leader such as Henry, the enterprise would have been a forbidding task: ruled by an infant king, however diligent his regents, England could not hope to win the war, for her resources could not support it. Henry V had won much, but at enormous cost, and even in his lifetime there had been complaints. Parliament had become less ready to vote funds and had refused to grant further taxation; he had had to rely on loans to finance his campaigns in later years. This brought the Crown near to bankruptcy and burdened it with crippling debts. Henry had been unable to pay even his servants' wages; how, then, was the completion of an English conquest of France to be financed?

Henry V's reopening of the Hundred Years War had been intended to launch England into a new era of prosperity and glory. Instead he had saddled her with decades of expense and humiliation, which would ultimately bring about the ruin of his house. Even the dual monarchy established by the Treaty of Troyes was a precarious institution that Henry might not have been able to maintain, had he lived. The French people resented it, and large parts of France were as yet unconquered. In fact, the activities of Henry V in France did more than anything else to foster the growing sense of nationalism in that kingdom.

After his death, it was inevitable that divided opinion about the continuance or otherwise of the war with France would ensure that the English magnates would group themselves into factions: those in favour of following the late king's example and prosecuting the war, and those who believed that a peaceful end to it was essential. These differences would institute half a century and more of government by factions, which in itself would undermine law and order and the stability of the realm and even of the Crown itself. Worse still, the throne had now passed from a strong and respected man to a helpless baby, consigning England to the uncertainties of minority government. Not for nothing was it commonly said, 'Woe to thee, O land, when thy king is a child.'

5

The Child King

Henry VI succeeded his father at the tender age of nine months on 1 September 1422. On 11 October his grandfather, Charles VI, ended his miserable existence on earth, and Henry was proclaimed King of France also, in accordance with the terms of the Treaty of Troyes. In France, however, most people refused to acknowledge him, holding that the Dauphin should succeed his father. For the moment, though, the English held the upper hand, for Burgundy was all-powerful in France, and Burgundy was a staunch friend to England.

Henry V had expressed the fond wish that his son would one day go to Constantinople and 'take the Turk by the beard', and there were fervent hopes in every quarter that the infant king would grow up to emulate the auspicious example of his father. As the chronicler William Worcester put it, upon his life England's weal depended.

The most pressing problem in 1422 was the establishment of a regency government. Henry V's will, which no longer survives, instructed that Bedford should be Governor of Normandy and Regent of France, and that Humphrey, Duke of Gloucester, be Protector of England and guardian of the young King, with the support of the Earl of Warwick. However, the wishes of a deceased monarch held no force in law.

On 28 September the magnates swore allegiance to Henry VI. They then made plans for the minority government, summoning Parliament in the King's name and establishing a regency council made up of the most influential lords and bishops in the kingdom. Gloucester was appointed Protector and Defender of the Realm and the Church in England and principal councillor until such time as the King came of age; the appointment was at the King's pleasure, which meant in effect that the Council could revoke it at any time. The lords of the Council were reluctant to allow Gloucester sovereign power and would not permit him to bear any title 'that should import authority of governance'. His duties were restricted to keeping the peace and summoning and dissolving Parliament, and when Bedford was in England Gloucester was to give precedence to him. Gloucester repeatedly asserted that Henry V had intended him to enjoy sovereign authority, but to no effect: the lords of the Council were adamant that he was just a figurehead acting as the King's commissioner, whose actions were subject to their consent. For this state of affairs Gloucester blamed his uncle, Bishop Beaufort, whose influence was never to be underestimated and who had himself wished to be named regent. Gloucester had opposed this vociferously, and now the Duke was convinced that Beaufort had had his revenge. During the minority it would in effect be the lords of the Council who exercised the sovereign prerogative on the King's behalf, and behind this there was naturally a degree of self-interest on the part of the magnates.

The Queen was not given any political role in the regency, and at Henry V's request, Thomas Beaufort, Duke of Exeter, and Bishop Beaufort, young Henry's great-uncles, were given responsibility for the safe-keeping and nurture of the King.

The lords confirmed Bedford's appointment as Regent of France. His task was a thankless one, for he had to maintain Henry V's conquests there, protect the interests of the dual monarchy, and proceed to the conquest of those parts of France not yet under English rule. To support him in this he counted on England's ally, Philip of Burgundy, who had reasons of his own for bringing about the destruction of the House of Valois.

John of Lancaster had been born in 1389 and created Duke of Bedford in 1414. In 1423, to cement his friendship with Burgundy, he married the Duke's sister Anne. He had had considerable experience of government, and Henry V, trusting his brother completely, had appointed him Regent of England during his French campaigns after the death of the Duke of Clarence. As Governor of Normandy, Bedford established a policy of conciliation, making it clear he would honour the ancient traditions of the duchy. He was a wise, just, enlightened and respected statesman and a brave soldier whose men recognised his integrity. Those who harassed the indigent population could expect severe and immediate punishment, for Bedford's chief aim was to make English rule acceptable to the French, and in this he enjoyed moderate success. During his lifetime English interests in France were more than satisfactorily protected. Nevertheless, Gloucester, jealous of his elder brother, never ceased criticising him, and seemed on occasion to be doing his best to wreck the vital alliance with Burgundy. But then Gloucester, no realist, was his own worst enemy.

Born in 1390, Humphrey of Lancaster had been created Duke of Gloucester in 1414, and may have attended Balliol College, Oxford. He was one of the best educated princes in mediaeval England, a lover of classical learning, and the internationally renowned patron of humanist scholars as well as writers such as Titus Livius of Forli, Leonardo Aretino, John Lydgate and John Capgrave. His donation of 263 books to the University of Oxford provided the foundation for Duke Humphrey's Library at the Bodleian, although the collection was dispersed in the sixteenth century.

Gloucester was intensely ambitious, and his single aim in life was self-promotion. Although in fact he enjoyed considerable power, it was never enough for him, and he was consistently jealous of the precedence accorded to Bedford and the wealth and influence of Bishop Beaufort. His arrogance, irresponsibility, volatile temper and insistence on single-mindedly furthering his own interests, whether or not these were at variance with the common weal of the country, all constituted a bar to the fulfilment of his ambitions.

Gloucester had been given a command – and been wounded – at Agincourt, and had served Henry V on later campaigns; he was a good soldier, anxious to win military glory. Henry V had been his hero; he was loyal to his brother's memory and resolved to pursue his war policy, which, to Gloucester, was a sacred trust. He was a pious man, if a promiscuous one – his sexual excesses are said to have undermined his health by the time he was thirty. He was also gracious in manner and affable to all classes, and it was this that made him popular with the common people and caused them to dub him 'Good Duke Humphrey'. The magnates, who knew him better, might well have called him something rather different.

Bishop Beaufort, Gloucester's chief rival, was a shrewd politician who was intellectually the Duke's superior – Gloucester was seldom to get the better of him. The Bishop was by far the most dynamic of Gaunt's sons by Katherine Swynford, and saw himself primarily as a European churchman. His main ambition was to become pope, but although he became a cardinal in 1426, it was a dream that would never materialise.

The chronicler Edward Hall describes Beaufort as 'rich above measure of all men'. He had profited immensely from the wool trade and had used his wealth as a bridge to power. His loans to the Crown – which during the period 1406–46 amounted to over £213,000 – bolstered the depleted royal finances. Gloucester tried to accuse

Beaufort of usury, then condemned as mortal sin by the Church, but could uncover no proof that Beaufort was actually charging interest on his loans. Examination of the Bishop's accounts has only recently proved that he did indeed make hefty profits. Beaufort was not only out to gain wealth, but was also to use that wealth to buy the power to challenge Gloucester's leadership of the Council and gain political supremacy himself.

Beaufort exerted enormous influence over the young King, who would come to regard him as 'a very dear uncle to me, and most liberal'. Throughout the minority, the Beauforts were to be a united and powerful faction. Exeter was the King's guardian; his nephew Edmund Beaufort was a member of the Council (Edmund's elder brother Somerset was at this time a prisoner of the French), and the Cardinal ruled all.

Queen Katherine, denied by the provisions of her husband's will any political role in the regency, was at least allowed to have her son with her during his early years. After Henry V's funeral she took the baby to Windsor, remaining there in seclusion with him for a year. Thereafter, they frequently stayed either at Hertford Castle or Waltham Palace, residing at the Palace of Westminster only on state occasions. Katherine played the part of Queen Dowager to perfection. She never involved herself in politics and was in turn accorded all the honours due to her rank. Her roles were purely domestic and ceremonial.

Gloucester and the Council were concerned about her future, for she was still an attractive girl in her early twenties, and it was inconceivable that she would not wish to remarry at some stage. The difficulty lay in whom she would marry when the time came. There was no precedent for a queen dowager remarrying in England, and if Katherine married an English lord he would almost certainly have political ambitions and influence over the young King. Her marrying abroad could cause equally serious political complications. Fortunately, as yet, the Queen was preoccupied with her son and showing no inclination to remarry, so the problem could be shelved for the time being.

The regency Council was made up of about twenty lords and bishops. One of its unofficial priorities was to safeguard aristocratic interests, and members were rewarded by occasional grants and the voting of substantial salaries. Apart from this, there was comparatively little corruption. Most members were genuinely concerned that the kingdom should be governed properly and that the King's prerogative be preserved. The Council, in a bid to unite the nobility and commons, did its best to maintain the policies of Henry V, and enjoyed some success. Nevertheless, the minority of the young king provided an ideal opportunity for an already powerful aristocracy to expand its power-base even further, and divisions on the Council itself were reflected in the formation of noble factions, rivals greedy for the rewards of high office.

The Council was dominated by Gloucester and Beaufort, whose squabbles were to influence English politics for the next twenty-five years. The rivalry between these two men was intense and deadly: each tried to bring the other down by cunning or force, and their bitter divisions had by 1424 split the Council. Gloucester was convinced that the war with France should be continued, but Beaufort, prompted by the success of French armies led by Joan of Arc and financial constraints at home, was convinced by 1430 that an honourable peace was the best solution. Bedford tried to arbitrate between Gloucester and Beaufort when he was in England, but without much success. Most councillors, however, tried not to let the rivalry between the two men interrupt the normal functioning of government, and were anxious to have the Council present a united front. Many were also concerned about law and order, which was declining at a local level, though this was not yet the major problem it would later become. When the Earl of March quarrelled with Gloucester, in the interests of unity he was hastily moved out of contention's way to Ireland, where – like his father and grandfather before him – he served as the King's Lieutenant, at the exorbitant salary of 5000 marks per annum.

The minority was therefore an unexpectedly peaceful period. No voices were raised to challenge the King's title, nor were there any rebellions. Given the problems it faced, the regency Council governed responsibly and fairly well.

Early in 1423, the redoubtable and respected Richard de Beauchamp, Earl of Warwick, was appointed the King's legal guardian. On 21 February, Dame Alice Butler, a lady described as 'expert and wise', was appointed his governess, and the Council, in the King's name, gave her 'power to chastise us reasonably from time to time' because 'in our tender age it behoves us to be taught and instructed in courtesy and nurture and other matters becoming a royal person'. Nor would Dame Alice be 'molested, hurt or injured' in years to come for beating her sovereign.

Henry VI's first public appearance was at the opening of Parliament in November that year, when he was nearly two. On Saturday 13 November Queen Katherine brought him from Windsor and lodged at Staines for the night. On Sunday morning, Henry was carried out to his litter which was waiting to take him to Kingston, but 'he shrieked, he cried, he sprang, and would be carried no further. Nothing the Queen could devise might content him.' He was yelling so much she thought he was ill. At length, 'they bore him again to the inn and there he abode all day. On the Monday he was borne to his mother's car [litter], he then being merry or glad of cheer, and so they came to Kingston.'

On Wednesday 16 November 'he came to London, and with merry cheer, on his mother's lap in the car, rode through London to Westminster, and on the morrow was so brought to Parliament', again on his mother's lap on a movable throne drawn by white horses. 'It was a strange sight, and the first time it was ever seen in England, an infant sitting on the mother's lap, before it could tell what English meant, to exercise the place of sovereign direction in open Parliament. Yet so it was – the Queen illumined that public convention of estates with her infant's presence.'

This account, which appeared in a London chronicle of c.1430, was later used as evidence of Henry VI's early inclination towards sanctity, for it was believed that his refusal to travel on a Sunday betokened incipient holiness. Modern parents might well describe his behaviour as a temper tantrum typical of a two-year-old, but people in the fifteenth century were more apt to see portents in such things.

In January 1425 the Earl of March died of plague at Trim Castle in Ireland, aged thirty-three. His body was brought back to England and buried in the collegiate church at Stoke Clare in Suffolk, near the tombs of his forbears. He was the last of the male line of the Mortimers and had left no legitimate issue, therefore his claim to the throne, his wealth and estates, and the earldoms of March and Ulster should by right have been inherited by his sister Anne's son, Richard of Cambridge, now fourteen years old. However, the Council, on 22 May 1425, resolved to grant custody of March's lands to Bishop Beaufort and entrust Baynard's Castle to Queen Katherine. As Richard's father had been attainted there was nothing he could do about this, and the Mortimer inheritance remained in the hands of the Crown for some years to come. The other – and more dangerous – prize that Richard ought to have inherited from his uncle, the Mortimer claim to the throne as heir-general of Richard II, was not acknowledged by anyone, nor would it be for many years to come.

However, from 2 February 1425 Richard was allowed to style himself Duke of York, as heir to the uncle who had died at

Agincourt. By this time, the young Duke was already a married man. Some time before 18 October 1424 (the exact date is not known) he had married Cecily Neville, the youngest daughter of Ralph Neville, Earl of Westmorland by Joanna Beaufort. Cecily had been born in 1415 at Raby Castle in County Durham, and because of her good looks was popularly known as 'the Rose of Raby'. She was her father's twenty-second child, and many of her brothers and sisters had married well; thus by virtue of his marriage York found himself closely related to most of the great magnates of England, which in the future would prove useful for building up a powerful affinity.

Cecily's father had had to purchase Richard's marriage from the Crown, which held him in wardship, at a cost of 3000 marks. In December 1423 Richard had gone to live at Raby Castle with Westmorland's younger children, which enabled him to become well-acquainted with his bride. His father-in-law paid out 200 marks a year for his maintenance, and presumably considered this money well spent because Richard was a great matrimonial prize by virtue of his birth and hoped-for inheritance. The Council doubtless felt that the Earl was the right man to be entrusted with the upbringing of York, since Westmorland had been a loyal supporter of the House of Lancaster since 1399 and would ensure that his charge was raised in such a way as to prevent him from getting any ideas about his own dynastic status.

In April 1425 the Queen once again brought the King to London. When the procession stopped at St Paul's, Gloucester lifted Henry down from the litter and then he and Exeter led the three-year-old to the high altar, where he dutifully said his prayers and looked gravely about him. He was then carried out into the churchyard and, to the people's delight, placed on a horse and taken in procession through the city. Two days later he went with his mother to open Parliament. So appealing did he look that the crowds watching cried out their blessings, saying that he appeared to be the very image of his famous father, and expressing hopes that he would grow up to display the same martial zeal.

Around this time, the Council decided that the King needed some companions of his own age, and decreed that all noble boys in royal wardship should be brought up with Henry at court. On 19 May 1426 the King was knighted by Bedford, then he in turn conferred knighthood on some of his young companions and Richard of Cambridge, who on that same day was formally restored to the dukedom of York. Later that year, the Duke of Exeter, who had been responsible for the King's upbringing, died.

In 1427, Henry's first 'master' was appointed. He was John Somerset, a monk in Gloucester's service, but he died when Henry was nine, after teaching him French and English and inspiring him with a love of the Christian faith, so that he could recite all the divine offices by heart. Many books were bought for the boy, including devotional treatises, Bede's *History of the English Church*, and a work entitled *On the Rule of Princes*, which set out how a king ought to behave and how he should set a moral example to his people. Henry was not the only boy to benefit from such instruction, for each of the royal wards in his household was appointed a schoolmaster of his own, thus forming an exclusive and privileged school.

In 1427, as he approached his sixth birthday, the young King was removed from the care of women. He now resided in turn at the castles of Windsor, Berkhamsted, Wallingford or Hertford, and saw his mother only infrequently, though the bond between them remained close. He never failed to choose pretty gifts for her at New Year, such as the ruby ring given him by Bedford, which he presented to her in 1428.

On 1 June 1428 the King's guardian, the Earl of Warwick, was also appointed his Governor and Master, with sole charge of the young sovereign and orders from the Council in the King's name to instruct him in good manners and courtesy, letters and languages. Like Alice Butler before him, Warwick was authorised 'to chastise us from time to time, according to his good advice and discretion'. Warwick did not spare the rod, but Henry VI had the advantage of being educated by one of the finest minds of the age.

Warwick was the son of one of the Lords Appellant who had rebelled against Richard II in 1388. He had rendered distinguished service as one of Henry V's foremost generals during the Normandy campaign, and remained in France after the death of his master, serving Bedford with similar loyalty and brilliance. The Emperor Sigismund, who had met Warwick in England, was so impressed by his chivalry that he dubbed him 'the Father of Courtesy'. Courtesy was certainly one of the disciplines he instilled in the young Henry VI, along with kindness and piety, for which the Earl was renowned, having made the challenging pilgrimage to Jerusalem.

The Rous Roll, written by the antiquarian John Rous in the 1480s to commemorate the deeds of the earls of Warwick, has a line-drawing of Henry VI's governor in full armour, with the child king sitting on his arm. Warwick was indeed a man to be respected, and he believed in discipline and character training. Henry's upbringing was strict but fair, and it was not long before he began, for awe of his tutor, 'to forbear the more to do amiss and intend the more busily to virtue and learning'. From Warwick he learned literacy skills and languages, as well as the knightly training in horsemanship, swordplay, tilting, self-defence and military strategy – all of which the Earl was well qualified to teach him. Henry was to show little interest in these accomplishments later on, though the precepts taught by Warwick would remain with him all his life, giving him the strength to face adversity and humiliation.

Some time between 1425 and 1429, Queen Katherine formed a romantic attachment to a Welshman called Owen ap Maredudd ap Tewdwr (Tudor). Their affair is surrounded in mystery. Little is known of Katherine's personal life, although she and her retinue lived in the King's household until at least 1430, and during this period she seems to have borne Tudor at least one child. However, concealing a pregnancy might not have presented such a problem because women's gowns of the period were high-waisted with full gathers in the front.

Many later chroniclers claimed that Katherine had actually married Tudor in secret; indeed, it was not until the seventeenth century that the legitimacy of their union was questioned, and then on spurious grounds. What is likely is that the wedding had to be kept private because in marrying a man so far below her in rank the Queen had 'followed more her own appetite than her open honour', according to the Tudor chronicler Edward Hall. The earliest reference to the marriage appears in 'Gregory's Chronicle' for 1438, where it is stated that the common people knew nothing of it. The Council and the King were almost certainly aware of the union but left the couple unmolested so as to avoid scandal attaching itself to the royal house.

The Tewdwrs, or Tudors, as they later became known, were a prosperous gentry family from Anglesey, north Wales. They had supported Glendower's rebellion and had consequently been dispossessed of all their lands. A senior branch of the family eventually had the estate at Penmynydd restored to them and, taking the name Theodore, lived there in obscurity until the seventeenth century, ignored by their more famous relatives.

Owen Tudor saw service in France in the retinue of Sir Walter Hungerford, who later became steward of Henry VI's household. It may have been through him that Tudor acquired the post of Keeper of the Wardrobe to Queen Katherine. Hall describes him as 'a goodly gentleman and a beautiful person, garnished with many gifts of nature', though 'Gregory' calls him 'no man of birth, neither of livelihood'. He was never knighted, and his income was at most £40 per annum. He was naturalised in 1432 and treated thereafter as an

English subject of Henry VI, but he did not adopt the anglicised version of his surname – Tudor – until 1459.

Many fanciful and unsubstantiated tales have attached themselves to the love affair between Katherine of Valois and Owen Tudor. Most are romantic, some lurid, and nearly all are probably apocryphal, but what does emerge from them is that Katherine, who is said to have been stirred by carnal passion, took the initiative, ignoring all the warnings of her ladies that Tudor was no suitable match for her. It is impossible now to substantiate later tales that he fell into her lap while dancing, or she watched him swimming nude; the truth of their relationship is obscured by a veil of legend.

What is certain is that Katherine bore Tudor several children, and that those who survived infancy became staunch supporters of the House of Lancaster. The eldest child was Edmund, born around 1430 at Much Hadham Palace in Hertfordshire, a brick-built twelfth-century manor owned for eight hundred years by the bishops of London which still stands today. The second son was Jasper, born in approximately 1431 at the Bishop of Ely's manor at Hatfield in Hertfordshire. In 1432, Katherine's third pregnancy was near term when she visited the King at Westminster, but her labour began prematurely and she was obliged to seek the help of the monks of Westminster Abbey, where she was delivered of a son, Owen. The baby was taken from her at birth and reared by the brethren; Vergil says he became a Benedictine monk at the Abbey, where he seems to have been known as Edward Bridgewater. He died and was buried there in 1502. Vergil also mentions a daughter who became a nun, but no other source refers to her.

Throughout the 1420s the war with France had continued under Bedford's direction. In 1423 the English were victorious at the Battle of Cravant, and again in 1424 at Verneuil. By the end of 1425 they were in control of Maine and Anjou.

In 1428, the Earl of Salisbury defied Bedford's warning and took the offensive against the Dauphin's forces, laying siege to the city of Orléans. Bedford was uneasy because he was aware that, despite government propaganda aimed at raising popular support for the war, fewer Englishmen than ever now wanted to fight against the French, and Parliament was refusing financial support for the war because resources were scarce.

Hitherto, the Dauphin had controlled that part of France which was south of the Loire and outside the English-owned duchy of Aquitaine. By 1428 his fortunes were at a very low ebb and his people were demoralised. At this moment there appeared at his court a peasant girl, Joan of Arc, who claimed to have heard angelic voices instructing her to free France from English rule. At length, the Dauphin was persuaded to allow her to lead the defence of Orléans. What followed was a resounding victory for the French, which marked a turning point in their fortunes while, conversely, the English could date the decline of their hold on France from the appearance of Joan of Arc. Their defeat at Orléans in 1429 was the first major setback they had suffered since the death of Henry V. Worse was to follow.

After another victory at Patay in 1429, Joan led the Dauphin to Rheims. There, in the cathedral which had seen the hallowing of his royal ancestors, he was anointed and crowned King Charles VII on 18 June in her presence. Even now perhaps the English could have retrieved the situation. They did not, for the simple reason that their war effort was hampered by bitter squabbling between the nobles on the Council.

In England, too, there was a coronation, on 5 November, when Henry VI was crowned in Westminster Abbey. It was a long ordeal for a child not yet eight, but Henry bore it well and with gravity, for all that the crown was too heavy for him to wear with comfort. Few celebrations marked the event; in London, the conduits did not run with free wine, as was customary, because the Council was worried that the King might see drunken people in the streets. Instead, wine was distributed by the cup to each person. Despite this, there were such huge crowds lining the streets that several people were suffocated. Some pick-pockets ended the day in prison, and there was even alternative entertainment at Smithfield, where a heretic was burned at the stake.

The ritual of coronation should have marked Henry's assumption of personal rule, but clearly he was still too young to exercise sovereign power. The Council would continue to exercise it for him for several more years, under the authority of Gloucester and Beaufort, who were still at each other's throats. The coronation seems to have turned young Henry's head, for soon afterwards Warwick was complaining to the Council that he was growing far too aware of his royal estate, 'the which cause him to grudge with chastising'. The Council had Henry before them and warned him that, king or not, he had to obey his governor. But Warwick was not always the stern disciplinarian, and he seems to have had a deep affection for his charge. In 1430 he had made a little harness trimmed with gold for the King's horse, and procured for him some toy swords, 'for to learn the King to play in his tender age'.

In 1430, much to the gratification of the English, Joan of Arc was captured by the Duke of Burgundy, who sold her to his ally, Bedford. In May 1431, after being convicted of witchcraft, she was handed over by the Church to the secular authorities and burned at the stake at Rouen in the presence of Cardinal Beaufort. However, her death did not herald a revival of English fortunes in France.

Henry VI was in Rouen at the time of Joan's trial, but he was not present at her execution. Soon afterwards he went with the Cardinal to Paris. Bedford was desperate to retrieve the situation in France before it was too late, and had decided that Henry should be crowned King of France in Paris to counter the effect of Charles VII's coronation the year before. Accordingly, Henry's took place at the cathedral of Notre Dame on 16 December 1431.

The French did not want an English king. Fired by a new and vibrant spirit of nationalism, they were determined to oust the invaders and have Charles VII as their ruler. Even as Henry was being crowned in Paris, crowds were rioting in the streets and some of the nobility were hastening to Charles's aid. The coronation was one of Bedford's few failures, and he knew it. Judging the mood of the French people to be dangerous, he sent Henry home to England almost immediately, thus ending the King's first and only visit overseas.

After a joyful welcome back home, Henry settled down to his studies again. He was progressing well, having read many chronicles of English history and become particularly interested in Alfred the Great, whom he was later to try, unsuccessfully, to have canonised. In 1432, at eleven, Henry was still headstrong, and so rebellious at times that his hard-pressed governor again complained to the Council of the boy's wilfulness. The lords assured him of their support. It seems that Henry greatly resented his royal person being beaten for misdemeanours, and was fond of threatening Warwick with dire retribution when he came of age. The Council, however, made it plain to the King that Warwick's disciplinary measures were enforced with its full approval. It also empowered the Earl to dismiss any of the King's companions who distracted him from his studies and exerted a subversive influence over him.

Richard, Duke of York, came of age in 1432, when he was twenty-one. Two years earlier he had been given the important office of Constable of England, which carried responsibility for England's military defences, and in 1431 had attended Henry VI in France. Now, on 12 May, York was recognised as Earl of March, Ulster and Cambridge by hereditary right, notwithstanding the attainder against his father. However, he was only allowed to take possession of his estates after agreeing to pay the King, within five years, the sum of £1646.0s.6d (£1646.02½p) for the privilege of doing so. In 1433 he was made a Knight of the Garter.

Despite his vast wealth and his nearness in blood to the throne – and probably because of it – York was not given a place on the King's Council nor involved in the government of the kingdom. There were those about the King who feared he might make a bid for the throne if he were allowed too much power, and it was decided to employ him in a strictly military capacity.

York was now the owner of great tracts of land in Wales, Ireland and thirteen English counties. The greatest concentration of his estates was along the northern Welsh Marches. From his uncle, March, he had inherited the fabulous wealth of the Mortimers, making him the richest magnate and greatest landowner in England. He also owned the great castles at Ludlow and Fotheringhay, and Baynard's Castle in London. In 1436, his income was at least £3231, possibly twice as much, and by 1443-4 his income from his Welsh Marcher lordships alone had risen to £3430 net. Despite his loyalty to the King, this wealth, and his powerful family connections, made him potentially a force to be reckoned with.

The year 1433 saw the emergence of two disastrous trends in Lancastrian history. The first was the decline of Burgundy's friendliness towards England. After Anne of Burgundy, Bedford's wife, died in childbirth in 1432, Bedford married Jacquetta of Luxembourg, the beautiful daughter of the Count of St Pol. Burgundy was against the marriage for various political reasons, and from then on relations between England and her greatest ally began to cool.

By now, it was obvious that England no longer had the resources to support the war. Bedford was ill, and his chief desire was to negotiate an honourable peace with the French before England was ignominiously defeated. Predictably, Gloucester blocked every attempt he made to persuade the Council that this was the best course of action, knowing that if the war ended Bedford would return to England and oust him from power. By 1434 Burgundy was already negotiating his own peace with Charles VII, and before the year was out had written to Henry VI formally breaking their alliance. The young King cried when he saw that Burgundy had not addressed him as King of France, and when the news of the Duke's disaffection broke in London there were riots, and Flemish aliens, subjects of Burgundy, were lynched. It was clear, however, that without Burgundy's support the English cause in France was lost.

Cardinal Beaufort and many others on the Council agreed with Bedford that peace with France was the only solution, but Gloucester was adamant: Henry V's policies must be carried out until their final objective was achieved. Deadlock had been reached.

The second trend was illustrated by the emergence of William de la Pole, Earl of Suffolk, as the dominant influence over the royal household. Suffolk was appointed its steward in 1433, thanks to his avuncular friendship with the young King. But he was a greedy, ambitious, self-seeking man, and saw his appointment as the ideal opportunity to feather his own nest.

The de la Poles were descended from a Hull merchant who had gained royal favour after lending money to Edward III. Suffolk's grandfather, Michael de la Pole, had been a favourite of Richard II, who had conferred upon him the earldom of Suffolk. His son, the 2nd Earl, had supported Bolingbroke in 1399 and been rewarded with substantial lands in East Anglia. He died at Harfleur in 1415, and his son, the 3rd Earl, fell at Agincourt.

William de la Pole was uncle of the 3rd Earl. For seventeen years he had served the House of Lancaster loyally in France, where he had cultivated a friendship with the Earl of Salisbury. Salisbury was a supporter of Cardinal Beaufort, and in 1430, after Salisbury's death, Suffolk married his widow, Alice Chaucer, granddaughter of the poet Geoffrey, and aligned himself with the Beaufort faction. By 1434 he was an enthusiastic advocate of peace with France.

He was a man of pleasant appearance and manner, and a competent soldier imbued with high chivalric ideals. Like many magnates, he frequently placed his own interests before those of the realm, although he did sincerely believe in the necessity for peace, the only policy he ever consistently supported. His enthusiasm for any other policies depended upon how popular they were among his supporters and the public, for he would do nothing to jeopardise his own position.

Suffolk was not well-endowed with lands, which was why he was so anxious to acquire wealth, and he now began to exert considerable influence over the King. The boy was completely won over by his charm, and responded by enriching Suffolk with a steady stream of grants of lands and lucrative appointments.

Thanks to Warwick's thorough training, Henry now had a precocious interest in politics, much to the Council's dismay. The lords were not prepared to have a twelve-year-old boy interfering in government, even if he were the King. Moreover, it was becoming apparent that he was easily led, and the Council. perceiving this, warned him in 1434 to avoid becoming entangled in court intrigues and swayed by persons who were trying to influence him. Occasionally he attended meetings of the Council, and on one occasion acted as mediator between Gloucester and Beaufort. Like everyone else he was weary of the enmity between his uncles, and once he imperiously commanded them to stop quarrelling over the limits of each other's authority.

By the autumn of 1435 it was obvious that the French had rejected the Treaty of Troyes, and there were further heated debates on policy in England, Gloucester wanting to sustain the treaty by intimidation, while Beaufort, more realistic, was insisting on peace. The European powers held a peace conference at Arras in northern France, and the English sent an embassy. However, their ambassadors made unreasonable demands and proved obdurate when it came to surrendering Henry VI's claim to the French throne. Walking out in high dudgeon, they left Burgundy free to negotiate a peace treaty with France, and undermined the credibility of the peace party in England, leaving Gloucester temporarily in control.

As Burgundy and France discussed their alliance, Bedford died at Rouen on the night of 14–15 September 1435. Six days later the Treaty of Arras was signed by Philip and Charles, heralding the end of Lancastrian domination in France. When Henry VI heard the news he wept uncontrollably.

Bedford's death, following hard upon the victories of Joan of Arc and Burgundy's desertion, wrecked English fortunes in France and signalled the collapse of the Plantagenet empire. It also spelt tragedy for England because no one but Bedford could hold in check the rivalry and ambitions of Gloucester and Beaufort. After his death their constant elbowing for power became more intense, particularly since Gloucester now replaced his brother as heir-presumptive to the throne, and felt that this should ensure him appropriate precedence.

There was also the problem of who should replace Bedford in France at this critical time. There were few men of his calibre and this was not a decision that could be made in undue haste. Meanwhile, Gloucester's views prevailed, and the remaining English armies descended on the occupied territories in France with a ferocity calculated to terrify the rebellious inhabitants into submission. This scorched earth policy cost the English little in expense but a great deal in the longer term, because it made the French doubly determined to get rid of them.

The events of the autumn of 1435 prompted the young King, now nearing fourteen, to voice his own views on policy and take a greater interest in politics. Beaufort and Suffolk managed to convince him that his father's policy could not be sustained any longer and that peace was the only realistic solution.

Early in 1436 the Council decided that York should replace

Bedford as Governor of Normandy and Regent of France. Although he was young he was the premier magnate of the realm and his rank demanded high office. The appointment would hopefully satisfy his ambitions and prevent him from trying to meddle in politics in England. However, York lacked experience in military matters and received little support from the Council or Parliament, the latter consistently failing to grant him sufficient funds. Instead, he was expected to finance his men, his campaigns and his administrative costs out of his own pocket. He enjoyed little success against the French, who re-took Paris in April 1436, driving out the English whose authority was now confined to Normandy, Gascony, Aquitaine and the Calais Pale. All York gained was military experience, though this would stand him in good stead in the years to come.

As if all this was not bad news enough for Henry, in 1436 he realised that his mother was dying, probably from cancer. Some time that year, pregnant with her last child, Queen Katherine withdrew to the Abbey of Bermondsey, a foundation much favoured by royal and noble ladies, to be nursed by the sisters there. Suffolk was entrusted with the care of her children by Tudor, and the King was kept informed of her progress. There is no evidence to substantiate later allegations that the Council had just discovered the Queen's marriage and had her incarcerated at Bermondsey as a punishment.

However discreetly her withdrawal to Bermondsey had been managed, the royal family could not escape scandal entirely. Bedford's young widow, Jacquetta, created a furore in 1436 when she married a Northamptonshire squire, Richard Wydville, who was far below her in rank and had only his looks to commend him. The gossip died down eventually, and the couple settled at Grafton, where they produced sixteen children. History, however, had not heard the last of the Wydvilles.

At Bermondsey, Katherine's health deteriorated fast. On 1 January 1437, knowing she was approaching what she herself described in her will as 'the silent conclusion of this long and grievous malady', she made her last testament. In it she did not refer to Owen Tudor or their children. Instead, she nominated Henry VI as her executor and asked him to ensure 'the tender and favourable fulfilling of my intent', which is not specified, but which he must have known about. Almost certainly he had visited her during her illness, and almost certainly her request alluded to her children and perhaps her husband.

The Queen gave birth to a daughter who did not long survive, and then on 3 January, having endured pitiful suffering, she died. The

King was enthroned in Parliament when they brought him the news. Katherine was buried with royal honours in the Lady Chapel of Westminster Abbey, but the fine tomb raised to her memory by her son was destroyed when the chapel was demolished to make way for the Henry VII Chapel in 1509, and thereafter her corpse remained above ground in an open coffin as one of the curiosities shown to visitors. In 1669 the diarist Samuel Pepys saw it and daringly embraced and kissed it, 'reflecting that I did kiss a queen'. In the eighteenth century Katherine's bones were still firmly united and thinly clothed with flesh resembling tanned leather, and it was not until 1878 that they were decently laid to rest beneath an ancient altar slab in Henry V's chantry chapel.

After Katherine's death, Owen Tudor sought to return to Wales, but was overtaken by Gloucester's men and imprisoned in Newgate. His offence is nowhere recorded, and in fact the whole matter was kept very secret. It may be that the Council, having been reluctant to move against Tudor while the King's mother was alive, now wanted him punished for compromising her honour. This is the reason given by Vergil, writing in the reign of Tudor's grandson, Henry VII. But the Council's discretion was in vain, for while Tudor was in Newgate, news of the arrest quickly became public knowledge, as did his marriage to the late queen.

Katherine's children by Tudor were now given into the care of Katherine de la Pole, Suffolk's sister, who was Abbess of Barking. Edmund and Jasper, and perhaps their sister who later took the veil, went to live at Barking Abbey in Essex, and the Abbess was paid £50 for their keep. She provided them with food, clothing and lodging, and both were allowed servants to wait upon them, as befitted their status as the King's half-brothers.

By the end of 1437, the Council, divided by squabbling factions, had ceased to rule effectively, and the corruption and inefficiency that had already pervaded local government in many areas were beginning to affect central government also. Suffolk's influence over the royal household had extended to the Council, where he had grouped about him a nucleus of lords committed to peace with France, headed by Cardinal Beaufort, who had long been its advocate. The war had depleted the treasury, and the Crown now stood on the verge of bankruptcy, its revenues having fallen by more than a third. The King owed £164,815 to his creditors, and could not pay it, for his annual income was then only £75,100. Nor was the Council able to devise any solution to these problems.

Matters were no better in France, where it was predicted that it was only a matter of time before the English were expelled from the territories they still held. York, with the help of the great military strategist, John Talbot, Earl of Shrewsbury, had managed to drive a French force out of Normandy, and the Council, knowing his term of duty was due to end in April 1437, asked him to stay on. York did not consider the financial inducements sufficient, and was angered by the government's failure to repay monies owed to him, and he refused and came back to England. Once again, the Council faced the problem of who was to take command in France.

Henry VI had now, at the age of sixteen, not only to confront these troubles but also to assert his authority over the lords of the Council, who had for so long held the reins of government. On 12 November 1437 he declared himself of age and assumed control. With the ending of the minority, the Council reverted to its traditional role of advisory body to the King, even though its powers had been immeasurably strengthened by fifteen years of autonomy. Once he had established himself, Henry VI reappointed all its members to the positions they had formerly occupied, making each conditional upon the holder agreeing not to settle weighty matters of state without first consulting the King. Henry's coming of age released Warwick from his duties as governor, and he was appointed the King's Lieutenant in France in place of York, holding this office with honour until his death in 1439.

Although the young King firmly supported Beaufort's peace policy, he was neither prepared to relinquish the French lands still held by England nor the title of King of France. He was too weak and inexperienced to stand up to Gloucester, especially when the Duke warmed to his favourite theme, the sacred duty of fulfilling the wishes of Henry's mighty father. To bolster his position, Henry tried to buy support by bestowing extravagant gifts and grants of land and money on those whom he believed to be his friends. The Council, alarmed at his profligate generosity, was soon warning him against excessive liberality and reminding him of the need to conserve money.

The appearance in England at this time of a strong and determined ruler might have saved the situation, with the power of the nobles being diverted to other causes, law and order being effectively enforced, and even the war with France successfully prosecuted or brought to an honourable conclusion. Henry VI was not a strong king and never would be; nor was he ever interested in winning military glory. Therein lay the tragedy of the House of Lancaster.

6

A Simple and Upright Man

In 1910, Henry VI's skeleton was exhumed at Windsor. Examination showed that he had been a strongly built man, about 5'9" tall, with brown hair and a small head. The portrait of him in the Royal Collection at Windsor, which dates from about 1518–23 and is probably a copy of an original from life, shows a chubby-faced, clean-shaven youth in a black gown furred with ermine and crimson sleeves, a gold collar and a small black bonnet. One contemporary described him as having a childlike face, and this portrait bears out that description.

In the National Portrait Gallery another portrait shows him in later life, with a far more angular and care-worn face. He had heavy-lidded eyes and a full underlip, and was inclined to stoop and bow his head.

In youth he enjoyed dressing in fashionable clothes, on one occasion appearing in a purple chaperon or cloak, a large round headdress with tippet, and a light blue gown known as a houppelande which swept the floor and had tight sleeves, a high scarlet collar, padded shoulders and a crimson belt with a gold buckle. As Henry grew older, however, he came to believe that rich apparel was a worldly vanity, and appeared wearing broad-toed shoes like those of a countryman, a long gown with a round hood like that of a burgess, and a long tunic, every item of a dark grey colour. His courtiers complained that he dressed 'like a townsman', and his commons, who expected their sovereign to look and dress like a king and to carry himself with regal bearing, made similar criticisms. So little did Henry care for his clothes that in 1459 he presented his best gown to the Prior of St Albans. His embarrassed treasurer then discovered that the King had no other gown suitable for state occasions, and no money to purchase another, and had to buy it back for fifty marks. Henry was not pleased.

John Whethamstead, Abbot of St Albans, described Henry as a simple and upright man. Commines calls him 'a very ignorant and almost simple man'; even John Blacman, who wrote a hagiography of Henry at the behest of Henry VII, uses the word 'simple' to describe him, and in 1461, Whethamstead accused Henry of 'excessive simplicity in his acts'. In each case the word '*simplex*' should be translated to mean gullible or guileless; it was not until the seventeenth century that the word 'simple' was used to describe a half-wit or idiot. Nevertheless, gullibility was not a desirable quality in a king: Waurin says that all the evils that befell England during Henry's reign were due to his simple-mindedness.

Although Henry had been comprehensively educated, was well-read and had a love of learning, he was not particularly clever. John Hardyng describes him as being 'of small intelligence'. He lacked perception, and on one occasion even pardoned four nobles convicted of treason, along with three others who had plotted to kill him.

He had a strong sense of fairness and, wishing to see justice available to all, ensured that he was accessible to his subjects: 'Upon none would he wittingly inflict any injustice,' wrote Blacman. Once, Henry was riding through London when he saw a blackened object on a spike above Cripplegate and asked what it was. Told it was a quarter of a traitor who had been false to him, he commanded that it be removed, saying, 'I will not have any Christian man so cruelly handled for my sake.' Yet he showed no such qualms when he voluntarily witnessed the massed hangings of thirty-four rebels in 1450.

In general, though, Henry was a kindly soul, gentle and generous, honest and well-intentioned, and too humble and virtuous by far successfully to rule a country sliding slowly but surely into political anarchy. He never lost his temper, looked after his servants well, and was not interested in acquiring riches, his prime concern being the salvation of his soul. When a certain nobleman presented him with an expensive ornament of gold filigree, he hardly glanced at it, much to the donor's chagrin. Indeed, Henry's qualities were manifold, but they were not the qualities required of a sovereign.

There was nothing in Henry's early years to indicate that he might be mentally unstable, but during early manhood he suffered from spells of excessive melancholy and depression which hindered his ability to lead a normal life. In the 1440s he was described as being 'not steadfast of wit as other kings have been', and prior to 1453, the year in which he suffered his first really incapacitating mental illness, several of his subjects were hauled before the justices, charged with having referred to the King as a lunatic, or even as being childish, for which they were punished. Given the state of England at that time, they might have been forgiven for believing such things. Henry VI was no lunatic, but we must conclude that his mental health was never very stable.

Henry's piety is legendary, yet the question now has to be asked: was he as pious as later writers, who supported Henry VII's bid to have him canonised as a Lancastrian saint, would have it? The answer is probably not.

There is no doubt that Henry VI was a religious man and that his personal piety was genuine. Blacman says that, at the principal feasts of the year, 'but especially at those when of custom he wore his crown', he wore next to his skin a rough hair shirt. He was 'a diligent and sincere worshipper of God, more given to devout prayer than to handling worldly things or practising vain sports or pursuits. These he despised as trifles.' He feared God and avoided evil. He would not transact any business on Sundays or holy days, nor would he allow his courtiers to speak during services, bring their hawks into church, or wear their swords or daggers there, and he would remain on his knees throughout the service in perfect silence, his head bowed. When going about his daily duties he was constantly engaged in meditation and prayer, withdrawn into a world of his own to which he could retreat from the harsh realities of political life.

It is true that he was rather more than conventionally pious, but then so were many people at that time. Because he was the King, his piety attracted attention. By the time he was twenty-five he was famed for it throughout Europe, and Pope Eugenius IV, impressed by the King's charities and care for the poor, awarded him the highest papal honour, the Golden Rose. There was, nevertheless, a more cynical reason for this award – Eugenius wanted money from the Church in England and hoped Henry would assist him in obtaining it.

The King's piety generally endeared him to his subjects, although there were those who were privately of the opinion that he would make a better monk than a king. He was forever exhorting his magnates to prayer, and, knowing that it was in their interests to do so, they acquiesced, for Henry could be very generous to those he favoured.

Like his father, another pious man, Henry VI was merciless to Lollards and other heretics, and many were burned at the stake during his reign. Unlike Henry V, he did not found any religious houses or endow many chantries. Towards the end of his reign, sermons preached before him were censored beforehand by the Council so as to avoid the King being confronted by any embarrassing criticisms.

It would be fair to say that Henry saw himself as a guardian of public morality. He never took the Lord's name in vain, could not abide swearing, and refused to tolerate it in his presence, gently admonishing or severely chiding any noble who disobeyed this edict: 'Everyone who swore was abominable to him.' His strongest oaths were 'St John' or 'Forsooth and forsooth!'

He had no time for the vagaries of fashion, believing that the revealing clothes of the period led people into promiscuity, an opinion shared by many contemporary moralists. Blacman says, 'He took great precautions to secure not only his own chastity but that of his servants,' and was so concerned about immorality at his court that he was not above keeping 'careful watch through hidden windows of his chamber' on ladies entering his palace, 'lest any foolish impertinence of women cause the fall of any of his household'.

He was excessively prudish and much offended by nudity, often quoting Petrarch on the subject, saying, 'The nakedness of a beast is in men unpleasing, but the decency of raiment makes for modesty.' When he visited the Roman baths at Bath, he saw men 'wholly naked, with every garment cast off, at which he was displeased', and fled with embarrassment from the scene, 'abhorring such nudity as a great offence'. One Christmas time, a certain lord, probably for a malicious prank, 'brought him a dance or show of young ladies with bared bosoms who were to dance in that guise before the King, who very angrily averted his eyes, turned his back upon them, and went out to his chamber, saying, "Fie, fie, for shame!"'

Shortly before Henry married at the age of twenty-three, the papal envoy to England reported that he lived more like a monk than a king and 'avoided the company of women'. Blacman says that as a youth he was 'a pupil of chastity'. He was 'chaste and pure from the beginning of his days and eschewed all licentiousness in word or deed while he was young'. He was fond of reading moral treatises and other improving literature, and firmly believed that the spread of such works would lead to more virtuous behaviour on the part of his subjects. Indeed, his chamberlain, Sir Richard Tunstall, recalled how the King would spend much of his leisure perusing books and chronicles, or, on holy days, the scriptures.

Like his father, Henry was a patron of music, and was the first king to appoint a master for the children of the Chapel Royal, while under his auspices the first degrees in music were awarded by the University of Cambridge. He himself was no mean composer and the manuscript of his *Sanctus* is still preserved at King's College, Cambridge.

Education was one of Henry's chief passions, and he was especially anxious to promote the spread of literacy among his subjects: in fact, he was more enthusiastic about education than he was about governing his realm and righting its wrongs. He was a generous patron of scholars and a great benefactor of the universities of Oxford and Cambridge. During his reign a great many grammar schools were founded, catering for boys from the newly prosperous middle classes and for poor boys who might not otherwise obtain a good education and could benefit from the charitable places available.

Henry's chief interest was in his two great academic foundations, Eton College and King's College, Cambridge. Not only did he found these two institutions, but he also devoted great care and expense to their buildings. Blacman states that he 'graced the laying of the foundation stones with his presence, and with great devotion offered his foundations to Almighty God'.

Since he was seventeen, Henry had wished to found a college dedicated to prayer and charity, where the sons of poor families could benefit from a free education. 'The King's College of Our Lady of Eton beside Windsor' was founded in 1440, with provision for a provost, a schoolmaster, ten priests, four clerks, six choristers, twenty-five poor and indigent scholars, and twenty-five feeble and poor old men. Tuition was free. In 1443 the King raised the number of poor scholars to seventy and cut the number of poor men to thirteen. The Lower School at Eton, which is still in use, dates from this time, the college hall and chapel from a few years later. Henry was concerned that, being near the court at Windsor, 'the young lambs should come to relish the corrupt deeds and habits of his courtiers'. If he found any boys within the castle boundaries, he would promptly send them back, telling them his court was no place for the young. He liked nothing better than to visit Eton, and would give the scholars money and bid them be good boys, 'gentle and teachable, and servants of the Lord'.

King's College, Cambridge was founded in 1441 to provide further education for boys who had completed their studies at Eton. The college buildings and chapel are still numbered among the chief glories of the University of Cambridge. There was an element of laying up treasure in heaven about Henry's foundations, for in lavishing so much expense and care on them he was consciously aiming to eclipse similar foundations such as the schools and colleges founded by William of Wykeham in the fourteenth century.

Henry spent lavishly on his educational projects, his palaces, and – above all – his favourites, with little regard for his depleted treasury. He was easily manipulated and exploited by unscrupulous courtiers, who took advantage of his extravagant generosity; he, in turn, lacked the perception to judge the worthiness of its recipients. He was an unworldly man, basically shy and naive, who had little aptitude for dealing with people. He was too simple to adopt a political role, too open and honest, lacking in cunning and the ability to dissimulate. He was sensitive, not only about the Lancastrian title to the throne, but also about attempts to limit his royal authority, which – given his long minority and the difficulties he faced in asserting his authority – is perhaps understandable. As a man he was virtuous and good; as a king, he was a disaster.

Henry VI's chief weakness was allowing himself to be dominated by political factions, who frequently manipulated him into making unwise decisions and who were chiefly concerned with promoting their own interests. He had a peculiar talent for surrounding himself with the most rapacious, self-seeking and unpopular magnates, in heeding whose advice he showed a marked lack of political judgement. Nor did he make much attempt to stand up to those he disagreed with. Whoever controlled the King controlled the country; throughout Henry's reign, therefore, the government of England was carried out according to the wishes of whichever faction was able at any given time to influence him.

Few kings can have inherited so many problems: a kingdom near bankruptcy, a Council divided by factions, a legal system corrupted by local magnates and their armed retainers, an aristocracy that was growing ever mightier and losing its integrity, and a war that could not be won but which was draining the country of its resources. None of these problems was Henry's fault, but his failure to address them effectively made their escalation his responsibility.

Waurin wrote: 'The King was neither intelligent enough nor experienced enough to manage a kingdom such as England.' Although Henry's chamberlain, Tunstall, says that he did spend a good deal of time 'diligently treating of the affairs of his realm with his Council', he left much of the business of government to whichever faction was in power, and when he did assert control it was sometimes only to make serious mistakes. Lord Chief Justice Fortescue, who remained faithful to Henry in prosperity and dire adversity, was yet a realist when it came to assessing his sovereign's limitations, and in his treatise *The Governance of England* he stressed the need for a strong and united Council to protect the King from his own follies and extravagance, especially when it came to the profligate giving away, or alienation, of crown lands.

People inevitably compared Henry VI to his father, usually to his detriment, but criticism of him was rarely voiced out loud. Because of his virtues and his inherent goodness, even his most unruly nobles respected him, and the universal reverence for an anointed monarch acted as a brake on those who might have rebelled against him. Those who did rebel, in the cause of good government, aimed their complaints at the nobles who controlled the King, not at Henry himself. His favourites naturally shielded him from such complaints, while Henry himself was inordinately sensitive to any implied criticism of himself and his abilities as king. Those who dared openly to take him to task for his shortcomings – Gloucester in the early years, York later on – provoked in him deep suspicion of their motives. To such men he could be – and was – vindictive and dangerous.

A king's most important function was to protect and defend his subjects, therefore he had to be an efficient warrior and general, capable of planning campaigns and winning battles. Henry VI was the complete antithesis of this, categorically refusing to take the field against his fellow Christians. He did not share the enthusiasm of his magnates for martial endeavour, and they in turn were shocked and astonished that the son of Henry V should display such marked lack of interest in military glory. Although Henry rode at the head of his armies during the Wars of the Roses, he remained by his standard while battles were fought and awaited the outcome, leaving the planning of strategy to his commanders. He never fought any campaigns in France, and therefore earned the dubious distinction of being the first English king since the Norman Conquest of 1066 never to have led an army in battle against a foreign foe.

Conversely, although he desired peace with France on his terms, he made little effort to endear himself to his French subjects, and never set foot in France after 1431. This was a fatal policy in an age when monarchical government was expected to be carried out on a personal level.

Unlike Richard II, who had sought peace with France because he had feared the effect of war upon the Crown's finances, Henry VI's wish for peace was inspired by his piety and his distaste for the carnage and waste of war, and above all by the views of his uncle, Cardinal Beaufort. To pursue a peace policy in the current political climate was a bold move but, predictably, it was not at all popular in England. Fired by Henry V's victories and the acquisition of an empire in France, the vast majority of his English subjects were greedy for more conquests and more glory, and were convinced that, given the right strategies, the present dismal trend of the war could be reversed. Their view was that the only person who could possibly benefit from a peace policy was Charles VII. Already it had created divisions at court, which could only be to Charles's advantage, for the English magnates now preferred to fight each other in the Council chamber than confront the enemy on the field in France.

Henry VI's court was a dull place compared with the later courts of the Yorkist and Tudor sovereigns. Like all mediaeval courts it was itinerant, moving from palace to palace throughout the year so that royal homes recently vacated could be cleaned and their larders restocked.

Westminster was the chief royal residence and the administrative centre of government. Within the palace were to be found the Exchequer, the Court of Common Pleas and the Court of King's Bench, but it was also a luxurious royal home. Visitors gazed in wonder at the beautiful St Stephen's Chapel, decorated in 1350–61 with murals depicting the family of Edward III, and at Henry III's Painted Chamber, the walls of which were covered with frescos of scenes from the Bible. Then there was the Star Chamber, built by Edward III and so called because of its ceiling, which was painted as blue as the night sky and patterned with gilded stars. The private chambers of the royal family were sumptuous indeed, with beds hung with cloth of gold and satin, and made up with deep feather mattresses, pillows embroidered with the arms of England, and coverlets furred with ermine. The whole effect of the state apartments was one of magnificent colour and splendour, calculated to impress foreigners and so convince them of the wealth and might of the island kingdom.

Westminster was really an amalgam of three palaces: the Great Palace, which was the official seat of government; the Privy Palace, which housed the royal apartments; and the Prince's Palace, where the royal family normally lodged. These were all stone buildings, probably two storeys in height. Courtiers and servants are thought to have been accommodated in adjacent timbered dwellings. In front of the palace stood thirteen stone statues of the kings of England, from Edward the Confessor to Richard II, the latter having commissioned them. Richard had also erected a new gateway with marble pillars and a campanile.

There were two halls: the White Hall, which housed the Court of

Chancery, and Westminster Hall, which, along with the fourteenth-century Jewel Tower, is all that survives today of the mediaeval palace, most of which was burned down in Henry VIII's reign. Originally there had been a Great Hall, built by William Rufus in the Romanesque style and covered with murals. Richard II had rebuilt this as Westminster Hall, employing the great architects Henry Yevele and Hugh Herland, who designed and executed the magnificent hammerbeam roof which may still be seen today, as well as the high windows. This new hall, one of the biggest in Europe, was decorated with Richard II's emblem of the white hart, and was the ceremonial centre of the palace.

Richard II had carried out improvements to the royal residences on a vast scale, having them painted, gilded and modernised. The walls of the royal apartments at Westminster, Windsor and the Tower of London were painted with heraldic or allegorical designs in brilliant colours. Sadly, few of these murals survive, and then only in fragments. Richard also modernised Eltham Palace in Kent, a favourite residence of English queens since the early fourteenth century. Here he built a bath house, a painted chamber and a dancing chamber, while the windows were of stained glass and the surrounding gardens had been laid with turf. Richard had also built a range of apartments for visiting magnates, along with new domestic offices, including a spicery and a saucery, and a lower court beyond the moat.

Henry VI loved Eltham, and built there a study library where he could keep his treasured books. This room had seven great windows fitted with 42 square feet of stained glass depicting birds and monsters. In 1450, however, in the early evening of a February day, a lightning bolt struck the palace and destroyed a substantial part of it, including the hall, a store-room, a kitchen, and other rooms. Henry's study seems to have survived.

In the royal apartments in the Tower, Richard II had installed 105 square feet of glass painted with fleurs de lys and the royal arms of England, as well as floor tiles depicting heraldic leopards and white harts, and murals of popinjays and fleurs de lys worked in gold and vermilion.

By the end of the fourteenth century tapestries were being hung on the walls of royal and noble residences, sometimes to block draughts, but usually to add colour and luxury to masonry or plaster. The most popular subjects commissioned by the purveyors of tapestries were battles, scenes of heroism, allegorical and mythological characters, courtly pastimes or religious subjects.

Henry V owned tapestries depicting Edward the Confessor, the

Arthurian legends, the Emperor Charlemagne, the Roman Emperor Octavian, Pharamond – a legendary King of France – a tournament, allegorical subjects such as 'The Life of Love' or 'The Tree of Youth', a lady in a tent, the Annunciation, the Five Joys of Our Lady, and the Three Kings of Cologne. These tapestries were almost certainly still hanging in the palaces of Henry VI.

Each year, there were several religious festivals at which the King kept great state, and on these occasions hundreds of nobles, gentry, knights and squires would come up from the country to see him wearing his crown and feasting in public. All would be fed and lodged at the Crown's expense. Those who wished to gain access to the King might wait for weeks, for the sovereign was at the centre of an intricate web of patronage manipulated by predatory nobles and besieged on every side by those seeking appointments, redress in law or some other mark of favour. His courtiers tended to group together in factious cliques that produced an atmosphere of suspicion, jealousy and intrigue.

The court customarily set trends in codes of manners, dress and taste, and it was normally the monarch who was the arbiter of such fashions, but Henry VI considered himself above such worldly vanities, preferring to encourage public morality and private piety. He did extend his patronage to literature, music, art and architecture, but his court could not be described as the centre of culture or learning as later courts were.

Henry VI's household was large, unwieldy and corrupt. Its officers abused his patronage and wasted the Crown's resources, with catastrophic consequences for the economy, earning themselves great unpopularity among the magnates, most of whom were excluded from this privileged circle. In 1433, during the minority, it had cost £13,000 a year to run the royal household; by 1449 the annual cost was £24,000. Even in 1433, the household was £11,000 in debt, and that figure rose steadily over the years. Complaints were made by the Commons in Parliament about the bad influence exerted over the King by his household, that he was unduly extravagant in his gifts to household officers, and that his favour to them was destroying the impartiality of royal justice. Henry, however, paid little heed. As long as he had sufficient money for his foundations, he was content. From time to time he would put pressure on the Exchequer to relieve his household from its mounting debts, but he had little incentive to do more because he himself had a private income drawn mainly from the duchy of Lancaster. Parliament was concerned, however, and in 1440, responding to a petition from royal servants whose wages had long been unpaid, it announced that

£10,000 a year would be made available for the next five years through taxation, to help clear the debts of the royal household. The King's subjects, who had to foot the bill, were not best pleased.

One night in January or February 1438, Owen Tudor, with the help of a priest, escaped from Newgate gaol, 'hurting foul his keeper' in the process. In March he was recaptured and returned to prison. However, by July he had been moved to the custody of the Constable of Windsor Castle. He remained there two years before being released on a huge bail of £2000 in July 1439, on condition that he agreed not to attempt to go anywhere near Wales. On 10 November the King was 'moved by special causes' to grant him a general pardon for all offences committed before the previous October; again, his original offence was not specified.

From then on, Owen Tudor never looked back. The King, 'by especial favour', granted him a pension of £40 per annum out of his own privy purse, and Tudor settled down to a life of comfortable obscurity for the next twenty years. Lodged in the royal household until around 1455, he was treated with respect and kindness by the King, his stepson, who made him several grants of land and in 1459 increased his annuity to £100. In February 1460 he was appointed Keeper of the King's Parks in the county of Denbigh, and we may assume that by this date he had been allowed once more to take up residence in his native Wales.

In 1459 an unnamed Welshwoman bore Tudor a bastard son, David Owen, at Pembroke Castle. When Owen Tudor's grandson, Henry Tudor, invaded Wales in 1485, David joined him and was knighted; after Henry became King Henry VII a few days later, Sir David Owen grew in prosperity, married an heiress and probably settled in Sussex, where he is buried in the priory church of Easebourne, near Midhurst.

As well as providing for his stepfather, Henry VI also took care of his half-brothers, Edmund and Jasper Tudor. Sometime after March 1442 he arranged for them to be brought from Barking Abbey to live at court. Here, says Blacman, Henry was at great pains to do his best for 'the Lords Edmund and Jasper in their boyhood and youth, providing for them most strict and safe guardianship, putting them under the care of virtuous and worthy priests, both for teaching and for right living and conversation, lest the untamed practices of youth should grow rank if they lacked any to prune them'. It was a dull regime for two lively boys, and the sources do not even record that they received any knightly training, although they must have had some, since both were later given responsible military commands.

The King's obvious concern and affection communicated itself to Edmund and Jasper, and fostered fraternal bonds that would endure for life.

From the time Henry VI assumed control of the government in 1437 Cardinal Beaufort and his family prospered. Never before had a king been so generous to his relations. By 1441, eleven members of the Beaufort family had been appointed to the office of sheriff, thus dispersing their influence through eleven English shires. The Cardinal's ally, Suffolk, who was being groomed as his political heir, also benefited from this largesse, for during those years his wealth and influence increased enormously.

Gloucester, who had campaigned to continue the Hundred Years War throughout the 1430s, now found himself and his supporters in a minority on the Council. Thanks to the enthusiastic support of the King, Beaufort's views had prevailed, and Gloucester was left virtually in political isolation, his influence with his nephew diminishing daily. It was now obvious to most of his fellow Council members that Gloucester's policies were too unrealistic to be successful, and that since the Treaty of Arras England's hopes of conquering France were nil.

Beaufort's first peace embassy to Charles VII, in 1439, ended in failure. The Cardinal concluded that England had to offer better terms and greater concessions, and that a royal marriage should be negotiated in order to seal the peace. That year, as a temporary replacement for Warwick, the Cardinal's nephew, John Beaufort, Earl of Somerset, was appointed Lieutenant General of France, and awarded the exorbitant salary of £7200 per annum.

In 1440, Charles of Valois, Duke of Orléans, who had been held a prisoner in England since being captured at Agincourt in 1415, was released by the English in the hope that his liberation would predispose the French to discuss peace terms once more. Gloucester saw through this ploy and asked the Council if Henry V would have released the Duke without an enormous ransom.

York supported Gloucester, being already disillusioned with the faction fighting in England and angered by the way in which the government had let matters deteriorate in France. With the Duke's support, Gloucester accused the Cardinal and his party of influencing the King against him and York, but his protests were in vain. The Council was now dominated by Beaufort and his cronies – Suffolk, John Kempe, Archbishop of York, Adam Moleyns, Bishop of Chichester, and the earls of Northumberland, Stafford and Huntingdon – while the King had little time for the outdated policies of his uncle of Gloucester.

York, at any rate, could be disposed of. On 2 July 1440, the Council once more appointed him Lieutenant General of France for a period of five years, with expenses of £20,000 per annum. York was perhaps the only man of stature and rank who could fill Warwick's place. He had gained some experience of governing France during his previous tenure, and was also aware of the difficulties involved. Whatever his personal views on the Cardinal's policy, his brief was to come to terms with Charles VII and work towards the negotiation of the desired peace treaty. At the same time he would have to cope with the rapidly deteriorating situation in the English-occupied territories with only minimal support from home. His expenses never arrived.

Somerset, however, was reluctant to relinquish his lucrative position to York, and for some time after the latter's appointment he continued to draw his salary. As York did not take up his appointment until 23 June 1441, there was no official objection to him doing so, and by the time York arrived in Normandy with 500 soldiers Somerset had resigned his commission and left for England without waiting to hand over formally to his successor.

During his time in office York governed admirably and, says Waurin, 'had many honourable and notable successes over the French. Everything he did was highly commendable, not only for himself but also for the honour and furtherance of the Crown of England and for the exaltation of his master the King, whom he served with due reverence and loyalty.' To bolster his position in France, York built up an affinity of influential supporters, men such as Sir William Oldhall, who had served under Bedford and were prepared to offer their loyalty to his successor, men who, above all, were disgusted at the way in which the war had been handled by the government in London, and who were convinced that, even now, the situation was not irretrievable.

At home, their ally Gloucester's vociferous protests were proving an embarrassing obstacle which, if reported in the wrong quarters, might well jeopardise the expected peace talks. Something had to be done to silence him, it was felt, or at least to undermine his credibility.

The plot to discredit the Duke was almost certainly the brainchild of Cardinal Beaufort, his ancient enemy, who was supported by most of his party, including Cardinal Archbishop Kempe, and – above all – the King. The outcome of the plot proved just how vindictive Henry VI could be when his prerogative was challenged.

Gloucester's marital history had been complicated. He had entered into a bigamous union with the already-married Jacqueline of Hainault, who bore him no children, then, when he tired of her, he obtained an annulment and married his mistress, Eleanor Cobham, who was a mere knight's daughter and had already presented him with two bastards. Beaufort's plan was to attack Gloucester through his duchess, whose reputation was such that people would easily believe the worst of her. Eleanor seems to have played right into the Cardinal's hands. Not content with being Duchess of Gloucester, she was all too aware that, if the King died, her husband would ascend the throne and she would be Queen of England. She had dabbled dangerously in witchcraft, having her horoscope cast to predict what her future held – a practice much frowned upon by the Church – and, far worse still, made a wax image of the King and melted it in a fire.

In June 1441 Eleanor was attending a dinner in London when she was arrested on a charge of witchcraft. She was tried in an ecclesiastical court along with several accomplices, and all were found guilty. Eleanor's clerk, Roger Bolingbroke, was hanged, drawn and quartered, while Margery Jourdemain, known as the Witch of Eye, was burned at the stake. Eleanor herself escaped relatively lightly, being sentenced to perform three public penances. However, when these had been carried out a secular court condemned her to perpetual imprisonment for treason. She was incarcerated first at Chester, then at Kenilworth Castle, a luxurious royal residence, and later on the Isle of Man. She died either in 1446 or 1457, still in captivity.

Gloucester, knowing how precarious his own position was, and guessing his enemies would swoop upon him as an accomplice if he openly supported his wife, kept silent throughout Eleanor's trial and condemnation, even though he must have realised who was responsible for it.

Although there was never any evidence that Gloucester had been involved in his wife's crimes, his political credibility and influence were radically diminished after her conviction. His position on the Council was irrevocably weakened, and he only attended meetings infrequently thereafter. He was not sufficiently crushed as to cease criticising the King's peace policy, but his was now a discredited voice. After twenty years, Beaufort had finally vanquished his rival.

7

'A Queen Not Worth Ten Marks'

With Gloucester chastened and quiescent, Cardinal Beaufort was free to concentrate all his energies on procuring the desired peace with France, a project he worked on ceaselessly throughout 1442. But by the spring of 1443, the prospect still seemed remote, for negotiations had again broken down and there seemed little hope of reviving them. This unhappy state of affairs was mainly due to the dogmatic insistence of the English on Henry VI being recognised as the lawful king of France, even when it was obvious that the French were gaining the ascendancy in the war. King Charles's ultimate objective was to reconquer the territories taken by the English, but in the meantime he was insisting on them being held of him, as overlord, and that was not acceptable to Henry VI.

At this point Charles and his son, the Dauphin Louis, invaded the province of Gascony, part of the duchy of Aquitaine. The English had been expecting an attack on Normandy and were so preoccupied with preparing its defences that when they realised what was going on they were too late to halt the French in the south. In April 1443, the Council appointed Somerset Lieutenant and Captain General in Aquitaine without reference to York, who was furious at the snub, for his command extended to the whole of France. To make matters worse, Somerset's military career had so far been a non-event. He had been captured at the Battle of Baugé in 1421 and had spent seventeen years as a prisoner of the French. He had therefore had little experience of warfare or politics, and proved to be an amateurish and incompetent commander.

In August 1443 Somerset was created Duke of Somerset and Earl of Kendal and given command of an expeditionary force which he was to lead into Gascony, again with no reference to York. Somerset attempted to mollify the Duke, sending him word that he would be a shield 'betwixt him and the adversary', and assuring him it was not his intention 'to do anything that might prejudice in any wise the power that my cousin of York hath of the King in this country of France and Normandy'. Nevertheless, it appeared that York had been deliberately slighted, and to crown it all, while York was receiving very little financial help from London, Somerset's expedition was generously funded.

Worse was to come. York was expecting much-needed reinforcements in Normandy, but he soon learned they had been diverted to Gascony where Somerset's campaign ended in ignominious failure, although not before he had managed to anger England's ally, the Duke of Brittany. He was forced to return to England in shame without having accomplished anything.

In Rouen, York seethed with resentment. He was now in severe financial difficulties, thanks to the government's failure to forward his £20,000 annuity, which was meant to cover not only his salary but also the wages of his soldiers and administrators. Thus he had to pay them himself or face desertions or mutinies. The Council were under the complacent impression that York was doing very well on the proceeds of Norman taxation, but in fact the Duke hardly received any money from this source because it had all been diverted to other necessary causes.

Fat was added to the fire when York learned that the government had agreed to pay the ineffectual Somerset an annual pension of £25,000. This spurred the Duke to write to the King asking for his annuity to be paid to him forthwith, as provided for in the terms of service agreed upon at the time he took up his commission. Henry had the audacity to reply that, as so much money had been spent on equipping and provisioning Somerset's army, he hoped York would 'take patience and forbear him for a time'. York would not. In vain did he petition again and again for payment, not only of his expenses but of the debts owed him by the Crown. Throughout two terms of office he had subsidised the government of Normandy and military campaigns, and was now so financially embarrassed that he was forced to pawn one of his prized possessions, a heavy gold collar adorned with precious stones and enamelled white roses of York and hung with a huge, spear-pointed diamond. Apart from the crown jewels, this collar was the most priceless item of jewellery in England. York was the wealthiest of Henry's magnates, but he had beggared himself in his master's service, and would only have parted with this collar in extreme necessity.

York's petitions were ignored. However, when government money did become available — which was not often — Somerset was given priority claim to it, to clear his private loans. York saw clearly that, while the incompetent Somerset enjoyed the favour of the King, he himself was to be left out in the political wilderness, with no redress for his grievances. It was at this point that his anger and frustration crystallised into a deadly enmity against Somerset, whom he rightly perceived to be his chief political rival. In this lay the origins of the long-standing feud between York and the Beauforts, a feud that would not be resolved other than by death.

By 1441, Henry VI had conceived 'an earnest desire to live under the holy sacrament of marriage'. Like any young man he was anxious to secure a bride who was personable and attractive, and to this end he insisted on being sent a portrait of any suitable candidate. None of these likenesses, alas, has survived.

Henry was also convinced that he should conclude a marriage alliance that would cement the hoped-for peace with France, and from 1441 to 1443 was considering a match with the daughter of the Count of Armagnac, Burgundy's rival. Then in the autumn of 1443 Cardinal Beaufort proposed Margaret of Anjou, Charles VII's niece by marriage, a suggestion that was enthusiastically supported by Suffolk, who had little difficulty in persuading the Council to agree to the match. Philip of Burgundy had suggested Margaret as far back as 1436, but Charles VII had then vetoed it. Now, apparently, the Duke of Orléans was urging it. Naturally, Gloucester opposed the idea, if only because Beaufort had suggested it, but Gloucester had no influence with the King, who was enthusiastic at the prospect of marrying Margaret.

While an official approach was made to King Charles through an embassy of bishops, headed by the Cardinal himself, the young King used his own methods of procuring information about his proposed bride. There was on parole in London a French knight of Anjou called Champchevrier, who had been captured by Sir John Fastolf. Henry was acquainted with this knight and, knowing the man had seen Margaret, Beaufort and Suffolk briefed him to sing her praises to the future bridegroom. Soon Henry was enraptured by Champchevrier's eloquent descriptions of the rare endowments which nature had bestowed on the princess, and which more than compensated for the fact that she had no dowry.

Henry wanted a miniature of the lady, but this presented a problem, because the English ambassadors had not yet commenced formal negotiations, nor was there any certainty as to how their proposal would be received. The whole matter required careful diplomatic handling, but Henry dispatched Champchevrier to the court of Lorraine, where Margaret and her parents were residing, to obtain a portrait secretly.

Meanwhile, Sir John Fastolf had learned that his prisoner had apparently broken parole and escaped back to France without waiting to be ransomed, a most dishonourable act on the part of a knight. Because a ransom was due, Fastolf was entitled to ask Charles VII if his prisoner might be returned to him; such were the laws of chivalry. Fastolf did just this, and Champchevrier, with a portrait already in his possession, was arrested by French soldiers on his way back to England. Granted his request to see King Charles, he confessed to him the reason for his visit to France. Charles was secretly pleased to learn it, for he too could see the advantages of an alliance between England and France. Champchevrier was released and allowed to return with all speed to England, Charles having urged him to impress upon Henry VI the benefits of a marriage with Margaret of Anjou.

Henry duly received her portrait, a miniature by a renowned but anonymous French artist in the pay of Suffolk, and instantly fell in love with it. By October 1443 he was writing to Suffolk and describing the sitter as 'the excellent, magnificent and very bright Margaret'.

Margaret of Anjou was born in March 1429 at Pont-à-Mousson, Lorraine. She was the daughter of René, Duke of Anjou and titular King of Naples, Sicily and Jerusalem, by Isabella, daughter of Charles the Bold, Duke of Lorraine. Baptised at Toul, she was reared in infancy by her father's old nurse, Théophanie la Magine, and spent her early years moving between the castle of Tarascon on the River Rhône and the old royal palace at Capua in Naples. Her mother, herself a gifted woman, saw that she was well-educated, tutoring her herself and perhaps arranging for her to have lessons with the scholar Antoine de la Salle, who taught her brothers. In childhood Margaret was known as 'la petite créature'.

René of Anjou has been described as a man of many crowns but no kingdoms. Born in 1408, his early political career had been chequered. He inherited the duchy of Anjou in 1434, but it was then occupied by the English. In 1435 he had claimed the kingdom of Naples, but had to cede his title to Alfonso of Aragon. René nevertheless continued to call himself King of Naples and Sicily, though it was as empty a pretence as were his claims to be King of Jerusalem and Hungary.

In 1441 René returned to France where, thanks to the marriage of his sister Marie to Charles VII, he built up a sphere of influence at the

French court. The friendship between Charles and René dated back to their childhood, when both had been as brothers at the court of René's father at Angers. Now he found himself a member of the King's council and an honoured courtier, who was constantly at Charles's side at tournaments, courtly ceremonies and banquets. He also campaigned on the French king's behalf in Normandy and Lorraine. By 1444 René, despite his landless status, was a considerable power at the French court, and the Milanese ambassador observed that he was 'the one who governs this entire realm'.

René lived in some style, surrounded by luxuries such as silks and porcelain imported from as far away as China. He was a highly cultivated and talented man, a gifted artist and poet, whose illuminated manuscripts are arguably the best-executed of the period. He was also a musician of some renown. His small but brilliant court attracted all kinds of talented people seeking patronage. Most of all it was famed for its tournaments, which René raised to an art form, and for its artificial creation of a pastoral idyll inspired by the new humanism sweeping across Europe from Italy.

René had five children, including his heir, John of Calabria, Yolande, who was married to a Burgundian nobleman, and Margaret, whom the Burgundian chronicler Enguerrand de Monstrelet describes as one of the younger daughters. During her childhood her father had considered several possible husbands for her, including the Emperor Frederick III. In 1443 he sent her to live with her aunt, Queen Marie, at the French court, and early in 1444 was considering a match for her with Burgundy's son, Charles, Count of Charolais. But René's ancestral territories of Maine and Anjou were still in the hands of the English, and when he learned of Henry VI's interest in his daughter he saw a means of getting them back.

Margaret spent a year at the French court, where she won golden opinions for her beauty and character. The Burgundian chronicler Barante wrote: 'There was no princess in Christendom more accomplished than my lady Margaret of Anjou. She was already renowned in France for her beauty and wit and her lofty spirit of courage.' Already she had an admirer in the courtly tradition: Pierre de Brézé, Seneschal of Anjou, had conceived an entirely proper and chivalrous passion for her, and carried her colours at jousts, calling himself her 'Chevalier Servant'.

In January 1444 it seemed that peace with France was within England's grasp, for in that month an agreement was reached between Henry VI, Charles VII and Philip of Burgundy that their commissioners should meet shortly at Tours to discuss peace terms and a possible marriage alliance between England and France. Also present would be René of Anjou, father of the prospective bride.

In February an English embassy headed by Suffolk travelled to the French court at Tours. Suffolk appears to have been unenthusiastic about his mission, almost certainly because he had belatedly realised that peace with France would not be popular with the English people, and as a result he did not wish to be too closely associated with it. In vain he had pleaded with the King to send someone else, but Henry, for once, was obstinate. He had great confidence in Suffolk's ability to succeed in his task, and Suffolk therefore had no choice in the matter. Even Gloucester now realised that prolonging the war was hopeless, although he was urging the King to negotiate an advantageous peace while he was still in a position to dictate terms. He would have been horrified to learn that Henry believed by this time that peace could only be achieved by making concessions to the French, even secretly if need be.

Suffolk and his entourage landed at Harfleur in March 1444, magnificently equipped at great cost to the Exchequer. In April he was courteously received by René and Charles, and given all the trappings of a state welcome. Peace talks then commenced. Suffolk made a formal request for the hand of Margaret of Anjou, to which René readily agreed, but he warned the Duke that he was penniless and could not provide his daughter with the customary dowry. He then had the temerity to demand that England return to him the counties of Maine and Anjou as part of the terms of the marriage treaty, and this demand was backed by King Charles. Suffolk referred the matter back to the Council in England, knowing full well that the cession of Maine and Anjou in return for a queen who brought no financial advantage whatsoever would be bitterly unpopular in England. Unfortunately Henry VI had just learned that the Count of Nevers was on the point of offering for Margaret, and knew he had to act quickly.

Suffolk later claimed that Bishop Moleyns urged Henry to agree to the French demands, but the Bishop declared on his deathbed that Suffolk himself had been the one to persuade the King. The extent of Suffolk's involvement in the matter is now never likely to be established, but ultimately, of course, the responsibility for the decision was Henry's. There is no doubt that he and his Council were conscious of just how aghast the people of England would be when they learned that their king had blithely ceded the hard-won counties of Maine and Anjou back to the French. And it was because of this awareness that, in conveying their acceptance of the terms,

Henry and his councillors insisted that the agreement be kept a secret until the matter was a *fait accompli*, which would not be for some time to come. It was hoped that by then the English would be able to see the benefits of an alliance with France. Above all, Gloucester must not know of the agreement.

Suffolk was thus empowered to agree to the cession of Maine and Anjou in return for the English being allowed to retain Aquitaine, Normandy and all the other territories conquered by Henry V. At the same time Henry VI agreed to waive Margaret's dowry and undertook to pay for the wedding out of his own privy purse. Already, anticipating a happy outcome to negotiations, he was making strenuous efforts to raise money for this purpose. Meanwhile, at Tours, Suffolk was arranging a two-year truce; the demands of King Charles were such that a peace treaty was not possible at this stage. The marriage, however, was to be a stepping-stone to such a treaty, or so it was hoped.

Throughout the negotiations, Margaret was at the castle of Angers with her mother. In early May both ladies travelled to Tours where they were lodged with King René in the abbey of Beaumont-les-Tours. Here on 4 May, Suffolk visited them to pay his respects to his future queen, and apparently he was much impressed with her beauty and her bearing. On the 22nd the Treaty of Tours was signed, providing for the marriage of Henry VI and Margaret of Anjou and including a secret clause committing the English to the surrender of Maine and Anjou. René had at the last minute appealed to the clergy of Anjou, who granted a tenth and a half of their revenues to provide the bride with a trousseau and pay for the betrothal celebrations.

Two days later Margaret and Henry VI were formally betrothed at Tours. The occasion was celebrated with magnificent festivities at court, with King Charles and King René leading the nobility of France in procession through the city. The papal legate, Piero da Monte, Bishop of Brescia, officiated at the ceremony and Suffolk stood proxy for King Henry. Afterwards a banquet was held at which Margaret was accorded all the honours due to a queen of England.

Back in England, on the 27th, John Beaufort, Duke of Somerset, died unexpectedly at Wimborne in Dorset, and was buried in the nearby Minster. There were rumours that, unable to come to terms with his humiliating failure in France, the Duke had taken his own life. He left no son, but an infant daughter, Margaret Beaufort, born on 31 May 1443, through whom the Tudor sovereigns would ultimately inherit their claim to the throne of England. Margaret became a ward of Suffolk, who later brought her to court and made plans to marry her to his son, John de la Pole.

Somerset was succeeded, not as duke but as earl, by his brother Edmund Beaufort. Now aged about thirty-seven, Edmund had been created Earl of Dorset in 1442 and Marquess in 1443. His meteoric rise was due in no small part to the efforts of his uncle, Cardinal Beaufort, who meant to ensure that his policies and family ambitions would survive his own death. As with his brother, Edmund was deferred to as a prince of the blood royal, and as such he rapidly became very influential at court, where he stood in high favour with the King. In the years to come, the new Earl of Somerset would play a central role that reflected the dynastic and political importance of the Beauforts in the history of the fifteenth century.

The death of Somerset also brought his ally Suffolk to greater prominence. Suffolk had enjoyed the confidence of Henry VI for more than a decade, and during those years he had grown rich and powerful, having created a widespread network of support within the royal household and the country at large by ensuring that his supporters were preferred to influential positions, both in local and central government. His influence over the royal household was so great that in 1445 he was able to exert it in favour of the appointment of his ally, Adam Moleyns, to the see of Chichester. Moleyns was not the only bishop who owed his mitre to Suffolk.

The main beneficiary of Suffolk's influence with King and Council was Suffolk himself. By 1444 he was the King's chief political adviser. He genuinely supported the peace policy, but this, and his obvious self-interest and political inconsistencies, had made the commons loathe him and refer to him as 'Jackanapes'. The Burgundian chronicler Georges Chastellain describes Suffolk as a second king. Certainly he was in control of the King's prerogative of patronage. He was jealous of his power and suspicious of his fellow magnates, and was prone to make accusations against his political rivals without first obtaining proof of their alleged misdeeds. He may well have supported Beaufort in poisoning the King's mind against Gloucester by insinuating that Gloucester's ambitions were dangerous.

Suffolk's had not been the only star to rise. By the mid-1440s certain noble families such as the Nevilles and their rivals the Percies had expanded their influence and grown powerful, as had those families who were related to the King – the Beauforts, the Staffords and the Hollands. Henry VI, whose immediate family consisted of his uncles Gloucester and the Cardinal and his Tudor half-brothers, relied on the extended Lancastrian family to bolster his throne, and to its members he assigned the chief posts at court and in his household.

In the 1440s Henry showed his favour to his kinsmen by creating dukedoms for them: the Beauforts became dukes of Somerset, the Staffords dukes of Buckingham, and the Hollands dukes of Exeter. With only a very few exceptions dukedoms had hitherto been reserved for immediate members of the royal house, but there was ample and worrying evidence that these new dukes now regarded themselves as royal princes.

On 27 June 1444 Suffolk returned to London, where he was received with great rejoicing. The Treaty of Tours and the truce were laid before Parliament for ratification; Gloucester's party made loud protests about both, but Duke Humphrey himself voiced no criticism, and even made a speech in Parliament thanking Suffolk for arranging them, in the belief that both truce and marriage had been negotiated on terms advantageous to England and without making any substantial concessions. Henry VI rewarded Suffolk by raising him to the rank of marquess.

It was some time before arrangements were made to escort Margaret to England. There was an exchange of cordial letters between the sovereigns of England and France, and Charles VII prepared a safe-conduct for Margaret to carry on her journey. On 7 November, Suffolk again crossed to France, with an embassy as splendid as the one he had led before, and accompanied by the earls of Shrewsbury and Salisbury, and also by his wife, Alice Chaucer, who was to act as principal lady-in-waiting to the Queen on the journey home. After arriving in France, Suffolk travelled to Nancy, arriving there in January.

Margaret had probably spent the intervening months at the French court, which in February moved to Nancy for her proxy wedding. In March, Charles VII and King René arrived, fresh from success-fully suppressing a Burgundian-inspired revolt by the citizens of Metz, and shortly afterwards the proxy ceremony took place. Again Suffolk represented his sovereign, and Louis de Herancourt, Bishop of Toul, officiated. The bride wore a gown of white satin embroid-ered with silver and gold marguerites, her emblem, and marguerites appeared everywhere, on clothing, hangings, canopies and banners.

After the wedding a ceremonial banquet was held, attended by the King and Queen of France, the Dauphin, King René, and a host of French lords. The feasting continued for a week, accompanied by miracle plays and eight days of tournaments, hosted by René and presided over by Charles VII's mistress, Agnes Sorel, as 'the Lady of

Beauty'. All combatants wore garlands or devices of marguerites in honour of the bride, and her champion Pierre de Brézé broke a lance with Suffolk.

At the end of the festivities, it was time for Margaret to leave for England. Two miles from Nancy Charles VII formally took leave of her, saying he feared he had done nothing for her by placing her on one of the greatest thrones of Europe for it was scarcely worthy of her. Then he commended her to God, and uncle and niece wept bitterly on parting. At Bar-le-Duc Margaret said farewell to her parents; it was an emotional leave-taking, and René was so overcome that he could not speak.

On 15 March, Margaret entered Paris where, on the following day, she received a stately welcome at the Cathedral of Notre Dame. Later that day her brother, John of Calabria, formally delivered her into the safe-keeping of Suffolk. The Duke of York, who had come with an escort of six hundred archers, came forward to bid her welcome on behalf of King Henry, and presented her with a palfrey caparisoned with crimson and gold velvet sewn with golden roses, a gift from her husband. Cannon saluted and church bells pealed as the Queen's cavalcade rode through Paris.

On the 17th the Duke of Orléans rode with the English to Poissy on the Norman border, whence York escorted them by river to Rouen, the English capital in France. The next day, Margaret arrived in Pontoise, and was York's guest at two state dinners; relations between the thirty-three-year-old Duke and the fifteen-year-old Queen were noticeably cordial, and there was no hint of the deadly enmity that would one day divide them.

Parliament had voted £5,129.2s.5d. (£5,129.12) against the cost of bringing the new queen home to England, and the Council had dispatched an escort of fifty-six ships. Not surprisingly, expenditure exceeded the available funds by about £500. On 3 April, Margaret's party came to Harfleur, whence they travelled along the coast to Cherbourg, where the English fleet awaited them.

Prior to their departure, Suffolk did his best to prepare Margaret for her future role and advise what was expected of her. He was concerned, however, about her poverty-stricken state. Henry VI might have been content to take a queen without a dowry, but there had been complaints in England that for all René's magnificent titles he had 'too short a purse to send his daughter honourably to the King, her spouse'. Gloucester had openly deplored the lack of dowry and had accused Parliament of having 'bought a queen not worth ten marks'.

René had provided his daughter with a trousseau of sorts. A furrier

had supplied 120 pelts of white fur edging for robes, and a merchant
of Angers had provided eleven ells of violet and crimson cloth of
gold at thirty crowns per ell, plus a thousand small pieces of fur. But
that was about all. Before she left France, Margaret had been obliged
to pawn some silver plate to the Duchess of Somerset so that she
could pay her sailors' wages; she then had to buy cheap, second-hand
plate at Rouen with which to replace it. But at least she was well
provided with attendants, for her household and escort comprised
five barons and baronesses, each paid a daily rate of 4s.6d. (22½p),
seventeen knights at 2s.6d. (12½p) each per day, sixty-five squires at
18d. (7½p) and 174 valets at 6d. (2½p) each, as well as 1200 other
persons at least, including yeomen and sumptermen.

The crossing to England was terrible: the sea was turbulent and the
rolling of the ship made Margaret ill. On 9 September her ship, the
Cock John, was beached at Porchester, Hampshire, but no reception
awaited the Queen's arrival because she had not been expected. The
mayor and other local worthies, apprised of her coming, hastened to
lay carpets on the beach, while large crowds gathered to greet her,
but Margaret was too sick to walk, and Suffolk was obliged to carry
her ashore. Her clothes, according to the assembled dignitaries,
looked like rags. The Duke carried her to a nearby cottage, where
she fainted, and she was later taken to a convent to recuperate. The
next day, however, she was sufficiently restored to be rowed in state
to Southampton, where she was saluted by seven Genoese
trumpeters from the decks of two galleys. Suffolk was now so
concerned at the Queen's lack of decent apparel that he immediately
summoned a London dressmaker, Margaret Chamberlayne, to
attend her.

Henry could not wait to see his bride. The Milanese ambassador
records that he dressed as a squire,

> and took her a letter which he said the King of England had
> written. When the Queen read the letter the King took stock of
> her, saying that a woman may be seen over well when she reads
> a letter, and the Queen never found out that it was the King
> because she was so engrossed in reading the letter and she never
> looked at the King in his squire's dress, who remained on his
> knees all the time. After the King had gone, Suffolk said, 'Most
> serene Queen, what do you think of the squire who brought the
> letter?' The Queen replied, 'I did not notice him.' Suffolk
> remarked, 'Most serene Queen, the person dressed as a squire
> was the most serene King of England.' And the Queen was
> vexed at not having known it, because she had kept him on his

knees. Afterwards the King wrote to her, and they made great triumphs.

Their meeting was destined to be further delayed, however, because soon after arriving at Southampton Margaret fell ill again and was taken to another convent to be nursed. Henry wrote to the Lord Chancellor: 'Our dear and best beloved wife the Queen is yet sick of the labour and indisposition of the sea, by occasion of which the pox been broken out upon her, for which cause we may not in our own person hold the feast of St George in our castle of Windsor.' Fortunately, Margaret recovered within a few days, and spent her convalescence planning her trousseau with the dressmaker. The King, meanwhile, rewarded the master of the *Cock John* with an annuity of twenty-one marks for life for having 'conveyed his beloved consort safely to England'.

8

The Daisy Flower

Despite his efforts, Henry had raised very little money to pay for his wedding. He had pawned the crown jewels, but then realised he needed them for the ceremony, and was forced instead to pawn some of his personal jewellery and plate to retrieve them.

On 23 April 1445 Henry VI married 'the most noble Lady Margaret' in a quiet ceremony at the abbey of the Premonstratensian monks at Titchfield in Hampshire. The 'venerable Master William Ayscough, Bishop of Salisbury' and confessor to the King, officiated and gave the young couple his blessing. Henry placed on Margaret's finger a ring set with an enormous ruby which had been given to him at the time of his coronation by Bishop Beaufort. Margaret also received an original wedding gift from an unknown admirer – a lion, which was brought to her at the abbey and then promptly dispatched at considerable expense to the royal menagerie at the Tower of London.

After the wedding the King and Queen spent several nights at Titchfield Abbey, and the Charter Rolls record that the abbot and convent were well rewarded for their hospitality. The chronicler John Capgrave, for whom Henry VI could do no wrong, predicted that 'this marriage will be pleasing to God and the realm, because that peace and abundant crops came to us through it'. The marriage itself looked not to be so fruitful. Henry was twenty-three, Margaret sixteen; their wedding night is not likely to have seen the flowering of any grand passion, since the King's confessor, Bishop Ayscough, had warned him against self-indulgence and having his 'sport' with his bride, advising him not to 'come nigh her' any more than was necessary for the procreation of heirs. As Margaret did not produce an heir for eight years, we may conclude that Henry took his confessor's advice to heart.

Others were not so immune to his wife's charm, for all contemporary sources agree that Margaret was beautiful. Chastellain called her the exemplification of 'all that is majestic' in woman, and one of the most beautiful women in the world. 'She was indeed a very fair lady, altogether well worth the looking at, and of high bearing withal.' She had, he added, excellent manners. A Milanese envoy described Margaret as 'a most handsome woman, though somewhat dark'. Whether he meant her hair – which was very long – or her skin is not clear, but the surviving manuscript illustrations of Margaret portray her as blonde or auburn-haired; the ambassador, however, had seen her, the illustrators had probably not.

The best surviving representation of Margaret of Anjou is a head and shoulders profile relief on a medal struck in 1463 by Pietro di Milano and now in the Victoria and Albert Museum. A copy is in the Bibliothèque Nationale in Paris. Both show Margaret with upswept hair wearing a crown. This sitter bears more than a passing resemblance to a noble lady painted by René of Anjou in a tournament scene in his manuscript *Le Livre de Tournois*, now in the Bibliothèque Nationale. This lady is evidently of high rank, for she is attended by a bevy of well-dressed ladies, and is shown standing at the right of the page, inspecting the helms of jousters. Did René here depict his own daughter? It is tempting to think so.

Margaret appears in several authenticated manuscript illustrations. The most famous is one in which she and Henry VI are being presented with an illuminated copy of John Talbot's *Poems and Romances*; it dates from c. 1450–3 and is now among the King's MSS in the British Library. There is a fanciful portrayal of Margaret's wedding in the Royal MSS in the British Library, and a beautiful picture of her and Henry kneeling before the altar in Eton College chapel in the manuscript of Ranulf Higden's *Polychronicon*, now in Eton College Library. Margaret appears as an older woman, hooded and at prayer, in a manuscript owned by the Worshipful Company of Skinners of the City of London, of whose guild – then the Fraternity of Our Lady's Assumption – she was patron.

There are fifteenth-century carvings of Henry and Margaret at Lambeth Palace in London. A corbel head said to portray Margaret is in the porch of the parish church of Henley-in-Arden, while her head and Henry's are shown in relief on a five-hundred-year-old bell that once hung in Valle Crucis Abbey in North Wales and is now at Great Ness Church, Shropshire. In nearby Wrockwardine Church is an ancient chair carved with an illustration of Queen Margaret confronting a robber, a famous episode from the Wars of the Roses. Finally, there is a stained glass window in the church of the

Cordeliers at Angers, showing Margaret kneeling in prayer, but this is an eighteenth-century copy of a fifteenth-century original.

Margaret's mother and grandmother were strong, capable women, and she took after them in many respects. She was intelligent and courageous and had great strength of character, which was apparent even in her youth. Charles, Duke of Orléans was of the opinion that 'this woman excelled all others, as well in beauty as in wit, and was of stomach and courage more like to a man than to a woman.' She was talented and valiant, but she had also inherited the hauteur and pride of her royal forebears, and could be domineering, ruthless, autocratic, hot-blooded and impulsive. She had a quick temper, and her changeable moods often irritated her male contemporaries, who complained that she would often change her mind 'like a weathercock'. She could be vindictive, quick to repay the smallest slight or insult, and was therefore not a person to be trifled with.

Margaret's native tongue was French, but she quickly learned to speak English well, applying herself with her usual energy to the task of learning the language of her adopted land. She was highly literate and particularly loved the works of Boccaccio, which were in light-hearted contrast to the pious tomes that made up her husband's reading matter.

Margaret quickly became the dominant partner in the marriage. She had energy and drive enough for two, and Henry accepted her tutelage without protest; he had, after all, been dominated since infancy by a succession of strong characters, and Margaret was another such. Blacman says that Henry 'kept his marriage vow wholly and sincerely, even in the absences of the lady', which in later years 'were sometimes very long', through force of circumstances. Nor, 'when they lived together, did he use his wife unseemly, but with all honesty and gravity'. He was a generous husband, anxious to ensure that Margaret lacked for nothing. She seems to have conceived a genuine affection for Henry, referring to him in her letters as 'my most redoubted lord'.

In many ways they were unsuited: Margaret was in most respects the complete antithesis of Henry, and probably viewed his willingness to forgive his enemies and opponents as a weakness. Instinctively, she began to shoulder his burdens and responsibilities, and he let her, being content to allow someone else to take the initiative. Nevertheless, from the first they were deeply loyal to each other, spending as much time as possible together.

The physical side of marriage was of no great importance to Henry at least, and here again he was failing in his duty as king, for it was a king's responsibility to provide for the succession. This failure rebounded on Margaret in time, for in that age infertility in a marriage was regarded as a dereliction of duty on the part of the wife. In a queen such a lack was a national disaster, for the provision of an heir was crucial to the well-being and stability of the realm.

The royal marriage represented a triumph for Beaufort and Suffolk, but the English people in general did not want peace with France: they wanted glorious victories and conquests against their old enemy. The young Margaret represented a peace they regarded as ignominious, and they disliked her for it. Later, when it brought England only defeat and humiliation, she was held responsible, however unjustly. In addition her belief in the peace policy strengthened Henry's resolve to pursue it in the face of public opposition.

And there was much of that. Later it would be said that, from the time of his marriage, King Henry never profited. Gloucester seized every opportunity to voice his disapproval and, although he was not, to begin with, personally hostile to Margaret, he did his best to engender distrust of her in the minds of the people. As a result of this, and the inbred Francophobia of the English, the marriage was never popular. Gloucester, and many others, felt that the truce constituted a threat to England, in that it gave the French time in which to re-arm and plan a decisive assault on England's remaining territories in France. Nor would this have been difficult, for during the years of truce the English forces in France were in some disorder, lacking consistent or effective leadership and undermined by lawlessness and lack of discipline.

The royal marriage also led to increasing bitterness between court factions. From the first Margaret identified herself vigorously with Beaufort's party, in the belief that she was helping her husband. By her willingness to support a particular faction she did much to exacerbate the divisions in court and household. Automatically placing herself in opposition to Gloucester and York, she thus, probably in youthful ignorance, made enemies of both of them.

In the opinion of the Duke of Orléans, 'England had never seen a queen more worthy of a throne than Margaret of Anjou. It seemed as if she had been formed by Heaven to supply to her royal husband the qualities which she required in order to become a great king.' The Milanese ambassador wrote in awe-inspired tones of 'the magnificence of the Queen of England'. From the first, Margaret was every inch a queen, having a commanding presence and a haughty manner. Etiquette at her court was rigorously formal. Duchesses, and even princes of the blood, were obliged to approach the Queen on their knees, and on one occasion the mayor of Coventry found that when he was escorting Margaret from his city he was expected to carry his mace of office, which he had only hitherto done for the King.

Margaret's motto was 'Humble and loyal', but she was also ambitious and loved power for its own sake. She used her rank and influence to secure the advancement of her favourites, and thereby ensured that the court party remained dominant. Headstrong and inexperienced, she was unable to assess the damage she was doing to her reputation. In France and Italy, where she had spent her formative years, rule by factions was accepted as a necessary evil, but in England it was bitterly resented. Unfortunately, Margaret never learned to understand the prejudices and fears of her husband's subjects, and would not have paid much heed to them even if she had, believing that it was not their place to question the decisions made by their betters.

Not since the time of Isabella, the 'She-Wolf of France', wife of Edward II, in the early fourteenth century, had a queen of England ventured to involve herself to any degree in politics. Margaret made it clear from the first that she was to be no passive consort, content to remain in her husband's shadow. She had a fine brain and meant to use it, even though the business of government was then considered to be a male preserve. By thrusting herself forward and taking the initiative on the King's behalf, Margaret confirmed the suspicions of those who suspected that she would have preferred the ineffectual Henry to concentrate his energies exclusively on his prayers and his foundations, so that she could get on with the serious business of ruling England in his name.

The Queen's willingness to involve herself in politics drew much adverse comment from all classes. It did not, of course, happen overnight, but was a gradual process. The more she discovered just how inept Henry was, the more she was driven to make decisions for him. She certainly had enough self-confidence to do so. But until 1453, when the whole political scene shifted and changed, Margaret's opponents, despite their criticisms, were not overly concerned about her influence because she was childless and would have no power whatsoever if the King died. She herself seems to have realised this, and until then she trod a fairly cautious path, aware of the precariousness of her situation.

Margaret made the most of the financial advantages of her position. Despite the state of the treasury, she did not lack for material comforts, although she spent comparatively little on herself. She wasted no time in obtaining a licence to export wool and tin wherever she pleased, thereby evading customs duty and the strict rules of the Merchants of the Staple at Calais. As the Paston Letters confirm, 'she spareth no pain to sue her things to an intent and conclusion for her power'. She did, however, attempt, with some success, to boost England's wool trade by importing skilled craftsmen from Flanders and Lyon, and she also tried to introduce silk weaving into England, bringing in foreign weavers, encouraging women to join the trade, and becoming patron of the Sisterhood of Silk Women, a guild based in Spitalfields, London.* Margaret also paid for the fitting out of English merchant ships destined for ports in the Mediterranean.

The Queen's Wardrobe Book for the year 1452–3 survives. It shows that she did not lavish large sums on clothes. The only items she bought were bolts of silk and cloth of gold, which were imported from Venice and cost £72.12s.6d. (£72.62½), and jewellery and items of goldsmiths' work amounting to £125.10s.0d. (£125.50). These were, of course, luxury items, but a queen was expected to attire herself in a manner worthy of her rank, for it was an age that set much store by outward appearances.

Margaret attended Mass daily and offered 4d on each occasion, unless it was a holy day or royal anniversary, when she gave more. She patronised many charities and gave liberally to them, as well as giving financial help to members of her household who were ill or getting married, or to those who had suffered bad luck, such as the two Newmarket men whose stable had burned down during a royal visit; to them, she gave £13.6s.8d. (£13.33).

Margaret is often credited with being the foundress of Queen's College, Cambridge, but this is not strictly true. The college was founded in 1446 as St Bernard's College by Andrew Docket, Rector of St Botolph's, Cambridge, who urged Margaret to become patroness the following year. Margaret petitioned the King to grant a new charter to the college and rename it Queen's College. In 1448 Henry did this, donating a sum of £200, but it was Docket who bore the lion's share of the cost of the foundation. There is no evidence that the Queen gave any financial endowment, although she certainly took an interest in the college, sending her chamberlain, Sir John Wenlock, to lay the foundation stone of its chapel in 1448.

Wenlock is listed in Margaret's Wardrobe Book as the head of her household, earning £40 per annum. The Queen maintained a large establishment, but found it hard to meet the cost of it because she was generous to those in her service and assiduous in obtaining

---

* The Spitalfields silk industry was still flourishing in the early nineteenth century.

promotion for them. Those members of her household in holy orders could realistically hope to be preferred to a prebend or deanery if they gave good service; two brothers, William and Laurence Booth, became successive archbishops of York thanks to the Queen's favour.

There were other officers in the Queen's household – the Clerk of the Closet, the Private Secretary, the Clerk of the Signet and the Clerk of the Jewels, while two Knights of the Board (table) earned forty marks per annum each. Margaret had five female attendants; one was Dame Elizabeth Grey, daughter of Sir Richard Wydville and wife of Sir John Grey; none could have then predicted that Elizabeth would one day be Queen of England. Another attendant was Elizabeth, wife of the powerful James Butler, Earl of Wiltshire, one of the foremost members of the court faction and a great admirer of the Queen.

In the lower ranks of the Queen's servants were ten 'little damsels', two chamberwomen, grooms, pages of the robes, pages of the beds, pages of the bakery, scullions, kitchen staff who worked in the buttery and pantry, the Queen's gardener – who was paid 100s. (£5.00) per annum – twenty-seven esquires whose salary bill was £143.4s.4d. (£143.22) annually, and twenty-seven valets at £93.15s.6d. (£93.77½) a year. The Queen paid £7 a day to the treasurer of the King's household for the maintenance of her own household, although she often found to her dismay that some of the money due to her as part of her dower, the income settled on her by the King through Parliament, was paid late. She therefore had to stretch such resources as she had to the limit.

Margaret's influence made the court once again the hub of fashionable society. In the year of her marriage Henry VI ordered that the Queen's apartments at Eltham Palace be rebuilt with a new hall, scullery and range of lodgings for the Queen to use prior to her coronation. In other royal palaces his wife's apartments had to be renovated as they had not been used for more than a decade. In these refurbished apartments Margaret entertained royally and encouraged a livelier atmosphere at court. She hunted frequently, ordering that the game in her forests be preserved exclusively for her use, and that bloodhounds be especially trained for her.

Margaret's chief mentor after her marriage was Suffolk, though rumour soon had it that they were lovers, and Gloucester later accused Cardinal Beaufort of turning a blind eye to the fact and even encouraging such wickedness. But no contemporary chronicler, however hostile, ever hinted that there was anything improper in the relationship.

When Suffolk met Margaret he was forty-eight and she fifteen. He was a suave, experienced man of the world with cultivated charm, while she was a young, untried girl about to leave her family and the land of her birth for a strange husband and a new life. Suffolk was kindly and avuncular, and made no secret of his admiration; she was flattered and susceptible to his warmth. His party had arranged her marriage and therefore she supported it.

Suffolk even saluted Margaret in romantic verse:

> How ye lover is set to serve ye flower . . .
> Mine heart is set and all mine whole intent
> To serve this flower in my most humble wise
> As faithfully as can be thought or meant
> Without feigning or sloth in my service.
> For wit thee well, it is a paradise
> To see this flower when it begin to spread
> With colours fresh enewed, white and red.

This poem is a typical example of the kind of courtly doggerel that was then fashionable, it being socially acceptable for knights and lords to write in such terms of a lady whose rank precluded any closer relationship. Nevertheless, the enemies of Margaret and Suffolk made political capital out of their friendship and spread scurrilous rumours about it.

Suffolk used Margaret's confidence and loyalty to his own and his party's advantage, and in return protected her from criticism, keeping her in ignorance of public opinion and dissident voices in Council and Parliament. Together they made a formidable political team, for the court faction headed by Beaufort and Suffolk controlled both King and government; Suffolk even manipulated his adherents so as to ensure that important decisions were taken independently of the Council.

On Friday, 28 May 1445, the Queen rode from Eltham Palace to Blackheath, where she was officially welcomed by the Lord Mayor of London, his aldermen and sheriffs, all clad in scarlet and attended by guildsmen in blue gowns with embroidered sleeves and red hoods. Gloucester, attended by four hundred retainers, then escorted her to his palace of Placentia at Greenwich.

On the following day, Margaret made her state entry into London, coming up river by barge to Southwark and entering the city by London Bridge, above which was a device representing 'Peace and Plenty'. She then processed through the streets of the capital, which were decorated with a profusion of marguerites in her honour, beneath triumphal arches, and alongside fountains sprouting ale and wine. At several points the cavalcade halted so that the Queen could watch miracle plays and pageants, with verses composed by Lydgate. Although she made a fine sight in her white damask gown and coronet of gold, pearls and precious stones, seated in a chariot pulled by two white horses caparisoned in white damask, some of the people were less than enthusiastic about their new queen, for Gloucester's supporters had already stirred up anger among them over Margaret's lack of a dowry. Others greeted her merrily, though, sporting daisies in their caps or hoods.

On Sunday, 30 May, Margaret was crowned at Westminster Abbey by Archbishop Stafford. The coronation was followed by a splendid banquet in Westminster Hall and three days of tournaments.

Parliament now conferred upon the Queen a dower of land worth £2000 per annum and an annuity of £4666.13s.4d. (£4666.67), the same amount as had been assigned to Katherine of Valois. The money was to come from the revenues of the duchy of Lancaster and the duchy of Cornwall, customs dues and the Exchequer.

On 2 June, Suffolk announced to Parliament that a French embassy would shortly arrive for the purpose of discussing a permanent peace to supersede the truce, which was due to expire in April 1446. There was, of course, a hidden agenda, of which Parliament knew nothing, and when the embassy arrived on 13 July it brought the predictable request that Henry VI cede Maine and Anjou to King René without delay, as provided in the Treaty of Tours. Now that the marriage was completed, Henry was expected to fulfil his part of the bargain. Henry prevaricated and dithered, even when the envoys produced letters from King Charles to him and the Queen, urging him to honour his promise, and saying this would be the best means of achieving a permanent peace. Henry played for time, and the only benefit to result from the meeting was an extension of the truce for three months, until July 1446.

Meanwhile, Gloucester was making his anti-French views known, much to the King's embarrassment, and when he saw the ambassadors again on 15 July, Henry spoke contemptuously of his uncle, while Suffolk informed them that the King no longer had any regard for the Duke. Thus Henry publicly dissociated himself from Gloucester's policies.

In the late summer of 1445 Henry recalled York from Normandy, since the Duke's five-year term of duty was at an end and there was apparently no question of him serving a further one. York's enemies had been busy: Waurin says that, despite York's obvious qualities, envy reared its head among the princes and barons of England, and was directed at the Duke, who was gaining in honour and prosperity. What is more, he prospered far too much for the liking of those who did not devote themselves loyally to the benefit of the King and his country. Above all, envy prompted Somerset, who despised the Duke of York and found a way to harm him. Somerset was well-liked by the Queen. She worked on King Henry, on the advice and support of Somerset and other lords and barons of his following, so that the Duke of York was recalled to England. There he was totally stripped of his authority to govern Normandy, which he had done well, and for some time, and despite his having acted commendably throughout the whole English conquest of France.

The way the tide was turning had been made clear to York earlier that year with the appointment of Sir Thomas Hoo, a member of Suffolk's affinity and hostile to York, as Chancellor of Normandy.

York returned in the autumn. The Crown still owed him £38,677; he was a wealthy man, but even he was crippled by the loss, and his financial problems only exacerbated his feelings of bitterness. To make matters worse, he now learned that Somerset was to replace him in France, an appointment that amounted to a slap in the face to one who had carried out his duties responsibly and effectively and who would have welcomed a second term of office. The appointment was also catastrophic from a military point of view, for Somerset was not nearly as experienced a commander.

York believed he could have achieved more in Normandy had he received adequate support from the government in England, though it would not have been in the interests of the peace party at court to have him making conquests in France. Waurin says that Somerset and Margaret had pointed out to Henry VI that 'Normandy was costing him a lot to maintain in wages to the soldiers that he was keeping there', and they even recommended that the duchy 'should be handed back to the French in order to avoid all these expenses'. Henry was not yet prepared to concede that much, but he certainly did not want York winning golden opinions.

Despite his just grievances, York met with scant sympathy or support in England. Most people at court were openly supportive of the King's peace policy and preferred not to identify themselves with a man who had backed Gloucester's call for a more aggressive stance in foreign policy. Out in the cold once more, York fell back on the support of his small circle of loyal friends, men who had served him well in Normandy and who were angry that he was so badly treated by a King and Council who should have been grateful to him.

But worse was to come. In Parliament Bishop Moleyns accused York of misgovernment and financial malpractice in Normandy. The court party did not want him at court or in the Council, interfering in politics, and were now so confident that they dared to accuse the man who was technically second in line to the throne of such crimes. York himself believed that Suffolk was behind the plot to disgrace him; placed as he was, he could hardly have been unaware of it, and from that time on relations between York and Suffolk, which had been quite friendly in France, grew icy.

York defended himself ably against Moleyn's accusations, summoning officials from Normandy who testified that the Bishop had offered bribes to York's soldiers to complain about his failure to pay them. Against all expectations, York was cleared of suspicion. Nevertheless, he now knew that while the court party controlled the King he could never expect preferment.

In October 1445, René of Anjou wrote to Henry VI, urging him to surrender Maine and Anjou. That same month a second French embassy arrived in London in response to Henry's request for a further extension of the truce.

Urged by her father and uncle, Queen Margaret began to exert pressure on Henry to do as they wished and honour the treaty. First she pleaded and cajoled, then she nagged, raged and threw tantrums; still Henry prevaricated. On 17 December, Margaret wrote to King Charles and promised to do all she could to obtain Henry's compliance. Whatever wiles she employed had their effect, for on 22 December the King himself gave Charles a solemn written undertaking to cede Maine and Anjou to René by 30 April 1446, this undertaking being given 'to please the King of France and at the request of his wife'.

Characteristically, Henry did not bother to inform his officers who were stationed in Maine and Anjou of what was to happen, nor did he wait for the approval of the Council. But somehow rumours of his secret arrangement leaked out, unleashing a storm of protest. His subjects, from Duke Humphrey downwards, considered they had been betrayed. Yet it was Suffolk upon whom most of the opprobrium fell, for it was he who had arranged the Treaty of Tours.

Henry ignored the storm and did nothing until the last minute. Then on 30 April, knowing that he could delay no longer, he sent orders to the governor of Maine and Anjou to evacuate the provinces, preparatory to ceding them to the French. This confirmation of the rumours sparked a further wave of protests, and when the governor defied the King and refused to obey there was general jubilation. Such was the mood of the people that Henry dared not force the issue.

Margaret was not so timid. In May she reminded the King of his promise to Charles VII, begging him to keep his word. He would not listen, being too fearful of his subjects' reaction. Margaret was being subjected to a barrage of pressure from the French king, but she could do nothing to move her husband, and negotiations with France over Maine and Anjou dragged on throughout the rest of the year without reaching a conclusion satisfactory to either side. King Charles became increasingly exasperated by Henry VI's dilatoriness, and in the winter made efforts to force him to surrender the territories, dangling the carrot of extending the truce until January 1448. Still Henry dithered.

Margaret, meanwhile, hoping to cement further the truce between England and France, had proposed a marriage between York's four-year-old heir, Edward, Earl of March, and Madeleine, daughter of Charles VII, but although Suffolk gave the proposal his backing, nothing came of it. Nevertheless, the suggestion was a tacit acknowledgement of the dynastic importance of York, and may well have been intended also as a means of diverting the Duke's interests towards French politics.

In December 1446, an incident occurred which gave the court party cause to wonder whether York might be secretly plotting to seize the throne. York's armourer, John Davies had as an apprentice a villein, William Catour, who claimed to have heard Davies say that the crown belonged by right to York. Suffolk had the man hauled before the Council to repeat his accusation, while York, who realised that others might believe – or try to allege – that he himself was implicated in Davies's treasonable assertion, demanded that the armourer be brought to justice and punished. Davies denied having said any such thing, but his judges decreed that he and Catour should undergo trial by combat, using single sticks. The trial took place at Smithfield, in the presence of the King, the Queen and the whole court. Catour was victorious, and it was therefore deemed that God had given His verdict. Davies was hanged and his body burnt. From now on, the Queen and her party would be suspicious of York and his dynastic intentions.

When Gloucester had found out that Suffolk had, seemingly without consulting Council or Parliament, secretly promised to cede Maine and Anjou to the French, his anger had known no bounds, and his violent and vociferously expressed opposition to the court faction's policies had won him much popularity among a disenchanted populace who regarded him as their champion. Those who knew that it was not against Suffolk but the King that Gloucester's fury should have been directed were therefore concerned to curb 'Good Duke Humphrey's' public speeches, lest he should unleash a scandal that would compromise the throne itself.

Gloucester, far from heeding warnings to temper his criticisms, became ever more outspoken, and by December 1446 the King and the court party knew that something would have to be done to silence him, lest he discover and broadcast the truth. He had also incurred the enmity of the Queen, who regarded his censures as insults to herself which could not be forgiven or forgotten, and he had fallen out with most of his fellow councillors. Gloucester seemed unaware of the peril in which he stood. Abbot Whethamstead of St Albans states that 'satellites of Satan' had poisoned Henry's mind against his uncle, who was 'so respected and loved by the people and so faithful to the King'.

The Duke was causing so much dissension that Henry VI, in vindictive mood, decided that the Duke must be silenced once and for all. He was supported in this resolve by Queen Margaret, Suffolk, the ageing Cardinal Beaufort, and Somerset, who had all managed to convince their royal master that Gloucester was in fact plotting a coup, with the intention of setting himself up as king and immuring Henry and Margaret in religious houses. Margaret was so convinced of his evil intentions that she begged Henry to order his arrest. The King, however, decided that his uncle should be summoned to answer certain charges before Parliament.

In February 1447 Parliament met at Bury St Edmunds in Suffolk, a region where the de la Poles exercised a great deal of influence and Gloucester very little. On the 10th, in bitter weather, the King and Queen arrived at the head of a great army, and the King formally opened Parliament in the refectory of St Edmund's Abbey. The next day was devoted to a discussion of the Queen's jointure.

Gloucester had as usual received a summons to attend Parliament, but he was entirely unaware of the conspiracy against him, and when he arrived at Bury on the 11th he was surprised to receive an order to wait upon the King without delay. When he came into the royal presence he was confronted, not only by his unsmiling sovereign, but also by a hostile group that included the Queen, his old enemy the Cardinal, Suffolk and Somerset. Suffolk wasted no time in charging Gloucester with plotting treason against the King and the realm, and of spreading rumours against the Queen's honour, rumours that named Suffolk as her lover. Gloucester hotly denied this but Margaret said coldly, 'The King knows your merits, my lord.'

Gloucester was allowed to retire to his lodgings while the King decided what was to be done with him, but when he arrived there he was overtaken and arrested by a deputation of lords including the Duke of Buckingham and the Queen's steward, Viscount Beaumont, who was also Lord High Constable of England. Beaumont charged him in the King's name with high treason and informed him he was to be placed under house arrest.

Gloucester remained in his lodgings for twelve days. On 23 February 1447 he died there. The cause of his death has never been properly established. Contemporary rumour had it that he had been strangled, suffocated with a feather bed, or 'thrust into the bowel with an hot, burning spit'. No one pointed any finger of suspicion at the King or Queen: it was Suffolk who was deemed guilty of his enemy's alleged murder, although if this had been the case he would hardly have acted without the King's sanction, for Gloucester was a prince of the blood and heir presumptive to the throne. Nor would Queen Margaret or Cardinal Beaufort have given the order for Gloucester's assassination without Henry's knowledge or approval.

There is no evidence, however, that Gloucester was murdered. His great friend Abbot Whethamstead believed he had died from natural causes, and modern historians have tended to agree with him. The Duke was fifty-seven, and had ruined his constitution by physical excesses and debauchery over many years. There is no doubt that his arrest came as a shock to him, and every possibility that it may have hastened his end, perhaps from a stroke, for he lay for three days in a coma before expiring. Nevertheless, his passing was certainly timely, and undoubtedly many in high places wanted him out of the way as an embarrassment and a political liability. Gloucester's wife had tried to bring him to the throne by witchcraft, and although he had not been implicated, it is clear that Henry VI had never again trusted him and was all too ready to believe the lies of his detractors.

Gloucester was buried, as he had wished, in the Abbey of St Albans, where his tomb still survives. He left no legitimate issue. After his death, 'Good Duke Humphrey' became something of a legend. People remembered his charities, his generosity and his patriotism, and forgot his self-seeking ambition and anachronistic policies. It was those who were commonly believed to have murdered him who were perceived as the enemies of the state.

9

Murder at Sea

The death of Gloucester left York heir presumptive to the throne until such time as the Queen bore a son – or Henry named Somerset his heir.

In every respect York was the perfect heir presumptive: wealthy, respected, experienced in warfare and government, and already the father of a growing family with healthy sons. He had a better claim to the throne than Henry VI himself, though few dared voice this opinion, but the Duke by his overt loyalty to the King had already demonstrated that his ambitions did not include a crown. Nevertheless, he had the resources and the ability to pursue his claim if he so wished, as the court party was well aware, and for this reason, York was not acknowledged as Henry's heir. Instead, the question of the succession passing to the Beauforts was raised, and although the matter was ultimately left in abeyance, once again York's rights were overlooked.

York had been dismayed by Gloucester's death, which left no one but himself to lead the opposition to the court party, who he believed were doing untold damage to the kingdom. As Gloucester's political heir, he knew himself to be particularly vulnerable, for had not Suffolk just persuaded the King to charge his late uncle with high treason? What might the over-powerful Suffolk now do to York? The Moleyns affair had proved just how malicious the court party could be. York, therefore, was reluctant to assume Gloucester's militant stance. From now on he would tread a careful path, ever wary of his enemies' motives, yet ever zealous to reform the present regime and gain a voice on the Council.

Physically York was not the most prepossessing of men. He was short in stature and stout, with a square-shaped face and dark hair;

his youngest son, later Richard III, was said to bear a strong resemblance to him. No portrait of York survives, and there are only two extant representations with any claim to authenticity. One is in a stained glass window donated to Cirencester Church before 1443 by two of York's squires. This shows his head and shoulders, adorned with a coronet and his famous gold collar with enamelled roses. His face is clean-shaven and his hair cut in the military style affected by Henry V. He has heavy-lidded eyes, a prominent nose and a small mouth. In Penrith Church, Cumberland, is an engraving showing the Duke with long hair and a forked beard; this is a copy of a lost original, and its authenticity is unsubstantiated.

York was a man of considerable intelligence, who could speak and read Latin. He was a political conservative, a proud, serious, even austere man, aloof, remote in manner, and difficult to warm to. He was not popular among his fellow magnates and did not see any reason to cultivate their friendship. His mother had died at his birth and the execution of his father when he was four may have led to a certain coldness in him and an insistence on keeping his own counsel. On occasion, he could act impulsively without consulting anyone else, sometimes with disastrous consequences. Indecisiveness was periodically another of his faults, as was inconsistency. He was courageous in battle and an able commander, but even here his record was marred by occasional stubbornness and recklessness. His arrogance was a constant bar to success in every field.

York, like Gloucester, desired to see the government formulate an aggressive war policy against France, as Henry V would have wished. He was also genuinely concerned about the misgovernment of the court faction and resolved to eliminate the endemic corruption and indiscriminate patronage of its regime. There was, naturally, an element of self-interest in this: York could only gain from the court party being publicly discredited. Moreover, winning the support of the magnates to do this would prove difficult: most were either in awe of the ruling clique or hoping to gain some advantage from supporting it, while others believed that not to support a faction so openly favoured by the King would have appeared as crass disloyalty.

York, however, preferred to distinguish between loyalty to the King and loyalty to a faction that was doing him no service. To York, loyalty to the King meant demanding the reform of the government and the dismissal of all the corrupt advisers and time-servers who were dragging the reputation of the Crown into the dust with their own. If the King could not see how badly the kingdom was suffering from misgovernment, York and the few others who supported him could, and meant to do something about it – as well as furthering their own interests along the way.

York now began to promote himself as the champion of good government and reform, and this was how the people soon came to regard him and why he rapidly gained popularity with the commons. There were those, however, who did question whether York was sincere about reform. His enemies said he was as guilty of oppressing his tenants by intimidation and the perversion of justice as other lords, citing the case of his steward on the Isle of Wight, who was said to live 'like a lord, with as rich wines as could be imagined', as a consequence of his extortion and corruption. There is in fact little evidence that such practices were widespread on York's estates. Certainly there was a degree of self-interest in his aims, but his later record is proof that his concerns about misgovernment were indeed genuine.

York's favourite residence seems to have been his castle at Fotheringhay in Northamptonshire, which was situated on an imposing site above the River Nene and was surrounded by a thriving market town. Today, only fragmentary remains testify to the existence of this magnificent castle and the adjacent buildings adjoining the collegiate church. Mounds of earth to the south of the church are all that remains of the college quadrangle and library. The church, however, survives as a monument to the House of York, and is decorated with York's personal badge, the falcon and fetterlock; here are the tombs of his family, and here, too, he himself would one day be laid to rest.

The mightiest fortress owned by York was Ludlow Castle, the ancient stronghold of the Mortimers, which was situated on a commanding and strategic position on the Welsh Marches, and would become the chief headquarters of the House of York during the Wars of the Roses. The castle dates from Norman times, and massive remains survive today. In the inner bailey is an unusual circular twelfth-century chapel, as well as the luxuriously appointed domestic ranges, built by the Mortimers in the fourteenth century.

York's London residence was to become Baynard's Castle on the banks of the Thames. It stood in Upper Thames Street between Blackfriars and St Paul's Wharf, not far from where the River Fleet flowed into the Thames. Built in the eleventh century by one of the Conqueror's companions, a knight called Baynard, it had passed into the hands of the powerful de Clare family and been rebuilt with stone walls and ramparts in the twelfth century. Later, it was acquired by Gloucester who, after a disastrous fire in 1428, built it anew with battlements and strong fortifications, so that it resembled Warwick

Castle. On the Duke's death it reverted to the Crown, and Henry VI eventually granted it to York, who is first recorded as living there in 1457.*

In these residences York lived in some splendour with his duchess, Cecily Neville, a proud woman of robust health who bore him thirteen children. She lived to be eighty, a remarkable age in those days, having witnessed the deaths of four dukes of York and the creation of the future Henry VIII as the sixth duke. Richard and Cecily appear to have been an amicable, even happy couple. She accompanied him on all his overseas tours of duty, and several of their children were born abroad. Cecily's piety was legendary, and as she grew older, her life was increasingly dominated by religious offices and prayers. She rose at seven, attended eight services, and was in bed by eight o'clock every evening. Occasionally, though, she would take some wine or indulge in 'honest mirth'. Later on, political propaganda would accuse her of playing her husband false with a French archer called Blaybourne, and of foisting upon the Duke two bastard sons, but her renowned piety makes nonsense of this, as indeed she did herself when she protested very vehemently against being so unjustly slandered.

The Yorks' children were born over a period of seventeen years, from 1438 to 1455. There were eight boys and five girls. Four of the boys, Henry, William, John and Thomas, died young, as did two of the girls, Joan and Ursula, who was the youngest child. The surviving children were Anne, born 1439 at Fotheringhay, and married before 1447 to Henry Holland, Duke of Exeter; Edward, born 1442 at Rouen, and styled Earl of March during his father's lifetime; Edmund, born 1443 at Rouen and created Earl of Rutland in 1446; Elizabeth, born 1444 at Rouen; Margaret, born 1446 at Fotheringhay; George, born 1449 at Dublin Castle; and Richard, born 1452 at Fotheringhay, a frail child whose survival of infancy surprised everyone. Cecily's will of 1495 refers mysteriously to 'my children, Katherine and Humphrey', but these names do not appear in any contemporary list of York's issue, and were probably his grandchildren, Katherine and Humphrey de la Pole. All of Richard

---

* Baynard's Castle was again rebuilt after the Wars of the Roses, but was destroyed in the Great Fire of 1666. In 1972, during excavations for an office block, its foundations were discovered. These showed that the castle had been built around an irregular quadrangle. Surviving engravings depict a rectangular-shaped house with a double courtyard, above which soared a hexagonal tower. On the river side, the walls rose straight up from the water, while houses either side were built on stilts.

and Cecily's children were descended thrice over from Edward III, through Lionel of Antwerp, John of Gaunt and Edmund of Langley.

After Gloucester's death, the vultures descended. The Queen was given his manor of Placentia at Greenwich, a magnificent house set in lovely 'gardens of pleasaunce'. Margaret immediately arranged for extensive building works to be undertaken there: new latticed windows were installed, others were re-glazed, terracotta floor tiles bearing the Queen's monogram were laid, and new pillars carved with marguerites were erected outside. A great chamber was built for the Queen's own use, as well as a parlour and a gallery overlooking the gardens, where an arbour was put up. Finally, new tapestries were hung. In the refurbished house – now a palace – 'disguisings' or pageants were mounted for the entertainment of the King and court.

Gloucester's greatest rival did not long enjoy his triumph. Cardinal Beaufort was now well over seventy and nearing death. By 1447 he had virtually retired from political life, although his party remained dominant under the leadership of the Cardinal's protegés, Suffolk and Somerset. On 15 March 1447, Beaufort died at Wolvesey Palace at Winchester; he was buried in the nearby cathedral, where a fine effigy wearing a cardinal's hat adorns his tomb.

With his death, the government lost one of its chief financial mainstays. The Cardinal left one last bequest of £2000 to the King but Henry refused it because he felt that his uncle had given him enough during his lifetime. 'The Lord will reward him,' said Henry. Beaufort's nonplussed executors protested, urging that the money be used for the King's educational foundations; Henry, to their relief, agreed.

Somerset was now head of the powerful Beaufort family, and was also the King's nearest Lancastrian relative. Again there were rumours that he would be named heir presumptive despite the existence of letters patent barring the Beauforts from the succession. Somerset, having inherited his uncle's fortune, was now a very wealthy man, and was accorded precedence as a full prince of the blood. The King relied heavily on his counsel and showered him with gifts and honours, which aroused the resentment of other magnates, especially York, who justifiably regarded Somerset as a threat to his own position.

Together with Suffolk, Somerset now led the court party, both men enjoying the full confidence of the King and Queen. Suffolk was at the zenith of his power: around this time he was promoted to the influential offices of Chamberlain of England, Captain of Calais,

Warden of the Cinque Ports, Chief Steward of the Duchy of Lancaster north of the Trent, Chief Justice of Chester, Flint and North Wales, and steward and surveyor of mines for the whole country.

With Gloucester dead, there was no one to lead the protest about the surrender of Maine and Anjou, and in the spring of 1447 a French embassy arrived to conclude the matter. This provoked another storm, but again it was not the King who was the object of his subjects' patriotic indignation – it was Suffolk, who had become the scapegoat for Henry and his councillors and was widely perceived as the villain of the piece. If he had been unpopular before, he was now loathed. The people blamed him for the downward slide of England's fortunes in France and for giving up Henry V's conquests in return for a dowerless queen.

In May, Suffolk offered the Council a satisfactory explanation of his actions, but this did not mollify the commons, who were now blaming him for all the ills that had befallen the realm, especially the faction-fighting in Council – for which he was, to a degree, responsible – the government's failure to pay its soldiers in France, the embargo placed on the import of English cloth by the hostile Duke of Burgundy, and the near-bankruptcy of the kingdom.

By 27 July negotiations with the French were complete. Henry VI agreed to surrender Maine by 1 November provided compensation was paid to his garrison in the province. On the following day he appointed commissioners to transfer Maine and Anjou to Charles VII.

The Queen also shared in the unpopularity of the court party. In June the keeper of Gloucester Castle arrested a man who had been overheard lamenting the coming of the Queen to England, a sentiment probably shared by many of the King's subjects. For them, Margaret was irrevocably associated with Suffolk and the loss of Maine and Anjou, and neither the Queen nor the Earl improved matters when they attempted to evade customs duties on the export of wool and alienated the English merchants, who had hitherto been staunch supporters of the Crown.

With the deaths of Gloucester and Beaufort the Queen's influence grew. Every letter signed by the King was now backed up by a similar one from the Queen, who demanded that she be kept informed on all political matters, especially negotiations with France and military and financial affairs. State papers and reports on seditious persons were submitted for her inspection, and neither Suffolk nor Somerset, nor their associates Cardinal Kempe, Bishop of Chichester, and Lord Say, would act without Margaret's approval.

It could therefore be said with some truth that an eighteen-year-old girl was effectively ruling England.

By the end of 1447 it was apparent that the emergence of the Queen on to the political stage had given birth to a new factional rivalry to replace that of Gloucester and Beaufort. Beaufort's peace party had become the court party, headed by the Queen, Suffolk and Somerset, which controlled the King and the government. The opposing faction comprised a group of lords who had, for various reasons, been excluded from this charmed circle, mainly because they upheld the ideals for which Gloucester had fought for most of his career, or were critical of the ruling party. This faction now looked to York to lead them.

The court party feared York, had consistently blocked his attempt to participate in government, and had been searching for ways to neutralise his influence. As with Gloucester, they wanted him out of the way. On 9 December 1447 he was appointed the King's Lieutenant in Ireland for a term of ten years. This ill-conceived appointment was the brainchild of Suffolk, and it was obvious to York that he was being sentenced to virtual exile. Hence he managed to delay his departure for two years.

York had rendered loyal service, digging deep into his coffers to finance his expenditure on behalf of the Crown. Not once had he displayed any inclination to press his superior claim to the throne. Yet Henry and his advisers now treated him as an enemy; and by their wholly unjustifiable slights against one who was a prince of the blood and premier magnate of the realm, they made him an enemy.

November came and went, and still Henry VI had not handed over Maine and Anjou. In February 1448, Charles VII, tired of his prevarications, led his armies into Maine and laid siege to the city of Le Mans. When the garrison claimed it could not hold out, Henry at last agreed on a formal surrender, which took place on 16 March and was conditional upon the truce being extended until April 1450. In England, the surrender was greeted with anger and bitterness. A worried Queen urged Henry to promise financial compensation to dispossessed English landowners returning from Maine, which he did, though the money was never forthcoming and this created more ill-feeling. So did the fact that the Queen's father had fought at King Charles's side in Maine, which did not endear Margaret any more to the English though in fact it had caused her great distress. Naturally, it was she and Suffolk who bore the brunt of public opprobrium.

In the spring of 1448 the King demonstrated his confidence in the leaders of the court party by creating Edmund Beaufort Duke of

Somerset, which meant that his twelve-year-old son Henry was now styled Earl of Dorset, and William de la Pole was created Duke of Suffolk. This was the first time that ducal rank had been conferred on anyone other than members or relatives of the royal family, and reflects the enormous influence and prestige enjoyed by Suffolk. Possibly Henry wished to raise the two men at court to equal rank with York, and it may have been in response that York began using the surname Plantagenet, which had been in abeyance since the twelfth century, when it had been borne by Count Geoffrey of Anjou, father of Henry II.* York adopted it in order to emphasise his royal connections and proximity to the throne, implying, perhaps, that it should have been he who was advising the King, not an upstart like Suffolk or a magnate tainted by bastard descent such as Somerset. There is no evidence, however, that York at this date had any designs on the throne, and it would be more than a decade before he himself would dispute Henry's title.

In 1448, York's chief concern was that the King would repudiate Henry IV's letters patent and declare Somerset his heir. He felt, quite justifiably, that the elevation of Somerset was a deliberate attempt to block his own political and dynastic ambitions, and knew that it was Suffolk and Somerset, and not the King, who were responsible for his political exile. Thus the rivalry of York with the two men now crystallised into a deadly political feud that would have serious repercussions throughout the next two decades. The situation was such that a man could not support one side without being deemed the enemy of the other.

Somerset and the Queen began a whispering campaign, spreading rumours that York, by calling himself Plantagenet, was plotting treason, intending to mount a coup and take the throne. Tainted with suspicion and impeded by his own aloofness and arrogance, York found it increasingly difficult to win the support of his fellow magnates. At length, says Waurin, in 1449, York was 'expelled from court and exiled to Ireland', this being 'provoked by the Duke of Suffolk and other members of his party', including Somerset, who was 'responsible for these deeds' and 'overjoyed' at the Duke's departure. York's post was no sinecure, for Ireland at that time was a land riven by tribal feuds and struggles. His achievements there were modest, but he did win the favour and affection of the Anglo-Irish

---

* Geoffrey had been called Plantagenet after his emblem the broom flower (*planta genista*), a sprig of which he wore in his hat. Although his son and successive kings until the mid fifteenth century are now referred to as the Plantagenets, none of them had actually used the name.

settlers and even some of the native Irish, thus establishing a long-standing affinity between Ireland and the House of York.

That same year, at a salary of £20,000, Somerset, as Governor of Normandy and chief commander of the English forces in France, took up residence at Rouen, capital of the duchy. His appointment, says Waurin, was 'due to the solicitation and exhortation of the Queen and of some of the barons in power'. The truce with France still held, but the Duke was assured that his allowance would be paid even if war did break out. There is, however, no evidence that he ever received it.

As commander-in-chief Somerset was a failure, having neither ability nor capacity for the job. Waurin says he carried out his duties 'so negligently that afterwards, due to his misconduct, the whole country was returned to the control of the King of France', and in fact his term of office marked the beginning of the end for the English in France. In March 1449, Henry VI himself, urged on by Suffolk, broke the truce and reopened hostilities, authorising an attack on the Breton town of Fougères, which the English speedily occupied. The onslaught made nonsense of Henry's much-vaunted desire for peace and effectively amounted to a new declaration of war. It gave the French the opportunity they had been waiting for, and in June they launched a full-scale attack on Normandy, determined to reconquer it. In July, Charles VII formally declared war on England.

Fears were voiced that the French offensive would lead to the 'shameful loss' of Normandy, the centre of English power in France, 'which God ever defend', and by 15 August, according to the chronicler Henry Benet, 'about thirty fortified towns in Normandy were lost'. Charles VII's status among the monarchs of Europe was now in the ascendant, and his victories gave both him and his subjects new confidence and the impetus to carry to a successful conclusion what had been begun.

In the late summer of 1449, his armies overran Normandy and began an assault upon Rouen, which had been in the hands of the English for thirty years. Somerset agreed to discuss terms and to withdraw from Rouen if the French would leave the English in possession of the towns they held along the Norman coast. This was agreed, and in October the Duke surrendered Rouen to the victorious French, handing over the veteran John Talbot, Earl of Shrewsbury and others as hostages. The cheering citizens, who regarded King Charles as their liberator, then flung open the gates and welcomed him and his army with ecstatic rejoicing. Somerset, says Benet, 'fled to Caen'. The French were now determined to have all, and soon broke their agreement with the Duke. In December, the ports of Harfleur – so dearly won by Henry V – and Honfleur fell to Charles VII.

By now, the disastrous effects of the peace policy were plain to see, and the mood of the English people was ugly. Rumours were spread alleging that Margaret was not René's daughter but a bastard, and therefore unfit to be Queen of England. Public anger was also fuelled by high food prices and the profligate alienation of crown lands. In July, Parliament had ventured to suggest that an Act of Resumption be passed, which would revoke all grants of land and annuities made by the King since his accession, but Henry, manipulated by those who had profited by such grants, had refused to authorise it; instead, he had dissolved Parliament.

But it was Suffolk who was the real target of the people's hatred. Few Council records for this period survive, which suggests that the Duke had often acted independently of the Council and taken upon himself much of the important business of government. He was doing the House of Lancaster no favours, for its prosperity depended upon a Council that was publicly perceived to be united and equitable. Instead, thanks in no small measure to Suffolk, it was riven by factions, excluded from decisions affecting the weightier affairs of state and its reputation was now such that many people had lost all confidence in it, seeing it purely as the focus for the private ambitions of the landed aristocracy.

The virulent criticisms of Suffolk greatly alarmed the Queen, and she urged Henry to deal forcefully with his fractious subjects. He, who had also to consult Parliament on the critical situation in France, summoned it to meet on 6 November. There were many who perceived that Suffolk was unlikely to survive this latest storm with his power intact; his supporters, guessing that this was the end for him, hastened to dissociate themselves from him, some even resigning from their posts in the royal household. His enemies were poised for the kill.

The Lords and Commons combined to bring Suffolk down. The process began when the Duke's long-standing enemy, Lord Cromwell, rose in Parliament and publicly accused Sir William Tailboys, Suffolk's squire, of plotting to kill him. Suffolk denied that he knew anything about such a plot, but this did not help Tailboys: people believed him guilty, and he was fined £3000.

In Ireland, York was being kept informed of what was happening in England and holding himself in readiness to support the attack on Suffolk, anticipating that the fall of the favourite would provide an opportunity for him to elbow his own way on to the Council. His

informants had already told him that there were others of like mind
to himself who desired reform of the administration and would be
glad to see Suffolk go.

On 9 December Adam Moleyns, Bishop of Chichester, resigned
as Lord Privy Seal. Moleyns, a political animal rather than a
churchman, was a member of the court party, a former supporter of
Suffolk who now believed that the Duke had abused his power and
should be ousted from it. On 9 January, he was in Portsmouth,
attempting to explain Suffolk's misdeeds to an angry and unruly
mob of sailors who were about to embark for Normandy. He had
also brought their wages, long unpaid, but when he handed them
over, the sailors found that they had received far less than was their
due. They shouted abuse at the Bishop, denouncing him as the
betrayer of England, and when he haughtily reminded them that
they were insulting a man of God, his manner so incensed them that
they fell on him and mortally wounded him. Later, it was alleged
that, as he lay dying, he accused Suffolk of being responsible for the
loss of Maine and Anjou. After the murder Parliament, which had
been in recess over Christmas, refused to reassemble. Thus began the
violent, watershed year of 1450.

Suffolk was frantically trying to consolidate his position. Early in
1450, with the help of the Queen, he secured a great matrimonial
prize for his son John – his ward, the seven-year-old Lady Margaret
Beaufort, a very wealthy little girl who was also the direct
descendant of John of Gaunt and had a better claim to the throne than
her uncle, the Duke of Somerset, whom many expected to be named
heir-presumptive. Margaret's claim had until now largely been
overlooked because she was female and a child, but an ambitious
husband, with the means and determination to do so, might well be
successful in pressing it.

The significance of this betrothal was not lost on Suffolk's
contemporaries, some of whom drew the unlikely conclusion that he
was in fact plotting the overthrow of Henry VI in order to secure a
crown for his son and thereby establish the de la Pole dynasty on the
throne of England. Others believed, perhaps correctly, that the Duke
hoped to persuade the King to recognise Margaret Beaufort as his
heir. Either way, the confusion surrounding the future succession
proves that at the time the people of England had no clear idea as to
who had the best claim to succeed a childless Henry VI.

When Parliament finally reassembled on 22 January, Suffolk felt it
appropriate to justify his rule. He reminded the assembly how
loyally his family had served the Crown, both in England and
against the French, and declared he had been of late the victim of

'great infamy and defamation', and was much misunderstood. He swore he had never betrayed his king or his country. Was it likely he would do so for 'a Frenchman's promise'?

The Commons were unimpressed. Suffolk's day was done; there had to be a scapegoat for the recent disasters and humiliations in France and misgovernment at home. On 26 January an angry Parliament petitioned the King that he be arrested and impeached, and the Duke was sent to the Tower of London while the Commons prepared a Bill of Indictment. The Lords had decided to keep a low profile until specific charges were made. While the Duke was in the Tower, there was a great armed presence of the watch of the city of London about the King and in the capital, 'and the people were in doubt and fear of what should befall, for the lords came to Westminster and Parliament with great powers as men of war'. Influenced by York, the Council sent officers to Norfolk to put a stop to the local tyrannies there of Suffolk's agents, Thomas Tuddenham and Henry Heydon.

On 7 February the Commons presented the King with a formal petition to indict Suffolk. There were many charges, the most serious being that in July 1447 Suffolk had treasonably plotted an invasion of England with the French ambassador and had divulged secret intelligence to the French. He had promised to cede Maine and Anjou to Charles VII 'without the assent, advice or knowing of other [of] your ambassadors', which had led directly to the loss of Rouen and other towns in Normandy. He had also plotted the deposition of King Henry with the intention of setting on the throne his own son John, whom he had betrothed to Margaret Beaufort, 'presuming and pretending her to be next inheritable to the Crown'. Not once was the Queen's name mentioned.

On 12 February, the King, using his royal prerogative, commanded that the charges against Suffolk be referred for his own decision, even though the Commons wanted the Duke arraigned at the bar of the Lords. Then Henry dithered for a month. His frustrated Commons, meanwhile, added on 9 March other charges to the petition, accusing Suffolk of 'insatiable' covetousness leading to the embezzlement of crown funds and taxes and the impoverishment of the monarchy, and influencing the appointment of sheriffs who would 'fulfil his desires for such as him liked'. He had committed 'great outrageous extortions and murders; manslayers, rioters and common, openly-nosed misdoers, seeing his great rule and might in every part of your realm, have drawn to him and been maintained and supported in suppressing of justice, to the full heavy discomfort of true subjects'. Much in these charges was certainly justified, but there is no evidence that Suffolk planned to make his son king, nor that he had plotted with the French. Nor was he the only magnate to indulge in bribery and corruption on a grand scale.

Henry VI refused to allow any of the charges to be formally examined by Parliament. Instead, on 17 March, he called upon Suffolk to answer them. The Duke denied them all, describing them as 'too horrible to speak more of, utterly false and untrue, and in manner impossible'. The Chancellor then informed him that the King held him 'neither declared nor charged' a traitor 'in respect of matters mentioned in the first bill'. Because the Commons were loudly baying for Suffolk's blood, the King conceded that there might be some truth in the second set of charges. The Queen, anxious to save the man who had arranged her marriage and been father-substitute and support to her ever since, had persuaded Henry that a sentence of exile should be sufficient to satisfy the Commons. When the storm had blown over and a suitable time had elapsed, Suffolk could be brought back and restored to favour. The King agreed to this, and sentenced Suffolk to exile for five years from 1 May.

The Commons and the people were furious. To them, it seemed that parliamentary justice had been circumvented by those whose proper function it was to enforce it. By his intervention the King had saved Suffolk's life: the mood of Parliament was such that, had the Duke stood trial, he would undoubtedly have been condemned to a traitor's death. The Lords were angry because they had not been consulted as to Suffolk's fate. The Londoners, in particular, were incensed by the sentence: when the Duke was released from the Tower on 18 March, he went to his house at St Giles to prepare for exile, but a mob tried to force an entry, intent upon lynching him, and he was obliged to escape by a back door. Frustrated of their prey, the Londoners seized his horse and assaulted his servants instead. The Duke took refuge at his country seat at Wingfield in Suffolk, where he remained during the six weeks prior to his banishment. An emotional farewell letter to his son still survives, in which he urges the boy to be loyal to God and his sovereign.

On Thursday, 30 April, Suffolk sailed from Ipswich for Calais and exile with two ships and a little pinnace, which (according to a letter written by William Lomnour of London to John Paston in Norfolk on 5 May) he sent ahead with letters 'to his trusted men in Calais to see how he should be received'. Later that day, in the straits of Dover, the Duke's ship was intercepted by a fleet of small vessels which had been lying in wait for him, 'and there met with him a ship called the *Nicholas of the Tower*'. The *Nicholas* was not a pirate ship, as some later historians have suggested; Benet describes her as 'a great vessel', and she was in fact part of the royal fleet, her master being Robert Wennington, a ship-owner of Dartmouth.

Rumour later had it that, when Suffolk saw this ship approaching, he asked what name it bore, and when he was told he remembered an old seer who had once prophesied that if he could escape the danger of the Tower, he should be safe. Now 'his heart failed him'. The master of the *Nicholas* 'had knowledge of the Duke's coming from them that were in the pinnace', and now he sent his men in a small boat to Suffolk to say 'he must speak with their master. And so he, with two or three of his men, went forth with them in their boat to the *Nicholas*, and when he came there, the master bade him, "Welcome, Traitor!"' Suffolk was on the *Nicholas* 'until Saturday following, and some say he was tried after their fashion upon the articles of his impeachment and found guilty. And in the sight of all his men' – presumably Suffolk's small fleet was following – 'he was drawn out of the great ship into a boat, and there was an axe and a stock, and one of the lewdest of the ship bade him lay down his head'. If he co-operated, he was told, 'he should be dealt with fairly and die on a sword'. So saying, the sailor 'took a rusty sword and smote off his head with half a dozen strokes, and took away his gown of russet and his doublet of velvet, mailed, and laid his body on the sands of Dover. And some say that his head was set on a pole by it.' The head and body lay rotting on the beach for a month until the King gave orders for their removal to Wingfield Church for burial.

Suffolk died a much-hated man, and many rejoiced at his end. Political songs vilified him and gloatingly recounted his fall. The identity of his killers has never been established; presumably they acted on the orders of men who felt that the Duke should be made a scapegoat, or of those who wished to see him suffer a just punishment for his crimes, a punishment that the law had failed to provide.

Suffolk's widow, the indomitable Alice Chaucer, broke the news of his death to the Queen, who was so grief-stricken that she could not eat for three days and wept continually during that time. After that, anger surfaced, and the desire for retribution. Suffolk might be dead, but she still had Somerset and other powerful supporters who would help her avenge him. But the days when the court party could rule unchallenged were now numbered, and there remained the deadly enmity between York and Somerset as the gravest threat to peace between the contending factions.

10

John Amend-All

By 1450 the Lancastrian government had not only lost much of its credibility, but it was also bankrupt, with massive debts amounting to £372,000, increasing by about £20,000 each year. York was still owed £38,000. The cost of maintaining the royal household was a staggering £24,000 a year, twice what it would be twenty years later, while the King's basic revenues yielded a mere £5000 annually. Other sources of income raised his annual budget to £33,000 – not nearly enough to live on and pay his debts as well. Thus the debts grew ever larger and the Crown's capacity to pay ever less. Hitherto the government had relied on loans from Italian merchants and bankers, but even they were now wary of lending more money, being aware of the precarious state of the nation's finances, and in the decade from 1450 they advanced only £1000 in total. Nor would Parliament vote sufficient taxation to meet the Crown's debts or fund the war in France, which was still a major drain on the economy. Even members of the King's household went unpaid and were forced to petition Parliament for their wages.

Under the influence of the court party, Henry VI had given away royal lands and estates on an unprecedented scale, and had thus lost the revenue from rents and dues on them. He had also lavished large sums on Eton and King's College, and been criticised by Parliament for it. The court faction, whose members were the chief beneficiaries of Henry's generosity, were milking the country dry, and had strongly resisted all attempts by Parliament to pass Acts of Resumption which would deprive them of their ill-gotten gains. There was no likelihood, therefore, of any immediate improvement to the Crown's financial problems.

The people of England were largely united in their desire for political stability, firm government, and the restoration of law and order. They were aware that the court party was manipulating the administration of law to the benefit of its individual members and their affinities, and that it so monopolised the King and the Council that there was little hope of any effective opposition emerging. The anonymous author of *An English Chronicle* wrote: 'Then, and long before, England had been ruled by untrue counsel, wherefore the common profit was sore hurt and diseased, so that the common people, what with taxes and other oppressions, might not live by their handiwork and husbandry, wherefore they grudged sore against those who had the governance of the land.'

The wealthy and influential London merchants were loudest in deploring the endemic disorder, being particularly anxious to see stable government restored, so that the economy could recover. Their sympathies naturally lay with those who opposed the court faction, and later they would support York in his struggle against that faction.

People were also appalled by what had been happening in France. Early in 1450 English troops began returning from Normandy, having fled before the victorious advance of the armies of Charles VII. In small groups, 'in great misery and poverty', they trudged along the roads that led from the Channel ports, begging and stealing as they went. Pitiful and starving as they were, some terrorised the countryside; a few were arrested and hanged. Others caught the imagination of a people infuriated by the humiliation of defeat, compounding their grievances against the government.

There was growing disorder in parts of Wales, which posed yet another problem for those in power. The Welsh in these areas suffered from neglect by absentee lords or exploitation by rapacious ones, such as William Herbert of Raglan. Herbert was York's steward in the lordship of Usk in south-east Wales, and he was ambitious, greedy and totally unscrupulous. Contemporary chroniclers gave him a bad press: the annalist of Gloucester Abbey called him 'a cruel man, prepared for any crime', while the author of the *Brief Latin Chronicle* describes him as 'a very grave oppressor and despoiler of priests and many others for many years'. Herbert was by no means the only oppressor of the Welsh: the native-born Gruffydd ap Nicholas subverted royal authority to devastating effect.

The trouble was that Henry VI was incapable of exercising that authority. He tried to keep in touch with his people by going on frequent progresses, but this did not distract them from the misgovernment and corruption of the court party. It was also apparent that Henry was unable to control his magnates and this, together with the loss of England's possessions in France, led to a general loss of faith in his ability to govern effectively. Public loyalty to the House of Lancaster was therefore strained, although few dared to criticise the King outright. In July 1450 two Suffolk farmers were arrested because 'they falsely said that the King was a natural fool and that another king must be ordained to rule the land, saying that the King was no person able to rule the land'. It was true, but such candour was ruthlessly punished. It says much for the reverence in which Henry VI was held that there were only isolated incidents such as this. It was the court faction which bore the brunt of public criticism.

With a weak king, a Council whose authority had been undermined, and a divided parliament, central government was weak, ineffective, and unable to control an aristocracy whose chief function was to make war. It was not that Parliament and the Council had ceased to function altogether, but that such government as they did provide was virtually ineffectual against the tide of disorder and injustice that was sweeping the country. By the 1450s it was being said that

> the realm of England was out of all good governance, for the King was simple and led by covetous counsel, and owed more than he was worth. His debts increased daily, but payment there was none. Such impositions [taxes] as were put to the people were spended in vain, for he kept no household nor maintained no wars.

The murder of Suffolk had angered many of the King's supporters, among them William Crowmer, Sheriff of Kent, and Lord Say, the ruthless and greedy Treasurer of England. Both men were convinced that Kentishmen had been involved in the murder, and throughout Kent rumour now had it that the two lords had vowed to turn the county into a deer park. Kent was an area particularly suggestible to rebellion because it had suffered a number of coastal attacks by French pirates, while a decline in trade had hit its ports. Those same ports, and the roads leading out of them, had also witnessed a steady stream of ragged, embittered soldiers returning from France, the embodiment of England's humiliation.

On 24 May 1450, three weeks after Suffolk's death, Whitsun was being celebrated all over the land, and in Kent the people gathered as usual for the festival. But this was a gathering with a difference for it signalled a political revolt orchestrated by intelligent men who were aware of the violent public feeling against the corrupt officials of the royal household and the magnates of the court faction who had abused their power. Many towns and villages in the Weald of Kent and beyond had armed and equipped all their able-bodied men, and on this day the constables of the county summoned hundreds of men to Ashford, where they formed an armed band and marched towards London. One of their leaders, Jack Cade, had incited the people by publicly declaring that the Queen meant to avenge her lover Suffolk by razing to the ground the houses of Kentish peasants and farmers.

Thus began what became known as Cade's Rebellion, a well-planned and organised movement that posed a serious threat to the government. When news of it reached London, the King and court were at Leicester, where Parliament was in session. Henry VI was thus fortunate in having his lords and their retainers to hand, and had no difficulty in amassing a large army, which marched at once for the capital. He even, for once, donned armour, and the sight of him riding at the head of his men through the streets of London heartened and comforted the citizens.

Jack Cade was a prosperous gentleman whom Benet describes as 'a most bold and subtle man': the men of Kent had chosen him to lead them because of his status and reputation in the local community. The warrant later made out for Cade's arrest states he had been born in Ireland and had served in the household of a Sussex knight. He then, it alleges, murdered a pregnant woman, but this allegation may have been an attempt to portray Cade as a vicious criminal and so destroy public sympathy for him. His talent as a military leader suggests he had seen active service in France, and he was, to begin with, a strict commander who controlled his men well, forbidding looting and hanging those who disobeyed his orders.

Cade appealed to the popular imagination by inventing catchy names for himself which yet had a certain political significance. First he used a clerical alias, 'Dr Aylmer', then he called himself 'John Amend-All'. Latterly he had used the more provocative 'John Mortimer' to emphasise his sympathy for the Duke of York and other opponents of the government. By using the name Mortimer as a rallying cry he was reminding the people that there was an alternative to the present regime, and that the House of Lancaster had usurped the throne and set aside Richard II's true heirs. It also denoted symbolic kinship with York, though many people at the time believed there was also a literal kinship.

Cade published a manifesto listing a catalogue of grievances against the government, grievances that were shared by most members of Parliament and several magnates, and by the nation at large. He cited the alienation of crown lands, the imposition of cruel taxes, the financial state of the realm, the use of bribery and corruption in the appointment of local government officials, the perversion of justice by royal favourites, the rigging of parliamentary elections, the loss of England's lands in France, the corruption of the court faction, the slighting of York, and the government's failure to deal with piracy around England's coasts. There were also complaints about individuals, former supporters of Suffolk such as Thomas Daniel and John Trevelyan, William Booth, the Queen's chancellor, Sheriff Crowmer and Lord Say.

Cade demanded that, to redress these wrongs, the King should resume all the lands he had given away and dismiss Suffolk's supporters from the Council; he should order sweeping reforms of the judicial system and also lift wage restraints. There should be curbs on government spending and an enquiry into whether England's losses in France were the result of treason. Finally, Gloucester's murderers should be brought to justice – it was still widely held that the Duke had died of foul play. These demands were hardly revolutionary, indeed, they were all eminently sensible and moderate, and they were not primarily aimed at the King but at his corrupt officials.

Nor was Cade supported by a rabble of peasants. This was not a second Peasants' Revolt but a rebellion by well-informed, practical men who were realistic about what they might hope to achieve. They believed in the justice of their cause, and looked upon themselves as campaigners and protesters rather than rebels. Some of them were supporters of York. Few had suffered any particular economic hardship: there was no agrarian depression in Kent, and in recent years Kentish farm labourers had enjoyed increased wages. The list of pardons issued after the rebellion shows that Cade's army, estimated by Benet at 5000, comprised men from all classes of society and included one knight who had fought at Agincourt, seventy-four gentlemen, three sheriffs, two members of Parliament, eighteen squires, and a substantial number of local officials, sailors, churchmen, tradesmen and yeoman farmers. They came mainly from the south-eastern counties, but their concerns were the concerns of people in every part of the realm.

Henry VI concluded that York was the prime mover behind Cade's rebellion, and that he had incited it from his safe base in Dublin. Consequently, he was sure that the rebels' intention was to make York king. Since the Duke's criticisms of the present regime were common knowledge, it is hardly surprising that Henry should link him to the rebellion, but there is no contemporary evidence that York or any of his affinity were connected in any way with Cade's uprising. York, though, was no doubt anxious to be kept informed of its progress by his friends in England; Cade had, after all, demanded that York be recalled to take his rightful place in Council and at court.

Early in June, a scarlet-clad Cade led his well-disciplined army on to Blackheath, where it encamped as if preparing for war. The King, then lodging at the Priory of St John at Clerkenwell, sent representatives to parley with Cade, who in turn presented them with a copy of his manifesto. Henry passed this on to the Council, whose members rejected out of hand all its demands. The Londoners, meanwhile, were preparing to defend themselves, positioning cannon along the banks of the Thames and blockading the river with barges. The royal army, 20,000 strong, was camped in Clerkenwell Fields outside the city walls.

The King commanded the rebels to go home. Thinking he would turn his army on them, and knowing they could not hope to prevail against it, Cade ordered a retreat to Sevenoaks in Kent. Here, he waited for reinforcements from Sussex. The court party knew that the King had the advantage, but Henry was reluctant to take the offensive against his subjects. Nevertheless, his advisers persuaded him that it would help his cause to do so: the presence of the sovereign at the head of an army and the sight of the royal standard fluttering in the breeze would have the power to quell the most hardened of rebels.

As Henry prepared to lead his army in pursuit, someone – probably the Queen, so terrified for her husband's safety that she had refused to leave his side – persuaded Henry to split his army in two: half remained with him at Blackheath, the rest, under the command of Sir Humphrey Stafford and his brother William, marched on Sevenoaks, where a bloody skirmish lasting two hours took place. The rebels suffered heavy losses, but still succeeded in overcoming the royal forces. The Stafford brothers were killed, and those of their company who did not share the same fate scattered in panic.

When news of this disaster reached Blackheath, the King's soldiers mutinied, declaring themselves to be Cade's men, and ran riot through London, burning and looting the houses of those who supported the court faction and crying out that they would have the heads of the King's wicked counsellors. This was all too much for Henry, who – at Margaret's urging – fled to Greenwich. The Queen wanted Lord Say to accompany them, but he declined to do so, knowing that the rebels might well pursue him and so endanger the royal couple.

In the morning Henry's demoralised nobles attempted to muster the remainder of the royal army on Blackheath, but were alarmed when a man began shouting, 'Destroy we these traitors about the King!' Other voices now began clamouring for the blood of Lord Say, Thomas Daniel and other members of the court party. The King ordered the arrest of Lord Say and Sheriff Crowmer, and consigned Say to the Tower and Crowmer to the Fleet Prison, more for their own safety than to please the rebels. In the meantime, the Archbishop of Canterbury and most of the Council had prudently taken refuge in the Tower, which was under the command of its royal governor, Lord Scales.

The King issued a proclamation to the effect that all traitors would be arrested, and set up a commission whose members were instructed to bring to justice the extortioners and corrupt advisers and officials against whom Cade and the men of Kent had made their accusations. But, says Benet, 'Cade and the men of Kent were not thus appeased'. On 25 June, the King quitted London and travelled to Kenilworth, leaving a fearful and ineffectual Council headed by Archbishops Kempe and Wayneflete to deal with the crisis. His retreat left the way clear for Cade to march again on London.

By now, the whole of south-eastern England was in a ferment. Men came in droves, flocking to join Cade from Essex, Sussex and Surrey. Inspired by his qualities of leadership, they were confident he would lead them to victory. Almost to a man they remained loyal to the King, believing he had been ill-served and deceived by those in power, whose heads the rebels now meant to have. Royal government had virtually collapsed; the Council was helpless, and unwilling to confront Cade. Simultaneous risings had broken out in Wiltshire and the Isle of Wight, where Lancastrian officials were the targets of mob violence.

On 29 June the rebel army returned in high spirits, its ranks swelled by deserters from the royal army, and quickly occupied Blackheath before the Londoners guessed what was happening. Cade was now arrayed like a lord in a handsome helmet and a brigandine – an armour-plated jacket – studded with gilt nails. On his shoes he wore the purloined spurs of Sir Humphrey Stafford.

On that same day, in the chancel of Edington Church in Wiltshire, William Ayscough, Bishop of Salisbury, was preparing to celebrate mass. Ayscough, a close friend of Suffolk, had officiated at the marriage of the King and Queen, but was generally blamed for their lack of an heir because it was well known that, in his capacity as chaplain, he had urged the King to avoid marital intercourse as far as possible. Yet in other respects Ayscough was a worldly bishop, spending the minimum of time in his diocese and the maximum time at court, where preferment was more likely to be had, and where he was a prominent member of the court faction. He was notoriously acquisitive and therefore 'evil beloved' by the commons.

So evil beloved, in fact, was he that as Ayscough turned to the altar, his congregation rose in fury and dragged him out of the church to a nearby hill. Here, in a frenzy of violence, they hacked him to death. His murderers then stripped the corpse naked and tore his bloody shirt to pieces. Later, they 'made boast of their wickedness', and took away as many of the Bishop's belongings as they could carry.

The murder was almost certainly the result of a whispering campaign by rebel agents sent to fan the flames of discontent among the people of the south-western counties. Judge Gascoigne was of the opinion that Ayscough was killed 'because he was the confessor of Henry VI and did not remedy the defects around the King nor depart from the King because these were not remedied'. His murder was chilling evidence of the mood of the people, and the bishops of Lichfield and Norwich were also threatened with violence by angry mobs at this time.

On 1 July the rebel army reached the Surrey shore of the Thames and Cade, still calling himself John Mortimer, took up residence at the White Hart Inn in Southwark, which became his headquarters. At the same time the Essex rebels were grouping outside Aldgate. Many Londoners, poorer people as well as some aldermen and several wealthy merchants, some of whom had financed Cade, supported the rebels' demands and were in favour of opening the city gates to them. The Lord Mayor hastily consulted his aldermen as to whether he should do so, and only one, Robert Horne, demurred, which made him so unpopular that the mayor cast him into prison for his own safety.

In the late afternoon of the 2nd, the drawbridge at the far end of London Bridge was lowered and Jack Cade led a band of his followers through it, pausing to cut the ropes of the drawbridge with his sword as he passed. He came like a conqueror, wearing a gown of blue velvet beneath his brigandine, and sporting the helmet and gilded spurs of a knight, to which he had no entitlement. He carried a shield studded with gold nails and an unsheathed sword and his squire walked before him carrying a sword as if it were the King's sword of State.

As he entered London Cade was presented with the keys of the city and many broke from the watching crowds and ran to join him. He then led his company along Cannon Street and so to the London

Stone in Candlewick Street.* Tapping it lightly with his sword, he cried: 'Now is Mortimer lord of this city!' Later he dined with the civic authorities, having his meat carved by a gentleman, as a lord would. At night he returned to Southwark, where the bulk of his army was encamped, but some of his men stayed in London and terrorised the citizens by their threatening behaviour.

At eleven o'clock the next morning, says Benet, 'Cade came to London again and rode through the city brandishing his drawn sword.' He was clad in the same blue velvet gown, embellished with sable furs, and a straw hat. This time he was accompanied by a larger force of his men and their mood was ugly. They were determined upon vengeance and their quarry was Lord Say and Sheriff Crowmer. Cade went to the Fleet Prison to take Crowmer, while a detachment of his men marched to the Tower, where Lord Scales gave in to their demand and surrendered Lord Say, who was hustled off in no very gentle manner to the Guildhall. Here, he and twenty others who had been rounded up by Cade's men were brought before the justices to be indicted for treason and extortion. Lord Say haughtily demanded the privilege of trial by his peers, as was his right as a nobleman, but, says Benet, 'when they heard this the common people wished to have him killed at once in front of the justices'. A priest was hastily summoned, 'and so he made his confession and was afterwards led by the junior officers and the men of Kent to the Standard in Cheapside, where he was beheaded forthwith'. Crowmer, meanwhile, had been taken out of the city via Aldgate, to Mile End, where he met a similar fate.

Cade had the two heads impaled on spears and ordered that Say's body be stripped naked; the ankles were then bound and tied to a horse, which dragged the bleeding torso, its arms outstretched, through the streets of the city, the rebels following bearing their grisly trophies. At Aldgate they were greeted enthusiastically by the men of Essex, and those carrying the severed heads made them 'kiss' to roars of coarse laughter. Cade then ordered that the heads be displayed on London Bridge, as was customary with traitors, and that Say's body be taken to the Hospital of St Thomas in Southwark for burial.

Many of Cade's men were by this time out of control and causing havoc in the city. He himself, puffed up with triumph, was no longer interested in disciplining them; indeed, he allowed his Kentishmen to ransack and loot the house of Philip Malpas, a wealthy alderman,

* A Roman monument, thought by historians to have marked the centre point of their road system.

though Malpas was warned beforehand and managed to remove himself and most of his valuables to a place of safety. Cade himself, joining the looters, seized some jewels that York had left in pawn with Malpas; these he later abandoned, and they were recovered and returned to the alderman.

Many of Cade's followers – respectable, honest men who had taken no part in the killing or looting – were appalled to see their leader stoop to theft. In that moment much of Cade's credibility melted away; he could no longer pose as the champion of justice. Says Benet, 'When the people of London realised that Cade was breaking the promises he made in his proclamation they turned against him.'

Cade was now desperate for money, having none left with which to pay his men. He had asked foreign merchants in London for arms and cash, but they had refused him. Now, having broken his own code of conduct, he could not prevent his men from stealing and pillaging. In desperation, he forced Master Curtis, a city merchant in whose home he dined that day, to give him some money, but it came too late. As soon as his army had returned to their camp at Southwark the Lord Mayor and aldermen met with Lord Scales to discuss how best to prevent Cade and his rabble from returning to the city.

The next evening, towards ten o'clock, soldiers from the Tower garrison, led by Captain Matthew Gough, made their way furtively to London Bridge. When Cade's men tried to enter the city they were strongly resisted. A furious battle then broke out, which lasted until eight the next morning.

London Bridge had not been built to serve as a battleground. Shops, houses and a chapel were crowded along its sides, and the central thoroughfare was only eight feet wide. Here, the press of fighting men was having truly horrific consequences. Citizens were screaming in terror, houses literally shook to their foundations, and panicking mothers, their babies in their arms, leapt into the river. Gough was killed, but even so, Cade realised that the rebels were losing ground, and gave orders to fire the drawbridge. This cut off the Tower force from his own, and he withdrew at last to the Surrey shore. Forty-two Londoners and two hundred Kentishmen had been slain, some by having been pushed into the Thames.

Scales, having ordered that the gates of London be locked, still feared what Cade might do next, so, acting on the advice of the Queen and several bishops, he sent Cardinal Kempe to parley with him. The Cardinal was empowered, on behalf of the government, to promise Cade and his men 'charters of pardon' if they would lay down their arms and go home. Cade agreed, on condition that the demands in his manifesto be met. Kempe assured him they would be, promising that the King's commission would investigate all grievances.

Government clerks set to work, hastily drawing up the promised pardons; Cade's was made out to 'John Mortimer'. Most of the rebels then dispersed and went home, but Cade told his remaining men that their cause could not be considered as won until Parliament had agreed to their demands. On 8 July, he retreated with his small force to Rochester by river, sailing along the Thames in barges full of stolen goods. The next day he made an unsuccessful attempt to besiege Queenborough Castle on the Isle of Sheppey. The Sheriff of Essex and many others were now hunting him down, and on 10 July he was publicly proclaimed a traitor and 1000 marks were offered for his capture. The free pardon granted at Southwark was revoked on a technicality as it had been issued to John Mortimer, not Jack Cade.

Many of Cade's followers had deserted him, and the authorities were hot on his trail. He fled into Sussex, south to Lewes, where he hid in the surrounding woods, and thence to Heathfield, where he concealed himself in a garden. Here, however, he found himself cornered by armed men led by Alexander Iden, Sheriff of Kent. He defended himself bravely but was quickly overcome and mortally wounded by the Sheriff himself. Broken and bleeding, he was dragged off towards London, but died on the way, cheating the executioner. His body was stripped naked and taken to the capital in a cart, but the Council were apparently in some doubt as to whether the right man had been arrested and would only accept that it was Cade when the corpse had been identified by the innkeeper's wife at the White Hart in Southwark. Then the head was smitten off and boiled and the skull was placed on a spike above the drawbridge on London Bridge, facing towards Kent as a warning to any future rebels. The torso was quartered and the quarters displayed in towns in the disaffected areas. Sheriff Iden was rewarded with a substantial pension for life and appointed Keeper of Rochester Castle. Benet says that Cade had been condemned 'not according to the law, but according to the King's wish'.

Indeed, Henry was bent on having his revenge. The King and Queen had returned to London on 10 July, but only after order had been restored by the Council. Henry then presided over the trials of other rebels captured by the authorities in Kent and himself passed sentence of death upon every one. Eight were executed at Canterbury, twenty-six at Rochester, the King being present on each occasion of what was referred to as 'the harvest of heads'.

The rebellion had achieved nothing. The King's commission was dismissed and no changes were made; the court party remained supreme. However, what had been made strikingly manifest by Cade's uprising was the inability of King and Council to cope successfully with such a crisis. A king was supposed to lead his armies, protect his people and enforce justice, but this king had fled, and in his absence the government of the realm had all but broken down. What had also been made alarmingly clear was how easy it had been for the insurgents to occupy the capital.

Cade's rebellion did not signal the outbreak of the Wars of the Roses, nor was it a part of those wars, but the frustrations engendered by its failure were undoubtedly a contributory factor. The grievances and demands published by Jack Cade were the same grievances and demands that Richard, Duke of York, would voice not so long afterwards. Hence the rebellion may be seen as a prelude to war; certainly it had been the most serious crisis of Henry's reign so far.

'A Great Division Between York and Lancaster'

In France, the situation was grave. In July 1450 Somerset formally surrendered the city of Caen to the French, along with all his artillery. Most people in England considered this an unnecessary and dishonourable act, but Somerset was aware of the hopelessness of the English cause and knew very well that he would have no further use for cannon in France. On 1 August, he rode into London, 'many poor soldiers with him'.

York, learning of Somerset's surrender, concluded – as did many others – that the Duke's incompetence had led to the loss of so much of Normandy, and wrote to the King demanding that his rival be apprehended as a traitor. Henry reluctantly acceded to his 'dear cousin's' request, and summoned Parliament, but Somerset, informed of what was afoot, pleaded his case with the Queen, who was sympathetic and promised she would not permit any charges to be laid against him. Henry bowed to his wife's wishes and even went so far as to reward Somerset for his services in France: instead of finding himself in the Tower, the Duke was appointed Constable of England and readmitted to the Council. Margaret's enemies promptly spread rumours that she was cuckolding the King with Somerset.

News from France did not improve matters. On 15 August a small English army led by Sir Thomas Kyriell had been soundly defeated by the French at Formigny; it was now only a matter of time before all Normandy was in the hands of Charles VII. By the end of August the last English garrisons had surrendered to the invader and the French had reconquered the duchy. England's only remaining possessions in France were Calais, captured by Edward III in 1347, and the duchy of Aquitaine, which had been annexed to the Crown on the marriage of Henry II to Eleanor of Aquitaine in the twelfth century. Aquitaine was of prime economic importance to England because of the wine trade centred on Bordeaux, which had made many London merchants wealthy over the centuries.

'Cherbourg is gone,' lamented a Paston correspondent, 'and we have not a foot of land left in Normandy.' The loss of Normandy signalled the end of English dominion in France and of the dual monarchy, although English sovereigns would continue to style themselves as King or Queen of France until the reign of George III. It was regarded as an ignominious and humiliating defeat which should never have happened, and which had irredeemably tarnished the honour of England; moreover, it had fatally undermined the credibility of a government whose policies had led to defeat.

News of Somerset's reception in England had made York extremely angry, and when he learned of the ugly mood of the English people, he quickly made up his mind to return from Dublin to consolidate his own position and secure for himself at last the power and influence he had been denied for so long. He received disturbing reports that the court party were plotting to indict him for treason, and without requesting the King for permission to leave his post, took ship for the Welsh coast and from there rode to Ludlow. Here he was joined by Lord Dudley and the Abbot of Gloucester, speedily raised an armed force of 4000 men and marched towards London. His return created a sensation. Many people welcomed him, and his ranks swelled with supporters, so much so that Benet says that by the time he reached London his army was 50,000 strong, a figure which must be an exaggeration but gives some idea of the strength of public feeling.

One man who received a summons from York to join him was Sir Thomas Tresham, Speaker in the recent Parliament. Tresham rode out at once from his manor of Sywell, Northamptonshire, but was ambushed and murdered on the road by a gang of ruffians. At an inquest into the murder, the coroner's jury was intimidated by those same ruffians, who threatened to kill them unless they returned a verdict of suicide. Such was the fear they inspired that no one dared arrest them.

It was from subversions of justice such as this that the common people hoped York would deliver them. Despite Somerset's political pre-eminence, York was the magnate with the greater territorial power, and should have the means to prevail over his enemies. All those who had suffered from the rapaciousness and corruption of the court party welcomed the Duke as a saviour come to deliver England from political anarchy, while the court faction and the Queen viewed

York's return as a greater threat to their power than the loss of Normandy.

When the Council learned that York was making for London it sent an armed force to arrest him which he successfully evaded. On 29 September 1450 he arrived at Westminster and entered the palace, demanding an audience of the King. Henry had shut himself in his apartments, but York hammered at the door of the King's privy chamber and insisted on being admitted, whereupon a petrified Henry agreed to let him in and 'graciously' received him. York assured him of his loyalty but then swung to the attack, urging the King to implement certain reforms and complaining that justice was being subverted. He also insisted that Henry dismiss his corrupt advisers and summon Parliament to deal with the abuses in government, and that he also make himself available to York for consultations on matters of state. Henry answered that he would appoint a committee to consider York's suggestions, although he had no intention of doing any such thing.

York's interview with the King had been conducted in such a manner that, according to the Paston Letters, 'all the King's household was and is afraid right sore; and my lord has desired many things which are much after the desire of the common people, and all is upon justice and to put all those who are indicted under arrest under surety or bail, and to be tried by law'.

York was hailed, as he had intended he should be, as the champion of good government, the man who would restore England's honour and rid the King of his corrupt advisers. Among the common people he already enjoyed considerable support, and he also found himself joined in opposition by all those of noble or gentle birth who had suffered under, or fallen out of favour with, the present regime; one was the Duke of Norfolk, who remained a staunch supporter and friend. Some came to York complaining about the intimidating behaviour of Suffolk's old retainers, Tuddenham and Heydon, in East Anglia, 'and cry out upon them and call them extortioners, and pray my lord that he will do sharp execution on them'.

It is significant that York made no attempt at this time to press his claim to the throne. He came instead with the purpose of leading an opposition party and thereby reforming the government and gaining conciliar power for himself, though the Queen and many of the magnates believed there was a more sinister reason, and acted accordingly in a hostile manner. Yet the most York wanted at this time was to be formally recognised as heir presumptive, for undoubtedly he was concerned about Somerset being named heir in his place.

On 30 September, York submitted to the King two bills of complaint. One listed personal grievances, and was obviously an attempt to forestall an attainder. It set forth York's claim to be heir presumptive, his request to be paid the £30,000 still owed him by the Crown (£8000 had in fact been repaid already of the original £38,000) and a complaint about having been excluded from the King's counsels. The other bill was a catalogue of grievances that reflected the concerns of the people of England at large. By reiterating abuses that had been highlighted in Cade's manifesto and identifying himself with the miseries suffered by the King's subjects, York was making an overt and successful bid for popular support and public sympathy. Now, the gauntlet thrown down, he retired to Fotheringhay to await Henry's response.

York's demands for personal recognition and reform, coupled with the humiliation of the loss of Normandy, aroused Henry at length to the realisation that his cousin had to be appeased if he was to remain loyal; accordingly, he admitted York at last to a newly constituted 'sad and substantial Council'. But there was a catch: Henry explained to the Duke that he could not act on the advice of one man alone – notwithstanding that he had done so with Suffolk and was now doing the same with Somerset – and that therefore the Council would discuss York's proposals for reform and implement them as they saw fit. In other words, York would have a political voice at last, but no one would necessarily heed it.

There was an added complication in that York and Somerset, those deadly rivals, were now both on English soil, which created a potentially explosive situation. York would find that, from now on, he had a great deal of support from the Commons in Parliament and the people, but very little from his fellow councillors or from the Lords in Parliament, all of whom resented his haughty arrogance.

On 6 November Henry VI opened Parliament at Westminster. York had used his influence to get men of his own affinity elected, and as a result they were the dominant party. The attending magnates brought with them a massive armed presence; London was packed and lodgings were not to be had anywhere, while an armed confrontation between the affinities of York and Somerset was expected daily. York was supported by his powerful brother-in-law, Norfolk, who arrived with a great following and 'six clarions before him blowing'. For the first time it was recorded that there was 'a great division between York and Lancaster', which led to riots in the streets. When York arrived from Fotheringhay late in November, he too brought 3000 armed retainers.

Parliament tried to stay neutral and would not discuss the merits of the King's councillors: it was readier to talk about the provision of a fixed income for the royal household. But the Commons, who supported York, demonstrated that support by electing his adherent, Sir William Oldhall, as Speaker. Oldhall was a wealthy Norfolk landowner who had known the Duke for many years, serving him first as a councillor in Normandy and latterly as his chamberlain; he was an influential man, with powerful friends and relations.

Under Oldhall's auspices, the Commons demanded, and got, an Act of Resumption providing for the return of all Crown lands alienated during the past twenty years and the establishment of a committee whose function was to oversee any royal grants proposed in the future. They also secured a promise from the King that efforts would be made to restore law and order in the shires.

While Parliament was sitting, York's falcon and fetterlock badge mysteriously appeared all over the city of London each night, only to be torn down every morning and replaced by the royal arms, which were in turn removed the following night. The Lord Mayor, anxious to maintain order, put on his armour each day and rode through the city with a band of soldiers 'harnessed defensibly for war'. He also ordered the crying of a proclamation forbidding the people to speak of or meddle 'with any matters done in the Parliament'.

When York came to Parliament he publicly criticised the government's policy of ignoring the demands of the people and taxing them heavily while rewarding royal favourites and allowing them – already rich men – to keep their wealth. But if York had entertained hopes of removing his enemies by constitutional means he was destined to be frustrated.

Many were angry that York's complaints had been ignored. On 30 November, says Benet, a crowd of Londoners and

> the armed men who had come with the nobles learned that neither the King nor the nobles had spoken of punishing the traitors whose actions were a scandal throughout England, in particular the Duke of Somerset, whose negligence was responsible for the loss of Normandy. So they cried out thrice in Westminster Hall to all the lords, saying, 'Give us justice! Punish the traitors!'

After the death of Suffolk, the Queen had turned to 'our dearest cousin, Edmund, Duke of Somerset' to take his place in her counsels and as leader of the court party. Her friendship extended not only to the Duke but also to his wife, Eleanor Beauchamp, one of her closest confidantes. Within two years the Queen would award Somerset an annuity of £66.13s.4d. (£66.67p) for 'his good and laudable counsel in urgent business'. Favouring Somerset could only alienate York, but the Queen already regarded him as her enemy, and when York returned from Ireland she made it very clear that it was Somerset, and Somerset alone, who, with her favour and the King's, would enjoy prominence in the government.

York's influence, however, prevailed for the time being over the Queen's, and on 1 December he had his way when Somerset was impeached by Parliament: the Duke was condemned to imprisonment in the Tower of London and taken there the same day. Having netted – or so he thought – the biggest fish, York made plans to snare other members of the court party, but the King and Queen refused to accept the judgement of Parliament and Margaret ordered Somerset's release only hours after his imprisonment had begun.

York's supporters were incensed. That afternoon, after Somerset had returned to Blackfriars, about a thousand of them marched on his house with a mob of angry citizens, meaning, says Benet, to kill him. They dragged him to a waiting barge, 'but the Earl of Devon, on the Duke of York's request, calmed them and prudently arrested their leader, who was taken in secret to the Tower, so as not to provoke the common people'. When Somerset returned home he found that his house had been stripped of all his possessions, and the looters had also ransacked the homes of men who were friendly to him.

On 3 December, the King, angered by this treatment of his favourite, put on armour and rode through the streets of the city at the head of a procession of lords, knights and 1000 soldiers. This had the effect of quelling the rioters but not the ill-feeling of his subjects at large. Somerset nevertheless remained high in royal favour and was soon afterwards appointed chamberlain of the royal household.

Parliament reassembled in January 1451, after the Christmas recess. An angry Commons now submitted to the King a petition demanding the removal from court of twenty-nine persons who had been 'misbehaving about your royal person and in other places, and by whose undue means your possessions have been greatly amenused [abused], your laws not executed, and the peace of your realm not observed'. The list was headed by Somerset's name and included also those of Suffolk's widow, Alice Chaucer, William Booth, Bishop of Chester, Thomas Daniel, John Trevelyan, Thomas Tuddenham and Henry Heydon. Many of those named had also been denounced in Cade's manifesto, and not only were they to be exiled from court, but they were also to be deprived of their lands and tenements.

Henry VI declared testily that he 'was not sufficiently learned of any cause why he should banish his favoured advisers in such a way', but was persuaded to agree to the removal of everyone but the magnates listed and a few personal servants. The rest he promised to banish from court for a year. Thanks to York's influence the notorious Tuddenham and Heydon, and several more of Suffolk's former supporters, were brought before judicial commissions in East Anglia and charged with extortion and other crimes. York also tried to have the murderers of Sir Thomas Tresham indicted, but this time without success, and far from banishing William Booth, the Council promoted him to the archdiocese of York. Henry did not keep his promise to banish his evil advisers either.

The Lords in Parliament, a majority of whom were members of the court faction, knew very well that if York gained full control of the government, many of them would be replaced by opponents such as the Mowbrays of Norfolk, the de Veres of Oxford and the Howards, all magnates of York's affinity. This would mean a huge shift in the balance of power, both at national and local level, and too many vested interests were at stake for the Lords to risk that happening.

Without the backing of a majority of the aristocracy, York found his hard-won influence gradually slipping from his grasp, while control of the King and the administration reverted by degrees to the court party. Seeing York's power diminishing daily, Henry VI defiantly refused to dismiss Somerset, who had quickly regained his former eminence at court, and early in 1451 Henry appointed him Captain of Calais, an important and influential post. Notwithstanding the fact that he had just presided over the ignominious loss of Normandy, Somerset was now to be in command of the largest garrison maintained by the English Crown. By May 1451, the court party, headed by the Duke and the Lord Chancellor, Cardinal Kempe, had regained its position once more, despite the worsening situation in France, where the French were making serious inroads in Gascony and Aquitaine

The mood of the times was apparent when one of York's supporters, Thomas Young, a member of the Duke's council and a member of Parliament for Bristol, persuaded the Commons to submit a petition to the King requesting that 'because the King had no offspring, it would be for the security of the kingdom that it should be openly known who should be heir apparent and [Young] named the Duke of York.' Young had naively hoped to deflect any ideas the King may have had of making Somerset his heir, but his proposal provoked a horrified uproar amongst the Lords and incurred the rare displeasure of the King, with the result that the unfortunate Young soon found himself a prisoner in the Tower. This was an infringement of his right as a member of Parliament to speak freely without fear or favour, and it in turn angered the Commons, who petitioned for his release. The King passed the petition to the Council, which ignored it, and Henry abruptly dissolved Parliament the same month.

The case of Young illustrates how factional contentions were interfering with the processes of Parliament, and also points to a crystallisation of political opinion in favour either of Lancaster or York. As for York himself, after Parliament was dissolved he found himself in an isolated position, distrusted more than ever by the King and most of the magnates.

On 30 June 1451 the French occupied Bordeaux, the capital of Aquitaine. The inhabitants of the city did not look upon their 'liberators' as friends, for they regarded themselves as English, the city having been a jewel in the Plantagenet crown for three hundred years. The fall of Bayonne, another Aquitainian city, followed a few weeks later and on 23 August the duchy of Aquitaine itself surrendered to Charles VII. News of this engendered great shock and dismay in England, especially among the merchant community, who were concerned about the future of the lucrative wine trade.

England was in a state of high tension, characterised by intermittent outbreaks of rioting, mainly in the West Country. By the autumn of 1451 it was obvious that Henry VI had no intention of implementing any plans for government reform; he had closed his ears to complaints and was content, in his blinkered way, to let things remain as they were. France might be all but lost, his government in England corrupt and rotten to the core, local government and justice subverted, and disorder and anarchy prevalent throughout the realm, yet Henry seemed genuinely unaware of the seriousness of the situation, and his advisers and councillors were too busy looking to their own interests to care. Nor had the pressing question of the succession been answered.

The King was still deeply in debt. How much so had been made dramatically clear the previous Christmas when, on the feast of the Epiphany, the King and Queen had arrived at the high table for the customary feast to find themselves confronted by a distraught steward of the household, who broke to them the news that there was no food, as the tradesmen who supplied the palace had refused to deliver any more on credit.

York was now faced with the bitter knowledge that the only way to make Henry do anything was by using force; reluctantly, he realised there was no alternative. The spectre of civil war was looming ever closer as that autumn York began to prepare for a confrontation with the King, or rather, with the court party.

Rumours of an imminent armed conflict between the opposing factions were already rife, and the Duke meant to capitalise on the nation's fears. In the autumn he instigated the first of the many propaganda campaigns launched by the House of York, beginning in September by writing to influential people in Norfolk, a county much disrupted by disorder and injustice, with a view to rousing support for reform of the government by peaceful or other means. In November, he sent Sir William Oldhall to encourage the people of East Anglia to rise in protest against the abuses in government. Then he gave out warnings of a possible rebellion.

The Queen hated and feared York, and by the beginning of 1452 she and Somerset had managed to convince the King that the Duke was plotting a coup that would lead to him seizing the crown. In fact, York's agents were now putting it about that 'the King was fitter for a cloister than a throne, and had in a manner deposed himself by leaving the affairs of his kingdom in the hands of a woman who merely used his name to conceal her usurpation, since, according to the laws of England, a queen consort hath no power but title only'. Such propaganda served only to inflame Margaret's temper. That there was truth in it is revealed by a study of the Queen's Wardrobe Book for 1452–3, in which the extent of her influence over the government is to be seen by the number of grants made 'by the advice of the council of the Queen'.

Knowing that York was planning some sort of confrontation, Margaret decided to take action. When the Scottish Earl of Douglas visited the court that winter, she eagerly sought to win his friendship, knowing he could command military support from one third of Scotland. Douglas was sensitive to the Queen's concerns and promised he would bring an army to Henry's aid if the King was unable to prevail against York.

By enlisting the aid of Douglas, Margaret demonstrated that she was completely out of touch with the prejudices of the English. A single-minded woman, she was unable to perceive that, although to her the Scots represented a much-needed ally, to her husband's subjects they were traditional enemies, whose military presence on English soil had for centuries been feared and resisted. It was perhaps fortunate for her that Douglas was murdered not long after his return to Scotland, which meant that she could no longer rely on substantial Scottish support.

York's propaganda was beginning to take effect. The King sent to inform the Duke, then at Ludlow, that he was most displeased with his defamation of the characters of his most trusted advisers. On receipt of this letter, York met with John Talbot, Earl of Shrewsbury, and Reginald Boulers, Bishop of Hereford, and solemnly declared to them that he was a true liegeman of the King, asking them to convey to Henry VI his willingness to swear his loyalty upon the Holy Sacrament in the presence of two or three lords if the King would be pleased to send them to Ludlow. Instead, on 1 February 1452, Henry dispatched the clerk to the Council from Westminster to summon York to a meeting of the Council at Coventry, a city with strong Lancastrian sympathies. York, sensing a trap, refused to obey the summons.

Queen Margaret, whose spies had informed her that York was mustering an armed presence, now set about urging Henry to do the same. He refused, and his wife, in desperation, resorted to emotional blackmail, asking what would become of her if he was killed. Reluctantly he agreed to issue commissions of array for the raising of a royal army.

On 3 February, York issued a manifesto addressed to the burgesses and commons of Shrewsbury, which read: 'I signify unto you, that with the help and supportation of Almighty God and of Our Lady and of all the company of Heaven, I, after long sufferance and delays, though it is not my will or intent to displease my sovereign lord, seeing that the Duke [of Somerset] ever prevaileth and ruleth about the King's person, and that by this means the land is likely to be destroyed, am fully concluded to proceed in all haste against him with the help of my kinsmen and friends.' He went on to blame Somerset for England's disastrous losses in France and for the King's failure to respond to the grievances which York had laid before him the previous year. Somerset, he complained, was continually labouring about the King for his, York's, undoing. Finally, he asked that the town of Shrewsbury send to him in this cause 'as many goodly and likely men as ye may'. Similar letters were sent by the Duke to other towns likely to offer support.

York, accompanied by Lord Cobham, had now left Ludlow and was leading his force towards London. His aim was to take the capital, and he sent heralds ahead requesting that the citizens allow his army peaceful passage. The Londoners' response was to man their defences. They knew only too well that supporting York would be construed by the government as treason, and, lacking powerful leadership, were reluctant to commit themselves to rebellion. On 12 February the clerk to the Council arrived back at Westminster and conveyed York's defiance of his summons to the

King, warning Henry of what the Duke was planning. At the same time the Council received news that the Earl of Devon was raising men in the West Country and preparing to join York. Two days later the King appointed the Duke of Buckingham and Lord Bonville as chief commissioners to deal with the rebels in the west.

The royal army had now assembled, and on the 16th the King, Queen and all the court marched with it out of London towards Coventry, hoping to intercept York. The next day the Council found out that York had incited seven towns to rebellion, including Canterbury, Maidstone and Sandwich, where bitter memories of Cade's rebellion were still fresh; and the King issued an indignant mandate to Lord Cobham, castigating him for his failure to obey the royal summons to arms and commanding him to attend upon his sovereign without further delay.

Between 19 and 23 February there were public demonstrations in support of York in East Anglia, but the royal army lay between the demonstrators and York, and none rode to join him. Nevertheless, the Duke managed to evade the royal army and press on towards London. The King learned of this while lodging in Northampton, and took counsel of his lords, who advised turning back towards Dunstable and London. By now, Henry had been joined by an impressive array of magnates – the dukes of Exeter, Buckingham and Norfolk (who could not bring himself to support York in a rebellion that might be construed as treason), the earls of Salisbury, Shrewsbury, Worcester and Wiltshire, and Lords Beaumont, de Lisle, Clifford, Egremont, Moleyns, Stourton, Camoys and Beauchamp – and they now urged him to write to York, forbidding him to take any step that might be interpreted as rebellion. Henry did so, sending his letter by the Bishop of Winchester, Viscount Bourchier and Lord Stourton. On the following day he sent to the Lord Mayor of London, forbidding him to allow York to enter the city.

Finding London barred to him, the Duke swung his army south and waited three days at Kingston, trying to ascertain the strength of the royal army and perhaps hoping for reinforcements. Then he crossed the Thames at Kingston Bridge and headed towards Dartford. The King's army gave chase, and on 27 February rode through London and set up camp at Southwark. Henry himself followed the next day, lodging that night at the Bishop of Winchester's palace by the Priory of St Mary Overie in Southwark.

On 29 February, York reached Dartford, and by 1 March his men had pitched their camp at nearby Crayford. Here, York deployed his men in battle order, splitting the army into three divisions, or 'battles' as they were then known. He himself commanded the centre or 'middleward' division, Devon the southern flank and Cobham the northern flank, nearest to the south shore of the Thames. In front of the army was drawn up a large number of cannon, which were intended to confront the royal army as it came along Watling Street. Whethamstead says that York had also fortified his ground with pits and other fortifications.

On 1 March, the King and his army moved to Blackheath, and thence crossed Shooter's Hill, and so came to Welling in Kent, where they camped for the night. The next day the royal army marched to within three miles of York's position.

York had a well-equipped army in a strong defensive position. Benet believed he had 20,000 men against the King's 24,000. The anonymous author of *An English Chronicle*, doubtless relying on unreliable rumours, says that York's army was 'not strong enough for the King's party', but in the Arundel MSS it says that both armies were equal in strength and that York had 'great stuff and ordnance'; in the nearby Thames he had seven ships laden with supplies, which could also facilitate flight if need be. But York lacked the aristocratic support that had so readily been made available to the King, and his expected reinforcements from Kent had not turned up.

Neither side was keen to fight. York was convinced that his show of force might be interpreted as an act of treason aimed at the King, and was relieved when, on the morning of 2 March, the Queen sent the bishops of Ely and Winchester and the earls of Salisbury and Warwick to negotiate a peaceful settlement. They commanded York, in the King's name, to return to his allegiance. York said he would willingly do so if Somerset was punished for his crimes against the state; he said 'he would have the Duke of Somerset or die therefor', and he also demanded to be acknowledged as the King's heir. The deputation agreed to lay his demands before the King.

Back in the royal camp, the two bishops asked Cardinal Kempe to keep the Queen occupied while they spoke with the King. In her absence they urged Henry to agree to York's demands. At length he gave his consent, and ordered that a warrant for Somerset's arrest be drawn up. No one was to tell the Queen what was afoot. The bishops then returned to York and told him that the King would agree to his demands on condition that he dismiss his army forthwith. Believing he had scored a victory, York ordered his force to disband, and his men began to pack up and make haste to their homes. That evening, the royal army withdrew to Blackheath.

On the following morning, Somerset was arrested, but the Queen saw him being marched away and demanded to know what was happening. When the Duke told her, Margaret exploded in fury and ordered the guards to let him go. She then went to Henry's tent with Somerset in tow. A few minutes later, around noon, York, accompanied by Devon and Cobham and forty mounted men, entered that same tent, intent on making his peace with Henry. He was surprised and dismayed to find Somerset and the Queen there, but controlled himself and knelt before the King, presenting him with a list of articles of accusation against Somerset. Suddenly, however, it dawned on him that he had interrupted a furious quarrel between the King and Queen, a quarrel which was immediately resumed in his presence and in which he found himself embroiled. Even Somerset joined the fray. York now realised, to his horror, that he was helpless in the hands of his enemies. The Queen was loudly demanding his arrest, but although the King refused to order it, he agreed that Somerset should remain at liberty.

York was then forced to travel with the court to London, riding ahead as if he were a prisoner, at the King's command, and obliged to swear a solemn public oath in St Paul's Cathedral 'that he had never rebelled against the King and would not rebel against him in the future'. Then he was allowed to retire to Ludlow – that he had not been imprisoned or executed was due to the fact that the court party dared not risk the consequences of proceeding against the hero of the common people, and also to the fact that the gullible Council had just received reports that York's heir, the Earl of March, had mustered an army of 11,000 men and was marching on the capital. Had they realised that March was not quite ten years old they might not have responded so readily to propaganda obviously put about by York's supporters.

The abortive campaign of 1452 may be considered the first military confrontation of what later became known as the Wars of the Roses. More soldiers were present than at the first actual battle, and certain precedents were established, the most important being that a show of armed force had been followed by a parley, both sides trying to avoid a confrontation. This pattern would be characteristic of the early battles of the Wars of the Roses.

York's failure resulted from his inability to co-ordinate the isolated pockets of political unrest that he himself had stirred into a cohesive movement, while the support of Talbot of Shrewsbury, the renowned hero of the French wars, undoubtedly contributed to Henry's success.

On 7 April the King issued a general pardon to all those who had risen against him, from which York was not excluded, and on 12 August following, in the same spirit of reconciliation, Henry visited

York at Ludlow Castle during the annual royal progress. But the court party had no intention of extending the hand of friendship to York; instead, they successfully excluded him from the Council. Humiliated and disgraced, the Duke was once again left in political isolation, and for the next year or so the court party, led by Somerset with the backing of Cardinal Kempe, who became Archbishop of Canterbury in 1453, was once again supreme.

From 1452 onwards the Queen endeavoured to court popularity with the people, believing that the best way to earn it was by reconquering Aquitaine and restoring peace to Henry's disturbed territories. In March 1452, the King received a letter from the citizens of French-occupied Bordeaux, begging for deliverance from the conquerors. But there was no money with which to finance an armed expedition, and though there were plenty of good soldiers ready to defend England's honour, there was nothing to pay them with. Margaret wrote, explaining the problem, to her kinsman Philip of Burgundy, who responded warmly and sent a large sum of money to finance the army and a fleet of ships. The King was therefore able to dispatch Talbot to France with a small but efficient force of 3000 men. On 17 October, Talbot marched on Bordeaux, whose citizens took heart and evicted the French garrison, and the city was restored to English hands. This unexpected good news, together with tidings that the friendship between Charles VII and Burgundy was deteriorating, served to lighten the mood of the people of England. After Bordeaux fell to Talbot, other towns in western Gascony speedily expelled the French and welcomed the Earl's army with rejoicing. It seemed that the tide of war was turning.

Campaigning ceased in the winter, and the King's thoughts turned to his half-brothers, Edmund and Jasper Tudor, who were now in their early twenties and very dear to him. In the spring of 1452 both had accompanied the Queen on a progress through the Midlands, visiting the Pastons at Norwich and Alice Chaucer at Wallingford. The brothers had then become members of the King's immediate entourage. On 23 November, Henry raised them to the peerage, Edmund being created Earl of Richmond in Yorkshire, and Jasper Earl of Pembroke. These were royal titles that had previously been borne by the King's late uncles of Bedford and Gloucester, and as such the Tudor brothers were given precedence over all other Englishmen below the rank of duke.

After spending Christmas at Greenwich, the King and Queen returned to London where, on 5 January 1453, at a magnificent ceremony in the Tower of London, Henry invested his half-brothers with the trappings of their earldoms, giving them rich gowns of velvet and cloth-of-gold, furs, saddles, and fine caparisons for their horses. On the 20th, the new earls were summoned to Parliament for the first time. From now on they would be given a voice in government and admitted to the King's counsels.

Henry was generous to his half-brothers and gave them several grants of land and money; each enjoyed an annual income of around £925. Edmund was endowed with the estates of the honour of Richmond to support his new rank, but Jasper had to wait for the lands belonging to the honour of Pembroke, because they were held by someone else. When in London, Edmund was allowed the use of Baynard's Castle – later to be the city residence of York – while Jasper owned a house in Brook Street, Stepney. Edmund prospered in his earldom of Richmond as a result of exporting his wool from Boston in Lincolnshire. The estates that Jasper later acquired were mainly in south Wales, and his wealth therefore lay in coal-mining and in trade centred on the port of Milford Haven.

In return for all this the Tudors would remain utterly loyal to Henry VI till their lives' ends, protecting his interests in the regions under their control and serving on his Council. They would also support him against York. Jasper was particularly popular in Wales because of his paternal connections, and those lands under his rule became firmly Lancastrian. As York also had great territorial interests in Wales, the principality would come to play an important part in the Wars of the Roses.

Early in 1453, the heroic Talbot swept through the region around Bordeaux, recapturing town after town. These successes, the first the English had enjoyed in thirty years, gave rise to cautious optimism back home. But when, in the spring, Talbot wrote asking the Queen to send reinforcements, Parliament hesitated and made excuses, leaving Talbot fuming and kicking his heels in frustration at what he saw as unnecessary prevarication.

Nevertheless, the success of Talbot in the Bordelais ensured that for the time being Parliament's loyalties lay firmly with the government and not with York. When it met at Reading on 6 March, it had been purged of all the Duke's supporters, and was primarily Lancastrian. The Tudor brothers were present, taking their seats as the premier earls of England, and the Commons petitioned the King to recognise them as his legitimate uterine brothers, born of the same mother, and requested him to ensure that they were not disabled in law in any way as a result of their father being Welsh. The King graciously acceded to these requests and granted the estates of the earldom of Pembroke to the hitherto titular Earl Jasper.

This Parliament was much more amenable than its predecessor. It did pass an Act of Resumption, but it only applied to grants made to York and those who had supported him. It then voted the King and his immediate dependants a reasonable income from customs dues and the best of the estates that were to be resumed by the Crown. Generous provision was also made for the Queen, who was granted new lands as part of her dower.

Then, in response to a petition presented by the Commons, an Act of Attainder was drawn up against Sir William Oldhall, York's chamberlain and Speaker in the last Parliament. His crime had ostensibly been to support Jack Cade in 1450, and he was also charged with having stolen goods from Somerset, but it was really his support of York in 1452 that had given offence, although York was not mentioned in the attainder.

Oldhall fled to sanctuary at the priory church of St Martin-le-Grand near Newgate in London, but he was mistaken in thinking himself safe there, for one night a group of nobles of the court faction breached the sanctuary and dragged him out 'with great violence'. The Dean of St Martin's was outraged at this violation of the sacred law of sanctuary and made a strong complaint to King Henry, who, notwithstanding the protests of his lords, ordered that Oldhall be allowed to return to the church. However, when the attainder against him became law, his goods were confiscated and distributed among his enemies, Somerset receiving his estate at Hunsdon.

Clearly Parliament believed that York would rise again in rebellion, for it authorised the King to raise 20,000 archers at the expense of the shires and boroughs for six months' service, if and when they were requested for the defence of the realm. Finally, on 24 March, her betrothal with John de la Pole having been dissolved, Margaret Beaufort was given into the custody of Edmund and Jasper Tudor as their ward. Henry had probably already decided that she should marry Edmund and so bring him her rich inheritance.

In February 1453 the Queen had been distressed by the death of her mother, Isabella of Lorraine, after a long and painful illness, and donned dark blue mourning. However, in April she was cheered by the realisation that she was at long last to bear her husband a child – hopefully a male heir. Curiously, the Queen did not break the news to Henry herself, but asked his chamberlain, Richard Tunstall, to convey 'the first comfortable relation and notice that our most dearly beloved wife the Queen was *enceinte*, to our most singular consolation and to all true liege people's great joy and comfort', as the King later recorded. He was so delighted with the news that he rewarded Tunstall with an annuity of forty marks. He then commissioned his jeweller, John Wynne of London, to make a jewel called a 'demi-cent', and commanded him to deliver it 'unto our most dear and most entirely beloved wife, the Queen'. It cost £200, a great sum at that time.

Henry had meanwhile been quietly restoring to their former positions all those officers of his household who had been dismissed at York's request. The activities of these men had been the basis of many complaints made by York, Cade and others, but Henry never learned from his mistakes and by July 1453 they all had regained their former influence.

It was an unsettled and gloomy early summer, despite the Queen's advancing pregnancy. There was tension in the north between the Percies and the Nevilles, who had long been feuding. Talbot was beset on every side by the French in Gascony; and there was unrest and disorder throughout the kingdom.

Parliament had still not voted Talbot the reinforcements he so badly needed, and in the spring of 1453 Charles VII had taken advantage of this and invaded Aquitaine, bringing with him three armies, all of which converged on Bordeaux from different directions. By the middle of June the French had advanced as far as the town of Castillon, whose inhabitants smuggled out a desperate plea for help to Talbot. The Earl's instinct counselled caution, as did his captains, but his knightly principles would not allow him to abandon those in distress, and in July he occupied Castillon. Shortly afterwards he received intelligence that the French were withdrawing, but this was not true. On 17 July, Talbot led his men out of the town and gave chase to the 'retreating' army, which suddenly turned and confronted him. The French used their new artillery to devastating effect, pushing the English back to the banks of the River Dordogne, where Talbot was cut to pieces with a battle-axe. When the English soldiers learned of his death they quickly surrendered.

Talbot's death deprived the English of their best commander, the only man who could have stemmed the tide of the French advance on Bordeaux. News of the disaster and of the loss of one of England's greatest warrior heroes prompted a frantic Queen Margaret hastily to summon Parliament. Parliament now acted – too late. At the King's request it voted enough money to finance the 20,000 archers, who were to be dispatched with all speed to Gascony in the hope of saving Bordeaux. But corrupt bureaucracy and local inefficiency stood in the way and not a single soldier enlisted. On 19 October

1453 Charles VII entered Bordeaux in triumph, and graciously permitted the English garrison to sail for home unmolested. Thus ended three hundred years of English rule in Aquitaine, and thus ended also the Hundred Years War, which had dragged on intermittently since 1340 – a war England could never have hoped to win.

Of England's former possessions in France only Calais remained, and even that was only saved from the French because they had agreed not to cross territory owned by the Duke of Burgundy, and his dominions surrounded Calais on the landward side. Even Calais' economic importance was fading with the decline of the wool trade. Strategically, however, it remained an important military base, and would continue to be so throughout the Wars of the Roses, when it was used as a springboard, not for the invasion of France, but of England itself.

There was no avoiding the fact that the King himself was to blame for the defeat. His subjects felt that, had he shown something of the martial spirit of his father, France might not have been entirely lost. Instead England stood humiliated and disgraced. No one was more incensed than York, who had striven so hard and invested so much money in order to maintain Henry V's conquests. And to add insult to injury, Parliament failed to vote any compensation to those loyal inhabitants of the former English territories who had lost everything, nor was there any pay awaiting returning soldiers stunned by defeat.

It was no coincidence that the end of the Hundred Years War should coincide with the outbreak of the Wars of the Roses. The one was one of the chief causes of the other.

12

'A Sudden and Thoughtless Fright'

During the first days of August 1453, it became clear that Henry VI was unwell. He had been under severe strain in recent months and this was beginning to take its toll. On 15 August the King was at his hunting lodge at Clarendon, near Salisbury in Wiltshire, when he complained of feeling unnaturally sleepy at dinner. The next morning, he appeared to have completely lost his senses: his head was lolling, and he was unable to move or communicate with anyone. He had, state the Paston Letters, taken a 'sudden and thoughtless fright' that utterly baffled his contemporaries. It is possible that the immediate contributory factor was the shocking news of the defeat of Castillon.

The Queen and Council were extremely alarmed by this turn of events, especially as Henry's condition showed no signs of improvement as days, and then weeks, went past. Margaret took him back to Westminster and made every effort to conceal his incapacity from his subjects for as long as possible. If York, in particular, were to hear of it, she feared he would almost certainly try to seize power.

Margaret now found herself, at seven months pregnant, completely responsible for the government of England. At first she hoped to remain with her husband at Westminster, but it soon became clear that his illness could only be concealed by removing him to Windsor.

What Henry VI suffered in 1453 was a complete mental breakdown, which is hardly surprising given his character and the stress engendered by the catastrophes and tensions of his reign. Whethamstead says that 'a disease and disorder of such a sort overcame the King that he lost his wits and memory for a time, and nearly all his body was so unco-ordinated and out of control that he could neither walk nor hold his head up, nor easily move from where he sat'. Henry later said that he had been totally unaware of what was going on around him, and that all his senses were in a state of prolonged suspension. He was 'as mute as a calf', spending his days in a chair, looked after by attendants. Some medical historians have diagnosed his condition, on the evidence available, as catatonic schizophrenia – complete mental withdrawal from normal life. Other modern experts have described the illness as a depressive stupor. Henry's contemporaries had only one word for it: madness.

The genetic components that predisposed to Henry VI's mental instability were almost certainly transmitted through his mother, Katherine of Valois. Her father, Charles VI of France, had been insane for most of his adult life, and there were parallels between Henry VI's life and Charles VI's. Both had become king in childhood, both had been dominated by powerful uncles, and both grew up to be weak and indecisive. Charles had suddenly become insane in 1392 when, during an attack of raging mania, he had run beserk with a lance and killed four people before being overcome by his attendants. His madness had taken a different form from Henry's, for he had been continually subject to violent fits and delusions, sometimes believing he was made of glass and would shatter if touched; at other times he announced that his name was George, and seemed unable to recognise his wife and children.

Charles's illness was spasmodic, and he did have periods of lucidity. But when he was in the grip of insanity he foamed at the mouth, refused to wash, and quickly became filthy, infested with vermin and covered in sores. Like a dog, he would eat his food from the floor, using his hands and teeth. Walsingham says he 'never recovered completely, for he suffered fits of madness which recurred every year at the same season'. His illness had led directly to civil war between the factions at his court, and clearly there were fears that this would happen in England in 1453 as a result of Henry VI's insanity.

An anxious Council wasted no time in summoning a whole host of doctors. Henry's chief physician, John Arundel, was a specialist in mental illness, being Warden of the Hospital of St Mary of Bethlehem (later known as 'Bedlam') in Bishopsgate, an asylum in which nearly half the inmates were 'out of their senses', and which, by this period, was specialising in treating the insane. Mediaeval doctors understood very little about mental illness, but they did distinguish five types: phrenitis (acute inflammation of the brain), delirium (abnormal behaviour accompanied by fever), mania (violent behaviour), melancholia (depression and loss of interest in life), and amentia (loss of mental faculties). Madness was believed to result from an excess of black bile, one of the four humours that mediaeval doctors believed governed the body, an imbalance of which led to illness. Diagnosis was based on observation of the external symptoms. However, having diagnosed what was wrong with the patient, doctors were often at a loss to know what to do for him. Mad people who were not violent were usually left at liberty within the community, often the butt of cruel taunts or ridicule; violent patients were locked up. Legally, the King had custody of all mad persons. Now he was apparently one himself.

The King's doctors tried everything within their limited power: bleeding, head purges, ointments, syrup cordials, suppositories, removing the King's haemorrhoids, gargles, laxatives, baths, special waters, electuaries – medicinal powders mixed with honey or syrup – and even cautery. None of these often painful processes had any effect. Henry was described by the physicians as being *non compos mentis*, a term applied when the onset of mental illness took place sometime after birth. But there was every hope, they assured the Queen and Council, of his temporary or permanent recovery. Perhaps, they suggested, the King was possessed by devils. Accordingly priests were called in to exorcise any evil spirits that might have taken possession of the royal mind, but to no avail. After all the treatments had failed, the Council authorised the King's doctors to bleed him as often as they thought necessary in order to let the evil humours out of his body, and apply various head poultices or any other remedy that occurred to them or seemed appropriate.

Henry VI's illness was to prove calamitous in several ways. It put an end to all hopes of unity between the opposing factions in government. It brought the Queen, with her poor understanding of English politics, prejudices and customs, to the forefront of power. It deprived the country of its head of state, however ineffectual. It removed, for a time, the last check on the rapaciousness of the court party and on feuding magnates in other parts of the country. Finally, it plunged England into a national crisis at a time when the political situation could not have been much worse.

In October, weighed down with anxiety over the King, Queen Margaret withdrew to her apartments in the Palace of Westminster to await the birth of her child. A screen was placed in the Queen's oratory, blocking the door to her bedchamber. It would not be removed until she had been churched and purified after the birth. Nor were any men allowed to go beyond the screen; for the duration of her confinement the posts of her household officers were filled temporarily by gentlewomen. Margaret's Wardrobe Book records that money was kept in her bedchamber so that she could make offerings during services conducted by her chaplain in the oratory beyond the screen.

At ten o'clock in the morning of 13 October 1453, the Queen produced the long-awaited Lancastrian heir, a healthy boy who was called Edward. The Queen had him named after Henry VI's favourite saint, Edward the Confessor, on whose feast day the child had been born, and after Edward III and the Black Prince, both of whom epitomised the heroic ideals of knighthood. The infant prince bore the title Duke of Cornwall from birth.

Immediately following the birth, letters conveying the glad tidings were sent out to all parts of the kingdom. One such was displayed on 14 October in the nave of Canterbury Cathedral, where – as in churches all over the land – the congregation stood as the *Te Deum* was sung. Church bells rang out proclaiming the joyful news, and there was general rejoicing. But at Windsor, the prince's father was still in a stupor, and did not even know he had a son.

The birth of a healthy boy to the Queen resolved the long-standing problem of the succession and also put paid to any hopes York had entertained of being named heir presumptive or even inheriting the crown. Overnight, his status had been diminished, as had that of his rival, Somerset, who had himself expected to be acknowledged as the King's heir.

The same month the prince was baptised by Bishop Wayneflete of Winchester in a splendid ceremony in Westminster Abbey. The Queen chose as sponsors the Duke of Somerset, the Archbishop of Canterbury, and Anne, Duchess of Buckingham. The baby, wrapped in an embroidered chrysom cloth, was borne in to the church in a procession led by monks carrying lighted tapers, to a font swathed in twenty yards of russet cloth-of-gold. The Queen had paid £554.16s.8d. (£554.83p) for both cloth and christening robe. After the ceremony the prince was admitted to the Order of the Garter. The King, of course, had been unable to attend the christening; nor did the Queen, by custom, attend, for she was not supposed to appear in public until she had been churched.

The choice of Somerset as sponsor infuriated York, and it was not long before some of his supporters vindictively spread a rumour that Edmund Beaufort was the prince's real father. There is no evidence that York himself was the originator of such a slander, nor that it was true, but he nevertheless did nothing to contradict it.

By now, it was clear that the King was not going to make a quick recovery, and the Queen and her advisers realised that they could not conceal his illness indefinitely. Margaret considered the possibility of

Henry abdicating in favour of his son; she may have anticipated that, even if he did recover, he would not be able to cope with the stresses of kingship. But there were other considerations: with the infant prince elevated to the throne, Margaret could look forward to fifteen years in power as regent. The lords of the Council, however, when the Queen sounded them out on this idea, were unenthusiastic; most of them expected Henry to recover.

There yet remained the urgent problem of how England was to be governed during the King's incapacity. It was now clear that arrangements must be made soon for some kind of regency. The birth of a son and heir to the monarch necessitated the summoning of a great council of magnates, in order that the prince could be formally acknowledged as heir apparent to the throne. On 24 October, Somerset, in the Queen's name, summoned such a council. The fact that York's name was omitted from the list of those chosen to attend drew angry protests, especially from Norfolk, and Somerset was obliged to invite him after all, to 'set rest and union between the lords of the land'. But when York finally arrived, he wasted no time in gathering support against Somerset and the court party. He had now, at last, acquired powerful allies among the magnates.

In the north of England, the feud between the Percies and the Nevilles was a long-standing problem that had recently escalated. In July 1453, the Council was so alarmed by reports that the two families had mustered 5000 armed men between them that it issued directives to all concerned, commanding them to keep the King's peace. But by August the tension in the north had erupted into violence. On the 24th, members of the Neville family had been travelling to a family wedding at Sheriff Hutton Castle, near York, but had been ambushed on the way by Lord Egremont, the brother of Henry Percy, Earl of Northumberland, and a band of retainers and thugs from the city of York. The Nevilles gave a good account of themselves and repelled the attackers without any fatalities occurring on either side, but the skirmish, described by contemporaries as the Battle of Heworth Moor, was regarded in retrospect as 'the beginning of sorrows' and the first military action of the Wars of the Roses. This was because it drove the Nevilles to seek the powerful protection of York.

It was natural for them to do so. Since early 1453, Richard Neville, Earl of Warwick, had been involved in a bitter dispute with Somerset over the ownership of substantial lands in Wales that had formerly belonged to the Beauchamp family, in particular the lordship of

Glamorgan. Warwick had held this lordship since 1450 and had administered it well, but early in 1453 the King, with his usual bungling ineptitude, had granted it to Somerset. An enraged Warwick prepared to hold on to the lordship, even if it meant an armed struggle against the King. It was not long before he began to realise what York had had to contend with and to sympathise with him. The Nevilles had hitherto been Lancastrian supporters, due to family ties, but York was Warwick's uncle by marriage, as well as being the most important magnate in England, and although Warwick had until now remained neutral in the conflict between York and the court party, the King's treatment of him over the matter of Glamorgan had had the effect of permanently alienating him from the House of Lancaster and driving him to take sides. And whither Warwick led, many other members of the powerful Neville clan would follow.

From 1453, therefore, York was to enjoy the influential support of Warwick, one of the richest and most powerful noblemen in England, and his father, Richard Neville, Earl of Salisbury, whose sister Cecily was York's duchess. This formidable alliance, which would influence the history of England for the next two decades, posed the greatest threat so far to the House of Lancaster and made York a force to be reckoned with. Commines, the French historian, looking back on that fateful friendship, believed it would have been better for the Queen if she 'had acted more prudently in endeavouring to have adjusted the dispute' between the Nevilles and Somerset 'than to have said, "I am of Somerset's party. I will maintain it."' The alliance with York also created divisions within the Neville family itself, and some junior branches of it remained firmly Lancastrian. Matters were further complicated by the fact that prominent Lancastrians such as the Duke of Buckingham, the Earl of Northumberland and Lord Dacre were related to the Yorkist Nevilles by marriage, though split family loyalties were to become a common feature of English aristocratic life during the Wars of the Roses.

The Nevilles were descended from Geoffrey FitzRobert, who inherited Brancepeth and Sheriff Hutton from his mother, the heiress of Geoffrey de Neville, in the thirteenth century, and adopted his mother's surname. Geoffrey's grandson married another rich heiress and added large tracts of land in Yorkshire, as well as the great lordship of Middleham in Wensleydale to the family estates. Military success on the Scottish border in the fourteenth century had brought the Nevilles to prominence, and the disgrace of the Percies after the

Battle of Shrewsbury in 1403 had served them well, allowing them to establish their supremacy in the north where their territorial influence stretched from Yorkshire to the Scottish border.

The Nevilles had gained political prominence with the marriages of Ralph Neville, who was created Earl of Westmorland by Richard II, much to the chagrin of the Percies. Ralph married first Katherine Stafford, and then Joan Beaufort, daughter of John of Gaunt and Katherine Swynford. Between them, his wives had presented him with twenty-four children. Several sons married heiresses; Joan's eldest boy, Richard Neville, born around 1400, married in 1421 Alice, the heiress of the Montacute earls of Salisbury, became Earl of Salisbury in right of his wife, fathered ten children, and had a distinguished military career in France. His younger brothers, William, George and Edward, acquired the powerful baronies of Fauconberg, Latimer and Bergavenny, all by marriage. Some of Westmorland's daughters became the wives of great magnates, such as the dukes of York and Norfolk and the earls of Stafford and, indeed, Northumberland. Through these, and other connections, the influence of the Nevilles was extended and consolidated, and they were now one of the most powerful families in England. Shrewd and pragmatic, they did not shrink from dabbling in commercial enterprises, and grew ever more prosperous.

Ralph Neville, realising that his children by Joan Beaufort were of far greater dynastic importance than those born to his first wife, left only the earldom of Westmorland to his eldest son, arranging for the bulk of his lands to pass to Joan's son, Salisbury. These included the lordships and castles of Middleham and Sheriff Hutton in Yorkshire, both enlarged and modernised by Earl Ralph, Raby Castle in County Durham, and estates in Westmorland and Essex.

The most brilliant marriage of all was that made by Salisbury's son, another Richard Neville, who was born on 22 November 1428. In 1439, Richard de Beauchamp, Earl of Warwick, died, and was succeeded in the title by his son Henry. Henry died young in 1446, and his infant daughter and heiress, Anne, Countess of Warwick, followed him to the grave in 1449. Her heir was her aunt, another Anne de Beauchamp, Earl Richard's only daughter, who had been born in 1429, and was now the wife of Richard Neville. On the young countess's death in July 1449, the great Beauchamp inheritance and the earldom of Warwick passed to Richard Neville, who became, literally overnight, one of the greatest landed magnates in the country.

Warwick was the archetypal English magnate, whose chief motivation was the enrichment and promotion of himself and his family. He was power-hungry, acquisitive and arrogant, like most of his caste. Nevertheless, he had great abilities, being a man of considerable courage and a fearless fighter and renowned naval commander. He had been born to govern, hence he could also be ruthless and unscrupulous, thinking nothing of resorting to violence, and even murder, when he considered it expedient. He was a clever propagandist, forceful, persuasive and manipulative, full of energy and tenacity. He was not greatly interested in aesthetic things such as art, literature or architecture, nor was he more than conventionally pious. He used his wealth to buy the support and friendship of influential men and so built up his own power and military strength.

Warwick's personality was more charismatic by far than York's. While people might sympathise with York's grievances, their imagination was stirred by Warwick, who came to enjoy far more influence with all ranks of society because he had the common touch, coupled with lavish, open-handed hospitality and a ready wit.

No portrait or effigy survives to show us what Warwick looked like, nor do the contemporary sources contain any descriptions of his appearance. He appears in the Rous Roll in full armour, but bears a marked resemblance to all the other armoured males in the work: Rous made no attempt at portraiture, even though he knew and admired Warwick.

By 1453, 'there was none in England of the half possessions that he had'. Warwick owned land in eighteen counties and more than a score of magnificent castles, his main seat being at Warwick Castle, a massive fortress that had been rebuilt by the Beauchamps with a splendid new tower. The Earl also held hundreds of manors, and his territorial influence stretched from Cornwall to the mighty lordship of Castle Barnard in Yorkshire, while the greatest concentration of his lands lay in the west Midlands and south Wales. From these properties Warwick drew a huge income, and could also call upon formidable reserves of fighting men if need be. Indeed, his possessions were so extensive that he was regarded as of greater political importance than his own father, Salisbury, and was thought to be richer even than York. The splendour and extravagance of his household was already renowned, while his huge army of retainers and men of his affinity displayed on their livery of bright scarlet surcoats his personal badge of a white, muzzled bear and a ragged staff, a device inherited from the earls of Warwick.

This was the man who now became York's principal ally.

The great council assembled, and York, whose supporters had expressed doubts about the Prince's paternity, now argued that the

Queen's child could not be recognised as the heir to England unless he was first acknowledged by the King and then presented by him to the nobility as his heir, according to ancient custom. A delegation of twelve lords, spiritual and temporal, therefore took the prince to visit his father at Windsor in the hope that the sight of the child would arouse Henry from his stupor. But although they made several attempts to make him acknowledge and bless the baby, he remained impervious to what was going on around him, appearing 'uncurious and unconscious'.

The council was faced with a problem. Until the King had acknowledged his son, Parliament could not pass legislation confirming the child's right to the royal succession or make provision for him as heir. This situation only served to fuel the rumours that flourished during the winter of 1453–4, that the prince was a bastard, that he was not the King's son, and possibly not even the Queen's. It was alleged that he was either a changeling, smuggled into the Queen's bed after her own child had died, or the result of an affair between Margaret and Somerset. This was all too believable, given Henry VI's vaunted views on marital sex and the fact that the Queen had not conceived once during the first seven years of her marriage. The rumours were also given credibility by the fact that the people were not aware of the King's condition, and placed their own interpretation on why he had not recognised the child as his heir.

Warwick even went so far as publicly to refer to the prince as the offspring of adultery or fraud in front of a packed assembly of the magnates at Paul's Cross in London. The King, he said, had not acknowledged him as his son and never would. Margaret never forgave Warwick for this insult which was to prove so damaging to her honour. York prudently kept silent, but of course he had everything to gain from the rumours and the defamation of the Queen.

On 18 November Margaret was churched at Westminster, wearing a robe trimmed with 540 sables, and attended by the duchesses of York, Bedford, Norfolk, Somerset, Exeter and Suffolk, eight countesses including the Countess of Warwick, and seven baronesses. Then she returned with great determination to the political scene.

The birth of a son had consolidated the Queen's power and her standing in the country. Despite the rumours, she had no doubt that the King would eventually acknowledge the child, and as the mother of the heir apparent she meant to dominate the government and rule with the help of the court party. Motherhood had transformed her into a doting parent, fiercely protective of her son's rights, which she was determined to safeguard by any means in her power, and it was now that she emerged as the most bitter enemy of York and as the driving force behind Somerset. Her greatest ambition was to crush the House of York, which she regarded as the chief threat to her husband's throne and her son's succession. From this time on, therefore, the conflict between Lancaster and York was not so much a power struggle between Henry VI and York, but a contest for political supremacy between York and Margaret of Anjou, who was to prove the backbone of the Lancastrian cause.

York in turn was poised for a return to the centre stage of politics, and was courting support for a bid to become regent during the King's illness. The King's half-brothers, Richmond and Pembroke, concerned about the extent of the court party's influence over the King, supported his candidature, while the court party took every opportunity of advancing the claim of the Queen to be regent, though here Margaret's sex was against her since most of the magnates found the prospect of petticoat government repugnant and improper.

Because York had, by January 1454, won the support of several influential magnates, the court party made a final attempt to rouse the King. On 19 January the prince was again taken to Windsor, and when he arrived, according to the Paston Letters, 'the Duke of Buckingham took him in his arms and presented him to the King in goodly wise, beseeching the King to bless him; and the King gave no manner answer. Nevertheless, the Duke abode still with the prince by the King, and when he could no manner answer have, the Queen came in and took the prince in her arms and presented him in like form as the Duke had done, desiring that he should bless it, but all their labour was in vain, for they departed thence without any answer or countenance, saying only that once he looked on the prince and cast down his eyen again, without any more.'

Later that month, the Queen, 'being a manly woman, using to rule and not be ruled', made a determined bid for the regency. The Paston Letters record that she 'hath made a bill of five articles, desiring those articles to be granted: the first is that she desireth to have the whole rule of this land; the second is that she may make [i.e. appoint] the Chancellor, the Treasurer, the Privy Seal and all other officers of this land; the third is that she may give all the bishoprics of this land and all other benefices belonging to the King's gift; the fourth is that she may have sufficient livelode assigned her for the King, the prince and herself. But as for the fifth article,' the writer did not know what it contained.

Margaret was well aware of the fact that many magnates were hesitating, reluctant to associate themselves with York in case it appeared that they were in treasonable opposition to the King, and she tried to capitalise on this, cultivating the support of York's enemies. However, her arrogant and peremptory bid to assume virtually sovereign power and exercise the royal prerogative offended and alienated many of them; nor did the common people wish to be ruled by their haughty, unpopular French queen, and they made this very clear. It was at this stage that many lords, who might not otherwise have done so, first began to support York's bid for the regency.

In the capital the political atmosphere was tense, as if a major conflict was about to erupt: the Archbishop of Canterbury took the precaution of issuing weapons to all the male members of his household at Lambeth Palace, and told them to hold themselves in readiness to safeguard his person. Somerset's ally, the Earl of Wiltshire, was preparing to attend Parliament at the head of a large army of retainers, as were several other lords including Somerset himself: his billeting officer had secured for his armed supporters every lodging in Thames Street and the vicinity of the Tower. Warwick sent 1000 armed retainers ahead into London to ensure his safety; then, at the head of another private army, he escorted York into the city. The Duke was accompanied by his household and a large retinue, and also by his son, March, and the earls of Richmond and Pembroke, each with a military following.

Somerset's spies had not been idle, for they were 'going into every lord's house of this land', some disguised as friars, others as sailors on leave, their brief being to discover how much support the Duke and his rival York would be able to command in the coming Parliament. Rumours of the activities of Somerset's spies gave rise to some alarm among those who secretly supported York but were waiting to see how matters turned out before committing themselves.

When Parliament did actually assemble, so few lords turned up that fines were imposed on the absentees for non-attendance – the only occasion on which this penalty was used in the Middle Ages. Undoubtedly some had been intimidated, while others had preferred to remain neutral. Parliament met on 14 February, and though some of York's supporters attempted to raise the sensitive question of the prince's paternity, the Lords refused to listen to them, and confirmed the infant's title and status as heir apparent. York, like the other magnates, was required to acknowledge him as heir to the throne, but it was noticed that he did so with ill-concealed chagrin. Indeed,

Thomas Daniel and John Trevelyan and other members of the court party were so concerned about York's true intentions that they submitted to the Lords a bill providing for the safeguarding of the King and the prince. On 15 March 1454 Edward of Lancaster was formally created Prince of Wales and Earl of Chester, and made a Knight of the Garter; on 13 April, an annual income of £2000 was settled on him, and in June he was invested as Prince of Wales at Windsor.

It was March before the regency question was settled. In that month, Cardinal Kempe, one of the chief mainstays of the court party, died. His death made the election of a regent even more pressing, since his successor to the See of Canterbury could only be chosen by the authority of the King.

York now had the backing of a substantial number of peers who were anxious to prevent the Queen or Somerset (which amounted to the same thing) from seizing power. He had also neutralised one of the Queen's chief supporters, the parliamentary Speaker, Thomas Thorpe, against whom the Duke had brought a charge of trespass. Thorpe had been sent to the Tower and fined £1000.

Before reaching a decision, the lords of the Council made one further visit to the King to see if he showed any signs of recovery, but there were none. Says Benet: 'The King's Council perceived that, if the King did not recover, England would soon be ruined under the government of the Duke of Somerset, so the noblemen of the kingdom sent for the Duke of York.'

On 27 March the Lords in Parliament nominated York as regent under the title Protector of the Realm. He was to be chief of the King's Council, but would not have the title of 'tutor, lieutenant, governor or regent, nor no name that shall impart authority of government of the land, but the name of Protector and Defender, which importeth a personal duty of intendance to the actual defence of this land, as well against the enemies outward as against rebels inward, during the King's pleasure, and so that it be not prejudice to my lord Prince'. York was to enjoy the same title and powers that Gloucester had enjoyed during Henry VI's minority, with the same limits on his authority.

Parliament further provided that, if the King did not recover sufficiently to reassume control of the government, the office of Protector should devolve upon Prince Edward when he attained his majority. As this would not happen for at least fourteen years, the lords had demonstrated singular confidence in York by entrusting to him the governance of the realm for so long.

After his nomination had been approved, York asked the Lords for their help and support in the task that lay ahead, saying, 'I shall employ my person with you.' Parliament then drafted an Act formalising his appointment.

Almost the first thing he did after his nomination was to depose Somerset from all the offices he had held from the King and order his arrest. Somerset was in the Queen's apartments when the guard came to take him to the Tower, and this time Margaret was powerless to save him. Nevertheless, she defiantly visited him in prison and assured him of her continuing favour. Parliament would not agree to Somerset being brought to trial, which York had wanted, but the Protector was not a vindictive man, and now that Somerset had been removed from the political arena, he left him unmolested in the Tower.

On 3 April York was formally appointed Protector in a short ceremony during which he formally reaffirmed the oath of allegiance he had made to Henry VI at the latter's coronation, and signed the deed that named him Protector. This provided that, should he break his oath, he was to be dismissed from office. On the 10th, he appointed his ally Salisbury as Chancellor of England.

Shortly afterwards, York ordered the Queen to remove to Windsor to be with her husband, making it clear that her influence was to be confined solely to the domestic sphere; nor was the furious Margaret allowed to leave Windsor once she had got there. Her worst fears had been realised and, angry and frustrated at being deprived of the regency, she chose to believe that the magnates had chosen York as Protector because they were really aiming to make him king, and was convinced that it was only a matter of time before he made a bid for the crown. Her very helplessness added to her fears for her husband and son.

Although he was extremely busy at this time, York remembered to send Easter gifts of green gowns to his eldest sons, March, now twelve, and Rutland, aged eleven, who were then being schooled by their tutor, Richard Croft, at Ludlow. Edward wrote back to his father, congratulating him on his recent victory in Parliament, and thanking 'your noblesse and good fatherhood of our green gowns, now late sent unto us to our good comfort'. He asked if they might 'have some fine bonnets sent unto us by the next sure messenger, for necessity so requireth. And where ye command us by your said letters to attend specially to our learning in our young age, that should cause us to grow in honour and worship in our old age, and please it your Highness to wit that we have attended to our learning since we came hither, and shall hereafter.' Nevertheless, the boy ended with a complaint about 'the odious rule and demeaning' of

Master Croft. We do not know whether his father took any notice of it.

On 28 July, York appointed himself Captain of Calais in Somerset's place in an attempt to establish control of the English Channel in the face of attacks on English shipping by French pirates. He also sought to protect England's western shores and regions by asking Parliament to confirm his appointment as Lieutenant of Ireland. This time, however, his duties in Dublin were carried out by a deputy.

York proved to be a conscientious and able Protector. He made a vigorous effort to restore good government, and carried out the duties of his office efficiently and with integrity. His opponents had expected him to exact revenge upon them for all the years he had been slighted and excluded from government, but he behaved towards them with moderation, trying to work with them in the Council for the benefit of the realm. He was ably supported by Salisbury and Warwick, the three of them making a formidable and seemingly invincible triumvirate, representing between them the larger part of the landed wealth and territorial influence of the aristocracy. Warwick's younger brother, George Neville, aged only twenty, was already embarked upon a meteoric career in the Church. As secular appointments became vacant, York tried to consolidate his position by filling them with men of his affinity, and he also raised his kinsman Thomas Bourchier to be Archbishop of Canterbury.

One of York's main concerns was to restore order, especially in the north, where the Percies and Nevilles were still 'breaching the King's peace'. In May, he visited the area to curb the quarrelsome tendencies of the Percies. However, says Benet, they fled at his approach. He was also concerned about rumbling Lancastrian disaffection in the north and west, and in July he ordered that the pro-Lancastrian Duke of Exeter be held at Pontefract Castle as a hostage for the good behaviour of his affinity.

York made some headway in restoring the authority of the Council, signing warrants issued by it as 'R. York'. He attempted to sort out the Crown's finances, so that adequate provision could be made for the King's household without incurring further debts or draining the Exchequer. In November he had the Council draw up ordinances for the reduction and reform of the household, in the interests of economy and cost efficiency. Even Henry's Tudor half-brothers found their establishments reduced, each being allowed only a chaplain, two esquires, two yeomen and two chamberlains, an entourage equal to that of the King's confessor. Nevertheless

Richmond and Pembroke supported the reforms because they realised that they could only be in the King's interests. In fact, these household reforms were aimed primarily at the Queen, being an attempt to deprive her of the means with which to reward her favourites if she returned to power. Her household was reduced to 120 persons, and the Prince of Wales's to 38, which gave her further reason to hate York. Despite his efforts as Protector, York still failed to win over a majority of the peers. Some were suspicious of his motives and unwilling to trust him, and many still resented his manner.

On Christmas Day 1454, just as York was making some headway with the task of reforming the administration, 'by the grace of God the King recovered his health', emerging after sixteen and a half months from his stupor 'as a man who wakes after a long dream'. He had no memory of what had happened to him during his illness, and told his courtiers that 'he never knew till that time, nor wist what was said to him, nor wit not where he had to be whilst he had been sick, till now'. As soon as he could speak, he ordered that a mass of thanksgiving be celebrated in St George's Chapel, and requested that prayers be offered night and day for his complete recovery. On 27 December, he commanded his almoner to ride to Canterbury with an offering, and commanded his secretary to offer at the shrine of St Edward the Confessor in Westminster Abbey.

On the next day, in the afternoon, according to the Paston Letters,

> the Queen came to him and brought my lord Prince with her. And then he asked what the Prince's name was, and the Queen told him Edward, and then he held up his hands and thanked God therefor. And he asked who were the godfathers, and the Queen told him, and he was well pleased. And she told him that the Cardinal was dead, and he said that he never knew of it till then.

According to one account, Henry said that the Prince 'must be the son of the Holy Spirit', which led to some ribald conclusions on the part of York's followers. But there is no doubt that Henry accepted the Prince as his own child without hesitation. He had, after all, known of the Queen's pregnancy for some time before his illness and had not entertained any suspicions then as to the child's paternity, so there was no reason for him to do so now. He would prove a consistently kind and loving father.

'Blessed be God,' wrote Edmund Clere, an esquire of the King's household, to John Paston on 9 January 1455, 'the King is well-amended and hath been since Christmas.' The Bishop of Winchester and the Prior of St John's, Clerkenwell, had spoken to him two days earlier, 'and he spoke to them as well as he ever did, and when they came out they wept for joy. And he says that he is in charity with all the world, and he would that all the lords were so. And now he says Matins and Evensong, and hears his mass very devoutly.'

Nevertheless, the Croyland Chronicle makes it clear that Henry's mental health remained impaired for some years after his recovery, and there is other evidence that he never fully recovered from his first breakdown. He would, as the years passed, suffer short recurrences of it throughout his life. In 1461, Croyland wrote, 'The King, for many years, suffered an infirmity of mind; this mental weakness lasted for a long time.' His illness changed him. He became more unworldly and introspective, and turned to religion for consolation; it also left him at the mercy of his domineering wife and factious nobles. The royal authority would from now on be in the hands not just of a weak king, but a king debilitated by a long mental illness that might recur at any time.

Part II

The Wars
of the Roses

13

The Wars of the Roses

York's protectorate had not lasted long enough for his reforms of the Council and the royal household to be of any lasting value. On 9 February 1455 the King appeared unexpectedly in Parliament, to the delighted astonishment of all present, thanked the members for their loyalty and concern, and dismissed York from the office of Protector. He then dissolved Parliament, amid cheers from Lancastrian supporters. Benet says that York formally resigned his office to the King 'at Greenwich, after he had governed England most excellently and nobly for a whole year, miraculously pacifying all rebels and malefactors according to the laws and without great rigour, in a wonderful manner, and he resigned his office much honoured and much loved'.

As soon as York had stepped down, there was a Lancastrian backlash against his followers. Salisbury was dismissed, and his office of Chancellor given to Archbishop Bourchier, who was careful to remain neutral, although he later came to support the Yorkists. The Queen's favourite, Wiltshire, was made Treasurer, and the Duke of Exeter was set at liberty. Margaret, of course, wasted no time in demanding of the King that he release Somerset from the Tower, and on the 16th the Duke was set at liberty; the offices that York had taken from him, those of Constable of England and Captain of Calais, were immediately restored to him. 'Once more,' wrote Benet, 'the Duke of Somerset became head of the government under the King, although in the past he had almost ruined England with his misrule.' Back at court and restored to his former eminence, Somerset now plotted with the Queen to destroy York, while at the request of the Archbishop of Canterbury and the Duke of Buckingham, the King pardoned all those who had benefited from Somerset's imprisonment by receiving his confiscated offices.

On hearing the news of Somerset's release, York had retired in disgust to his northern stronghold, Sandal Castle, near Wakefield in Yorkshire, knowing that he was once again in the political wilderness and that Somerset would attempt to take revenge on him. Salisbury also rode north to his castle at Middleham; he too faced an uncertain future. But York and his allies had no intention of remaining out in the cold, and soon began discussing how best to deal with the problem of Somerset.

By March 1455, many Lancastrian lords had been reinstated in their former positions of honour, a policy seemingly calculated to provoke York. The Queen had recently cultivated the support of the Earl of Northumberland and Lord Clifford, both of whom were now committed Lancastrians. Neither had any reason to love York, for he was the ally of their greatest enemies, the Nevilles. Margaret was also whipping up aristocratic support for the House of Lancaster in Wales and the West Country. She was well aware that York enjoyed considerable influence in the Welsh Marches, and could foresee problems if her enemy was able to extend that influence along the whole of the Welsh border. Here were to be found the estates of Warwick, Sir William Herbert, Edward Neville, Lord Bergavenny, and the Duke of Buckingham. Buckingham was staunchly loyal to the King, but what of the others? Margaret therefore did her best to ensure the continuing loyalty of Jasper Tudor, and even set out to woo Herbert, who was of York's affinity. Herbert was not a man to be trusted, and for the next few years York and the Queen would compete with each other to win his loyalty. Later, after Pembroke established Lancastrian authority in western Wales, Margaret would redouble her efforts to enlist Herbert's support.

Soon after Easter, wrote Benet, another dispute arose between York and Somerset, 'for Somerset was plotting the destruction of York. He offered advice to the King, saying that the Duke of York wished to depose the King and rule England himself – which was manifestly false.' Then Warwick learned through his spies that Somerset was planning to hold a secret conference at Westminster, to which only those peers sympathetic to the court faction would be invited.

York and Salisbury were not prepared to wait and see what the Queen and Somerset would do. Urged on by Warwick, they were busy raising an army, for which they were recruiting men from the northern marches along the Scottish border. It would appear that these levies were summoned to muster at both Middleham and

Sandal. Early in May, Warwick began assembling a large force at Warwick Castle. As well as preparing for an armed confrontation, York, Salisbury and Warwick all wrote to the King protesting their loyalty. Their letters were intercepted by the court faction and never reached him.

Although the Queen and her supporters firmly believed that York had designs on the throne, there is no evidence at this time to show that he did. People might remember that the Lancastrian kings were usurpers, but they had nevertheless occupied the throne virtually unchallenged for half a century, recognised by Parliament and the people, and anointed and consecrated at their coronations. Even if York had wished to make a bid for the throne, very few nobles would have supported him. The risks involved were too great, and he was not sufficiently popular among them. Even if some of his supporters felt that the Duke had been ousted from the succession by a prince of questionable legitimacy, they did not voice their concerns at this time.

Early in May, the Queen and Somerset, instead of holding a conference at Westminster as planned, summoned a large number of Lancastrian magnates to a great council to be held at Leicester, a town at the centre of a region in which Lancastrian loyalties predominated. The main business on the agenda was to make provision for the King's safety 'against his enemies'. As York, Salisbury and Warwick were not invited to attend, there could be little doubt as to who these enemies were and what the true purpose of the council was to be. The Queen and Somerset had persuaded the King that York meant to seize his throne, and Henry issued a summons requiring him and his allies, Salisbury and Warwick, to present themselves before the council on 21 May. To York, this sounded ominously like a repeat performance of what had happened to the Duke of Gloucester in 1447, and he now made up his mind to pre-empt Somerset and strike first.

A colourful legend, enshrined in the plays of Shakespeare, relates that the Wars of the Roses broke out in the gardens of the Inns of Temple in London. York and Somerset were one day walking there and fell into an argument, in the course of which Somerset plucked a red rose from a nearby bush and said, 'Let all of my party wear this flower!' York, not to be outdone, picked a white rose to be the emblem of his party.

Sadly, there is no truth in the legend. York was in the north in May 1455, when the incident is said to have taken place, and there is no evidence that the red rose was used as a badge by the House of Lancaster at this date. Nevertheless, red and white roses have been grown in the Temple Gardens since the sixteenth century to commemorate the event.

The white rose was certainly one of the badges of the House of York, although York's personal badge was the falcon and fetterlock. Many modern historians claim that the Lancastrian red rose symbol was invented as propaganda by the first Tudor king, Henry VII. York Civic Records state that in 1486, while on progress in the north, he gave orders for a pageant to be held at York, incorporating 'a royal, rich, red rose, unto which rose shall appear another rich, white rose, unto whom all flowers shall give sovereignty, and there shall come from the cloud a crown covering the roses'. Thus evolved the Tudor badge of the Rose and Crown, representing the union of Lancaster and York, Henry VII having recently married Elizabeth of York. The Croyland Chronicle, written in April 1486, also refers to the red rose of Lancaster. There is evidence, though, that the red rose symbol dates from at least as early as the reign of Edward IV, for a Yorkist genealogy drawn up during this time, and now in the British Library, shows a bush bearing both red and white roses. It should be borne in mind that the rose badges were just two of a number of badges used by members of the houses of Lancaster and York.

What we now call the Wars of the Roses were sometimes referred to by contemporaries as the 'Cousins' Wars'. The phrase 'Wars of the Roses' was coined by Sir Walter Scott in his novel *Anne of Geierstein*, published in 1829, but the concept was by no means new and originated in fifteenth-century propaganda. A pamphlet of Sir Thomas Smith, written in 1561, referred to 'the striving of the two roses', while Sir John Oglander wrote in 1646 a tract called *The Quarrel of the Warring Roses*, and David Hume, in 1761, published *The Wars of the Two Roses*.

Modern historians date the outbreak of the Wars of the Roses to May 1455, when the first pitched battle took place, though, as we have seen, the conflict had been gathering momentum for some time before then.

Instead of obeying the royal summons, York mobilised his army and began the long march south to London, probably with the intention of intercepting the King before he left for Leicester. With him went his allies, Salisbury, Lord Clinton, Lord Grey of Powys, and Sir Robert Ogle, all with an armed following of their own, Ogle having '600 men of the Welsh Marches'. Viscount Bourchier and Lord Cobham may also have been among their number. In the middle of May, Warwick led his army of a thousand men across the heart of England, linking up with York and Salisbury on Ermine Street, the old Roman road. York's chief objectives were the annihilation of Somerset, the dispersal of the court party, and his own restoration to the Council, which would bring with it control of the King and the government.

By the 18th, Somerset and the council had been warned that the Yorkists were approaching London with 7000 well-armed men. Benet says: 'When the Duke of Somerset heard this news he suggested to the King that York had come to usurp the throne. For this reason, the King sided with the Duke of Somerset,' and authorised him to raise a small army.

On the 20th York's company arrived at Royston in Hertfordshire. Here its leaders issued a manifesto declaring to the people that they meant no harm to the King and that they had raised their army and marched south 'only to keep ourselves out of the danger whereunto our enemies have not ceased to study, labour and compass to bring us'. A copy was sent to the King with a covering letter in which York and his allies begged him not to believe the accusations made against them by their enemies, but again both documents were intercepted, this time by Somerset himself, who destroyed them.

York was hoping that Norfolk would rally to his support, but although the Duke led a force into Hertfordshire, he made no attempt to join either side, preferring to remain neutral for the present. York had tried on the way south to raise more aristocratic support for his cause, but with little success. His advance at the head of an army looked very much like rebellion, even treason, in view of his public oath that he would never again take up arms against his sovereign.

While he was still at Royston, York learned that Henry VI and Somerset were about to leave London at the head of an army. On 21 May the Yorkists marched into Ware, where they were told by their scouts that the royal army was advancing north along Watling Street. The Queen was not with them, having taken the Prince of Wales to Greenwich, where she remained during the ensuing hostilities. That same day, York sent a further appeal to the King, along with a copy of his manifesto. Neither got past Somerset.

Meanwhile, the King and his army had reached Watford, where they spent the night, leaving very early on the morning of the 22nd. York's scouts advised him that Henry was making for St Albans, and the Duke swung west from Ware to confront him. On the road to St Albans the King received intelligence that the Yorkist army was nearing the town. Buckingham urged Henry to press on to St Albans, meet York's threat head-on, and deal with it firmly, for he was convinced that York would prefer to negotiate a settlement rather than resort to military force. He was also aware that the Yorkist army was larger than the King's, and believed it would be safer to await reinforcements in the town than in an exposed position in the countryside.

By 1455 there was little remaining of the original fortifications that had encircled St Albans, just a thirteenth-century ditch, along which wooden barricades could be erected so as to prevent an enemy from entering the market-place. After arriving in St Albans early in the morning of the 22nd, the King commanded his soldiers to occupy the ditch and make it 'strongly barred and arrayed for defence', pitching his own camp in the market-place. York, meanwhile, had decided to camp in Key Field, to the east of St Peter's Street and Holywell Street (now Holywell Hill), and set his men to blocking the exits from the town on that side.

In 1460, the Milanese ambassador was informed 'that on that day there were 300,000 men under arms, and indeed the whole of England was stirred, so that some even speak of larger numbers'. This was a gross exaggeration. Benet says that Warwick arrived with 2000 men, York with 3000 and Salisbury with 2000, 'all well-prepared for battle'. It has been estimated that the royal army numbered 2-3000 men, and may have been short of archers. The Yorkists not only had a strong force of archers but also cannon. Henry had sent an urgent summons to local levies to reinforce his ranks, but they were not ready in time. Only eighteen out of the seventy peers were present at St Albans; thirteen, including Pembroke, were with the King. Others, including Oxford, Shrewsbury, Lord Cromwell and Sir Thomas Stanley, were still on their way.

The King's army was under the command of Buckingham, who was hereditary Constable of the realm and had been appointed the King's Lieutenant for the occasion. Thomas, 8th Lord Clifford, who commanded the Lancastrian vanguard, had earned a distinguished reputation as a veteran of the French wars and for his successes on the Scottish border. The Lancastrian army consisted mainly of knights, members of the King's household, and the affinities of those few lords who were with him, many of whom came from the eastern counties. Abbot Whethamstead of St Albans, who gives an eyewitness account of these events, states that the East Anglian lords and gentlemen were less warlike than the men of the north in the Yorkist army, 'for whom wheat and barley' – which they meant to have as plunder – 'are like gold and ebony'. The northerners were regarded as foreign savages in the south, and enjoyed a fearsome reputation as ferocious fighters and rapacious looters.

York's army was drawn up into three divisions, as was customary, commanded by himself and 'the captains of the field', Salisbury and Warwick, the latter having command of the reserve, who were on foot. With York was his thirteen-year-old son, March, who was receiving his first taste of battle, nominally at the head of a small company of seasoned border campaigners. Also with York was Sir John Wenlock, latterly chamberlain to the Queen, who had transferred his loyalty to the Yorkist cause, which he would support for some years to come.

The commencement of the battle was delayed for three hours, during which York made every effort to induce the King to listen to his complaints about the misgovernment of Somerset and other 'traitors'. York's messenger, Mowbray Herald, opened negotiations by entering the town 'at the barrier' at the north end of St Peter's Street, where he was challenged. The herald bore a message from York, suggesting that the King's army might wish to retreat to Barnet or Hatfield for the night while negotiations proceeded.

Because his army was the smaller, Henry knew it was to his advantage to negotiate a peaceful settlement, and he sent Buckingham, who was Salisbury's brother-in-law, to ascertain York's intentions. York told him that he and his company had come as 'rightful and true subjects', who desired only that the King deliver up to them 'such as we will accuse'. When Buckingham reported these words to Henry, the monarch became uncharacteristically wrathful. Goaded by Somerset, he sent Buckingham back to York with a peremptory message:

> I, King Harry, charge and command that no manner of person abide not, but void the field and not be so hard to make any resistance against me in mine own realm; for I shall know what traitor dare be so bold to raise a people in mine own land, where-through I am in great dis-ease and heaviness. And by the faith that I owe to St Edward and the Crown of England, I shall destroy them, every mother's son, and they be hanged, drawn and quartered that may be taken afterward, of them to have example to all such traitors to beware to make any such rising of people within my land, and so traitorly to abide their King and Governor. And for a conclusion, rather than they shall have any lord here with me at this time, I shall this day for their sake, and in this quarrel, myself live and die.

York had failed, thanks in part to the hostility of Buckingham who meant to have him accused before the council at Leicester. The King, in any case, had no intention of delivering Somerset into York's clutches. Instead, he ordered his standard to be raised in the market-place, had himself clad in plate armour, and mounted his warhorse, positioning it under the fluttering banner. Here he remained for the duration of the battle. Before the fighting commenced, he gave orders that only the lives of the common foot soldiers were to be spared: lords, gentry and yeomen might be put to the sword. Many of the royal soldiers were still hastening back to their positions, having drifted off into the town, seeking refreshment after Buckingham had gone to parley with York.

York, learning that the King refused to accede to any of his demands, grimly put on his helmet and ordered his trumpeter to sound the alarm which would warn his men that the battle was about to begin. He then made a speech to his troops, using many classical and biblical allusions, saying that he represented Joab, while King Henry was as King David, and together they would overcome Somerset. Thus commenced the Battle of St Albans, the first battle of the Wars of the Roses, some time between ten and twelve in the morning.

York and Salisbury opened the attack from the east, leading charges along St Peter's Street, Sopwell Street and other streets leading to the market-place, and ordering their men to storm the barricades at the end of them, but Lord Clifford and other Lancastrian commanders 'strongly kept the barriers' at every entry. As more Lancastrian troops rallied to the defence, York and Salisbury found themselves being pushed back. Warwick, hearing that their situation was critical, 'took and gathered his men together and furiously broke in [the town] by the garden sides, between the sign of the Key and the sign of the Checker in Holywell Street', according to an account in the Stonor Papers. Once in the town, he had his trumpets sounded, and his men responded 'with a shout and a great voice, "A Warwick! A Warwick!"' With his progress covered by archers to the rear, Warwick led a fresh assault on the barricades that left his opponents reeling, for they had not expected him to approach from that end of the town.

'The fighting', says Benet, 'was furious', as the market-place became crammed with soldiers locked in a furious combat. As Sir Robert Ogle led his contingent into the mêlée, 'the alarm bell was rung and every man went to harness', for many of the King's troops were 'out of their array', not having anticipated that they would be engaged so soon. Within half an hour it was over. As Henry's men, alerted by the bell sounding in the clock tower in the market-place, raced to defend him, Warwick's soldiers scythed mercilessly through the Lancastrian ranks until, says Whethamstead – a horrified witness to the carnage – 'the whole street was full of dead corpses'. The King's army, 'disliking the sight of blood', broke into disarray and withdrew in a stampede, knocking down and trampling underfoot the royal standard as they did so. The Stonor Papers record that the Earl of Wiltshire 'and many others fled, leaving their harness behind them coward'; Wiltshire, says the chronicler 'Gregory', was 'afraid to lose his beauty'. Many of the King's party were despoiled of their horses and harness, and the royal banner was retrieved and propped against a house wall, while Henry stood alone and deserted, watching the flight of his men as arrows rained down about him. The Yorkists had won the battle.

Warwick had specifically instructed his archers to target those about the King – members of the hated court party – and many fell, mortally wounded, near the royal standard. As the battle drew to a close, Henry was wounded in the neck by an arrow and, bleeding profusely, was urged by his remaining nobles to take shelter. As he ran to the nearby house of a tanner, he cried out angrily, 'Forsooth, ye do foully to smite a king anointed so!'

Buckingham received wounds to the face and neck and was taken prisoner by the Yorkists. Lord Dudley also got an arrow in the face, and Lord Stafford one in the hand. Henry Beaufort, Earl of Dorset, Somerset's heir, was so badly hurt that he could not walk and had to be taken home in a cart, as was Wenlock. Benet says that 'all who were on the side of the Duke of Somerset were killed, wounded, or, at the least, despoiled'.

Somerset himself had been engaged in desperate hand-to-hand fighting outside an inn called the Castle. Later, it was said that, seeing the sign above him, he was utterly dismayed because he had once been warned by a soothsayer to beware of castles. His opponent – who may even have been Warwick himself – saw him falter, struck home, and killed him. He was later buried in St Albans Abbey, and was succeeded as Duke of Somerset by his son, the nineteen-year-old Earl of Dorset, whom Chastellain describes as 'a handsome young knight'. A commemorative plaque now marks the site of the Castle Inn, which stood at the corner of St Peter's Street and what is now Victoria Street.

Other noble casualties of the battle were Warwick's great enemy, Henry Percy, 2nd Earl of Northumberland, and Lord Clifford, who were both slain while fighting in the streets. Their bodies were stripped and despoiled, and left naked to public view. Buckingham's son, Humphrey Stafford, suffered grievous wounds and later died of the effects of them, either in 1455 or 1458. Benet says that 'about a hundred people were killed, mostly Lancastrian soldiers'. Abbot Whethamstead requested York's permission to bury the dead, and begged him to show mercy in his hour of victory, as did Julius Caesar. Quoting Ovid, he asked that nothing be sought in addition to victory.

The outcome of the Battle of St Albans, one of the shortest campaigns of the Wars of the Roses, was that York was able to crush the court faction, which had been deprived of its chief mainstay, Somerset. Much of the blame for the Lancastrian defeat lay with Buckingham, whose judgement and strategies had been fatally flawed. The royal army had faced an almost impossible task in defending all the entrances to the town. They had had little time in which to prepare their defences, and Buckingham had probably made the mistake of relying on some of the buildings to offer a degree of protection.

York, accompanied by Salisbury and Warwick, now moved to take control of the King's person, which they found in the tanner's house having his wound tended. All his earlier bravado had evaporated at the realisation that his army had been defeated. The Stonor Papers record that, when the Yorkist lords came to the King, they fell on their knees 'and besought him for grace and forgiveness of that they had done in his presence, and besought him, of his highness, to take them as his true liegemen, saying that they never intended hurt to his own person'. Benet says that when Henry heard them declare themselves to be his 'humble servants, he was greatly cheered'.

York justified his actions to Henry by pleading that he and his friends had had no alternative but to defend themselves against their enemies. If they had gone to Leicester, as summoned, they would have been taken prisoner and suffered a shameful death as traitors, 'losing our livelihood and goods, and our heirs shamed for ever'. Henry seemed to accept this and 'took them to grace, and so desired them to cease their people, and then there should no more harm be done'. Outside in the town, the victorious Yorkist troops were causing havoc. Abbot Whethamstead was shocked to see them rampaging through the streets, looting as they went and leaving behind a trail of destruction. Even in the abbey they stole everything they could lay their hands on, and threatened to burn it down. Then others came, warning them that the King and York, accompanied by the magnates and councillors, had arrived in the market-place and ordered them to reassemble, ready to return to London. Thus the abbey was saved.

York himself had broken the news of Somerset's death to the King. Some historians assert that shock, grief, stress and the effects of the wound he had suffered caused Henry to lapse once more into insanity – it was, after all, only five months since his recovery. However, there is no contemporary evidence to support this, and another six months would elapse before York was again appointed Protector. In view of the length of the King's previous illness, it is likely that the appointment would have taken effect immediately if

Henry had displayed symptoms of mental instability. The last word
on the subject should be that of John Crane, who wrote to John
Paston on 25 May: 'As for our sovereign lord, thanked be God, he
has no great harm.'

The fact that a battle had taken place at all shocked many people,
even the participants, and provoked the Yorkists into offering
extravagant justification of their actions in which they attempted to
shift the blame on to Somerset and the court party and thus avoid
any suspicion of treason. Nevertheless, the fact remained that they
had taken up arms against an army led by their anointed king, and
this was enough, in the opinion of many, to condemn them as
traitors. To counteract this ill-feeling, York issued a broadsheet
giving his account of the battle and the circumstances leading up to
it.

St Albans had accentuated the deep divisions between the
magnates and the widespread grievances against the government,
which could now, it seemed, only be settled by violence. This
realisation acted as a brake for a time upon the warring factions.
Neither side had wanted an armed conflict; the King, in particular,
and most of his lords were determined that it should not occur again.
But the divisions between Lancastrians and Yorkists were now so
profound that it would need a committed effort on both sides to
preserve the King's peace. That an uneasy truce prevailed for the
next four years is sufficient testimony to the desire of both sides to
reach an acceptable settlement.

On Friday 23 May, York and Salisbury, preceded by Warwick
bearing the King's sword, escorted Henry VI back to London, where
he lodged at the bishop's palace by St Paul's Cathedral. 'As for what
rule we shall now have, I do not yet know,' wrote a Paston
correspondent. On Sunday the 25th, the Feast of Pentecost, the King
went in procession to St Paul's, wearing his crown, to reassure the
people that his royal authority had not been in any way challenged.
So potent was the power and mystique of monarchy that still no one
ventured to voice the opinion that Henry himself should bear the
ultimate responsibility for recent events. There were no calls for his
deposition, and no criticisms of his incompetence or poor
judgement.

News of the court party's defeat and the death of Somerset had
soon reached the Queen at Greenwich, causing her deep distress, and
the knowledge that York was now to assume the role of chief adviser
to the King in Somerset's place only added to her bitterness. York
was immediately appointed Constable of England, an office

Somerset had held, and was already filling the late duke's other offices with men of his own choosing.

In the week after St Albans, Buckingham, Wiltshire, Shrewsbury, Pembroke and other lords, all back at court, made peace with York and did their best to reconcile the two sides. Jasper Tudor was particularly anxious to devise with York a workable solution to the problems facing the government, and the two men spent many hours in London discussing these.

But although Somerset was dead, his faction remained. Its members were more hostile than ever towards York, and looked to the Queen, whose influence over a suspicious and resentful Henry VI was paramount, for leadership. York was aware of this, and he knew that some of the King's household would resist any attempt at reform. He also had to deal with the enmity of individual noblemen, who had good reason to feel bitterness towards him. Lord Clifford's twenty-year-old son John, now the 9th Lord Clifford, was so incensed against York that he would spend the rest of his life seeking to avenge his father's death, earning in the process the nicknames 'Black-faced Clifford' and 'Bloody Clifford'.

By the beginning of July York had established himself as the effective ruler of England. He had appointed his brother-in-law, Viscount Bourchier, Treasurer, and given Salisbury the influential office of Chancellor of the Duchy of Lancaster. Viscount Bourchier's brother, Archbishop Thomas Bourchier, remained as Chancellor, and was now demonstrating that his sympathies were leaning towards the Yorkists. However, York's continuing lack of general aristocratic support led him to rely heavily on the Nevilles and to pursue a policy of conciliation. The problem of the Queen had been dealt with by forbidding her to come to London. Other than that, however, he did not seek vengeance on those who had opposed him.

York ruled as before, with wisdom and moderation. On 9 July Parliament, summoned by the Duke in the King's name at the end of May, met at Westminster in the presence of the ailing Henry VI. Predictably this Parliament was packed with York's supporters. Sir John Wenlock, now Warwick's man, was Speaker. When the Lords and Commons had assembled, York and his fellow magnates renewed their oaths of allegiance to the King in the Great Council Chamber in the Palace of Westminster.

York ensured the passing of an Act which justified his recent uprising on the grounds that 'the government, as it was managed by the Queen, the Duke of Somerset and their friends, had been of late a great tyranny and injustice to the people', emphasised his efforts to negotiate a peaceful settlement, which had been frustrated by the King's advisers, and pardoned all those involved. At the same time, also under York's auspices, an Act was passed rehabilitating Humphrey, Duke of Gloucester, whose political heir York considered himself to be.

Parliament was also anxious to regulate the Crown's tortuous finances, and approved a new Act of Resumption, cancelling nearly every grant the King had made during his reign. The only exemptions were those grants to the Tudors made since 1452, but even these were unpopular with York and other lords, who felt there should be no exclusions. Nevertheless, Richmond and Pembroke had offered their support to York without compromising their loyalty to the King, and they were now exerting a moderating influence in this Parliament, though the time was fast approaching when, because of the ever-widening rift between Lancastrians and Yorkists, they would have to decide where their true loyalties lay.

After Parliament had completed its business – but not before Warwick had fallen out with Lord Cromwell over which side had initiated the recent hostilities – York dispatched the King and Queen, with the Prince of Wales, to Hertford Castle. Shortly afterwards Margaret took her child to Greenwich, and it may be at this time that Henry was showing once more signs of mental illness.

In October 1455 Edmund Tudor, Earl of Richmond, at last married Margaret Beaufort, the ceremony taking place at Bletsoe Castle in Bedfordshire. The groom was twenty-five, the bride twelve. She was a strong-minded child who would grow up to be one of the most formidable women of the age, renowned for her piety, her many charities, and her unwavering devotion to the House of Lancaster. She was intelligent, serious and high-minded, and her impeccable Lancastrian credentials, her great inheritance, and the fact that she was Somerset's niece, made her a fitting match for the King's half-brother. By this marriage Henry VI had hoped to build up a core of committed family support for the Crown; for Richmond, it meant rapid social advancement.

Margaret later claimed it had been revealed to her in a vision that she should wed Richmond and, being a very devout girl, she had wished to see the vision fulfilled. That the marriage would produce a future king of England none could have foreseen at the time, but the Lady Margaret Beaufort was a great believer in destiny.

Shortly after his marriage, Richmond was sent to protect Henry's interests in Wales. York also entrusted him with the task of subduing the Welsh rebel, Gruffydd ap Nicholas, who was encroaching upon the March lordships belonging to York and Buckingham. In November Richmond took up residence at Lamphey, Pembroke-shire, a remote palace owned by the Bishop of St David's and situated two miles north-east of Jasper's fortress at Pembroke.

In London that autumn York assumed complete control of the administration. Contemporary accounts are not specific as to what prompted this, but possibly the King had suffered another mental breakdown, something which is indicated by the Queen's request that she be entrusted with the care of her husband, whom York sent to her at Greenwich.

Margaret of Anjou, of course, had no intention of being relegated to the role of nurse – she meant to regain power for herself and her supporters and put an end to York's ambitions. In the wake of St Albans, many of her household had deserted her, but now, by letters and messages, she was secretly cultivating support for her cause. Those who offered their allegiance included Henry Beaufort, the new Duke of Somerset, his brother Edmund, Owen Tudor and his sons, Richmond and Pembroke, the Lord Chief Justice Sir John Fortescue, the new Earl of Northumberland and his kinsfolk, the Earl of Wiltshire, Lord Clifford, Lord Grey, and the sinister Sir William Tailboys, the member of Parliament for Lincolnshire, a county in which he exerted a pernicious influence. Some years earlier he had been imprisoned in the Tower and fined for attacking the Treasurer, Lord Cromwell, then in 1451 he had been outlawed for murdering a man, yet he had defied the law and remained in England. Now he was offering his dubious services to the Queen, who, desperate for support, was glad to accept.

On 12 November 1455 Parliament was recalled, and on the 17th or 19th York was again appointed Protector and Defender of the Realm with much the same powers as before, except that it was now up to the Lords to dissolve Parliament. York continued to act with moderation, insisting that everything he did be subject to approval by the Council, whose members should be chosen by the Lords, and that the 'politic rule and governance of the land' should be reserved to the Council.

For the rest of the year York and his allies concentrated on formulating a radical programme of reforms aimed at the royal finances and the resumption of crown lands. Parliament settled 10,000 marks a year on the Prince of Wales until he reached the age of eight, when the sum would increase to 16,000 marks annually, until his thirteenth birthday. York also obtained a writ reversing the sentence of outlawry passed by the Lancastrian government on his chamberlain Sir William Oldhall.

As before, York enjoyed substantial support from the Commons, although the magnates were, predictably, less enthusiastic about his reforms. Two of his previous supporters, Richmond and Pembroke, were absent from this Parliament, and many peers remained suspicious of York's true intentions. Suspecting that his calls for reform concealed a hidden agenda, they were particularly at pains to safeguard the rights of the Prince of Wales during the protectorate.

1   Richard II. His reign was one of the most disastrous in English history.

JOHANNES FILIVS QVARTV
EDVARDI TERTII REX
CASTELLÆ ET LEGIONE
CONSTABVLARIVS CAST
DE QVEENBOVRG ◦ ROVIN
TO OCTOBRIS AN AO
REGNI ELW ERT LANN
OELA 80 FR XCH 371

2 John of Gaunt, Duke of Lancaster. He saw his life's work as maintaining the honour and integrity of the English crown.

3 *Below left* Henry IV. The legitimacy of his title to the throne would remain a sensitive issue.

4 *Below right* Henry V. He possessed all the attributes required of a successful mediaeval ruler.

5 Humphrey, Duke of
   Gloucester, an intensely
   ambitious man who was
   Beaufort's deadly rival for
   power during the minority of
   the young Henry VI.

6 Cardinal Henry Beaufort, a
   shrewd politician who exerted
   enormous influence over the
   King.

7 Henry VI as a young man. He was 'neither intelligent nor
experienced enough to manage a kingdom such as England'.
(Jean de Waurin: *Chronicle*.)

8   Henry VI in later life. His severe nervous breakdown resulted in his withdrawal from normal life and precipitated the outbreak of civil war.

9   *Below left*   René, Duke of Anjou. Despite his landless status, he was a considerable power at the French court, and was rumoured to govern the realm in Charles VII's name.

10 *Below right*   Margaret of Anjou. She was beautiful, talented, courageous, autocratic, changeable and vindictive – 'more like to a man than a woman'.

11 Richard, Duke of York. He had a better claim to the throne than Henry VI, but preferred to promote himself as the champion of good government.

12 The Falcon and Fetterlock badge of the mediaeval duke of York. Duke Richard inherited the fabulous wealth of the Mortimers and became the richest landowner in England.

13 'The harvest of heads': the gruesome aftermath of Jack Cade's rebellion in 1450, a largely middle-class revolt against misgovernment by Henry VI's favourites.

14 A nineteenth-century portrayal of the outbreak of the Wars of the Roses: the Dukes of Somerset and York confront each other in Temple Gardens, London. This colourful scene, enshrined in the pages of Shakespeare, is fictitious, the stuff of legend.

15 Ludlow Castle, Shropshire: the mightiest fortress owned by York, and his headquarters during the Wars of the Roses.

16 Westminster Hall, London. Here, in October 1460, York formally laid claim to the crown of England.

17 Edward IV. Affable, handsome, promiscuous and generally indolent, he nevertheless brought stable government to England and was consistently victorious over his enemies in battle.

18 *Above left* Elizabeth Wydville. In his choice of wife, King Edward was 'governed by lust'; the marriage caused not only scandal but political disruption.

19 *Above right* Warwick the Kingmaker. Next to the King, he was the greatest man in England, and virtually controlled the government during the early years of Edward's reign.

20 George, Duke of Clarence, with his wife, Isabel Neville, and their son. Clarence, who wanted to depose his brother the King and rule in his place, was Warwick's natural ally in the late 1460s.

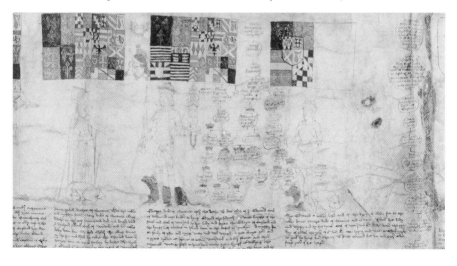

21 Edward IV sets sail from Flushing in March 1471. Although few believed he stood any chance of victory, he had no intention of retreating.

22 Edward IV watches the execution of the Duke of Somerset, last of the male Beaufort line, and twelve others, in May 1471. The King pardoned all the common soldiers who had fought against him.

23 The oratory in the Wakefield Tower in the Tower of London where tradition sets the murder of Henry VI, which took place on the night of 21 May 1471. He was the last surviving member of the House of Lancaster.

14

An Uneasy Peace

In February 1456 Henry VI appeared in Parliament and revoked York's appointment as Protector. Benet wrote: 'In front of the King the Duke resigned his office and left Parliament before the session was over,' although Henry, anxious to avoid a rift, had insisted that his cousin retain his place on the Council.

The King then reasserted his authority and ordered substantial alterations to York's Act of Resumption, adding to it a long list of exemptions. Many members of his household were relieved to learn that grants made to them over the years were not to be withdrawn after all. Although York could not approve of this, Lancastrians and Yorkists nevertheless co-operated in Council and Parliament during the next few months, and the Yorkists for a time retained a fair degree of influence, with York himself remaining the dominant voice on the Council. An uneasy peace would prevail for the next two years, thanks in no small measure to the moderating influence of the Duke of Buckingham.

London was no longer sympathetic towards the House of Lancaster; the merchants in the city had had enough of Henry VI's misrule and Queen Margaret's interference with their traditional privileges, and had come out strongly in support of York. When a riot occurred in London, the Queen, ignoring the fact that the city lay within the Lord Mayor's jurisdiction, sent in troops under Buckingham and Exeter, who were armed with a royal commission enabling them to try the ringleaders. The citizens were incensed by this usurpation of their rights and forcibly prevented the dukes from setting up their court. Bitter criticisms were levelled at the Queen, who had dared to challenge their fiercely protected privileges.

In the spring of 1456 Margaret, whose dislike of the hostile

Londoners equalled theirs of her, left London with the Prince. In April she stayed at Tutbury, and was in Chester by the end of May. She then took up residence at Kenilworth, all the time canvassing support for her husband against the Yorkists. During the spring and early summer Henry remained in the south in the company of Pembroke – in June, Pembroke was the only lord in attendance on the King at Sheen. Henry had come to rely heavily on his half-brother and to value his unquestioned loyalty.

With the Queen away, the King was also much under the influence of York at this time. On 20 April Henry appointed Warwick Captain of Calais, an office described by Commines as 'Christendom's finest captaincy', and it would be in this capacity that the Earl would gain his heroic reputation as a fine and dashing commander. York was behind the appointment; for he had long wished to reward Warwick for his crucial support at St Albans, and although the court party had tried to secure the post for their candidate, young Somerset, York had pre-empted them.

Securing Calais was a great achievement for the Yorkists. The Captain, or Governor, was the King's representative in the town. His was basically a military appointment, but he also enjoyed considerable judicial authority. The captaincy of Calais was the most important military command in the King's gift, and of such strategic importance that one is tempted to wonder why Henry VI allowed himself to be persuaded to bestow it on Warwick. Calais, in the years to come, would provide the Yorkists with a foreign base and a substantial garrison, whose loyalties were first and foremost to Warwick. Calais was also excellently placed for invading England or policing the Channel, and under Yorkist rule it would effectively become the seat of the opposition. Initially, Warwick had to win the confidence of the powerful Merchants of the Staple, who dominated the town and its wool trade, but by using financial inducements he achieved this with little effort, aided by the fact that those same merchants were heartily relieved that it was Warwick, and not Somerset, who had been placed in command.

After Warwick had left for Warwick Castle to prepare for his new duties, York rode north to Sandal Castle. It was now time for Henry VI to set out on his progress, and he and the Queen were reunited at Chester. In August they began a leisurely tour of the Midlands, ending up at the beginning of September at Coventry, where the King was accorded a warm welcome, with pageants mounted in honour of him and the Queen, who was lauded as the mother of England's heir. With Henry successfully wrested from York's clutches, Margaret had no intention of allowing the King to return to

London, and had already persuaded him to remove his court to the Midlands, the Lancastrian heartlands.

Thus Coventry became the seat of government for a time, and its castle the premier residence of the sovereign. Here, Margaret would create a centre of patronage, surrounding herself with artists, musicians and scholars in an attempt to recreate the splendours of former courts based in the palaces of the Thames valley. The citizens of Coventry, proud to be so honoured, were generous with gifts; on one occasion the mayor presented the Queen with oranges especially imported from Italy, a rare delicacy. Although Coventry Castle was the King's official residence, he himself preferred to stay in a nearby priory, while the Queen often lodged at the house of Richard Woods, a rich merchant. The royal couple may also have stayed at the manor of Cheylesmore, once owned by the Black Prince. Moving the seat of government caused endless administrative problems, since most of the great departments of state were based in London, but it served Margaret's purpose; on 24 September her chancellor, Laurence Booth, was entrusted by the King with the privy seal, thus allowing the Queen complete power over the administrative machinery of government.

Throughout the summer York waited to see what her next move would be, 'and she waited on him'. While York held back and the Queen played for time and moved her pawns, England went more or less ungoverned. London was the scene of riots and violence, particularly against Italian merchants who had been given preferential treatment and privileges by the court party. Trade suffered, there was a further deterioration of law and order in the shires, and French raids on the south coast of England.

In London the tension was palpable, and there were unfounded rumours that another battle had taken place, resulting in Warwick being 'sore hurt' and a thousand men slain. Placards were pinned to church doors bearing ballads that savagely attacked the government. According to 'Gregory's Chronicle', 'some said that the Duke of York had great wrong, but what wrong there was no man dared say'. York himself had realised by now that he had a new rival, the young Duke of Somerset, who was much favoured by the Queen and being groomed to fill his father's shoes.

The Queen was also cultivating the support of members of the royal household, and soliciting the favour of the people by promoting trade and industry, founding hospitals and schools, and displaying her young son in public wherever she went, earning herself unwonted popularity in the process. She made it a priority to win over with promises of future rewards the known enemies of the

Yorkist lords, especially in Cheshire and Lancashire, and she was even intriguing with England's enemies, the Scots. Rumour had it that she had offered them the counties of Northumberland, Cumberland and Durham in return for aid against York and his allies, and although there may have been no truth in this, it shows what many people believed the Queen capable of. Her negotiations with the Scots dragged on fruitlessly for two years; in 1457 she attempted to arrange marriages for Somerset and his brother with two Scottish princesses, but without success. Indeed, her concentration on building up her party, to the exclusion of all else, took precedence over the government of the country, which suffered accordingly.

Edmund Tudor, Earl of Richmond, had for several months been protecting King Henry's interests in Wales. For generations the Tudors and the House of Mortimer had been sworn enemies due to territorial rivalries in the principality. Nevertheless, Richmond had given his support to York because he believed that the latter's reforms could only benefit the King. But York was heir to the Mortimers, and his affinity in South Wales had recently taken it upon themselves to reassert his authority there. In the spring of 1456 the Queen had ordered Richmond to move against them.

Initially, the Earl enjoyed some success against the rebel Gruffydd ap Nicholas, who had now allied himself with York's supporters and seized and garrisoned several royal castles. Richmond wrested Carmarthen Castle from him and restored the authority of the King to the surrounding region. However, York himself was constable of Carmarthen Castle, and may well have resented Richmond's occupation of it, for in the summer of 1456, the Duke's adherents, Sir William Herbert, Sir Walter Devereux, and men of the Vaughan family, marched on Carmarthen, seized the castle, and took Richmond prisoner.

At this time, however, the King had good reason to be grateful to York, for on 15 August the King of Scots, taking advantage of the political situation, had invaded England with – according to Benet – '100,000 men, and burned twenty villages, but he was routed by the Duke of York'. Soon afterwards the King sent for York and Warwick to join him on his progress, and Benet says they 'were received most graciously' by Henry, 'though the Queen loathed them both'. Margaret was about to prove to York that she held the upper hand.

Once the King and Queen had settled at Coventry they summoned a great council of nobles to meet there. All the Yorkist lords were invited but, mistrustful of the Queen, having presented themselves in council, they withdrew and left Coventry without delay, 'in right good conceit with the King, but not in great conceit with the Queen'. York went to Ludlow, Salisbury to Middleham, and Warwick to Calais.

Margaret now persuaded Henry to dismiss York's partisans from office and replace them with men of her own party. On 5 October Henry Bourchier, York's brother-in-law, was replaced as Treasurer by Shrewsbury, who had recently quarrelled with Warwick and made an enemy of him. On the 11th Archbishop Bourchier was dismissed from the chancellorship, which was given to William Wayneflete, Bishop of Winchester, a prominent member of the court faction. News of these changes must have angered the Yorkists and aroused their anxieties, though the Queen as yet had made no move against her real adversaries. At his wife's behest, Henry VI summoned Parliament to meet at Coventry, so that the measures planned by the Queen's party could be implemented, a reassertion of the authority of the Crown as exercised by Margaret of Anjou.

That autumn, Richmond was released from captivity in Carmarthen Castle, although he remained in the castle, free to come and go. But he did not long enjoy his liberty. On 1 November he died, aged only twenty-six, probably of natural causes and possibly in an epidemic, although he may have succumbed to the effects of wounds received earlier in the year. There were even whispers of murder at the time, but no evidence exists to substantiate such claims, nor were any charges laid by the Lancastrians at the trials of Herbert, Devereux or the Vaughans, which took place some months later. Richmond was buried in the nearby church of the Grey Friars at Carmarthen; in 1536, in the reign of his grandson, Henry VIII, his remains and monument were removed to St David's Cathedral. Today, the shields, brass and inscription on the tomb are nineteenth-century replacements of the originals.

Pembroke was at court when he learned of his brother's death, and he immediately left for Wales to take his place and set his affairs in order. Edmund's death meant that all the properties jointly owned by the brothers came to Jasper, whose annual income was now increased to perhaps as much as £1500. Jasper was an honourable man, one of the King's most trusted counsellors, and he now realised he could no longer support York and remain loyal to the King. He therefore took steps to dissociate himself from the Duke, for the rest of his life devoting his services to upholding the right and authority of the House of Lancaster in Wales.

Pembroke was concerned about Richmond's thirteen-year-old widow. The late earl had not scrupled to consummate his marriage to one so young, and Margaret Beaufort was now six months pregnant. Jasper offered her a safe refuge at Pembroke Castle, and would be a tower of strength to her and her child for the next half century.

Both the Tudor brothers were held in great affection by the Welsh, and their deeds were commemorated in song by the bards, who sang of how a grief-stricken Jasper had taken Edmund's widow and unborn child under his protection and how he healed the terrible wounds, both emotional and political, that Edmund's untimely demise had caused. They voiced the feelings of their people when they compared Wales, bereft of Edmund, to a land without a ruler, a house without a bed, a church without a priest. The Welsh had great hopes of Jasper; he was never to let them down.

On 28 January 1457, Margaret Beaufort gave birth to her 'only beloved son' at Pembroke Castle. As his father's posthumous child, the infant was styled Earl of Richmond from birth. According to Welsh tradition, Jasper wanted him christened Owen after his grandfather, but the Countess insisted that he was to be named Henry after the King. No one dreamed that this obscure scion of the royal house would one day become the founder monarch of the magnificent Tudor dynasty.

Margaret was still only thirteen at the time of Henry Tudor's birth 'and of very small stature', according to her funeral sermon, delivered by Dr John Fisher. 'It seemed a miracle that of so little a personage anyone should have been born at all.' The baby was sickly and his survival of infancy was due only to his mother's diligent care. For the first five years of his life, he would live at Pembroke Castle in the care of his devoted parent and his uncle Jasper.

Early in 1457 Pembroke cultivated a friendship with Buckingham, both men uniting to defend their Marcher properties, and in particular the lordships of Newport and Brecon, from the depredations of men of York's affinity. In March, Pembroke and Margaret Beaufort were Buckingham's guests at his manor of Greenfield, near Newport, and it was probably on this occasion that plans were formulated for Margaret to marry Buckingham's younger son, Henry Stafford. This marriage, which took place about two years later, would cement the friendship between the two families and provide a secure home for the young widow, while Pembroke continued his efforts to establish a lasting peace in south Wales.

Meanwhile, disorder in England was escalating. The great magnates had now taken to paying pirates to plunder foreign shipping. The pirates – and the magnates – got away with it, but the English merchants suffered as a result because many foreign traders refused to send goods to England or charged more for them. In London, there were further riots against Lombard merchants, and many had their houses sacked or burned down.

Yet still the court remained in the Midlands. The Queen was more preoccupied with consolidating her power than with ruling England. In January she had ordered a vast stock of arms and ammunition to be delivered to the royal castle at Kenilworth, and she had also replaced Shrewsbury as Treasurer with Wiltshire, while the notorious Thomas Tuddenham had been made treasurer of the royal household. The household itself had now extended its web of corruption to the shrievalty of England. No less than sixteen sheriffs were in its pay, receiving regular wages as if they were on the royal pay-roll. In return they were expected to favour those who supported the Queen's party. Other sheriffs found themselves faced with demands for money in a kind of royal protection racket.

In April, Pembroke was appointed constable of the castles of Aberystwyth, Carmarthen and Carreg Cennen, in place of York. He carried out his new duties with diligence and success, even bringing to heel his old adversary, Gruffydd ap Nicholas, who would now remain faithful to the House of Lancaster for the remaining three years of his life.

Throughout the early months of 1457 the Queen's agents were busy hunting for Sir William Herbert, who had dared to seize Carmarthen and imprison Richmond the previous year. Herbert had remained at large throughout the winter, harrying the countryside of south-east Wales and undermining the King's authority. When he was at last captured, the Queen had him cast into the Tower of London. She wanted him executed, and York too, for she believed that Herbert had been acting on York's orders, although there was no proof of this. Buckingham, ever the peacemaker, dissuaded her, and York was sent back to Dublin to resume his duties as Lieutenant of Ireland.

At the end of March 1457, Herbert and his accomplices stood trial at Hereford in the presence of the King, the Queen, Buckingham, Shrewsbury and, possibly, Pembroke. Although all were found guilty and sentenced to be attainted for treason, Herbert received a royal pardon in June and the other attainders were reversed in February 1458. Herbert's pardon was enough to make him turn his coat, and for a time he and his brother Richard offered their loyalty to the Queen. His position was not easy, for most of his neighbours in south-east Wales were Yorkists, but he managed to balance the interests of all the parties, retaining the friendship and trust of the Queen as well as that of his former allies.

Warwick, meanwhile, had established himself in Calais, and had been made aware of the problems of piracy in the Channel, and its effect on the London merchants. He had also found out that these problems were unlikely to be dealt with by the King since Henry's navy comprised at that time just one ship. Warwick owned about ten ships, which he was soon using to good effect against French and Burgundian pirates; he also destroyed a hostile Spanish fleet.

Warwick was sensitive to the Londoners' feelings about the Italian aliens in their midst, and when he learned that three Italian ships had been granted a special royal licence to load their vessels at Tilbury with unlimited English wool and woollen cloth, he sent a small flotilla across the Channel and up the Thames estuary to capture them. His deeds were regarded by the Londoners as nothing less than heroic, and won him tremendous popularity. Here, at last, was someone ready to champion the cause of the merchants, who were the source of much of England's wealth yet were ignored and slighted by the Lancastrian government.

The Earl, who now spent much of his time travelling back and forth across the Channel, was at present building up a lavish establishment in London, where he kept open house, his aim being to court popularity by dispensing extravagant hospitality. When he was in residence there, six oxen were roasted every day at breakfast 'and every tavern was full of his meat, for whoever had any acquaintance in his household could have as much roast as he might carry upon a large dagger'. Waurin says that Warwick

> had in great measure the voice of the people because he knew how to persuade them with beautiful soft speeches. He was conversible and talked familiarly with them – subtle, as it were, in order to gain his ends. He gave them to understand that he would promote the prosperity of the kingdom and defend the interests of the people with all his power, and that as long as he lived he would never do otherwise. Thus he acquired the goodwill of the people of England to such an extent that he was the prince whom they held in the highest esteem and on whom they placed the greatest faith and reliance.

Warwick was the popular and charismatic face of the Yorkist party, having the dash and common touch that York lacked, and it was largely thanks to Warwick – and to Lancastrian misrule – that the Yorkist party increased its following during these years. The Earl's use of his great wealth to win it support was, naturally, not without self-interest, for he always had a sharp eye to his own self-aggrandisement.

Just how far Warwick was prepared to go to discredit the Lancastrians became apparent in August 1457. At that time the Queen was hoping to arrange a new peace treaty with France, so that she could call on her uncle, Charles VII, for military aid if necessary. As her go-between, she used one Dolcereau, who was the agent of her former admirer, Pierre de Brézé, now Grand Seneschal of Anjou, Poitou and Normandy, to carry highly sensitive communications to Richard de Beauchamp, Bishop of Salisbury, England's ambassador in France.

But that month Brézé himself landed a French fleet on the Kent coast, plundering and burning the town of Sandwich, which was almost destroyed. What made the raid so provocative was that the victorious French had been seen afterwards playing tennis in the smoking ruins of the town, before being eventually driven away by Sir Thomas Kyriell. The only comfort the townsfolk had was the satisfaction of knowing later that many Frenchmen drowned in the Channel, thanks to turbulent seas on the journey home.

The raid unnerved the English, who were alarmed at the government's inability to prevent it, and the Queen was the target of furious criticism. In an attempt to deflect public anger from herself she tried to pin the blame for the raid on Exeter, who had been Lord High Admiral for the past ten years. No one was fooled by her excuses, and the Yorkists immediately spread word that the Queen had actually invited Brézé to raid the English coast in order to discredit the exploits of Warwick. No one thought to criticise Warwick, who had not lifted a finger against the French, and had indeed decided not to intercept them knowing that anything they might do would stir up feeling against the Lancastrians.

This wave of criticism of the Queen gave rise to a fresh crop of rumours about the supposed paternity of the Prince of Wales which named the late Duke of Somerset or the Queen's current favourite, Wiltshire, as the child's father. Margaret herself told Chastellain later that her son was branded a 'false heir' born in 'false wedlock'.

Margaret incurred more opprobrium in September when she defied the King over the appointment of a new Bishop of Durham. She wanted her chancellor, Laurence Booth, to be preferred, while the King had nominated another candidate. Margaret secretly put considerable pressure on the Pope, and Booth was elected on 15 September.

At Michaelmas 1457 the court left Coventry. It had proved impossible for the administration to function effectively away from London, and reluctantly the Queen departed from her 'safe harbour' and returned south. She had rid herself of the Yorkists for the moment, but with Warwick in Calais and York in Dublin she did not feel safe. It was imperative that she be able to call upon an armed force if either of them threatened her position, yet such was the reputation of the government that she doubted if she could raise enough men to support her. There was only one solution to this problem, and the fact that she embraced it proves just how desperately insecure she felt.

The Queen introduced conscription, a measure hitherto employed in Western Europe only by the kings of France. That December she dispatched commissions of array to every shire, empowering the sheriffs to demand that every village, township and hamlet, according to its population and wealth, and as soon as she gave the command, provide the King with a number of able-bodied men and archers at its own expense, in order to defend the realm against the Yorkists. At the same time it was publicly proclaimed that Henry VI had written a letter to his Anglo-Irish subjects in Ireland, encouraging them to conquer that land (and hopefully kill York in battle in the process).

Henry VI was aware of the growing tensions at court and throughout his realm, but far from wishing to muster support for a new conflict he was determined to foster peace between the opposing factions. Whethamstead says he was fond of quoting St Matthew and saying that 'every kingdom divided against itself is brought to desolation'. In January 1458 he commanded that the magnates attend a peace conference at Westminster. It lasted for two months, but achieved only superficial success. One face was missing. One of the Queen's most valued supporters, the Earl of Devon, had died – some said by poison – at Abingdon Abbey in January, with Margaret at his side.

The fragile concord of the peace congress was brutally disrupted in February when the vengeful Lord Clifford arrived at the head of a large army at Temple Bar in the company of his cousin, the young Earl of Northumberland, and his kinsman, the Duke of Somerset. All three were demanding compensation for the deaths of their fathers at St Albans. So intimidated was the King that he had no choice but to agree. He commanded that York, Salisbury and Warwick collaborate to found and endow a chantry at St Albans, in which masses for the souls of the three dead lords and others killed in the battle could be sung in perpetuity. He also ordered the Yorkist lords to pay Clifford, Northumberland and Somerset a 'notable sum of money', which they did. York paid Somerset's widow 5000 marks, while Warwick paid the Clifford family 1000 marks. The chantry was duly founded the following March, and a proclamation was issued informing the people of what had been done.

The peace conference resulted in a staged public display of amity between the two warring factions. On 24 March 1458, which was Lady Day, the Feast of the Annunciation, there was an official ceremony of reconciliation between the King and Queen and the Yorkist lords which was afterwards referred to as the 'Loveday'. The King, followed by the Queen and York, walking hand in hand, the leaders of both factions, the Nevilles, the Percies and other lords, went in procession through the streets of London to St Paul's Cathedral, where a service of reconciliation was held. 'There was between them a lovely countenance', and they 'spared right nought in sight of the commonalty, in token that love was in heart and thought'.

The King and Archbishop Bourchier had laboured to bring about this reconciliation, and Henry was overjoyed that his initiative had produced such a visible result. 'Rejoice, England, in concord and unity!' exclaimed a popular ballad commemorating the occasion, and his subjects were only too glad to do so, hoping that this was a complete and final reconciliation. But Robert Fabyan, the Tudor chronicler, was nearer the truth when he referred to the event as 'this dissimulated Loveday', for lining the streets had been the retainers and supporters of the rival parties, many of them heavily armed, and most of them regarding each other with ill-concealed animosity.

Three days after the Loveday Henry and Margaret made a state entry into London and took up residence in the bishop's palace. York returned to Ludlow, Salisbury to Middleham and Warwick to Calais, and everyone waited to see what would happen next. The King, happily believing that his factious nobles were at peace with each other, kept Easter alone at St Albans Abbey. He was becoming more absorbed in his devotions and his foundations, retreating from political life, and leaving most executive decisions to the Queen.

When he arrived at Calais, Warwick began courting the friendship of Philip of Burgundy, whose ships he had recently so cheerfully plundered. The merchants of Calais and those in England were anxious to preserve the important trade links between England and Burgundy, and this was Warwick's response. By the summer of 1458 he had reached an understanding with Duke Philip and had dispatched Sir John Wenlock, now serving under him at Calais, to the Duke to negotiate on the King's behalf – without consulting Henry – a marriage between the Prince of Wales and a Burgundian princess. Afterwards, Wenlock went to France on Queen Margaret's behalf to open negotiations with Charles VII for the Prince's marriage to a French princess. Not surprisingly these negotiations were complicated and long drawn out, but they did have the advantage of keeping both France and Burgundy well disposed towards England for the time being.

For some time now Warwick had engaged in acts of piracy, on one notorious occasion ordering his ships out of Calais to plunder the fleet of the German merchants of the Hanseatic city of Lübeck. This attack violated a truce between the League and the English government, and the Germans had protested strongly to Henry VI about Warwick's behaviour. The Queen, who wished to oust the Earl from the captaincy of Calais, now saw her chance to get rid of him. She summoned him to London and ordered him to explain his actions before the Council.

Warwick responded to her summons by arriving in London at the head of 600 armed retainers, all wearing his livery. Margaret demanded of the Council that he stand trial for his crimes. On 31 July 1458 the Council instituted an enquiry, but after the first day Warwick publicly protested that the interrogation he had been made to undergo had been unduly rigorous, and that he believed there was a plot to discredit him. The Queen, he complained, had been acting insincerely on the Loveday, and had no regard for the glory of England's achievement on the high seas.

The next day, incited by Warwick's protests, his supporters – and there were many in London, including a number of aldermen – ran riot, demonstrating against the Queen and the authorities. In the confusion the Attorney General was murdered. The Queen commanded that pikemen be sent into the city to restore order, and when this had been done, those aldermen and citizens who had taken part in the riot were thrown into gaol. The outcome of the Council's enquiry is not recorded, but there was no doubt that the Queen's attempt to eliminate Warwick from the political scene had failed.

In the autumn Warwick again visited the court at Westminster. As he was passing through the royal kitchens, one of the King's scullions nearly impaled him on a spit. It was an accident, but Warwick and the retainers with him chose to believe that the scullion had been instructed by the Queen to murder him. A fight broke out between the Earl's followers and the royal servants, who rushed to defend the scullion. During the scuffle Warwick was set upon by the royal guard, though his men soon gained the upper hand, and the unfortunate scullion was seized by them and hauled before the Queen. Margaret knew that if she defended the man Warwick would accuse her of murder, so she ordered his execution. However, he was allowed to escape and flee to Yorkshire, while the Queen announced defiantly that the fight had been caused by Warwick's supporters at his instigation. Fabyan asserts that she then persuaded the Council to draw up an order for the Earl's arrest and committal to the Tower.

As soon as he heard that there was a warrant out for his arrest, Warwick left London and travelled at speed to Warwick Castle, and thence to the safety of Calais, where he would be protected by the garrison. In November, the Queen and Council, incensed at his escape, demanded that he surrender his post to Somerset. At this, Warwick boldly returned to London and stood defiantly before the Council, stating that Parliament had appointed him to his post, and therefore Parliament was the only authority that could revoke the appointment. Tempers were running high, and as he left the Council chamber he was attacked by retainers of Somerset and Wiltshire and only narrowly escaped. This time his claim that the Queen had tried to have him killed was almost certainly justified.

Warwick knew it was not safe for him to remain in England, and after a hurried consultation with his father, Salisbury, he returned to Calais, where he defiantly continued his attacks on the Lübeck fleet. It was probably this that drove the conciliatory Buckingham off the political fence and firmly into the camp of the Queen's party.

Margaret now knew she had to take decisive action against the Yorkists, and Warwick in particular. Late in 1458 she left London and during the following months travelled through Cheshire and Lancashire, cultivating support among the nobility and gentry and recruiting men. Davies' Chronicle claims she was prompted by her dread that the Prince 'should not succeed his father', and states that she 'allied unto her all the knights and squires of Cheshire, and held open household among them'.

It now seemed that a further confrontation between the Lancastrians and the Yorkists was inevitable.

15

'A Great and Strong Labour'd Woman'

'The Queen', wrote a Paston correspondent, 'is a great and strong labour'd woman, for she spareth no pain to sue her things to an intent and conclusion to her power.' None of her supporters now doubted that she would do her utmost to destroy the Yorkists. According to Croyland, Margaret, Northumberland and Clifford caused the Duke 'to stink in the King's nostrils even unto death, as they insisted that he was endeavouring to gain the kingdom into his own hands'.

It was obvious to everyone that Henry VI was no longer capable of leading an initiative against the Yorkists. The Queen's party needed a more inspiring figurehead, and who better than the appealing figure of the five-year-old Prince, a symbol of hope for the future? Margaret even tried to persuade Henry to abdicate in favour of his son, though he flatly refused. She continued to raise support in the north-west Midlands, and in Chester made the Prince bestow a livery of swans (the swan being Henry IV's personal badge, and his own) to all the gentlemen of the county, 'trusting through their strength to make her son king'.

The Queen spent the early months of 1459 at Coventry. In the spring Sir William Herbert urged her to take the field with her Cheshire levies, who were gathered around the city, before the Yorkists had time to unite in arms. Margaret saw the sense in this, and the Council approved it. In April, the Queen persuaded the King to issue writs commanding all his loyal magnates to meet with him at Leicester on 10 May 'with as many men defensibly arrayed as they might, and that they should bring their expenses for two months'. She also ordered that commissions of array be issued throughout the realm, conscripting young men from every town, village and hamlet. York responded by issuing a manifesto condemning conscription and asserting that this French innovation was unwelcome to all Englishmen.

Somerset and other nobles began to muster their private armies, and the city of Coventry sent the Queen forty able men at its own expense. In May, Pembroke was given a tower of the Palace of Westminster as his London headquarters, so that he could be at hand to defend the palace if it was attacked. Soon afterwards the King and Queen took the Prince on a progress through Warwickshire, Staffordshire and Cheshire in an attempt to rally support.

York and Salisbury were also preparing for war, at first resorting to propaganda which had proved successful on earlier occasions. In the early months of 1459 there appeared throughout London a proliferation of seditious bills and mocking verses against the Queen's government. Once again the Prince's paternity was questioned, and Margaret herself was accused of ruling like a tyrant through extortion and corrupt practices. This propaganda went home, especially among the merchant community, who at that time were making highly vocal protests against Lancastrian misrule and were already inclined to support York, even though Lancastrian counter-propaganda claimed that 'people in many places' were being 'deceived and blinded by subtle and covert malice'.

But favouring the Duke was one thing, rising in arms on his behalf and 'meddling betwixt lords' entirely another, and they were wary of taking any action that might be construed as treason. Thus York did not find it easy to enlist volunteers. He could, however, call upon his vast following of tenants and retainers to fight for him, as could Salisbury, and in the spring the two lords summoned their armies. However, with York at Ludlow and Salisbury at Middleham, they faced the problem of joining their forces before the Lancastrian army, concentrated in the Midlands, could intercept them.

The fact that the Yorkists were arming at all, even in self defence, was interpreted by the Queen as treason. Late in June, says Benet, 'the King held a great council at Coventry, which was attended by the Queen and the Prince. However, despite being summoned to attend, the Archbishop of Canterbury, the Duke of York and other lords' – including Salisbury, Warwick, George Neville, now Bishop of Exeter, the Earl of Arundel and Viscount Bourchier – 'were absent'. York and Salisbury had instead sent an urgent message to Warwick, warning him that the Queen intended their ruin and begging him to come to their aid.

Warwick speedily raised 200 men-at-arms and 400 archers, all of whom were issued with red jackets sporting his badge. These men were mostly professional soldiers who had seen active service in

France, and they were commanded by two veterans, Sir John Blount and Andrew Trollope, both of whom would attain renown during the Wars of the Roses; Trollope was the Master Porter of Calais, and Warwick had 'greater faith in him than any other'.

Leaving his uncle William Neville, Lord Fauconberg, in charge of the Calais garrison, Warwick crossed with his men to England, landing at Sandwich. He did not stop to raise a force in Kent, but pressed on to London, knowing that his services were urgently required by York. On 21 September he entered London unopposed, leaving it the next day through Smithfield, at the head of a 'very well armed force', making for Warwick Castle, where the Yorkist lords had planned to rendezvous. The plan was to go together to the King at Kenilworth at the head of their combined armies and lay their grievances before him.

The Queen's soldiers got to Warwick before the Earl did. He lacked enough men for a confrontation, and his scouts warned him that the King's army was marching north from Coventry and blocking any chance of him linking up with Salisbury. Warwick therefore had no choice but to turn west towards Ludlow, where York's army waited.

On the way, at Coleshill, Warwick was warned that the Queen and Somerset had sent a sizeable West Country force to intercept him. Just in time he managed to avoid it, and continued on his way. Salisbury, meanwhile, had left Middleham with a considerable following and, 'dreading the malice of the Queen and her company, which hated him deadly, took his way towards Ludlow'. No longer did the Yorkist lords entertain ideas of an appeal to the King. Their objective now was to combine their forces and march on London.

Margaret was recruiting in Cheshire when she learned of Salisbury's advance, and she and her commanders decided to intercept him as he marched through Staffordshire on his way to meet York. The Queen now issued a summons to Lord Stanley and other local magnates, commanding them to muster their retainers at once and join the King; then she turned back to Eccleshall Castle, where Henry joined her, having suffered a bout of illness at Coleshill. Margaret persuaded him that he must send 'a great power' of Cheshiremen, nominally under the command of the Prince of Wales but in reality led by James Touchet, Lord Audley, and Lord Dudley, to confront and apprehend Salisbury before he linked up with York. The main body of the royal army was to march to Eccleshall and remain with the Queen, where Audley was to bring Salisbury to her, alive or dead.

Of the two commanders Salisbury was by far the more

experienced and he had with him approximately 3-4000 well-armed men, possibly more. However, he was outnumbered by Audley's force, which comprised 6-12,000 men at least – the sources differ wildly and it is difficult to determine more exact figures. Salisbury's men were armed mainly with spears and bills and some cannon, but while Audley had many of the crack archers from Cheshire, whose reputation went before them, a lot of his recruits were inexperienced and ill-prepared for battle. Lord Stanley had asked the Queen if he might command the forward battle of her army, but the Prince's council thought his fellowship was too small and ordered him to join the main body of Audley's force. Piqued, he stayed where he was, six miles off, sending only 'fair promises' to Audley that he would join him. When he failed to do so, Audley and Dudley were left 'distressed', especially when they learned that Stanley's brother William had sent a detachment of soldiers to assist Salisbury.

On Sunday, 23 September Salisbury was approaching Market Drayton from Newcastle-under-Lyme when his scouts warned him that his route was blocked by Audley's army. He therefore drew up his forces in battle order on nearby Blore Heath, which was partly wooded and enclosed terrain. His centre wing was stationed on a small slope above the Hempmill Brook, while the left flank was concealed behind a hill protected by a stream. The weather was wet and the ground muddy, but the Earl set his men to digging ditches behind their line and driving sharpened stakes at an angle into the ground in front of the ditches. As an added precaution he ordered that the carts and wagons carrying the army's provisions be placed in a circle around his right flank as a protection against Audley's archers. He was now in a good defensive position; knowing himself outnumbered he realised that to take the offensive would be to court disaster.

When Audley's army approached, says Benet, 'Salisbury entered into negotiations with them, asking that they might permit his passage. When they refused to allow this, the Earl engaged in battle with them.' In fact, Salisbury seems to have feigned preparations for an advance or a retreat in order to lure Audley into ordering a charge. The ruse worked: Audley sent his cavalry thundering across the brook against the Yorkist centre, but it was repelled and had to fall back. Salisbury's men also retreated some way from the brook. Audley's horse charged again, and this time they breached the brook, which was no mean feat as it was a narrow stream with steep banks. Those in the vanguard of Audley's army dismounted and led their horses across, but as they climbed the far bank, Salisbury ordered his infantry to bear down on them. As the remaining Lancastrian cavalry galloped towards the brook, they were met with a hail of arrows from the Yorkist ranks, which shot their horses from under them and so unnerved the riders that 500 of them defected at once to the enemy. This was a blow to Audley, but he had little time in which to reflect upon it, for chaos now reigned on the battlefield.

After a fierce and bloody struggle on the slope, Audley's line broke and his men fled, being pursued by the Yorkists as far as the banks of the River Tern. During the rout Audley and many of his captains were brutally slain, and Lord Dudley was taken prisoner. After Audley's death many of his men deserted and returned to their homes.

By careful strategy and forethought, Salisbury had – against the odds – won a victory. The battle had lasted from one o'clock until five in the afternoon, but the rout went on until seven the next morning. About 3000 men perished, at least 2000 of them on Audley's side, and many were maimed or captured. Salisbury's cannon had been responsible for numerous fatalities, and a plaque in nearby Mucklestone Church records that for three days after the battle the Hempmill Brook ran red with blood. Legend has it that the Queen and the Prince watched the fighting from the tower of Mucklestone Church, their presence being commemorated by a modern stained glass window, while in the churchyard visitors may see an ancient anvil from a forge where the Queen was said to have had her horse's shoes reversed so that she could escape pursuit after Audley's defeat. However, it is unlikely that Margaret was in Mucklestone at all on that day, for the village was behind the Yorkist lines; she was probably awaiting news at Eccleshall Castle, ten miles away.

Today, it is hard to locate the site of Blore Heath. The decayed stone cross, erected in 1765 on the spot where Audley is said to have fallen, is concealed in a field to the left of the road leading from Newcastle-under-Lyme to Market Drayton, halfway up the slope where Salisbury's men were drawn up. The battlefield itself is on privately owned farmland.

After the battle the remnants of Audley's army fled to Eccleshall Castle, following the path of the brook. Henry VI was shocked and saddened to learn of the death of Audley and the defeat of his army, and was roused to anger against the Yorkists.

Salisbury wanted to press on to join York as soon as possible, but was aware that the Queen's main force was only ten miles away and would soon come after him. It was now nearing night, and very dark. The Earl cunningly entrusted his cannon to an Augustinian friar, who agreed to fire them off intermittently throughout the night, leading the Lancastrians to believe that the Yorkists were still encamped on Blore Heath. They did not discover the truth until the next morning, when the King and Queen rode over at the head of their army, determined to surprise Salisbury's force. All they found was the deserted camp, the frightened friar, and the battlefield strewn with corpses, and all they could do was order the capture of the Yorkist cannon. Salisbury, meanwhile, had gone to Market Drayton, where he camped that night.

Here he received a congratulatory message from the perfidious Lord Stanley, who promised he would secretly continue to support the Yorkists. The Queen had been angered by Stanley's failure to arrive on the battlefield with reinforcements, and had him impeached in Parliament for it, but her anger was short-lived, and she afterwards pardoned him.

Salisbury's triumph was short-lived. While he was at Market Drayton he learned that two of his sons, Sir Thomas and Sir John Neville, had been captured by the Lancastrians at Acton Bridge in Cheshire. Possibly they were searching for a safe house to rest in after being wounded at Blore Heath. Salisbury waited as long as he dared for further news of them before disconsolately pressing on. He left behind one of Sir William Stanley's cooks, who had been wounded fighting for him. When Shrewsbury's troops occupied Market Drayton later that day, they interrogated the man as to Salisbury's whereabouts, and he told them which road the Earl had taken.

Salisbury, however, arrived safely at Ludlow, followed soon after by Warwick. York had heard that the royal army, allegedly 30,000 strong, was advancing rapidly towards them. The Queen was bent on routing out the Yorkists and taking them prisoner, and her recruits were ready to fight 'for the love they bare to the King, but more for the fear they had of the Queen, whose countenance was so fearful and whose look was so terrible that to all men against whom she took displeasure, her frowning was their undoing and her indignation their death'.

The Yorkists led their great army, 25,000 strong, out of Ludlow, and marched towards Worcester, making for London, but the royal army blocked their way; the two came face to face on the road between Kidderminster and Worcester. While the royal army was being drawn up in battle order, with the King's standard displayed to proclaim his presence, York ordered a retreat into Worcester, having no desire to engage in battle with an army under the direct command of his sovereign. In Worcester Cathedral the Yorkist lords, after receiving the Sacrament, publicly swore an oath to render obedience and respect to the King's estate. This promise was enshrined on vellum and given to a deputation of clergy headed by the Prior of Worcester to take to the King, although Henry, under the influence of the Queen, ignored it.

When the King pursued him to Worcester, York moved on to Tewkesbury. Henry sent the Bishop of Salisbury to him, offering the Yorkist lords a pardon if they submitted, but they knew that to do so would put an end to all they had fought for, and Warwick publicly declined the offer. As the King then advanced on Tewkesbury, York crossed the River Severn, making for Ludlow and anxious to protect his Marcher lordships from possible sacking by the royal army. By protecting his own, however, York was forced to abandon his plans for cultivating wider support in the kingdom at large.

Having reached Ludlow, the Yorkist army encamped south of the town on the shore of the River Tern, near Ludford Bridge, an early fifteenth-century structure. On York's orders, his men fortified their chosen ground with carts and cannon, and laid ambushes and traps to halt the progress of the royal army. They also dug ditches and erected a palisade of stakes. On the evening of 10 October the King's army finally arrived, pitched its tents, and drew itself up in battle order.

By this time morale in the Yorkist ranks was low. Their leaders had no desire to engage in a war with the King, in fact their chief intent was to negotiate, not to fight. That evening they wrote to Henry VI suing for peace, protesting their loyalty to the Crown and their commitment to 'the prosperity of your common weal of this realm. Hereto we have avoided all things that might serve to the effusion of Christian blood, of the dread that we have of God and of your royal Majesty.' But they then referred to 'the great and lamentable complaints of your true, poor subjects, of robberies, ravishments, extortions, oppressions, riots, unlawful assemblies, wrongful imprisonments, universally throughout every part of your realm. Your said true subjects suffer such wrongs without remedy.' As for themselves, 'our lordships and tenants been of high violence robbed and spoiled'. The letter, however, was intercepted by servants of the Queen, who forged a reply saying that King Henry would meet his enemies in the field.

The King, meanwhile, wishing to avoid further bloodshed, had sent a herald to the Yorkists to proclaim a free pardon to anyone, except Salisbury, who would return to their allegiance within six days. In the dead of night, Andrew Trollope, who had served under Henry V, defected to the King with all his men, persuaded, according to Waurin, by a secret message from Somerset. The next morning, when York discovered them gone, he was desperately worried, not only because Trollope's men had been the best of his fighting force and been designated his advance guard, but also because Trollope could tell the royal commanders details of his army and planned strategies.

The King had between 40,000 and 60,000 men as well as a very considerable number of magnates, including Somerset and Northumberland, the latter's brother, Thomas, Lord Egremont, Buckingham, Exeter, Devon, Arundel, Shrewsbury, Wiltshire and Beaumont. All these lords had retinues and fellowships with them, and many would be rewarded for their services on this campaign. Henry had had weeks in which to recruit at leisure, while Warwick and Salisbury had not, and the Yorkists consequently had a smaller force of between 20,000 and 30,000 soldiers, some inadequately armed. Apart from March, York's seventeen-year-old heir, Lord Clinton and Lord Powys, the Yorkist lords had no other aristocratic support. York had expected to be joined by Sir William Herbert, but the Queen had persuaded him to remain loyal to Henry VI.

Many of the Duke's men were overawed at the sight of the royal standard fluttering at the other side of the bridge, and began to have second thoughts about where their loyalties lay. Some laid down their arms there and then and raced to join the King's army. York had to resort to desperate measures in an attempt to raise the spirits of his remaining troops, and announced that he had just heard news of the King's death, even producing witnesses and ordering masses to be sung. But the Queen was taking care to ensure that Henry was highly visible to all, and York's ploy was soon seen for what it was, losing him credibility with many of his men.

Buckingham persuaded the King to repeat his offer of a pardon, but as it was being proclaimed at the town gates, the Yorkist lords gave the signal for their guns to be fired at the royal lines. Even as the reports sounded, there were mass desertions from the Yorkist ranks, which led to panic among those remaining, many of whom now fled. Meanwhile, Henry VI, according to the official account in the Rolls of Parliament, had for once been rallying his army with a rousing speech, 'so witty, so knightly, so manly, with so princely apport and assured manner, of which the lords and the people took such joy and comfort that all their desire was to hasten to fulfil his courageous knightly desire'.

The situation was now hopeless for the Yorkists. At midnight on 12 October, York, Salisbury and Warwick announced to their captains that they were going into Ludlow to refresh themselves, and left their army drawn up in battle order with their standards and banners displayed. As soon as they were out of sight they fled, taking a few followers with them. Their desertion of their men at such a crucial time was regarded by their contemporaries as a cowardly and dishonourable act. On the morning of the 13th the remnants of the Yorkist army were obliged to kneel before the King and beg for mercy. Henry dismissed them; his quarrel was not with ordinary soldiers.

Now the Lancastrians streamed across the bridge and occupied the town of Ludlow, arresting many of York's chief supporters (who would later purchase their freedom) and systematically sacking the town and York's castle, robbing it of many of its treasures and furnishings. The royal soldiers ran out of control, drinking the taverns dry and smiting the heads off the pipes and hogsheads of wine, so that everywhere people were obliged to slosh through spilt drink and vomit. In a drunken frenzy armed men raided the houses of the townsfolk and stole away bedding, cloth and other goods. Then they turned to raping and assaulting the women.

York had not only abandoned his troops but also his duchess, who was powerless to stop the King's soldiers from sacking Ludlow Castle. When the soldiers stormed into the market place of the town, they found the Duchess of York, proud and stiff, holding the hands of her two youngest sons, George, aged eleven, and Richard, aged seven, and her thirteen-year-old daughter Margaret, all standing by the market cross. The Duchess was placed under arrest and consigned to the house and care of her sister, the Duchess of Buckingham, the King assigning 1000 marks a year for her maintenance during her captivity.

After Ludlow had been 'robbed to the bare walls', the King's men ransacked all the property of the Yorkist lords between there and Worcester, leaving their estates devastated.

Henry and Margaret had returned, meanwhile, triumphant to Coventry, where they disbanded their army, then rode to Worcester. It had not been an easy campaign. Food was in short supply and the King had shared the discomfort of his men, only resting on Sundays and sometimes lodging in a bare field with them, regardless of the weather. It was felt by the Lancastrians that the rout of Ludford had cancelled out Salisbury's victory at Blore Heath, and that the Yorkists were finished, though the royal victory was by no means decisive, for the Yorkist leaders were still at large and could strike at any time. Nor did the King have much chance of capturing any of them.

York had fled south to Devon, then sailed north to Wales, and crossed from there to Ireland, taking with him his son Rutland. Whethamstead says that when York arrived in Ireland, he was received like a second Messiah, although, like Ulysses, he longed to return home. Salisbury, Warwick and March made their way, by devious means, to Calais, arriving in early November. Soon afterwards, they were joined by Warwick's wife and two young daughters, Isabel and Anne.

Once in Calais, the Yorkist lords, accompanied by the loyal men of the garrison, plundered the countryside round about and took to piracy in the Channel, seizing or harrying merchant ships. They also began a hostile campaign against the English government, placing restrictions on English ships coming to Calais and disseminating virulent propaganda claiming they were the victims of the King's evil counsellors.

With York, Salisbury and Warwick out of the way, 'the Queen and those of her affinity ruled the realm as her liked, gathering riches innumerable,' states Davies' Chronicle.

> The officers of the realm, especially Wiltshire, Treasurer of England, for to enrich himself, peeled the poor people and disinherited rightful heirs, and did many wrongs. In this time the realm of England was out of all good governance, for the King was simple and led by covetous counsel, and owed more than he was worth. For these misgovernances, the hearts of the people were turned away from them that had the governance of the land, and their blessings were turned to cursing.

Margaret was again 'defamed and slandered, that he that was called Prince was not her son but a bastard gotten in adultery'.

Yorkist propaganda claimed that the Queen had persuaded the King to appeal secretly to Charles VII for military aid against York, and as Brézé's agent Dolcereau had been with Margaret during the recent campaign, it is likely that this was true and that she was indeed using Brézé as a go-between in the negotiations; he was still her friend, could be counted upon to support her, and by the end of 1459 he had certainly committed himself to her cause.

On 20 November Parliament, having been summoned at short notice, assembled at Coventry, packed solidly with the Queen's supporters, for which reason it became known as 'the Parliament of Devils'. As York had not submitted to the King, Margaret commanded Parliament to arraign him and his associates on a charge of high treason. A Bill of Attainder was drawn up that same day, in which York, Salisbury, Warwick, March, Rutland, Clinton, Wenlock, the Bourchier brothers, Sir William Stanley, Sir William Oldhall and others were all declared guilty of high treason and sentenced to forfeiture of their lives, estates, titles, honours and chattels. Should any of them return to England they would face arrest and the death penalty unless the King pardoned them. Duchess Cecily had been brought into Parliament and was made to witness her husband's humiliation. After the attainder was passed the sentence was proclaimed throughout England.

The confiscated estates, comprising a vast amount of landed wealth, were then distributed by the King and Queen among their supporters, a generous share going to Owen Tudor and his son Pembroke, who afterwards returned to Wales to stamp out Yorkist resistance there and prevent York from returning via the principality to England. Lord Clifford was given several lucrative offices that had been held by the Yorkist lords, and Somerset was appointed Captain of Calais in place of Warwick – a title he would hold in name only, as Warwick was still in possession of the town. Wiltshire became Lieutenant of Ireland, but York was already in control there and the Irish parliament was resolved to protect him, confirming him in that post and passing legislation to provide that anyone seeking his death or inciting rebellion against him would be deemed guilty of high treason. When Wiltshire sent a messenger to Dublin with a royal writ for the Duke's arrest, the hapless emissary was immediately charged with treason, brought to trial before York and sentenced to be hanged, drawn and quartered.

In the Parliament at Coventry, the magnates were obliged to swear a new oath of allegiance to Henry VI, which had been altered to include vows of fidelity to the Queen and the Prince of Wales also. The new oath was sworn by the archbishops of Canterbury and York, sixteen bishops, including George Neville, Bishop of Exeter, the dukes of Exeter, Norfolk and Buckingham, five earls and twenty-two barons. Parliament also assigned all revenues from the city of Coventry to the Queen, to be used for the benefit of the Prince, although she took this to include financing her war against the Yorkists. After Parliament's business was concluded she remained in Coventry for the winter.

Somerset was determined to drive Warwick from Calais and establish himself as its Captain. The desertion of Trollope and his men at Ludford Bridge had proved that not all members of the Calais garrison were loyal to Warwick. However, the majority were, and

Warwick also enjoyed the confidence of the Merchants of the Staple: Somerset would have to break that friendship before he could oust his rival. Margaret, exasperated by Warwick's tortuous political manoeuvring between Burgundy and France and realising that his presence in Calais posed a very real threat to her rule, was urging Somerset to action, and he therefore took ship with an army of retainers and attempted to land in Calais. The garrison remained loyal to Warwick, and the gates of the town were firmly shut to him. To make matters worse, Burgundy was showing friendship to the Yorkist lords, concluding a three-month truce with them so as to give them a chance to prepare for a new onslaught on England.

Warwick retaliated by impudently mounting a lightning raid on Sandwich, where some of the Duke's soldiers were stationed. Then, in November, Somerset arrayed an army of a thousand men under Trollope, and sailed again to the Calais Pale. This time he succeeded in capturing Guisnes Castle, an English stronghold near Calais. Warwick, in turn, captured Somerset's most important commanders, the new Lord Audley and Humphrey Stafford, while another, Lord Roos, deserted and returned to England. Somerset now had a base in the region, and from Guisnes he waged constant petty warfare on Warwick in Calais.

Back in England the Queen was furious to learn of Warwick's defiance and began raising reinforcements for Somerset. On 6 December some of Warwick's ships were seized and made secure at Sandwich, and four days later Lord Rivers and Sir Gervase Clifton began mustering a fleet and men nearby. The Council were at this time under the impression that the Yorkist lords lacked the resources to maintain themselves, let alone raise an army to invade England, but at the same time the government itself was at a disadvantage because it was now winter and the campaigning season was past. Nor were there sufficient funds left to finance a new enterprise.

In December, Master Judd, Master of the King's Ordnance, was commanded to survey the ordnance at all castles and fortified towns and ensure that it was in a good state of repair. The government ordered the arrest of any of the Yorkist lords the moment they set foot in England, and placed an embargo on trade with Calais, which was supposed to protect merchant shipping from piracy but in fact had a disastrous effect on the wool trade. When the Council tried to raise money for a new campaign, it was again accused of extortion, and London angrily refused to supply any soldiers for the King. To counteract the city's defiance the Council sent a priest to preach at Paul's Cross, 'charging the people that no man should pray for these lords, the traitors', but 'he had little thanks, as he deserved'.

On 21 December the government issued new commissions of array, but the mood of the people was ugly, and the loyalties of many were with the Yorkists. The hapless Master Judd, on his way back to London, was brutally murdered near St Albans. The Queen was aware of the public sympathy York enjoyed and feared that he might take advantage of this to press his claim to the throne, since he now had nothing to lose by so doing. The government dared not risk such a test of the people's loyalty.

In January 1460, Lord Rivers, his wife the Duchess of Bedford, and their son Anthony Wydville were lodged in Sandwich, where Rivers was assembling a fleet for the invasion of Calais. But before dawn on 15 January, Sir John Dynham, acting on orders from Warwick, landed without warning and occupied the town, gaining possession of several of Warwick's ships and capturing Rivers and his wife as they lay in bed; they also captured 300 of Rivers's men. All of them were hauled off to Calais, and Dynham's men also apprehended Anthony Wydville as he came riding into Sandwich to go to his father's aid.

When the Wydvilles arrived in Calais, the Yorkist lords kept them from entering the town until evening because they did not want them to excite the sympathies of the inhabitants. They were then held in captivity until 28 January, when they were brought before Warwick, Salisbury and March in a hall illuminated by 160 torches. According to the Paston Letters, the Yorkists began to abuse them, and Salisbury turned on Rivers,

> calling him knave's son, that he should be so rude to call him and these other lords traitors, for they shall be found the King's true liege men, when he [Rivers] should be found a traitor. And my lord of Warwick rated him and said that his father was but a squire and made by marriage, and that it was not his part to have such language of lords being of the King's blood. And my lord of March rated him in like wise.

Late in January Rivers's wife was allowed to return to England. The capture of her commander had caused great distress to Margaret of Anjou, and the government believed that his abduction heralded a Yorkist invasion and continued its efforts to raise an army. It was also provoked into tightening coastal defences and enlarging the navy. In fact, for the first five months of 1460 the Council was in a state of nervous tension, occupied with plans to re-take Calais and counteract any Yorkist invasion.

Pembroke was granted control of York's castle of Denbigh because the Council feared the Duke might make use of it as a centre of communication between himself and his supporters in England and Wales. Owen Tudor was also given a command at Denbigh, but York's retainers refused to surrender the castle. Pembroke besieged it, and it fell to him at last in May. He then rode on to Pembroke, to ensure that its defences were also in good order.

Late in January the Council issued commissions of array to the men of Kent, who were to join the King's army in the north. On 1 February Sir Baldwin Fulford was empowered to keep the seas, his objective being to destroy Warwick's fleet at Calais, but before his ships were ready to leave England's shores, the government received word that Warwick had gone to meet York in Ireland. He arrived there by 16 March. As soon as he had left Calais, Somerset made another futile attempt to breach the town's defences, but in a bitter struggle at Newnham Bridge many of his men were killed.

The Council seized the opportunity afforded by Warwick's absence to reappoint Exeter Admiral of England for a period of three years. It also requested the aid of a Venetian flotilla then at anchor in the Thames. The ships' masters all hurriedly disembarked and disappeared, not wishing to become involved, and the Council, thwarted, ordered the arrest of all Venetian merchants resident in London. By the end of April, despite a number of setbacks, the Council felt it was prepared to deal with a Yorkist invasion.

Throughout the winter, spring and summer of 1459–60, York and his allies were indeed planning a return, and were determined to launch one final, decisive offensive against the court party. Warwick's allies in England had made him aware of the government's unpopularity, and York's affinity had been rousing support for him in Wales. When Warwick visited York at Waterford in Ireland, they formulated plans for a two-pronged invasion of England, to be preceded by the now customary propaganda campaign. Then York was to land in the north, and the other Yorkist lords in Kent, where they would be sure of a welcome.

The Council soon discovered what was afoot and anticipated that Warwick would choose to invade through Kent. Exeter was provided with a new and efficient fleet of ships, and these were moored at Sandwich. On 23 May the Council appointed Osbert Mountfort, who had been Marshal of Calais in 1452, and one John Baker to raise and escort a body of reinforcements whose task would be to assist Somerset to escape from the Calais Pale. At Sandwich,

Mountfort recruited several hundred men, but was then held up as he waited for the wind to change.

Meanwhile, on the 25th, Exeter had sailed from Sandwich with fifteen ships and 1500 men to intercept Warwick. People in Kent and Sussex were looking daily for the Yorkist invasion force; the corporation of Rye paid 6d. to one John Pampelon to sail to Camber to see if anyone there had news of Warwick's coming. On 1 June, Exeter and his fleet lay off the coast of Cornwall. From here he could see Warwick's ships in the distance as they returned to Calais from Ireland. Exeter had far more ships, but by now he was not sure of his men who, disgruntled at short rations and poor wages, were openly voicing Yorkist sympathies. Consequently the Duke put in at Dartmouth and dismissed most of them. This left him with hardly anyone to man his fleet, since the government had failed to provide him with any money for new recruits. The Channel was now Warwick's.

After Warwick's return there in June, Yorkist supporters gathered in Calais. Many of the garrison would rather have driven Somerset out of the Pale than invade England, but Warwick overruled them. The Merchants of the Staple loaned the Earl and his allies a total of £18,000, and by committing acts of piracy against foreign merchant shipping Warwick raised further funds for the invasion, as well as boosting his popularity with the Londoners. He and the other Yorkist lords also mounted an extensive propaganda campaign through their friends in England. In Ireland, Warwick and York had drawn up a manifesto outlining their grievances and their intentions, and this was widely distributed. In it they asserted that the King was still led by evil counsellors, and castigated oppression by lords both spiritual and temporal. Henry, they said, had put himself above the law and banished 'all righteousness and justice' from the realm. The manifesto alleged that the King had been persuaded by his advisers to incite the native Irish to rebel against York; York even claimed to have seen letters from Henry urging them to conquer Ireland. It further alleged that the King had, by proclamations, guaranteed to all the men of Cheshire and Lancashire who fought for him that they would be allowed to take what they liked 'and make havoc' in the south, thus fuelling the southern prejudice against northerners. Clement Paston wrote: 'The people in the north rob and steal, and [have] been appointed to pillage all this country and give away men's goods and livelihood, and that will ask a mischief in all the south.' So successful was this particular piece of propaganda that proclamations were hastily issued in the names of the Queen and the Prince of Wales denying that the King had ever made such promises.

The Yorkist lords, says the chronicler 'Gregory', also 'sent letters unto many places in England how they were advised to reform the hurts and mischiefs and griefs that reigned in this land; and that caused them much the more to be loved by the commons of Kent and of London; and the commons of Kent sent them word to receive them and go with them in that attempt, and the most part of the land had pity that they were attaint and proclaimed traitors'. In fact, the Yorkists were putting it about that the King had not freely consented to the attainders passed the previous November, and that therefore his subjects need not obey the royal commissions of array.

They also wrote an open letter to the Archbishop of Canterbury accusing Shrewsbury, Wiltshire, Beaumont and other lords of preventing them from gaining access to the King and procuring their attainders, and stating that they would again request an audience of Henry to declare the 'mischiefs' for which these men were responsible. In this and other letters they asked for help, and assured everyone of their faithful allegiance to their sovereign.

This propaganda fell on fertile ground, for the commons were sick to death of misrule and readier than ever to support a loyal opposition. Only recently concern had been expressed in Parliament about the increasing violence and anarchy in English society, and there were continual complaints about riots, extortion and robberies, particularly in the north and south-west of England and in Wales. When the King ordered trade links with Calais to be severed, the people of Kent – already resentful of a government that constantly demanded men for service at unseasonable times of the year – were vociferous in their complaints. Few people in the south-east were ready to fight against their hero Warwick, who was perceived as a champion of Englishmen's rights against foreigners. Again, seditious bills were nailed to church doors, especially in London; these demanded the recall of York or repeated the old allegations about the Prince's paternity, some in the form of bawdy verses.

The King, for once, was not being idle. In late May he was to be found at Coventry, taking an interest in preparations for the defence of his realm. The Council had decided to appoint the royal castle of Kenilworth, which was well-moated and maintained, as his chief military base, and Henry rode there to see new fortifications being erected. He also sent for all the guns and armaments in the Tower of London, which filled forty carts; these would accompany the royal army throughout the coming campaign.

On 11 June a royal proclamation was issued, asserting that the King had consented freely to the Yorkists' attainders and commanding all men to obey the royal summons to array. Coventry supplied forty men, but the King was aware that it had also sent men to the Yorkists in the past. He noted – and complained about – disaffection and disloyalty among the citizens there and 'unfitting language against our estate', and the mayor was commanded to investigate these and punish all offenders.

The Queen and Prince were with the King at Coventry. Edward, now six and a half, had recently been 'committed to the rule and teaching of men', his governess, Lady Lovell, having been dismissed in March. But it was the Queen who remained the dominant influence in his life and who instilled in him her own ideals and prejudices.

The King and court remained at Coventry until at least 26 June, probably because the Council expected York to invade through Wales. York, however, was biding his time.

16

The Paper Crown

In June 1460 Lord Fauconberg, Sir John Dynham, and Sir John Wenlock crossed from Calais and occupied Sandwich, where they installed a large garrison and, with the willing assistance of the townsfolk, established a bridgehead for Warwick. Fauconberg also took Osbert Mountfort – still awaiting a fair wind – prisoner. The way was now clear for a Yorkist invasion of England.

On 26 June, Warwick, Salisbury and March landed at Sandwich with 2000 men. The Queen had sent ships to Calais to prevent them from sailing out of the harbour, but her sailors had mutinied and the Yorkist ships had passed unmolested. The Lancastrian government had long anticipated an invasion, but their preparations to counteract it proved inadequate; even Buckingham, who was constable of Dover Castle and Warden of the Cinque Ports, was absent from the area on the day the invaders landed, and seems to have taken few – if any – defensive measures.

Warwick knew the risks he was taking. His lands and the main spheres of his influence lay to the north and west, and before he could reach them he had to take London. Nor could he be certain of support from the magnates. But Warwick was held in much affection in south-east England. 'If aught come to my lord of Warwick but good, farewell ye, farewell I, and all our friends, for this land were utterly undone,' wrote a friend of the Pastons at this time. Hours after Warwick landed in Kent, Lords Cobham and Bergavenny rode to join him as he marched on Canterbury, as did numerous men of lesser rank.

On landing at Sandwich, Warwick had sent messengers to the other Cinque Ports, asking for assistance in the form of armed men and stressing that he came to remove the evil counsellors about the King. The mayor of Rye, receiving his message, cautiously sent to see if the mayor of Winchelsea was going to comply. Apparently the answer was yes, for both men led contingents from their towns to join the Yorkists. Archbishop Bourchier, who had hitherto acted as mediator between the opposing sides, was now heartily sickened of the Queen's misrule and was urging the men of Kent to rally to Warwick's banner, which they did in large numbers.

The Yorkist lords made their way that day to Canterbury. The Council had appointed three of its citizens to lead the defence of the city against the invaders, but the people of Canterbury were overwhelmingly Yorkist in sympathy and at dawn on the 27th these men met with the Yorkist lords at St Martin's Church, outside the walls, and agreed to surrender the keys of the city to them. Canterbury then joyfully opened its gates and afforded the invaders a warm welcome.

After Warwick, Salisbury and March had offered at the shrine of Becket and received the blessing of the Archbishop of Canterbury – who agreed to ride with them – they pressed on through Rochester and Dartford towards London, recruiting as they went. In their train was the papal legate, Francesco dei Coppini, Bishop of Terni. During the previous spring, Coppini had been sent to England by Pope Pius II to effect a reconciliation between the rival factions and 'quieten the people', so that England could provide him with men for a new crusade against the Turks. The Queen had not been interested in Coppini's offer to mediate, guessing that his sympathies lay with the Yorkists. This was true, but only because the Lancastrians had rebuffed him. The legate dearly wanted a cardinal's hat, and if his mission was successful he might obtain one. If he helped the Yorkists to power they might reward him by supporting the crusade. Coppini had with him 'papal bulls stating that the Pope had excommunicated Wiltshire, Shrewsbury and Beaumont and all others who had opposed the Duke [of York]'. His open support of the Yorkists swayed the opinions of several English bishops, who felt that they should follow the Pope's lead.

News of the invasion had reached London, and the mayor, aldermen and Common Council met to debate what they should do. At length they dispatched a messenger to warn the Yorkist lords that they would not be allowed to enter the capital. Warwick, however, had many supporters in London; merchants who had suffered as a result of the government's concessions to foreign traders were especially anxious to further his cause, and through their influence the Lord Mayor was persuaded to rescind his order. He may also have been swayed by the proximity and activities of several lords in or near the city – Bourchier, Bergavenny, Clinton, Say and Scrope –

who were preparing to join Warwick. At the end of June the Yorkist lords were informed that they could enter London provided their soldiers behaved themselves.

As the Yorkist army approached, prominent Lancastrians who were in the city, the Lords Hungerford, de Vesci, Lovell, de la Warre, the Earl of Kendal and the Duchess of Exeter, took refuge in the Tower of London, which was under the command of Lord Scales, a veteran of the French wars who deplored the decision of the city authorities to let in the Yorkists.

On 2 July, the gates of London were thrown open and the Yorkist lords rode into the city with a vast band of armed men. Estimates of their numbers vary between 20,000 and 60,000; the real figure, based on the evidence of Whethamstead and the London chroniclers, is likely to have been around 40,000, and at least 500 of them were on horseback. As the army began its progress across London Bridge, crowds of Londoners surged forward in welcome and two men were trampled to death. Lord Scales fired guns from the Tower, and during the next few days he would continue to do so, burning and hurting men, women and children in the streets but causing no harm to the enemy.

The first thing that the Yorkist earls did was to order the removal of the rotting heads of their supporters from London Bridge. On 3 July they addressed the Convocation of Canterbury at St Paul's Cathedral, emphasising the misrule of the Queen's party and reciting 'the cause of their coming into the land, how they had been put forth from the King's presence with great violence, so that they might never excuse themselves of the accusations laid against them'. They swore on oath on the Cross of Canterbury that they intended nothing contrary to the estate of King Henry, declaring that they wished only to lay their case before him in person and protest their innocence; they were, they said, prepared to die for their cause. But Coppini, in a letter to Pius II, wrote that, despite the strictures of Holy Church and his own role as an angel of peace, Warwick, Salisbury and March appeared ready to resort to armed force rather than peaceful negotiations in order to have their way.

On the 4th Coppini himself addressed Convocation, reading out a letter from the Pope to Henry VI, summarising and pleading York's case. The letter was afterwards presented to the King along with one from the legate, commanding Henry, on peril of his soul, to consent to the Yorkist demands.

The Yorkist lords were determined that this time they would gain control of the King and oust the court party for good. On the 5th Lord Fauconberg left London at the head of 10,000 men for the north. The Lancastrians were still anticipating that York would invade from Ireland and were therefore reluctant to move south to defend London, in case he raised Wales and the north behind them. Warwick and March soon followed Fauconberg north, leaving Salisbury, Cobham, Wenlock and 2000 men in London to lay siege to the Tower and hold the capital. In their train were the Archbishop of Canterbury, the bishops of Ely, Exeter, Rochester, Lincoln and Salisbury, the papal legate Coppini and the Prior of the Hospital of St John at Clerkenwell. They made first for St Albans, and then for Dunstable. Wet weather had made the roads virtually impassable, yet still men came to join them.

The King's commanders urged him to seek refuge in the Isle of Ely in the then almost impenetrable Fens, but the Yorkists somehow learned of this plan and moved their army to Ware, ready to intercept the royal army before it could evade them. There was no sign of it: Henry had in fact ignored his captains' advice and remained in Coventry, where the Queen had gathered a large army, and he now planned to march on Northampton. As he bade farewell to his wife and child, he kissed the Prince and commanded Margaret for her safety, not to join him unless she received from him a secret token known only to themselves. When the army left, Margaret rode with the Prince to Eccleshall Castle to await events.

The royal army encamped in a meadow outside Northampton, between the village of Hardingstone and Delapré Abbey. Here, the men dug deep ditches around the whole encampment, made a defensive palisade of sharp stakes, and blocked the road from London with cannon. Then the commanders drew the men up in battle order. They were not in the best strategic position because the nearby River Nene, then in flood due to two days of constant heavy rain, was not fordable and offered no means of escape in the event of a rout.

The commander-in-chief of the royal army, Buckingham, was probably anxious to get any battle over and done with as quickly as possible so that he could march on to London, relieve Lord Scales at the Tower and drive the Yorkists out of the capital. It was also imperative that Warwick and March be dealt with before they could be joined by York and Salisbury. Buckingham, however, certainly underestimated the military abilities of Warwick and the inexperienced March.

By Tuesday 10 July Warwick's army had arrived in Northampton. He now strove to avoid engaging the King in battle by sending the Bishop of Salisbury and Coppini to Henry with a request that he hear the grievances of the Yorkist lords. Henry refused, despite the added pleas of Archbishop Bourchier, and Buckingham accused the bishops of hypocrisy, brusquely advising the King to pay no heed to them. As far as he was concerned, the royal army was in an unassailable position and the King need not pander to traitors. A battle was now inevitable.

At mid-day the rain began again, rapidly turning the Lancastrian camp into a quagmire. Far from being unassailable, the royal army, which probably comprised 20,000 men, was only half the size of Warwick's force, and some expected reinforcements did not arrive in time to see action. Warwick was in command of the main battle of the Yorkist army; March, bearing aloft his father's banner, led the vanguard, ably supported by Lord Scrope, and Fauconberg was in charge of the rearguard. For the first time the Yorkists had mustered a substantial number of magnates – Bourchier, Bergavenny, Audley, Say, and possibly Clinton and Stanley were all present in the field, while most of the foot soldiers were from Kent, Sussex and Essex.

The royal vanguard was commanded by Lord Grey de Ruthin, a wealthy local landowner who had courted royal favour in the Coventry parliament and promptly ridden at the head of his retainers to obey the King's summons to arms. Prior to the battle, however, March received a secret message from Lord Grey that he would change sides and fight for the Yorkists if they would back him in a property dispute with Lord Fanhope. Grey may also have been offered inducements by Warwick, such as the promise of future high office in a Yorkist government, for he did indeed become Treasurer of England in 1463.

At two o'clock in the afternoon, watched by Coppini and the Archbishop of Canterbury, Warwick ordered his trumpeters to sound the call to battle, and the two armies advanced on each other, with the three Yorkist battles attacking the enemy simultaneously on different sides of the royal barricades. Warwick had ordered his men not to capture any magnates but to kill them, and not to lay violent hands on the King or the ordinary soldiers, especially those wearing the black ragged staff of Lord Grey's men.

March's advance across the Nene marshes was met with a deadly series of volleys from the archers in the Lancastrian centre, which caused many casualties. Despite this, they waded onwards through thick, viscous mud towards the royal entrenchment; the weather conditions were in fact so atrocious that Buckingham's cannon were soon lying deep in water and were rendered useless, while many of the royal cavalry were forced to dismount and fight on foot.

As the Yorkists approached the royal defences, Lord Grey signalled, and his men began to burst through the barricades in order to join them and assist them over the stockade, thus enabling them successfully to breach the Lancastrian entrenchment. This heralded the end of the battle, which lasted only half an hour and did not involve much in the way of hand-to-hand fighting. Seeing that the day was lost, many Lancastrian soldiers panicked and made desperate attempts to cross the swollen River Nene; few made it to the other side. The chronicler 'Gregory' relates the tale of Sir William Lucy, who lived near the battlefield and heard the desultory gunfire. He quickly hastened to the King's aid, but when he got there the rout was in progress. Alas for Sir William – John Stafford, a relation of Buckingham's, saw him coming. John had been conducting an illicit affair with Lucy's wife and now, in the chaos and confusion, seized his opportunity to murder his rival, an act typical of the lawlessness and self-interest of the times.

The Battle of Northampton ended in a resounding victory for the Yorkists, which was attributed to the fighting skills of 'the true commons of Kent', but was also due largely to the treachery of Lord Grey. About 3-400 men lay dead on the field, Lancastrian losses being heaviest. Buckingham, one of the mainstays of their cause, was among them. His son had predeceased him, and he was succeeded as second duke of Buckingham by his grandson, seven-year-old Henry Stafford. John, Viscount Beaumont, Constable of England, former steward to the Queen and one of her loyalest supporters, had also been killed, along with the Earl of Shrewsbury and Lord Egremont, who had been cut down by Warwick's Kentishmen outside the King's tent. Many Lancastrian casualties had drowned in the River Nene near Sandyford Mill. The dead were buried in nearby Delapré Abbey, which still stands, although much of its fabric dates from later periods. Yorkist losses were light. Today, little remains of the battlefield site, which is occupied by the Avon Cosmetics Company.

As the battle ended, Henry Mountfort, a Yorkist archer, captured the King and confined him to his tent. When it was clear that the day was theirs, Warwick, March and Fauconberg found him there alone, 'as a man born and predestinate to trouble, misery and calamity'. The three lords fell on their knees and craved the King's forgiveness for having taken up arms against him, emphasising that their only motive had been the desire to establish stable and just government, and assuring him of their continuing loyalty. Then March, who had not as yet sworn fealty to his sovereign, knelt and did him homage. For all their subservience, however, the Yorkist lords now had the

King in their custody. Later that day they conducted him in procession to Delapré Abbey and thence to Northampton. Meanwhile, Wiltshire and many other prominent Lancastrians had gone into hiding.

Queen Margaret had spent anxious days at Eccleshall Castle, awaiting news. When it came, it could not have been worse: the battle lost, many of her supporters dead or fled, and the King in the hands of the Yorkists, who would now control not only the sovereign but the government and the administrative departments of state. However, with the Queen and her son still at large, the Yorkists would have no scope for complacency.

Some Lancastrian prisoners taken in the battle, including the Lords Hungerford and Lovell, gave their captors the slip and rode to join the Queen, but others, including Lord de la Warre and the Earl of Kendal, transferred their loyalties to the Yorkists. Margaret decided it would be prudent to leave Eccleshall, and fled with her son and a few attendants through Cheshire to Wales. Near Malpas Castle, one of her servants, John Cleger, robbed her of her treasure and jewellery, and even threatened to kill her and the Prince, at which some of her retinue deserted her. However, as Cleger was rifling through her baggage, the Queen and her son managed to escape with the help of her remaining attendants and a courageous fourteen-year-old boy, John Coombe of Annesbury, with whom she and the Prince rode pillion to Jasper Tudor at Harlech Castle. Here she met with a warm welcome and was presented with many gifts. Her brother-in-law 'greatly comforted' her, 'for she had need thereof', though he was aware that he would not be able to shelter her for long.

Jasper was in control of York's castle of Denbigh, and he suggested that the Queen move there. 'Gregory' says she left Harlech by stealth 'for she durst abide in no place but in private' because 'counterfeit tokens were sent unto her, as though they had come from her most dread lord the King, but it was not of his sending, but forged things, for they that brought the tokens were of the King's house, and bade her beware that she gave no credence thereto, for the lords would fain had her unto London, for they knew well that all the workings that were done grew by her, for she was more wittier than the King'.

Giving out that she had gone to France to raise troops, Margaret went to Denbigh, where she was soon joined by Exeter and other prominent Lancastrians. On their advice, she now wrote to Somerset, Devon and other adherents, asking them to raise an army in the north and wait upon her at Hull. On 9 August, along with other royalist constables of Yorkist castles in Wales, Pembroke was ordered by the Yorkist Council to surrender Denbigh to York's deputy, Edward Bourchier. He refused, continuing to recruit Welshmen for the Queen and for the Prince of Wales, 'the hope of the British Isles', and York never regained his former supremacy in Wales.

In London, meanwhile, Salisbury, Cobham and the city's militia had besieged Lord Scales in the Tower, placing bombards and 'great ordnance' on the far side of the Thames and 'crazing the walls in divers places'. On 16 July, the King, escorted by the Yorkist earls, entered the City with a great retinue and was lodged in the bishop's palace, while Londoners 'gave Almighty God great thanks and praise' for the Yorkist victory. After nearly three weeks, Scales was ready to surrender. He was running out of food and had no hope of receiving any reinforcements; he had also given way to the panic-stricken pleas of the noble ladies who had sought refuge in the Tower. On the night after the surrender, Scales tried to escape by boat to the sanctuary at Westminster Abbey, but the London boatmen surrounded his vessel, dragged him out and murdered him, casting his bloody corpse, 'naked as a worm', on to the steps of the Priory of St Mary Overie in Southwark.

Queen Margaret had now left Denbigh and sailed from Wales around the coast to Berwick, intending to seek refuge in Scotland, where James II, whose mother had been a Beaufort, was a friend to the Lancastrians. The Scottish queen, Mary of Gueldres, advised of Margaret's coming, sent an envoy, Duncan Dundas, to escort her to Dumfries, where she and her son were warmly received. They were then lodged at Lincluden Abbey as guests of Queen Mary, and royally entertained there.

However, Scotland was just then in mourning because of the untimely death of its king, blown up by an exploding cannon while successfully besieging Yorkist sympathisers at Roxburgh. At the time of Margaret's arrival the regents were in Edinburgh for the late King's burial and the coronation of James III. James II's friendly relations with the House of Lancaster were to be maintained, however, by his widow and by the Bishop of St Andrews, who both headed the newly-formed regency council.

From Lincluden, Margaret wrote to Mary of Gueldres, begging for sanctuary and assistance against her enemies. Mary responded sympathetically and soon afterwards arrived at Lincluden with the young king to comfort Margaret and reassure her that help would be forthcoming. The two queens stayed at the abbey for twelve days, discussing what form that help would take. At length, Mary agreed to provide men and loan money for a campaign against the Yorkists on condition that Margaret surrendered the town of Berwick to the Scots. Margaret, having no understanding of the horror with which her husband's subjects would view this almost casual cession of one of the most fought-over border towns to their enemy, readily agreed. Mary then assigned the earls of Douglas and Angus to muster their retainers and accompany Margaret back into England. Such was the courage of the Queen that both these hardened warlords came to respect her; they were also gratified to hear her promise that there would be handsome booty for the taking in the prosperous south of England, so long as there was no pillaging and plundering north of the River Trent.

While these preparations for war were being completed, Mary invited Margaret to remain in Scotland, staying at Falkland Palace and other royal residences until she was ready to march into England.

York had in the past made several unsuccessful attempts to assume the role of chief counsellor to the King, to which he felt his birth and position as premier magnate of the realm entitled him. Now, after the success of the Yorkist lords' invasion, memories of previous short-lived triumphs convinced him that the only way to establish firm government and himself in power was to assert his right to the throne, thus reviving the long-dormant Mortimer claim.

By 1460, after long years of suffering the misrule caused by Henry VI's ineptitude, the English were beginning to question the right of the House of Lancaster to occupy the throne, and were showing signs of taking the claim of the Mortimers, vested in York, seriously. The whole issue of dynastic right would now be thrown open for public discussion and speculation. A Yorkist genealogy, prepared for propaganda purposes and now in the British Library, depicts Henry IV slicing through Richard II's line of descent with a sword, while an Old Testament prophet foretells of vengeance being visited upon Henry's descendants. Such seeds of propaganda fell on fertile ground in 1460.

York was descended from Edward III's second son through two females, Philippa of Clarence and Anne Mortimer, which made him Edward's heir general. Henry VI, descended in the male line from Edward's fourth son, was his heir male. Nowadays the question of legitimate right would be decided without question in favour of York, If, for example, the present Prince of Wales had an only daughter, and his brother Prince Andrew a son, the descendants of Prince Charles's daughter would inherit the throne as descendants of the Queen's eldest son. In the fifteenth century the law of primogeniture was never so strictly defined. Lord Chief Justice Fortescue put forward a hypothetical case in which a king 'has a daughter and a brother; the daughter has a son. The king dies without a son. Does the kingdom descend to the daughter, or to her son, or to the king's brother?' Fortescue concluded that the king's brother should succeed him because the woman is subject to the man. A woman, he declared, was not fit to rule or transmit a claim. Adam was superior to Eve because he was able to teach her the moral virtues of prudence, courage and temperance, and man was to woman as the soul to the body. When it came to the question of who should have the crown of England, however, Fortescue played it safe and suggested that the Pope should be asked to decide the issue.

York was not concerned with such legal niceties. He had had enough. His ineffective cousin must stand aside for the man who was determined and able to restore good government and rid the realm of corrupt advisers – Richard Plantagenet.

York, however, having failed to take into account the fact that hitherto few lords had actually supported him even in his quest for reform, did not now stop to consult with any of his followers or allies, nor did he try to cultivate sufficient support to back up his claim. He believed that right alone would be enough to win him the crown.

On 8 September 1460 York returned from Ireland and landed in north Wales, near Chester. From here he marched south to Ludlow and thence to Hereford. His duchess had been freed from house arrest after the Battle of Northampton, since when she had been living at Baynard's Castle with her younger children, awaiting her lord's return. As soon as York landed he sent a message asking Cecily to meet him at Hereford as soon as possible, which she did, travelling in a chariot, or litter, hung with blue velvet and drawn by four pairs of fine horses.

York had timed his return so that he would be in London when Parliament met in early October. He made no attempt to conceal the fact that he had come to assert his claim to the throne, and proceeded to the capital with as much state and ceremony as if he were already king. At Abingdon, he summoned trumpeters and had them issued with banners displaying the royal arms of England undifferenced – the sovereign's arms. And thus he came to London.

Somerset, meanwhile, had finally given up trying to wrest Calais from Warwick's garrison, and had recently been obliged to surrender

Guisnes to the Earl's men. Towards the end of September he too returned to England, and took up residence at Corfe Castle in Dorset.

Parliament assembled in Westminster Hall on 7 October. The King attended the opening ceremony but thereafter remained in the Queen's apartments in the palace. In this Parliament Lord Bourchier was made Treasurer of England and Warwick's brother, George Neville, Bishop of Exeter, was rewarded for his recent support by being appointed Chancellor. At that time he was about twenty-seven years old, a clever, cultivated opportunist who was not at all suited to his episcopal role, for he loved luxurious living and political intrigue. He was a great patron of scholars, corresponded with famous men of letters in other parts of Europe and amassed a respectable library of rare manuscripts. Chastellain describes him as a 'stately and eloquent man'.

On the 10th, York rode into London at the head of a great retinue, preceded by his trumpeters, whose banners astonished those who beheld them, and by his sword of state, borne upright before him. Gone was his former restraint and caution. His arrogant and dignified bearing proclaimed to all what his intentions were, and it was noted that from now on he would act 'more like a king than a duke'. Abbot Whethamstead accused him of the sin of pride.

In this manner he came to Westminster Hall, where Parliament was sitting. Dismounting at the door, and with his sword still carried before him, he strode through the assembled throng to the dais at the far end, on which stood the empty throne beneath a canopy of estate. Then, after bowing to the Lords, he placed his hand firmly on the throne, symbolically laying claim to it. As he did so, the Lords and Commons alike 'ran together and looked' incredulously. Then York turned to face them, expecting cheers of acclamation. Instead there was an embarrassed silence.

Nonplussed, he moved away from the throne, plainly furious. Nevertheless he announced undeterred that he 'challenged and claimed the realm of England as heir of King Richard II, proposing without any delay to be crowned on All Hallows Day following' – 1 November. The Archbishop of Canterbury cautiously suggested he obtain an audience of the King to discuss his claim, but this stirred York to anger. 'I know of no one in the realm who would not more fitly come to me than I to him,' he declared.

Nevertheless he marched out of the hall and made his way to the royal apartments where the King, having heard the commotion, had retired to an inner chamber. York was intent on seeing him, and coming to the door of the chamber he thrust aside the guards and burst in. Henry faced him calmly, but stood by his right to occupy the throne of his forefathers.

The reaction of most noblemen to York's astonishing act was one of profound dismay. How could they be expected to uphold his claim when they had all taken an oath of allegiance to Henry VI? That Henry should have inspired such loyalty after decades of misrule is testimony to the mystical power of the institution of monarchy at that time – perhaps the most remarkable aspect of the Wars of the Roses – and also the personal esteem in which Henry was held for his many virtues. Equally remarkable is the fact that Henry VI failed to capitalise on such support. Powerful magnates had not hesitated to depose Richard II – but Richard's tyranny had threatened their jealously-guarded privileges. Under Henry VI, many magnates had prospered.

Even Warwick and Salisbury were shocked and angered by York's behaviour. They had supported him in his calls for reform and in his attempts to gain power for himself, but this time they felt he had gone too far, and without even consulting them. Nor did they feel able to support his claim, for – in common with most magnates – they saw no reason why Henry VI, England's acknowledged and anointed king for the past thirty-eight years, should be deposed.

Warwick and his brother, Thomas Neville, wasted no time in going to York's lodging at Westminster to remonstrate with him. Men-at-arms filled the room, and Warwick saw the Duke at the far side, his elbow resting on a sideboard. Warwick was furious and told York so, and why, using 'hard words'. Young Rutland then came in and, seeing the Earl castigating his father, said, 'Fair Sir, be not angry, for you know that we have the true right to the crown, and that my lord and father here must have it.'

March, who was also present, could see that Warwick was in no mood for such talk, and realised that so powerful an ally must not be offended. 'Brother,' he said, 'vex no man, for all shall be well.' Warwick, controlling his anger, turned away from York and Rutland, and made a great show of speaking only to March.

Although the magnates quickly made it clear to York that they stood by their oaths of allegiance to Henry VI, he was determined to force the issue. On 16 October, sitting on the throne in Westminster Hall, he formally claimed the crown of England by right of inheritance and then submitted to the Lords in Parliament a genealogy showing his descent from Henry III. The Lords displayed few signs of approval and asked him why he had not put forward his claim before. He answered, 'Though right for a time rest and be put to silence, yet it rotteth not, nor shall it perish.'

Next day, the Lords respectfully asked the King for his views on the matter, and he asked them to draw up a list of objections to York's claim. The Lords then laid the matter before the justices, the serjeants-at-law and the royal attorneys, but all were extremely reluctant to express an opinion as to whether York's claim was valid or not, saying that it was not within their competence to do so, but was a matter for the King and York to determine between them. In fact, it was such a high matter that it was above the law and beyond their learning, and they referred it back to a higher legal authority – the Lords in Parliament.

There then followed much debate and poring over yellowing genealogies, statutes and precedents. The Lords warned York that the matter was proving difficult to determine, the stumbling block being their oaths of allegiance to Henry VI and their recent oath recognising Prince Edward as the future king. They pointed out that York had also sworn these same oaths and referred him to 'great and notable Acts of Parliament which be sufficient and reasonable to be laid against [his] title'. These Acts, they argued, recognised Henry's title, and should be relied upon as the ultimate authority on the matter.

York answered that the oaths made to Henry VI by the peers were invalid because the nature and purpose of an oath was to confirm the truth, and the truth was that he was the rightful king, not Henry, and the Lords ought to help him claim what was rightfully his. God's law, he said, governed inheritance, and that took precedence over all other laws.

Thomas Thorpe, Speaker of the Commons, later had some scathing words to say in Parliament about York's claim. But even though York was not yet king, he still wielded great power, and Thorpe soon found himself incarcerated in London's Fleet Prison, accused by York of trespass and theft. For this he was found guilty and fined, provoking protests in the Commons. It was to no avail, and the members had no choice but to elect another Speaker.

At length, the Lords grudgingly concluded that York did indeed have a better right to the crown than Henry VI, but by a majority of only five they decided that a change of dynasty was unthinkable at this stage. The Lords were now forced to a compromise, not so much because York had the better claim, but because they knew he had the power to make them acknowledge it.

On 31 October it was announced that the King and York were reconciled, and the next day, in St Paul's Cathedral, 'the King wore his crown and led a procession of dukes, earls and lords, as a symbol of concord'. Parliament now resolved that King Henry 'should enjoy the throne of England for as long as he should live', Prince Edward should be disinherited, and York should be proclaimed heir apparent and succeed to the throne on Henry's death. This was not the best compromise that York could have expected, and it reflected the Lords' antipathy towards him, for he was after all ten years older than the King and likely, in the natural course of things, to predecease him.

On 24 October an Act of Settlement – the 'Act of Accord', as it became known – was drawn up, enshrining the new order of succession in law. Four days later, Henry VI, under pressure from the few magnates who were present in Parliament – the rest having deemed it politic to stay away – agreed to its terms, and the Act became law. The King at once sent a message to the Queen, commanding her to bring the Prince to London, and warning that if she failed to do so she would be denounced as a rebel.

Now that the dynastic issue had been raised, the Wars of the Roses changed course. No longer were they primarily a struggle for supremacy between York and the Queen's party; instead, from now on they would be a struggle for the throne itself, with reform of the government second in importance. The unleashing of the dynastic dispute would have far-reaching consequences for the royal succession over the next twenty-five years and beyond, weakening the concept of legitimate title and fostering the ambitions of those whose might was greater than their right. From now on, also, the outcome of every battle would be regarded as an indication of God's approval of the claim of the victor.

In late October Parliament reversed the attainders against York and his followers, and restored to them their titles, lands and goods. On 8 November York was proclaimed heir apparent to the throne and Protector of England. All the lords spiritual and temporal swore allegiance to him as the King's heir, and he in turn swore allegiance to Henry and the lords, saying that for his part he would abide by all the conventions and compacts that had been agreed.

York now ruled England in the name of the King. He might reasonably have thought he was in an invincible position, but once again he would find that he was mistaken.

The Act of Accord provoked a furious political storm. The Queen had marched south with her Scottish recruits, who were reinforced as they went by large numbers of men from Northumberland, Cumberland, Westmorland and Lancashire. Many of the northern lords who joined her army cared little for the political issues at stake but were motivated rather by self-interest and the possibilities of plundering the prosperous and envied south. Meanwhile, Somerset and Devon were coming up from the south-west with a large force of gentlemen, knights and soldiers, marching via Bath and Coventry to York. Then Margaret learned that Lords Clifford, Roos, Greystoke, Neville and Latimer were on their way to join her.

When, at Hull, she received the news that Parliament had dispossessed her son of his inheritance, she was furious, and instantly stepped up her recruiting campaign, gathering an army of 15,000 men at Pontefract Castle, and placing them under the command of Somerset, Northumberland and Devon. By the time the army reached York, it numbered about 20,000. That the Queen had raised such an army so late in the year, when the campaigning season had long finished, is a tribute to her tenacity and energy, and also testimony to her fierce determination to protect her son's interests. What was more, the Queen had mustered her force so swiftly and stealthily that it was some time before York realised what was happening.

At York, Margaret made a formal public protest against the Act of Accord and challenged York to settle the issue of the succession by force of arms. She then summoned a council of war and informed the lords of her intention to march on London and deliver the King from the hands of his enemies. Those magnates who had not endorsed the Act shared her anger, and many more flocked to take up arms on her behalf.

Late in November, the Lancastrian army began to advance southwards from York. As they marched through Yorkshire the Queen took great pleasure in allowing her soldiers to sack the homes of tenants of York and Salisbury. They also raided York's castle at Sandal, where it was noticed by the superstitious that no herons had nested in the adjacent park that year.

As soon as York found out what Margaret was doing, he organised a fresh propaganda campaign which was calculated to instil fear of the Queen's savage northern hordes into the southerners, and began preparations to march north to deal with this new threat. The Queen and Prince had written to the Common Council of the city of London, requesting monetary and military aid, but their requests had been ignored. York, however, was granted a loan of 500 marks to finance his campaign. He was also in control of the royal arsenal of weapons in the Tower, and commandeered several guns to take north with him.

York and Salisbury, at the head of about 5-6000 men, rode out of London on 9 December, cheered on by waving crowds lining the streets and leaving Warwick behind to maintain order in the capital.

They marched north via Nottingham, recruiting on the way. Many of their scouts, or 'aforeriders', however, were killed in a skirmish with Somerset's men at Worksop, and at the same time Lancastrian scouts discovered that York's army was vastly inferior to their own.

York made for his castle of Sandal, two miles west of Wakefield, because, says Whethamstead, he desired to be among his own people and enjoy a comfortable lodging at Christmas. He also deemed his presence in the area necessary because his tenants had suffered harassment by local Lancastrian lords. Built in the reign of Edward II, Sandal Castle was a mighty fortress occupying an imposing position, though today it is a crumbling, roofless ruin. York arrived on the 21st and set his men to digging trenches around the castle and positioning their guns at strategic points around the walls, thus putting himself – theoretically at least – in a good defensive position should the Lancastrians attack. His plan was to await March's arrival from Shrewsbury with reinforcements before engaging with the enemy, and he settled down with his men to celebrate Christmas.

Somerset and Northumberland would have liked to besiege York in Sandal Castle, and in any case planned to prevent any fresh supplies from reaching him there. However, since they lacked the resources with which to conduct a siege, they decided that York must somehow be lured out of the castle and made to fight before March arrived. The Lancastrians certainly had the greater army, about 20,000 men to York's 12,000 at most, and they had also a substantial number of magnates, including Exeter, Somerset, Devon, Northumberland and Clifford. York had not a single peer in his army, apart from the ever-loyal Salisbury. While the Queen's captains included the experienced Sir Baldwin Fulford and Sir John Grey, who was husband to Lord Rivers's daughter, Elizabeth Wydville, one of York's captains of foot was a mere London mercer, John Harrow, who had served under Salisbury at the siege of the Tower in July. And although Lord Neville responded to York's summons, riding to Sandal with 8000 men, he then deserted to the Lancastrians. Even after this, York still underestimated the strength of his opponents.

By the end of December the Duke was in an increasingly precarious situation, though his captains believed that if he stayed in the castle until reinforcements arrived he would have nothing to fear. Discipline among his men was lax; many were allowed to go out foraging, thus broadcasting to the enemy that food supplies were running low, and his scouts were incompetent, failing to discover what the Lancastrians were planning. Sir Davy Hall, grandfather of the Tudor chronicler Edward Hall, advised York not to let his men out but to 'keep within his castle', but the Duke replied, 'Wouldst thou that I, for dread of a scolding woman, whose only weapons are her tongue and her nails, should shut my gates? Then all men might of me wonder and report to my dishonour, that a woman hath made me a dastard, whom no man could ever yet prove a coward!'

During the Christmas holidays, Somerset rode over to parley with York, and it was agreed that a state of truce would prevail until after the Feast of the Epiphany on 6 January; the royal commanders, however, had no intention of keeping it. For three days running they sent a herald with instructions to provoke York by insults into taking the offensive. The herald publicly sneered at the Duke's 'want of courage in suffering himself to be tamely braved by a woman'. On the 29th the Lancastrians selected 400 men, disguised them as Yorkist reinforcements, and sent them to join the garrison at Sandal. The deception worked.

It is not known for certain why York left the safety of Sandal Castle on 30 December. It was commonly believed at the time that fast-depleting provisions forced him to send out a foraging party to get more food. These men either attacked the waiting Lancastrians and were quickly driven back inside the castle, or were attacked by them. Another theory is that a band of reinforcements under Andrew Trollope, who had joined the royal army the night before, were also masquerading as Yorkist soldiers by parading in Warwick's livery; York, seeing them approaching the castle at dawn, either came out to meet them or, seeing through their disguises, decided to sally forth and take the offensive.

Whatever happened, the centre of the Lancastrian army, under Somerset, now advanced to a position near the castle and waited to engage in battle. At the same time, the right and left flanks of that army, commanded by Wiltshire and Roos, concealed themselves in the woodland on either side of the entrance to York's fortress. York obviously had no idea that the enemy was so near at hand, and in such strength, waiting to ambush him and his men. Nor did he listen to the repeated advice of his captains, who were still urging him to await reinforcements. Unsuspecting, he and Salisbury rode out at the head of their men across the drawbridge and cantered down the hill to the open fields south of the River Calder, an area known as Wakefield Green. With them rode York's seventeen-year-old son, Rutland. The waiting Lancastrian centre charged to meet them and there was a tremendous clash between the two armies, with the Yorkists fighting fiercely and bravely, believing they had the upper hand. But Somerset had been advised on strategy by Trollope, to devastating effect. As soon as the Yorkists had issued forth from the castle, he and his second-in-command, Lord Clifford, had sent orders to Wiltshire to take the castle, and to Lord Roos, telling him to block York's line of retreat. Suddenly, the two Lancastrian flanks emerged from the woods and descended on York's men, surrounding them on three sides 'like a fish in a net or a deer in a buckstall'. The Yorkists discovered that they were hopelessly outnumbered, but by then it was too late. Many were slaughtered, and the rest hastened to lay down their arms and surrender. York was pulled from his mount and killed in the midst of the fighting.

As the young Earl of Rutland left the field, accompanied by his tutor, Sir Robert Aspsall, Lord Clifford rode up and demanded to know who he was. Aspsall stupidly cried, 'Spare him, for he is a king's son, and good may come to you!'

'Whose son is this?' demanded Clifford, suspiciously, and then, without waiting to be told, for he had guessed the answer, drove his dagger into Rutland's heart, shouting, 'By God's blood, thy father slew mine! So will I slay the accursed blood of York!'

Later writers embroidered the story of Rutland's end, claiming that he tried to seek refuge in the house of a poor woman of Wakefield, but was followed there and dragged outside by Clifford's men. The woman is said to have shut her door as the boy beat frantically upon it, screaming to be readmitted as he was stabbed. The Tudor antiquarian, John Leland, claimed that the murder took place by Wakefield Bridge, and there is indeed a chapel that was once endowed by Rutland's brother Edward on that bridge; it dates, however, from 1357, so cannot have been built to commemorate the Earl's death. The site of the murder is more likely to have been the Park Street end of Kirkgate in Wakefield, because a cross was erected there to Rutland's memory.

Benet states that about a thousand men were killed in the battle; at least half of York's men who had ridden out of the castle with him were either killed or wounded. It was said that the wide expanse of Wakefield Green was covered with corpses. Salisbury's son, Sir Thomas Neville, was among them, as were Sir Thomas Parr, Sir Edward Bourchier and the London mercer John Harrow, men who were the backbone of York's affinity.

During the night after the battle Salisbury was captured by one of Trollope's men and taken to Pontefract Castle, where he was held prisoner. He bribed his gaoler to set him free, but as he was preparing to leave the castle, 'the common people of the country, which loved him not, took him out of the castle by violence, and smote off his head'. His death left Warwick the richest magnate in the realm, for he now added to his Beauchamp inheritance his father's intensive concentration of lands and power in the north, along with the earldom of Salisbury and the castles of Middleham and Sheriff Hutton, which would become Warwick's favourite residences in the years to come. Warwick now owned double the amount of land that any subject of an English king had ever owned before him, and was an enemy to be truly feared.

After the battle, some soldiers had retrieved York's body, propped it up against an ant-heap, and crowned it with a garland of reeds. They then pretended to bow to it, crying. 'Hail, king without a kingdom!' Lord Clifford ordered that the corpse be decapitated and the head impaled on a lance, along with that of Rutland, and when this had been done a paper crown was placed on York's head. His kinsfolk never forgave Clifford for his treatment of the bodies of York and Rutland, and vowed that they would not rest until their deaths had been revenged.

Tudor chroniclers, such as Hall and Holinshed, later asserted that Clifford took the heads of the three Yorkist lords to York and presented them to the Queen, saying 'Madam, your war is done. Here is your king's ransom.' She is said to have blenched at the sight, then laughed nervously, and to have slapped York's face, before ordering that the heads be placed on pikes above the Micklegate Bar, the main entrance to the city, 'so that York shall overlook the town of York', and that two empty pikes be placed next to them, ready for the heads of March and Warwick, 'which she intended should soon keep them company'. Although the heads of York, Salisbury and Rutland were indeed exhibited above the Micklegate Bar, their bodies having been quietly buried at Pontefract, there is no truth in this story. Margaret was not in York at the time, and had in fact returned to Edinburgh as a guest of the Queen of Scotland, staying there throughout late December, when the battle was fought. Only after she received news of the victory did she hasten south – clad in robes given her by Queen Mary, a long black gown and a black bonnet with a silver plume, and riding a silver jennet – to rejoin her army in Yorkshire.

Few magnates mourned York's death. He had not been a man to inspire affection among his peers. But the common people, whose champion he had professed to be, grieved for his passing. He was nominally succeeded as Duke of York by his son, March, who now became, at the age of eighteen, the premier English magnate. Henry VI, however, refused to acknowledge his right to succeed his father, nor would he allow him to bear the title Earl of Chester, as he was entitled to do as heir to the throne under the terms of the Act of Accord.

Some time after the battle a memorial to York's memory was set up by the road leading from Sandal to Wakefield, about 400 yards from the castle. This cross appears to have been dismantled in the 1640s. The present monument to the fallen was set up in 1897 in the grounds of Manygates School, and is adorned with a carving of York based on a now-vanished stone effigy that once stood on the Welsh Bridge at Shrewsbury. The site of the battle is now covered by modern houses and industrial units, but from time to time bones, swords, pieces of armour, spurs and other items have been dug up by local people.

After Wakefield, the battles of the Wars of the Roses were to become bloodier and the commanders more ruthless. Up to that time strenuous efforts had been made by both sides to avoid military confrontations. That era was past, and it was now tacitly accepted that major disputes could only be settled by violence.

On 2 January 1461 Warwick, in London, heard the news of York's defeat and death. March was still celebrating Christmas at Shrewsbury when a messenger came with the dreadful tidings, and he was 'wonderfully amazed' with grief. Spurred on by his determination to avenge his father's death and his brother's murder, the new Duke speedily raised an army, recruiting mainly in the Marcher shires and assembling his men at Wigmore and Ludlow. With him were Sir William Herbert and his brother Richard, Sir Walter Devereux, Roger Vaughan of Tretower, and other men of York's local affinity. York himself was dead, but his claim to the throne had passed to his son, who had every intention of enforcing it. And as the executed Salisbury had supported York, so his son, Warwick, would continue to support York's heir.

17

The Sun in Splendour

In the New Year of 1461 Margaret of Anjou was marching south from Scotland at the head of an army provided by Queen Mary, intent on consolidating the advantage gained at Wakefield and eliminating Warwick and March. She was on her way to link up with her main force, which was waiting for her near York.

On 5 January the two queens had come to an agreement whereby Margaret undertook to cede Berwick to the Scots in return for troops and the marriage of Prince Edward to Mary's daughter, Margaret Stewart. What Mary had been unable to provide, however, was money with which to pay the troops, and as Margaret was without funds herself she was again obliged to promise them unlimited plunder once they were south of the Trent. Word of this spread and, anticipating themselves growing rich on the spoils of war, many men of the north came to swell her army.

From January onwards the Yorkists were busily spreading propaganda against the Lancastrians, claiming that the recent wars and troubles were a manifestation of God's retribution and judgement on the realm for permitting the usurping House of Lancaster, founded by the murderer of Richard II, to remain on the throne, and for ignoring the rightful claims of the true heirs, York and his sons. Thanks to the Yorkist affinity, this propaganda permeated a wide area.

The view that the Wars of the Roses originated with the murder of Richard II is often believed to have been the official Tudor retrospective view on the matter, but in fact it was how the Yorkists perceived the struggle, and once the dynastic issue had been raised it is easy to see how this view was formulated, given the contemporary concepts of how God's approval or condemnation were manifested.

The Yorkists also began a scare-mongering campaign, warning of what the northerners in the Queen's army would do if they were victorious, and publicising the fact that she had licensed them to plunder the south: houses would be robbed, sacked and burned, womenfolk raped, lands ravaged, and citizens murdered. This appeal to the prejudices of the southerners against the northerners, who were perceived as an alien race of uncivilised savages, met with tremendous success, for recruits came forward in unprecedented numbers, eager to defend their own.

On 5 January, Warwick and other lords requested the Council for a loan for the defence of the realm and the Council granted him 2000 marks by a unanimous vote. Throughout January and early February a nervous government issued streams of commissions of array and warrants for the arrest of dissidents and persons uttering false tidings, holding unlawful assemblies, or hindering those trying lawfully to defend the King. On the 12th the city fathers of Norwich agreed to provide Warwick with 120 armed men. Five days later the Council ordered the town dignitaries of Stamford in Lincolnshire to put its defences in order, anticipating that Margaret would march that way as she advanced south down the Great North Road. On 23 January it was rumoured in London that the Queen's supporters and their retinues would 'be here sooner than men wean, ere three weeks'. By the 28th the Council knew for certain that 'the misruled and outrageous people in the north parts' were being led south in force by the Queen.

On 5 February, the Council ordered Sir William Bourchier and others to raise the Essex lieges and march with them to the King. The ports of Norfolk were told not to permit the shipment of provisions to the Lancastrian army, which was then at Hull. Nevertheless, provisions did get through, and the Council wasted a lot of time and effort in fruitlessly trying to discover who was responsible.

Castles were garrisoned, curfews imposed. On 7 February the Council ordered the seizure of Castle Rising in Norfolk, the home of a prominent Lancastrian supporter, Thomas Daniel, who had served the Duke of Suffolk and been a member of Henry VI's household. The Paston Letters imply that he was orchestrating a Lancastrian uprising, recording that he had 'made a great gathering of people and hiring of harness, and it is well understood that they be not to the King-ward, but rather to the contrary, and for to rob'. Daniel apparently enjoyed great influence in Norfolk and presented a danger to the Yorkists, but he escaped and rode north to join the Queen.

Margaret's intention was to march on London and deal with Warwick. Meanwhile, Pembroke and Wiltshire, who had raised an army of Welsh soldiers and French, Breton and Irish mercenaries, intended to march east from Wales to link up with the Queen's main force. But Edward of York had summoned the levies of Bristol, Staffordshire, Shropshire, Herefordshire, Gloucestershire, Worcestershire, Somerset and Dorset to meet him at Hereford, and after recruiting more men at Wigmore Castle, an old Mortimer stronghold, was also planning to march on London, intent on avenging the deaths of his father and brother. Warwick, who had been joined by Fauconberg, was holding the capital, and Edward meant to link up with him before the Queen got there, or intercept her before she reached the city.

Edward was moving east through Gloucestershire, therefore, when he learned that a large Lancastrian army led by Pembroke had left Wales and was making for the Midlands. He made a quick decision to swing his army round, march west, and dispose of this new threat before advancing on London.

Very early in the morning of Candlemas Day, 2 February 1461, Edward and his army came to Mortimer's Cross, which was – and still is – a hamlet of a few homes spanning a quiet crossroads between Ludlow and Leominster, in the midst of the Marcher territory once held by the Mortimers. On that morning a strange sight was to be seen in the sky above the astonished Yorkists – three suns appeared on the firmament 'and suddenly joined together in one'. This is a rare phenomenon called a parhelion, or mock sun, which occurs when light is refracted through ice crystals. Such things were, of course, not understood in the fifteenth century, and the Yorkist soldiers wondered what it portended, some crying out in fright. But Edward proclaimed that it was an omen of victory, saying to his soldiers, 'Beeth of good comfort and dreadeth not. This is a good sign for those three suns betokeneth the Father, the Son and the Holy Ghost, and therefore let us have a good heart, and in the name of Almighty God go we against our enemies!' He also construed the sign as foretelling the joyful reunion of the three sons (suns) of York – himself and his brothers George and Richard. At his words the entire Yorkist army sank to its knees in prayer, overawed by the vision. In time, Edward would incorporate those three suns into his personal badge, 'The Sun in Splendour'.

Contemporary chroniclers estimated that Edward had between 30,000 and 50,000 men in his army; the real figure was probably much less, and modern historians assert that it was nearer 5000. He certainly had a strong force of experienced archers and many retainers and tenants from his lordships in the Welsh Marches, men who were intent on preventing their property from being occupied by the enemy and on guarding the interests of their communities. Edward's chief captains were Lord Audley, Sir William Herbert, and Sir Walter Devereux, ably supported by Lord Grey de Wilton, Lord FitzWalter, and Edward's closest friend, Sir William Hastings, who was to serve him loyally until his death.

The approaching Lancastrian army was under the command of Pembroke, Wiltshire and Owen Tudor. The chroniclers say they had 8000 men, modern historians estimate about 4000, who were largely raw recruits, Welsh squires and mercenaries. Wiltshire was a poor choice for commander: he had been criticised both in 1455 and 1460 for his bad military judgement and lack of stamina in the field, and was not a leader to inspire confidence in untried men.

It is not recorded how long the Battle of Mortimer's Cross lasted, but it was certainly one of the bloodiest battles of the Wars of the Roses. As the sun rose, the Lancastrian army could be seen advancing from the west. Edward, relying on the advice of his friend Sir Richard Croft of nearby Croft Castle, positioned his men in Wig Marsh, thus blocking the road to Worcester. Because he had the River Lugg at his back, with its only bridge behind his lines, he was in a strong position, in command of the crossroads. As a precaution, however, he set his archers to guard the bridge and any places where the enemy might try to ford the river, while at Kingsland to the south his supporters were preparing to obstruct Pembroke if he came that way. Thus Edward had made it virtually impossible for the Lancastrians to avoid engaging in battle.

Wiltshire commenced hostilities by smashing the Yorkist right wing, but a similar onslaught by Pembroke failed to do the same at the Yorkist centre, commanded by Edward himself, and was repelled. Wiltshire returned to the mêlée to aid Pembroke, who was attempting to take the bridge, but both were soon overpowered. Wiltshire, however, managed to ford the river with his left flank and crushed the remnants of the Yorkist right wing. There then followed a lull in which the Lancastrian commanders, well aware that despite the crippling of his right wing Edward looked set for victory, debated suing for peace, but decided on one last attack, which was led by Owen Tudor. He tried to overcome the Yorkist left flank, but in vain, for they fought ferociously and drove a wedge through Tudor's force. He then led a detachment of men south towards Kingsland, hoping to find a way across the river there, but was surrounded and captured by local men of Edward's affinity, supported by soldiers of the Yorkist left wing. At this stage his men fled from the field in confusion and were chased by Edward's men as far as Hereford.

Edward's archers were now shooting deadly volleys of arrows into the Lancastrian cavalry, causing many deaths. The Yorkists quickly overcame the Lancastrian centre, pushing it south towards Kingsland and inflicting heavy casualties, so that the normally peaceful marshes and meadows around the village, where the fighting was most furious, were soon strewn with the dead and the dying.

As the Lancastrian centre collapsed, Pembroke realised that the day was lost and fled from the field, leaving his men – and his father – to the Yorkists, who now proceeded to butcher large numbers of the vanquished enemy. Four thousand men are said to have been slaughtered on that day, most of them Pembroke's, for Edward's losses were slight. Many Welshmen were taken prisoner, as well as several Lancastrian captains.

In 1799 an obelisk was raised to mark the site of the battle; it now stands outside the Monument Inn, while the battlefield, little changed in 500 years, may still be seen. The tomb of Sir Richard Croft is in the church beside Croft Castle, now owned by the National Trust. In 1839 a silver spur lost by a Lancastrian knight as he fled from the carnage was unearthed nearby, and is now in Hereford Museum.

On 3 February, Owen Tudor and other Lancastrian captains, including a knight and his two sons, an estate steward and a lawyer, were taken to the market place in Hereford to be executed. It is likely that Edward ordered the sentence on Tudor, Henry VI's stepfather, to avenge the death of his own father at Wakefield. The chronicler 'Gregory' states that, until the collar of his red velvet doublet was torn from his shoulders Tudor did not believe he would be beheaded. As realisation struck, he said sadly, 'That head shall lie on the stock that was wont to lie on Queen Katherine's lap.' Then, 'trusting that he should not be beheaded till he saw the axe and the block', he 'full meekly took his death'. His head was displayed 'upon the highest step of the market cross, and a mad woman combed his hair and washed away the blood off his face' before lighting over a hundred candles and setting them about him. His body was buried in the Church of the Grey Friars at Hereford, which has long since disappeared, and Welsh bards wrote a number of poignant laments in his honour.

After Mortimer's Cross, Wiltshire joined up with Pembroke and, heavily disguised, they went into hiding, Pembroke vowing 'with the might of Our Lord and the assistance of our kinsmen and friends, within short time to avenge the defeat'. He was mercifully unaware that this was the beginning of an exile that would last for a quarter of a century. Three weeks after the battle he was at his port of Tenby, where he could count upon the loyalty of the townsfolk, and on 25 February he wrote to at least two of his Welsh allies, trying to bolster their confidence in the Lancastrian cause and urging them to seek revenge on his behalf for the defeat at Mortimer's Cross and the execution of his father. He then fled abroad, leaving young Henry Tudor in hiding at Pembroke Castle, where the Yorkists later discovered him – by 1468 he was living under house arrest as the ward of Sir William Herbert at Raglan Castle. As for Pembroke, for the next two decades and more he would be a fugitive, moving between France, Scotland, Wales and northern England, ever constant in the cause of Lancaster, even in the face of total defeat.

While awaiting the Queen's arrival from the north, the Lancastrian army remained at Hull, where the civic council provided its men with food, since fresh victuals were unobtainable by boat from East Anglia thanks to Yorkist patrols off the coast of King's Lynn. On 12 January, Lord Neville's troops, growing restive, surged into Beverley and inflicted savage brutalities upon the citizens, a foretaste of what the south could expect.

By the 20th Margaret and her force had joined up with the main army at York where, on that day, a large gathering of Lancastrian nobles confirmed the agreement between Margaret of Anjou and Mary of Gueldres for the surrender of Berwick and the marriage of the Prince of Wales, and pledged themselves to persuade Henry VI to agree to it. News of this concord had been conveyed to the King of France, Scotland's ally, who was greatly pleased, and ordered that all the harbours of Normandy should be open to the Queen and her friends, should they have need of them. Margaret, believing that Charles would come to her aid himself, if need be, was now ready to march south, not stopping to consider how the English would view a queen who encouraged England's ancient enemy to invade her shores.

On that same day the Lancastrian army, under the command of Somerset and Northumberland, set off towards London, marching via Grantham, Stamford, Peterborough, Huntingdon, Royston and St Albans. Once they had crossed the Trent, the northern soldiers began robbing, raping, torturing, burning and looting at will, 'laying waste all the towns and villages that stood along their way', according to Benet. They sacked abbeys and priories, burned whole villages, barns, and even manor houses, after carrying off their treasures, and stole cattle and provisions. Because of the hardships of campaigning in winter it is likely that many were basically foraging for food, but their seizure of it meant near-starvation for country communities, especially as winter supplies were running low by that time of year.

Many people fled south from the wrath of the northerners, carrying with them dreadful tales of atrocities. The Croyland chronicler recorded the terror of the monks of his abbey and their neighbours in the nearby villages, who brought their few valuables to the abbot for safe-keeping, much to the dismay of the brethren.

> We collected together our precious vestments and other treasures, besides all our charters and muniments, and hid them in the most secret places within the walls. And every day the convent held processions and poured forth prayers and tears. All the gates of the monastery and town were guarded, day and night.

However, the Queen's soldiers mercifully passed them by at a distance of six miles. 'Blessed be God, who did not give us for a prey unto their teeth,' wrote the chronicler.

Croyland had heard that the royal army had now been reinforced by 'an infinite number of paupers and beggars, who had emerged like mice from their holes' eager for booty, and whose advance encompassed a line thirty miles wide. He tells how they committed many unspeakable crimes, 'murdering anyone, including clergy, who resisted, and robbing the rest, even digging up valuables whose whereabouts they discovered by threats of death'.

As the Queen's army advanced through the east Midlands, the men of the south and East Anglia were hurrying to arms. Clement Paston wrote: 'My lords that be here have as much as they may do to keep down all this country, for they would be up on the men in the north, for it is the weal of all the south.' Sir John Wenlock was busy arraying the levies of Hertfordshire and five other shires north of London. Reports of atrocities had caused many towns to switch sides, including Coventry, which had hitherto been chiefly Lancastrian in sympathy. Meanwhile, bands of Welsh soldiers, escaping after Mortimer's Cross, were hastening to join the Queen.

Warwick, who could be indecisive in a crisis, had dallied in London when he should have been busy raising an army in the

Midlands to counteract the threat posed by the advancing forces of the Queen. Instead, he waited until she had reached Hertfordshire before he began recruiting in London, Kent and the eastern and southern counties. On 12 February, the Council commissioned Edward of York, still making his way to the capital, to array the lieges of the west to march with him against the King's enemies.

On that same day, King Henry, accompanied by the Duke of Norfolk, rode out of London to Barnet, followed hours later by Warwick, who left the city for Ware with a great army and ordnance. Four days later the Queen's host came to Luton. Warwick had laid an ambush south of the town, with nets concealing spikes and caltraps, the latter being two rods of iron twisted together with cruelly sharp points which were strewn along the road to impede the passage of cavalry. However, a former Yorkist, Sir Henry Lovelace, espied them, and sent a message of warning to Margaret, who ordered her army to swing west and take the road to Dunstable instead of that to St Albans. At this time, some of her unruly troops were ravaging the countryside between Hitchin and Buntingford.

A detachment of Warwick's army under the command of a local butcher was waiting for the Queen at Dunstable, but fared badly in the ensuing skirmish, losing 200 men before being driven out of the town. The butcher, overcome with shame at his defeat, promptly committed suicide, and 'Gregory' is scathing in his denouncement of the man's inefficiency and cowardice. The royal army then proceeded down Watling Street towards St Albans.

On the 17th, King Henry rode into St Albans to rendezvous with Warwick, who was now awaiting the arrival of the Queen's advance guard. The Earl had a large army, the size of which is nowhere given precisely, and was supported by Norfolk, Suffolk's heir John de la Pole, and Arundel, none of whom could match him in military expertise and experience, and by the more reliable Lords Fauconberg, Bourchier and Bonville. He had divided his men into three groups, placing the weakest group, containing a large number of archers, in the town, and the other two outside it on the Harpenden and Sandridge roads, the latter being positioned on Nomansland Common. A sunken lane called Beech Bottom ran between these two wings and enabled them to keep in touch with each other.

Warwick also had a detachment of 500 Burgundian soldiers, who would shoot flaming arrows in the coming battle, and had rudimentary handguns called ribaudkins, which fired lead pellets, iron-headed arrows and 'wildfire' all at the same time. He also had a company of crossbowmen armed with pavises, large wooden shields studded with nails which screened the bowmen as they fired their bolts.

Warwick's Kentish recruits were captained by one of his most trusted retainers, Sir Henry Lovelace, who had the reputation of being the Englishman most expert in warfare, and may have fought for Jack Cade in 1450. Warwick had appointed Lovelace steward of his household, and had in former campaigns placed him in command of his advance guard or in charge of guns and supplies. He had been captured by the Lancastrians at Wakefield and condemned to death, but the Queen had spared him when, having been persuaded by Lord Rivers to switch his allegiance, he swore never again to take up arms against her. Margaret was so overjoyed to secure the services of this renowned warrior that she promised him £4000 and the earldom of Kent when the King came into his own again in return for his continuing loyalty. Lovelace marched south with the royal army, but after leaving Luton he rode to join Warwick's force, though he had no intention of fighting for his former lord, but was rather plotting to betray him.

Contemporary chroniclers estimated – doubtless with some exaggeration – that the Queen had 80,000 men in her army, which was captained by Exeter, Somerset, Devon, Shrewsbury, Northumberland, Clifford, Grey, Roos and other loyal peers. The advance guard was under the command of Andrew Trollope, and the main battle under Somerset, who had 30,000 horse. Sir John Grey was in charge of the cavalry. The Queen had only twenty-four southerners in her army, including five esquires and a grocer from London, and it would appear that both sides had hastily recruited untried men, who were difficult to train and discipline. A shortage of victuals did not improve matters, and by the time it reached St Albans the Lancastrian army was already disintegrating. Having got their booty from plundering, many of the Queen's northerners had deserted and gone home while often those who were left were useless in the field. However, when the time came for battle, the Lancastrian commanders managed to enforce discipline and effectively deployed their more reliable men, although some 'would not be guided nor governed by their captains'.

When Warwick reached St Albans he believed the Queen to be nine miles off, but she took him by surprise, entering the town, not as expected from the Verulamium end, but from the north-west, to the east of St Peter's Street. Warwick had deployed his archers in the streets and in several buildings including the Red Lion and Fleur de Lys inns in order to prevent the Queen's army from entering the town, but at dawn on 17 February her commanders tried to force entry. At first they were driven back by a deadly hail of arrows from the Eleanor Cross in the market place, and were obliged to retreat across the River Ver. On the farther bank they held a council of war, as a result of which Trollope decided to lead his advance guard along the narrow lanes to the north of Romeland and thence into St Peter's Street, avoiding barricades set up by the Yorkists. Despite heavy casualties from enemy arrows, they succeeded in driving Warwick's archers out of the town to Bernard's Heath, where the Earl made strenuous attempts to regroup them. It was now nearly noon, and snow was beginning to fall.

Before long Warwick had drawn up his men into a new line, stretching from Beech Bottom across the Sandridge Road. Caltraps had been scattered along the road, and the artillery and the Burgundians with their handguns were grouped in front of the line. As the Lancastrian vanguard under Trollope advanced, the Yorkists fired their cannon, but with little success because the falling snow had damped down the powder. Some of the handguns exploded or backfired, causing severe injuries to their owners – eighteen were burned to death by their own fire.

Behind Trollope came Somerset with the main battle of the royal army. The Yorkists tried again to bombard the enemy with their artillery, but it had now been rendered completely ineffective, and their arrows, shot into an adverse wind, were falling short of their targets. Nevertheless, the Lancastrians were finding it difficult to breach the Yorkist position, and Warwick might have won the day had it not been for the treachery of Lovelace, who had cautiously held back his troops until he saw that the tide was turning in favour of the Lancastrians, then deserted and raced to join them. The gap in the Yorkist lines left by Lovelace was soon targeted by the enemy commanders, who launched a charge of mounted knights, which shattered the Yorkist lines.

After this, it began to grow dark, and Warwick could see defeat approaching. His left wing was already in flight, and he therefore sounded the retreat and withdrew his centre from the field, drawing them up in a tight defensive position between Sandridge and Cheapside Farm, to the north of St Albans. Here he remained, fighting on until dusk fell.

Those of his army who remained in the field, hard-pressed, looked in vain for the Earl to return with reinforcements. The Lancastrians were causing confusion and it was impossible to ward off their onslaughts. But Warwick was preoccupied with disciplining his raw recruits, who made up the larger part of his army; many had deserted during the battle because they had not been adequately fed. The Earl had indeed tried to march his centre south to rejoin the fighting, but was thwarted by some of his captains, who urged him to withdraw altogether from the field and make for London. Although Warwick stubbornly insisted on relieving his men, by the time he got to them his left wing on Bernard's Heath were already fleeing the battlefield, running in panic in all directions, with enemy soldiers in grim pursuit who butchered the Yorkists when they caught them. Whethamstead, who was at the abbey of St Albans at the time of the battle and gives the most detailed account of it, says that those who escaped did so under cover of darkness. At the sight of the carnage, more of Warwick's inexperienced recruits ran for their lives.

As it was now dark and useless to struggle on further, and as it was obvious that the Lancastrians had scored a decisive victory – in fact, it was to be their most decisive victory of the war – Warwick sounded the retreat and withdrew the remnants of his army in an orderly manner from the field. He then marched west through the night with a force of 4000 men, aiming to link up with Edward of York. He left behind him a battlefield strewn with 2-4000 dead. Sir John Grey was among them.

After the battle, Henry VI was found seated under an oak tree, smiling to see the discomfiture of the Yorkists. Beside him stood the men Warwick had appointed to guard him, Lord Bonville and Sir Thomas Kyriell. Lancastrian officers immediately arrested them, but the King promised them that he would be merciful. Then he was escorted to the tent of Lord Clifford, where he was reunited with his wife and son. He rejoiced to see them after so many months apart, and embraced and kissed them, thanking God for bringing them back to him.

The people of St Albans, however, were horrified by the Yorkist defeat and its implications for them. 'Gregory' blamed it on Warwick's raw recruits, and the incompetence of his scouts, who had failed to warn him of the proximity of the Lancastrian army. Waurin and others held Lovelace to blame. Fortunately, most of the peers in the Earl's army had escaped; only the Lords Bonville, Berners and Charlton, and Warwick's brother John Neville had been taken prisoner.

On 18 February, at the Queen's request, the seven-year-old Prince, wearing a soldier's brigandine of purple velvet, received his father's blessing and was then knighted by him. Then came thirty others, who were dubbed knight by the Prince. Trollope was first in the line, and as he knelt, he said, 'My lord, I have not deserved it, for I slew but fifteen men, for I stood still in one place, and they came unto me.' William Tailboys was also honoured for his valour in the field.

There then followed a more macabre ceremony. Bonville and Kyriell were brought before the King, Queen, and Prince to be sentenced. In view of Henry's promise of mercy they expected to be dealt with leniently, for they had behaved honourably towards him throughout. But the Queen, intervening before her husband could say anything, turned to the Prince and said, 'Fair son, what death shall these two knights die?' There was a shocked hush as the child answered, 'Let them have their heads taken off.' Bonville, appalled, retorted, 'May God destroy those who taught thee this manner of speech!'

The executions of Bonville and Kyriell aroused fury among the Yorkists. Both men had been acting under orders, guarding the King, and had taken no part in the fighting. Bonville, however, had recently gone over to the Yorkists and was regarded by the Queen as a traitor, which was enough to secure his fate. The bloodshed did not end there, for several other Yorkist prisoners were brutally put to death on the Queen's orders.

The King and Queen and their retinues now went into St Albans Abbey to give thanks for the victory. At the porch they were received by the abbot and his monks with triumphal hymns, and processed inside for the service. Afterwards Henry and Margaret were shown to their rooms in the abbey's guest house, where they would lodge for the next few days.

News of Warwick's defeat reached London on Ash Wednesday, 18 February. From that day, 'we lived in mickle dread', wrote a Yorkist living in the capital, while Bishop Beauchamp told the Venetian ambassador that there was 'general dread' in the city at the news. One wealthy citizen, Philip Malpas, whose house had been sacked by Cade's rebels eleven years earlier, was so frightened that he fled abroad to Antwerp. As the wave of fear swept London, streets emptied as merchants shut up and locked their shops and people barricaded themselves inside their houses. Since Warwick had abandoned them, the Lord Mayor arranged for the city militia to patrol the walls, himself accompanying them. London had for years now been sympathetic to the Yorkist cause, and the reported behaviour of the Lancastrian army disposed the citizens even more in its favour. Already in the south-east there was a conviction that the Wars of the Roses had come to represent a conflict between north and south, and that the Lancastrian victory meant that the prosperous south now lay under a dire threat from the north.

On the 19th it was reported in London that Edward of York was in the Cotswolds. Warwick had ridden there at full speed and met up with him either at Burford or Chipping Norton. After he had greeted the Earl, Edward apologised 'that he was so poor, for he had no money, but the substance of his men came at their own cost'. Many, however, were more concerned about protecting their homes and families from the Queen's army than being paid to do so, and Warwick told Edward to be of good cheer, for the commons of England were on his side. The two men then formulated a plan to race for London and have Edward proclaimed king before the Lancastrians got there, both now realising that in this lay their only hope of victory.

Meanwhile, even as the King and Queen were being entertained by the Abbot of St Albans, Margaret's victorious northerners were enthusiastically pillaging and plundering the abbey and town and the countryside round about, creating a trail of destruction. Abbot Whethamstead persuaded Henry to issue a proclamation forbidding such behaviour, but no one took any notice of it, 'for they were all at liberty, and licensed, as they asserted, by the Queen and northern lords to plunder and seize anything they could find anywhere on this side of the Trent, by way of remuneration and recompense for their services'. In vain the Queen tried to stop them, promising pardon to all those who had committed any crimes, for they paid her no heed. Their violent behaviour was proof indeed that Yorkist propaganda had not exaggerated, and was so savage that it horrified the abbot, who could only conclude that these people had been brutalised by poverty and deeply resented the prosperity of the southerners. The King insisted that the Queen order them at least to spare the abbey from further harm, and this time she seems to have met with some success, though further afield, throughout Hertfordshire and Middlesex, her men were ravaging the countryside at will.

The royal army was now running desperately short of food, so the Queen sent a chaplain and a squire to the Lord Mayor of London with a peremptory demand for 'bread and victuals' and money. The frightened mayor hastily arranged for a number of carts to be laden with coin, meat, fish and other foodstuffs, but the pro-Yorkist citizens, emboldened by the news that Edward and Warwick were now marching together on London, rose in an angry mob, seized the carts and locked the city gates, mounting a guard over them so that no one could get in or out. The food they distributed among themselves and ate; as for the money, 'I wot not how it departed,' commented one London chronicler – 'I trow the purse stole the money!'

When the Queen heard how the Londoners had flouted her demands, she was so furious that she allowed her soldiery to plunder and lay waste the countryside of Hertfordshire almost to the gates of the capital itself. If the King and Queen had then regrouped their army and marched on London, 'all things would have been at their will', but Margaret failed to consolidate her victory. She and the King were fearful of further alienating the Londoners by unleashing their uncontrollable troops on the capital, and their captains may well have advised them to wait and intercept the Yorkists as they marched on London. Whatever the reason, Margaret hesitated – and as Lord Rivers soon afterwards certified to the Milanese ambassador, the Lancastrian cause was 'lost irredeemably'.

Upon receiving news of the victory at St Albans, the Lord Mayor of London had written to the King and Queen, offering his obedience, provided that they could assure him that the city would not be plundered or suffer violence. On 20 February the duchesses of Bedford and Buckingham were sent by Margaret to the mayor 'and reported that the King and Queen had no mind to pillage the chief city and chamber of their realm, and so they promised', wrote William Worcester. 'But at the same time they did not mean that they would not punish the evil-doers.'

The city fathers decided to send the noble ladies back to the King and Queen with four aldermen, in order to come to an arrangement whereby Henry and Margaret might enter their capital, providing that the city did not suffer plunder, punishment or violence. But the Londoners had heard too many reports of the atrocities committed by Margaret's troops, and were also heartily sick of Lancastrian misgovernment and their French queen. 'It is right a great abusion,' wrote one anonymous London commentator at this time,

> a woman of a land to be a regent; Queen Margaret, I mean, that ever meant to govern all England with might and power and to destroy the right line. Wherefore she hath a fall, to her great languour. And now she né wrought so that she might attain, though all England were brought to confusion, she and her wicked affinity certain[ly] intend utterly to destroy this region.

The citizens prevaricated and dithered: should they admit the Queen? News of the plundering of St Albans was the deciding factor. The Lord Mayor and a few of his aldermen were virtually the only persons in London who supported her, and they were, predictably, not very popular and were overridden by the angry citizens, who were fearful for their homes, womenfolk and possessions. The city's gates were closed.

Around 21 February, Margaret divided her army; the main body retired to Dunstable with her, while a detachment of the best troops was sent to Barnet, where it halted. Feelings were running high among the men, who were unpaid and underfed. Many were on the brink of mutiny, and the Queen knew she had to find food and money soon, or risk disaster. Moving to Barnet, she wrote two letters to the citizens of London, assuring them of her good intentions. Her commanders warned her not to proceed further south, urging her to return to the north and avoid forcing the issue with the Londoners, but the northerners, seeing their prospects of pillaging the capital and its environs receding, erupted in fury. Hundreds deserted, though, since the victory at St Albans had led to new recruits joining the Lancastrian forces, the army was kept more or less up to strength.

Margaret now sent back the deputation of ladies and aldermen to negotiate the terms of the capital's surrender, ordering the citizens to proclaim Edward of York a traitor and assuring them of an amnesty. They did not trust her, and with good cause, for her next move was to order 400 of her elite troops to march on Aldgate. Here they demanded admittance to the city, in the King's name, but the mayor, thoroughly cowed by the people, refused it. Another detail of the Queen's soldiers reached Westminster, but was roughly dealt with by indignant citizens, who drove it back with threats.

The widowed Duchess of York was then in residence at Baynard's Castle and becoming increasingly concerned for the safety of her younger sons, George and Richard, who might be taken as hostages for their brother's good behaviour if the Lancastrians entered the city. She therefore placed them on board a ship bound for Burgundy, where they would remain under the protection of Duke Philip until it was safe for them to return to England. She herself remained in London, praying for the safe arrival of her eldest son.

Realising that an attempt on London was impossible, Margaret ordered a retreat to Dunstable, hoping to allay the fears of the citizens. At the same time, Edward was approaching the capital. Prudently, he sent ahead a messenger to proclaim that the Lancastrians had given their soldiers licence to rob and assure the Londoners that he had forbidden his own troops to do so.

Margaret's retreat gave Edward the chance to advance on London unhindered, and the citizens, eager to demonstrate their support of the Yorkists, collected the then princely sum of £100, which was sent to Edward to help finance his soldiers. The Milanese ambassador informed his master that the enthusiastic support of the Londoners would probably mean that Edward and Warwick would triumph over their enemies.

On 27 February Edward of York, at the head of 20,000 knights and 30,000 foot soldiers, rode through the gates of London and took possession of the city. The Londoners welcomed him with rapturous acclaim as their saviour, the man who would save them from the Lancastrian menace. Even at eighteen he cut an impressive figure. The people cried, 'Hail to the Rose of Rouen!' and one punned, 'Let us walk in a new vineyard and let us make a gay garden in the month of March with this fair white rose and herb, the Earl of March!' At Edward's side rode Warwick, his strongest and most faithful ally, and there were fervent cheers for him also, who had long been a favourite with the Londoners. Edward rode to greet his mother at Baynard's Castle, while his army set up camp in Clerkenwell Fields outside the city walls.

It was no longer possible for Edward to claim, as his father had done earlier, that he had taken up arms in order to remove Henry VI from the influence of evil counsellors. People were now acknowledging that the endemic disorder was directly attributable to the weak government of Henry VI. This time, therefore, the Yorkists' intentions were to remove him from power and make Edward king. In fact, they had no alternative, for despite his warm welcome in London, he was not in a strong position, being technically an attainted traitor and lacking funds and the support of a majority of the magnates.

In order to test the mood of the people, whose allegiance was essential to Edward's success, on Sunday 1 March the Lord Chancellor, George Neville, addressed a crowd of citizens who were mingling with the Yorkist army in St John's Fields, declaring that Edward of York was the rightful king of England and that Henry of Lancaster was a usurper. When the Bishop asked the Londoners for their opinion, they shouted, 'Yea! Yea! King Edward!' and clapped their hands, while the soldiers drummed on their armour. 'I was there. I heard them!' wrote one chronicler. The next day Edward, accompanied by Warwick, Fauconberg and Norfolk, rode to Clerkenwell and reviewed his men, knowing that, whatever happened, he would need their services again before long.

Parliament was in session at this time, and therefore Edward must be seen to be elected king by the will of the people, whose assent would be expressed by their public acclamation of him. Evidence of such acclamation had already been displayed at St John's Fields, and on 3 March the Archbishop of Canterbury, the bishops of Salisbury and Exeter, Warwick, Norfolk, Lord FitzWalter and other peers held a council at Baynard's Castle, which resulted in all the magnates there present agreeing that Edward should be offered the throne. On the following day a deputation of lords and commons, led by Warwick, went to Baynard's Castle and presented a petition to him, begging him to accept the crown and royal dignity of England, while outside a crowd of Londoners was crying, 'King Edward! God save King Edward!' and begging him to 'avenge us on King Henry and his wife'. Edward graciously acceded to the lords' petition and was shortly afterwards proclaimed King Edward IV at Baynard's Castle.

Edward IV was not a usurper, as Henry IV had been, but the rightful heir to the crown of the Plantagenets legitimately restored to the throne sixty-two years after it had been usurped by the House of Lancaster. Yet although his claim to the throne had been acknowledged by the Lords in Parliament as superior to that of Henry VI, what really determined the issue was the fact that he was in control of the capital and had the military advantage over the Lancastrians. He had become king thanks to the efforts of a small group of magnates headed by Warwick, who had seen that the only way to maintain his position was to uphold the Yorkist claim.

On the day of his accession London's leading citizens were summoned to St Paul's, where they enthusiastically acclaimed their new sovereign when he arrived there after being proclaimed king. In the cathedral he made a thanksgiving offering to God, and then, at the invitation of the Lord Chancellor, went in procession to Westminster Hall where he took the oath required of a new monarch. Afterwards, attired in royal robes and a cap of estate, he was enthroned upon the King's Bench, to the cheers of the assembled lords, who then escorted him past huge crowds, waving and cheering, to Westminster Abbey, where the abbot and monks presented him with the crown and sceptre of St Edward the Confessor. He made more offerings at the high altar and at the Confessor's shrine before returning to the choir and mounting the coronation chair, which had been hastily placed there. He addressed the congregation, asserting his right to the crown. When he had finished speaking, the lords asked the people if they would have Edward for their king, at which they cried that they indeed took him for their lawful king. The magnates knelt one by one before him and paid homage, placing their hands between his, and afterwards the Abbey was filled with the glorious sound of a *Te Deum*: at its conclusion the King made yet more offerings before leaving the church and proceeding to the landing stage at the Palace of

Westminster, where he boarded a boat which took him back to Baynard's Castle.

Later that day his councillors came with plans for his formal coronation, but Edward vowed that he would not be crowned until Henry VI and Margaret of Anjou had been taken and executed or driven into exile. In his speech in Westminster Abbey Edward had declared that Henry had forfeited his right to the throne by failing to honour the Act of Accord and allowing his wife to take up arms against the true heirs. Henry was deposed, wrote Benet, 'because he ruled like a tyrant, as had his father and grandfather before him' – that is to say, without benefit of legal title. Warkworth says that 'when he had been removed from the throne by King Edward, most of the English people hated him because of his deceitful lords [but] never because of his own faults. They were therefore very glad of a change.'

On 5 March the Milanese ambassador, Prospero di Camulio, heard a rumour that Henry VI, learning of Edward's accession, had abdicated in favour of his son. The Queen, went the story, was so angry that she 'gave the King poison. At least he will know how to die, if he is incapable of doing anything else!' Although the rumour had no foundation in fact, it is testimony that the Queen's reputation was such that people believed her capable of the deed.

The House of York, in the person of Edward IV, was now established on the throne, but the deposed king and queen were still at large, and in command of a sizeable army. No one believed that the conflict would end here.

18

The Bloody Meadow

'And so, in field and town, everyone called Edward king.' His accession was hailed by his supporters and propagandists as the restoration of the true Plantagenet line. God would now, it was hoped, look benevolently upon the realm and allow peace and good government to be restored.

On 5 March the new king wrote to the city of Coventry, thanking the citizens for their loyal support. This was intended to forestall them from transferring their allegiance back to Henry VI, whose cause they had formerly supported so staunchly. Edward also rewarded Warwick for his inestimable service by appointing him Great Chamberlain of England, Captain of Dover, and Lord Warden of the Cinque Ports; he remained Captain of Calais.

After the Yorkists had entered London, Henry VI, Margaret of Anjou, Prince Edward and the entire Lancastrian army, 'having little trust in Essex, less in Kent and least of all in London, departed into the north country, where the foundation of their strength and refuge only rested'. With them went their prisoners. They marched to York, shocked and despondent, their men pillaging as they went and leaving havoc and misery behind them.

By retreating to the north the Lancastrians were effectively surrendering the military initiative to the Yorkists. Henry could have given the order to advance on the capital, but the royal troops were by now so disorderly and violent that he refused to do so, being appalled at the atrocities he had witnessed and guessing what the outcome would be and what damage it would do to the Lancastrian cause.

The royal army camped outside the walls of York, while Henry sent letters to his loyal lieges, listing 'the Earl of March's misdeeds' and commanding them to raise their people and attend him

'defensibly arrayed' with all speed. The Queen also called upon all
true subjects of King Henry to rally to his standard and appealed to
Mary of Gueldres for reinforcements. Mary responded with a small
force of men. Some chroniclers claim that within days Margaret
had increased the size of her army to 60,000 men, but the figure is
likely to have been nearer 30,000. Her generals, Somerset,
Northumberland and Clifford, now began to plan a decisive
campaign, and persuaded Henry and Margaret to remain in York
while they rode to face the enemy.

King Edward knew that if he did not take urgent steps to deal with
the Lancastrians he would never be secure on his throne; Henry VI
had to be overthrown in fact as well as in name. On 5 March he
dispatched Norfolk to East Anglia to recruit men, and the next day
sent Warwick north, accompanied by 'a great puissance of people',
to muster support for the Yorkists in his territories in the Midlands.
Two days later Warwick received commissions authorising him
to array the lieges of Northamptonshire, Warwickshire, Leicestershire, Staffordshire, Worcestershire, Gloucestershire, Shropshire,
Derbyshire, Nottinghamshire and Yorkshire. On the 11th Edward's
foot soldiers, recruited mainly in Wales and Kent, marched out of
London on their way north. With them went a number of carts filled
with weapons, guns and food.

Edward himself left London on the 13th, via Bishopsgate, and
marched north to St Albans with a great host whose ranks were
swelled by new recruits as he went. Rumours of the conduct of the
Lancastrian army were still driving many to support the Yorkists.
However, Edward's army was not much better behaved, at least to
begin with, for at St Albans, although Abbot Whethamstead asked
the new king to forbid looting, many soldiers defied the ban and
caused such extensive damage to the monks' quarters that the abbot
and his brethren were obliged to lodge in outlying manors until it
could be repaired.

Meanwhile, the King's mother, Duchess Cecily, remained in
London, working tirelessly to gain and maintain support for her
son's cause among the citizens, who were fearful as a result of
terrifying reports of the depredations of the Queen's northerners
that were filtering south. These made her task much easier, for the
Londoners' loyalty was now almost exclusively to the cause of
York.

On 16 March Edward came to Barkway, and the next day to
Cambridge, where he met up with Sir John Howard, newly arrived
from the abbey of Bury St Edmunds, where the abbot and convent
had raised £100 for the King, 'by way of love'. Coventry sent him

100 men, while other contingents were arrayed by the cities of Canterbury, Bristol, Salisbury, Worcester, Gloucester, Leicester, Nottingham and Northampton. By the 22nd Edward had arrived in Nottingham, where – after several false reports – he received certain intelligence that Somerset, Rivers and a strong force were positioned to defend the river crossing at Ferrybridge in Yorkshire. By the 27th he had reached Pontefract, 'collecting men in thousands', according to the Milanese ambassador. 'Some say that the Queen is exceedingly prudent, and by remaining on the defensive, as they say she is well content to do, she will bring things into subjection and will tear into pieces those attacks of the people.' Edward was now close behind the Lancastrian army, which was blocking the road to York, where lay Henry VI, Margaret of Anjou and their son. Hall says that nearly 30,000 Lancastrians were encamped nearby, and that Edward had 25,000 Yorkists, which would shortly be reinforced by the hosts led by Warwick and Norfolk.

Between them the two armies had between 60,000 and over 100,000 men – possibly two per cent of the total population of England – yet sources differ as to whether the Lancastrians had more than the Yorkists or were of equal strength. Whethamstead saw the coming conflict as a struggle between northerners and southerners, while Waurin says that the northern commanders were inferior to the southern ones.

The Lancastrian army was indeed predominantly northern and was under the command of Somerset, Exeter, Northumberland, Devon, Trollope, and the Lords FitzHugh, Hungerford, Beaumont, Dacre of Gilsland, Roos and Grey of Codnor. It included at least nineteen peers – proof that many magnates still felt that their first allegiance was to Henry VI – while the Yorkists boasted only eight: Warwick, Norfolk, Bourchier, Grey de Wilton, Clinton, Fauconberg and the Lords Scrope and Dacre (Richard Fiennes). Somerset, commander-in-chief of the Lancastrians, was just twenty-four, while King Edward, commander-in-chief of the Yorkists, was not quite nineteen. Somerset and Exeter were in command of the Lancastrian reserve, stationed in the village of Towton, not far from York, while the Yorkist vanguard was commanded by Fauconberg.

On 28 March King Edward sent Lord FitzWalter ahead with a force to secure the bridge over the River Aire, south of Ferrybridge, but they were ambushed by Lord Clifford, leading a large contingent of cavalry. So many were massacred or drowned that hardly any of FitzWalter's men were left, while he himself was killed and Warwick, who was with him, was wounded in the leg. When the news spread through the Yorkist ranks morale among the men plummeted. King Edward and his captains were worried that this would affect their performance in battle, but Warwick saved the day in dramatic fashion when he killed his horse in full view of the army and vowed that he would rather fight on foot and die with his men than yield another inch.

Meanwhile, King Henry had sent a message pleading for a truce to be negotiated, as it was Palm Sunday on the morrow, but King Edward refused the offer. He knew that a contingent of the main Lancastrian army, under Somerset and Rivers, was waiting two miles away, ready to crush the Yorkists if they overcame Clifford and tried to cross the river, and that if this campaign was to be successful then he must persist. Accordingly, he sent in the Yorkist vanguard under the command of John de la Pole, Duke of Suffolk, which managed to push the Lancastrians back to the end of the bridge. Messengers raced back to inform King Edward what was happening and he, seeing that reinforcements would be required, marched the main body of his army to Ferrybridge and commanded his men to go to Suffolk's aid, himself going on foot to fight with them.

At this point, in the midst of a violent struggle, the Lancastrians destroyed the bridge. The Yorkists, undeterred, built a narrow raft, intending to ferry their soldiers across, but it was seized by the enemy. Further furious fighting took place as the Yorkists made a successful but bloody attempt to recover it. Eventually they managed to cross the river a few miles upstream at Castleford, and set up camp on the other side amidst driving snow and freezing hail. In the end they had won the day, their victory having demonstrated to the enemy the new king's superior qualities as a general; by continually reinforcing his vanguard he had achieved victory, knowing that to do so was critical at this stage. The Lancastrians, although they had fought furiously, had lacked sufficient reinforcements, although they did manage to make off with a great number of Yorkist horses whose owners were fighting on foot with their king.

Lord Clifford, however, had been killed in the fight. As the Yorkists crossed the Aire at Castleford, Fauconberg was the first to go over, at the head of the vanguard. Clifford tried to trap him on the farther bank, and there was an intense struggle on Brotherton Marshes. Clifford fought with heroic courage, but seeing that his men were surrounded and no match for the enemy, gave the order to retreat via the valley of Dintingdale and the village of Saxton; he was by then so shattered with exhaustion that he unwisely loosened his gorget, and as he rode off a headless arrow embedded itself in his exposed throat and he died in great suffering. Edward had neither forgiven nor forgotten Clifford's brutal murder of young Rutland after Wakefield, and would have considered his brother's death well avenged.

That night, King Edward lodged at Pontefract Castle. At dawn on 29 March – Palm Sunday – both armies awoke to find themselves in the midst of a snowstorm. Shortly afterwards the Yorkists began their march north, and at eleven o'clock in the morning encamped on the hill south of the village of Saxton, ten miles south of York, with their backs to the village. When Edward drew up his men in battle formation, their lines stretched for a mile along the ridge. At the same time the Lancastrians moved north from Tadcaster along the road from London, via Stutton and Cocksford, and took up their position half a mile to the north of the Yorkists on high ground a hundred feet above meadowland and the village of Towton, six miles north of Ferrybridge. Below them the land sloped gently down to the valley.

The armies were now facing each other across what would shortly be known as the 'Bloody Meadow' and a field which is still called North Acres. From an offensive point of view the Lancastrians were in a commanding position and seemingly had the advantage. Behind the Yorkist lines lay the road to London and, beyond that, the River Aire: the Yorkists could easily be defeated by being pushed back along that road and trapped by – or in – the river. However, in the event of a Yorkist victory, the Lancastrian position was in reality horribly vulnerable. To their right, on the far side of the meadow, was a ravine, along which flowed a river called the Cock Beck, which was now in flood due to heavy rain and snow. To their left, a little way off in the direction of Selby and Cawood, lay the road to Tadcaster and the River Wharfe, which was also flooding. The only escape route for the Lancastrians, in the event of a rout, was by Tadcaster Bridge, across the River Wharfe.

'The lamentable Battle of Towton', the largest, longest, and one of the most important battles of the Wars of the Roses, took place on Palm Sunday in the midst of a thick blizzard that continued all day. As soon as both armies had taken up their positions, the fighting began. The chroniclers are maddeningly vague as to the tactics and strategies employed, and Waurin's is the only detailed, if unsubstantiated, account. Edward had brought with him plenty of artillery but there is no record of it being deployed during the battle – probably because of the appalling weather conditions.

At first, the Lancastrians were at a disadvantage because the wind was blowing the snow into their faces and they were unable to see the enemy properly or judge distances. Volley after volley of their arrows fell wide or short of the mark, and all they could hear through the swirling snow was the mocking laughter of Fauconberg's archers, which was accompanied by a deadly hail of heavy-shafted arrows that created havoc in the bewildered Lancastrian ranks. What the Lancastrians did not know was that the Yorkists had gathered up thousands of enemy arrows from the ground and were firing them back at them, moving deftly backwards, at Fauconberg's command, to avoid the next haphazard fall of yet more ineffectual Lancastrian arrows.

Before long the Lancastrians became aware of what was happening and of the terrible slaughter that was being wrought in their army, which had as yet gained no advantage. The order was given to lay down bows and arrows and charge into battle across the meadow. The Yorkists, likewise, dropped their bows and rushed into the fray, as Northumberland and Somerset advanced downhill with the Lancastrian vanguard, inflicting numerous casualties as they came and routing Edward's cavalry flank, which was chased from the field by Somerset's men.

There then followed one of the most terrible and bloody struggles in English history, as for two hours Lancastrians and Yorkists were locked in a vicious mêlée in driving sleet and bitter winds. By King Edward's command, no quarter was given nor any prisoners taken; even the common foot soldiers were not to be spared. Edward, remembering the fate of his father and brother, was bent on revenge. He himself was busy commanding his army, aiding his men, or helping to carry the wounded from the field. When his soldiers appeared to be flagging he dismounted in the thick of the fighting and rallied them, crying that he intended to live or die with them that day.

Warwick, in the thick of the mêlée, managed to maintain his position, although his men in particular were very hard pressed by their opponents. 'There was great slaughter that day at Towton,' wrote Waurin, 'and for a long time no one could see which side could gain the victory, so furious was the fighting.' So many had fallen that the snow was red with blood, yet throughout the battle reserve troops replaced those who had been killed or injured, or were collapsing from exhaustion; some of the latter were unable to rise and were trampled to death by the men who came to take their places.

As the afternoon advanced the fighting showed no signs of abating, and every foot of ground gained by one side would be violently recaptured by the other; thousands perished, and the air was split by the screams of the wounded and the dying. It was not clear who was winning until dusk fell, when at last the Lancastrians were driven back to the western side of the meadow. At this point, a strong force sent by Norfolk, who was terminally ill and unable to come himself, rode up from Saxton into North Acres and attacked the Lancastrian left flank. The Lancastrians, realising then that the day was lost and that they were all dead men unless they got away, fled the field. As their forces broke, the Yorkist cavalrymen raced to the horse park behind their own lines and mounted their steeds to give chase. As they thundered past, the King and Warwick, flushed with victory, yelled, 'Spare the commons! Kill the lords!' Their words went unheeded.

By evening, the already swollen waters of the Cock Beck had risen higher, thanks to the snow, yet for many of the defeated this was their only escape route, and before long almost the entire Lancastrian army was in full flight down the steep banks of the ravine, slipping on the snow and ice and plunging into the freezing waters of the flooding stream, which was soon filled with thousands of panic-stricken men, desperately struggling to escape from the fury and arrows of the pursuing Yorkist troops, who were systematically butchering every man they caught.

Most of the fleeing Lancastrians were making for a makeshift bridge of boards at Cocksford, but what they had not anticipated was the strong current in the stream. Many drowned, while others were shot by the enemy, whose arrows were falling thickly amid the snowflakes. The Yorkists were also racing for the bridge, and there was heavy fighting as they tried to prevent the Lancastrians from crossing it to freedom. The bridge had not been built to support a battling mass of men, and as it gave way with a sickening crack hundreds of Yorkists and Lancastrians plunged together into the icy, deep water below, where most of them drowned or suffocated in the press. As they gasped their last, struggling wildly in the water, horses' hooves trampled them, as more pursuers used their bodies as a bridge to the farther shore. Before long the Cock Beck was running red with blood all the way to the far-off River Wharfe.

As other Lancastrian fugitives came up to find the bridge gone, they were slaughtered by Wenlock's men or chased into and beyond Tadcaster. Yorkist soldiers pursued the fleeing Lancastrians for some time after the battle, and even smashed the bridge over the River Ouse at Tadcaster, where yet more vanquished soldiers drowned.

The battle lasted in total ten hours, from eleven in the morning until roughly nine at night, although the rout went on for longer, some fugitives being pursued nearly as far as York. When it was over, men dropped down with exhaustion and slept among the dead and wounded. The Yorkists had scored a decisive and overwhelming victory, but at a bitter price.

Towton was probably the bloodiest battle ever to take place on English soil. Casualties were high because large numbers of men had fought intensively in a somewhat confined space. When dawn rose on 30 March, the meadow and North Acres were thick with corpses. King Edward surmised that about 20,000 had been killed; his heralds, after surveying the carnage, estimated 28,000, a figure given by several contemporary chroniclers. However, this only applied to bodies lying on the field, and did not include those who perished during the rout, so the real figure was probably nearer 40,000. Of these, according to John Paston, 8000 were Yorkists, although on 8 April the Venetian ambassador reported Yorkist losses of only 800. Whatever the actual figures, all the contemporary accounts agree that the death toll was unusually high; in fact, the casualty lists for Towton were proportionately higher than those for the Battle of the Somme.

The people of Yorkshire remembered Towton as 'a great battle', according to the *Arrivall*, an official Yorkist account of events, but the memory was bitter because in that battle were slain 'many of their fathers, their sons, their brethren and kinsmen, and many other of their neighbours'. The slaughter of Towton broke the power of the great families of the north, and the Lancastrians lost some of their best captains: the Earl of Northumberland, Lord Randolph Dacre of Gilsland, Lord Scrope of Bolton, Sir Richard Percy, Lords Welles, Willoughby and Neville, and Sir Andrew Trollope were among the fallen. Lord Dacre, during a brief lull in the fighting in North Acres, had thought it safe to stop and refresh himself and, removing his helmet, used it to scoop up some water from a small tributary of the stream that flowed through the field. Unfortunately he was recognised by a young Yorkist soldier hiding behind a nearby elder tree, who raised his bow and shot Dacre dead. He was buried with his horse in the churchyard at Saxton; in 1861 the animal's skull was dug up, to the great astonishment of the villagers.

There were so many dead that it was said that blood was spattered on the snow-covered plain all the way from Towton to York. Because of the herculean task of burying so many thousands of bodies, King Edward gave extra wages to the gravediggers. A huge pit was dug at Saxton, in which hundreds of bodies, including that of Lord Clifford, were buried. Others were interred in another large pit in the Bloody Meadow, beside the bank of the Cock Beck; in the nineteenth century the soil in this spot was noted for producing rich, rank grass. Burial mounds are still visible at Low Leads, beyond Castle Hill Wood, by the battlefield, and a small wooden bridge across the Cock Beck now marks the spot where hundreds of Lancastrian corpses were piled high in water, mud and snow. In the 1850s, the owner of nearby Towton Hall had his cellars enlarged, and workmen found a large number of skeletons and bones buried beneath, belonging to men who had perished at Towton.

Relics of the fallen have surfaced over the years. A ploughman found a fifteenth-century ring inscribed: '*En loial amour tout de mon coer*'. 'Many a lady,' observed 'Gregory' mournfully, 'lost her beloved in that battle.' On another occasion a ring was found which bore the lion of the Percies and a motto, 'Now is thys'; it is now owned by the Duke of Northumberland. In the Castle Museum at York are a crossbow and a gisarm, or disembowelling knife.

Towton had a profound effect on everyone. Savagery on such a scale was thought shocking even in that warlike age, and the Milanese ambassador observed, 'Anyone who reflects at all upon the wretchedness of the Queen and the ruins of those killed, and considers the ferocity of that country and the state of mind of the victors, should indeed, it seems to me, pray to God for the dead, and not less for the living.'

Henry VI and Margaret of Anjou were in York when the battle was fought. Together with Exeter, Roos and Dr John Morton, a cultivated and intelligent cleric who would one day become Archbishop of Canterbury but who was now committed to supporting the House of Lancaster, they awaited news. When they were told of the terrible Lancastrian defeat, and that their army had been virtually annihilated, they decided on flight, 'packed up everything they could carry', gathered up their train, and fled from the city via Bootham Bar, passing north through the forest of Galtres, Margaret vowing fiercely that she would one day be revenged on the House of York. 'King Henry and his wife were overthrown,' wrote Waurin, 'and lost that crown which Henry IV had violently usurped and taken from King Richard II. Men say that ill-gotten goods cannot last.'

Edward IV might have scored a resounding victory, but it was an incomplete one, for Henry, Margaret and their son were still at large, focal points for resistance to Yorkist rule, and he would not be secure on the throne until they were either dead or he had them in his power. The Queen, in particular, would be a thorn in his side for some time to come.

'When King Edward had won the day at Towton he gave thanks

to God for his glorious victory,' wrote Waurin. 'Then many knights, earls and barons came into his presence, bowed to him, and asked him what they ought now to do for the best, to which he replied that he would never rest until he had killed or captured King Henry and his wife, or driven them from the country, as he had promised and sworn to do.' His lords advised him to make for York, because they had heard that the Queen and her supporters were there, but before they could depart the King ordered that the executions of forty-two Lancastrian knights and others captured during or after the battle be carried out. Many Lancastrians would now go into exile, while others, observed the Milanese ambassador, were 'quitting' King Henry 'and coming to tender obedience to this king'. The transfer of allegiance by so many lords meant that Edward was able to consolidate his position and become in fact, as well as in title, master of his realm. Many believed that, by according him so decisive a victory, God had declared His pleasure. There were still a number who regarded Edward as a usurper, but they were now in a minority; nor was the Lancastrian faction any longer in a position to challenge his authority. Nevertheless, although he was in control of most of England, the Lancastrians still held the English border counties in the north and several strategic castles in Wales.

Edward, knowing he needed to win support in the north, did show mercy to a number of northern magnates captured at Towton, including Northumberland's brother, Sir Ralph Percy. Others were allowed to escape and were later pardoned. Lord Rivers came to Edward and acknowledged him as the rightful king, whereupon Edward forgave his past support of the Lancastrians and promised him and his son Anthony Wydville pardons, which were issued the following July. By March 1463 both men had been admitted to the royal Council. The King also rewarded the men who had fought on his own side. Warwick's brother, John Neville, had shown such valour in the field that the King raised him to the peerage with the title Lord Montague.

On Good Friday, 3 April, news of the King's victory was delivered to the Lord Mayor of London; the Duchess of York learned of it the next morning when a letter from the King, written on 30 March, arrived. All her household gathered excitedly in the great hall of Baynard's Castle to hear her read it out. That Saturday, the Lord Chancellor, George Neville, announced the victory at Paul's Cross, and there was great rejoicing among the people. One rumour had it that Henry VI had been captured, but the Milanese ambassador shrewdly commented that 'vain flowers always grow in good news'. In Dover and Sandwich, huge bonfires were lit to signal the news to the royal garrison at Calais, where a third beacon was kindled in response.

On the morning after the battle King Edward rode in triumph to York, 'with great solemnity and processions', but as he approached the Micklegate Bar his face set into grim lines as he saw above him the rotting heads of his father, his brother, and his uncle of Salisbury. This dreadful sight turned him visibly grey with anger and sorrow, and he vowed that the Lancastrians would taste his vengeance and that those responsible for the deaths of his kinsfolk would be relentlessly sought out and slaughtered. When he arrived in York his first order was that the heads be taken down and decently interred at Pontefract with the corresponding bodies.

Edward received a warm welcome from the people of York. 'All the clergy came out to greet him,' says Waurin, 'and did reverence to him as their sovereign lord and prince, humbly begging him to forgive them if they had in any way offended him, and he freely forgave them [and] stayed a full week in the city with much joy and celebration.' Representatives from major towns in Yorkshire came and offered their submission, and he issued commissions of the peace for the arrest of any rebels. The King's officers soon discovered several Lancastrians in hiding in the city and rounded them up. Devon had barricaded himself in the ancient Norman castle, but had not the resources to defend it, so he too was taken, while Wiltshire was soon afterwards captured at Cockermouth and imprisoned. The King ordered that the Earl of Devon, Sir Baldwin Fulford and Sir William Hill, all prominent Lancastrians, be beheaded in York as an example to the citizens. Their heads replaced those of the Yorkists on the Micklegate Bar, grim reminders of the fate of those who rebelled against their lawful sovereign.

On 5 April, Edward celebrated Easter in York, having ordered his captains to recruit fresh soldiers. He then rode north with his army to Durham, and thence to Newcastle, in pursuit of King Henry and Queen Margaret, who were making for Scotland, accompanied by Somerset, Exeter, Roos and Morton. The city of Coventry had paid Warwick £14 for the expenses of hiring fourteen men to chase after the deposed King. By 7 April the fleeing Lancastrians were resting briefly in Newcastle; they then continued their journey to Alnwick, whence the Queen sent an urgent message to the Bishop of St Andrews, Regent of Scotland, begging him to issue a safe-conduct for their entry into that kingdom. At Wark Castle, near Carham, Henry and Margaret were besieged by a force of Yorkist adherents led by Sir Robert Ogle. Retainers of the late Earl of Northumberland gathered 5-6,000 men in order to relieve the siege, and their intervention enabled the royal party to escape through a little postern gate at the back of the castle and proceed in haste to Berwick. Here, while awaiting word from Scotland, they enjoyed a few days of rest; the Queen even went hunting and shot a buck. But they knew that this respite could not last.

In Scotland, Mary of Gueldres found herself in a difficult position. The Duke of Burgundy was her uncle, and he was hopeful of securing an alliance with Edward IV. A show of friendship by his niece to Edward's enemies could place this alliance in jeopardy. Warwick was well aware of the Queen Regent's dilemma and capitalised on it by using diplomatic pressure. Before long, he had extracted from her an agreement that the Scots would not offer military support to the Lancastrians. Nevertheless, he could not stop them from granting asylum to the dispossessed royal family, and the necessary safe-conduct was issued. Henry, Margaret, the Prince and 6000 followers crossed the border into Galloway. Henry sought refuge in the convent of the Grey Friars at Kirkcudbright, while his wife and son travelled on to the Scottish court, then at Linlithgow Palace, where Mary of Gueldres accorded them a sympathetic welcome and ordered that apartments be prepared for them. Margaret stayed here for a time, then at Durrisdeer, then at Dumfries, and finally at Lanark, before the Bishop of St Andrews arranged in July for her to move to more convenient lodgings in Lincluden Abbey near Edinburgh.

The Yorkists pursued their quarry almost to Scotland and, had they succeeded in capturing them, Edward IV would have been spared many problems in the years to come. But they failed, and returned south, much dispirited. Edward himself had arrived in Newcastle on 1 May, where he ordered the execution of Wiltshire, whose head was afterwards displayed on London Bridge.

Because the north of England was still strongly Lancastrian in sympathy, Edward dared not penetrate beyond Newcastle. The north would remain unconquered for some time to come, and Margaret of Anjou would capitalise on this, fuelling discontent against the Yorkists by propaganda and appealing to the loyalties of local landowners. On 18 April, Prospero di Camulio had prophesied: 'If the King and Queen of England, with the other fugitives, are not taken, it seems certain that in time fresh disturbances will arise.' He also predicted that 'before long, grievances and recrimination will break out between King Edward and the Earl of Warwick. King Henry and the Queen will be victorious.' Both these predictions were to prove strangely accurate.

It was not long before the Queen managed to persuade the Scottish government to conclude a treaty providing for the marriage of Prince Edward to James III's sister Margaret Stewart. In return, Henry VI would surrender Berwick, as already promised, and when he was restored to the throne of England would grant the Scots lands in England and make the Bishop of St Andrews Archbishop of Canterbury. Furthermore, England was to enter into a tripartite alliance with Scotland and France, her traditional enemies. When Edward IV learned of this agreement, he issued a proclamation, publishing its terms in full and accusing Margaret of 'exciting and provoking the greatest and largest cruelty against our subjects, unto the execution of her insatiable malice towards them'. He then wrote an angry letter to King James, saying, 'Whereas ye took and received our traitors and rebels, we require and exhort you to deliver [them] unto us without delay.' The regents, in James's name, refused; they would not break such an advantageous alliance, nor jeopardise the Princess Margaret's marriage.

Life was not easy for the Lancastrians in Scotland, however. Although Queen Mary took Prince Edward into her household to learn the knightly graces, his mother found herself in desperate financial straits. Having pawned her gold and silver plate to raise funds for a fresh onslaught upon the Yorkists, she had to resort to borrowing money from the Queen Regent. Between May and July Mary loaned Margaret a total of £200, but she had no means of paying it back. Before long she was 'in want of the absolute necessities of life', according to the French chronicler Le Moine. Nevertheless, for all her poverty, Edward IV feared her more 'than all the princes of the House of Lancaster combined'.

On 25 April, Margaret, in the name of Henry VI, formally ceded Berwick to the Scots. Needless to say, its surrender infuriated the English and presented the Yorkists with an excellent propaganda weapon. Nevertheless, the loss of the last English-owned fortified border town meant that Edward had lost an invaluable bridgehead for invading Scotland; it weakened his diplomatic bargaining position, and gave the French, Scotland's allies, a potential advantage. Worst of all, in Scottish hands Berwick became a centre for launching Lancastrian raids into Northumberland.

After dealing with several outbreaks of disaffection and disorder in the north, Edward IV left Newcastle on 2 May and returned to London, where he received a hero's welcome as the man who had saved the city from the brutality of the northerners. During the summer the King issued a stream of commissions of array, which testify to his fear that a Lancastrian invasion was imminent. Fauconberg was left in overall charge of the north, with instructions to safeguard it from Lancastrian attacks. In May, Geoffrey Gate was commissioned to safeguard Carisbrooke Castle and the Isle of Wight against invasion from the south, and in July, orders went out to Lord Ferrers, Sir William Herbert and Sir James Baskerville to raise the levies of Herefordshire, Gloucestershire and Shropshire for the defence of the realm against the King's enemies in Scotland and France. Edward was taking no chances.

In June, Queen Margaret led an army of Scotsmen, retainers of the earls of Douglas and Angus, into England. With her rode Prince Edward, Exeter, Lord Rougemont Grey, Sir Humphrey Dacre, Sir Robert Whittingham, Sir Henry Bellingham and Sir Richard Tunstall. Her objective was to take Carlisle, which she had also promised to the Scots, Her army laid siege to the town and burned its suburbs, but was driven back by a force led by Warwick's brother, Montague, whose task it was to guard the northern border from attack.

Undaunted, the Lancastrians, who had now been joined by Henry VI himself, who rode at their head, penetrated further south, making for Durham. But King Edward commanded the Archbishop of York to muster his tenants and have them prepare to join a force led by Fauconberg and Montague. When, on 26 June, the Lancastrian standards were raised at Ryton and Brancepeth, the levies raised by the Archbishop, which were now under the command of Warwick himself, repelled the invaders, who retreated north two days later.

Warwick began to root out Lancastrian rebels in the countryside bordering the River Tyne, and by July, thanks to his presence in the region, the Yorkists had gained a foothold in the north and were, by a gradual process, beginning to overcome Lancastrian resistance. On 31 July the King appointed Warwick Warden of the East and West Marches on the northern border, instructing him to bring the north to Edward's allegiance or reduce it to submission. A month later it was being reported in Milan that Warwick had prevented the Lancastrians from invading Northumberland. Edward was now relatively free to focus his attention upon Wales, where his enemies were still in control of several strategically placed strongholds, and wasted no time in dispatching an army to deal with them also.

On Friday, 26 June, Edward IV was conducted by the Lord Mayor and aldermen of London to the Tower, where custom decreed he must spend a night prior to his coronation. There he created twenty-eight Knights of the Bath, among them his brothers George and Richard, and a further five the following morning. These knights, clad in gowns of blue with white silk hoods on their shoulders, like those worn by priests, then preceded him in a grand procession through the streets of the city to the Palace of Westminster, there to lodge the night before his coronation.

On the morning of Sunday, 28 June 1461 Edward issued a proclamation promising his subjects good and just government, and condemning 'the oppression of the people, the manslaughter, extortion, perjury and robbery amongst them, the very decay of merchandise wherein rested the prosperity of the subjects' that had characterised Lancastrian rule. This touched a sensitive nerve in the London merchants, who had suffered much under Edward's predecessor.

Before leaving the palace, Edward created his brother George, then twelve, Duke of Clarence: later that same year he would be made a Knight of the Garter. The King's youngest brother, Richard, was just eight, and would for a time remain under their mother's care.

That Sunday, Edward was crowned in Westminster Abbey in a ceremony of great splendour, amidst public acclaim. 'I am unable to declare how well the commons love and adore him, as if he were their god,' wrote one London merchant. 'The entire kingdom keeps holiday for the event, which seems a boon from above. Thus far he appears to be a just prince, and to mean to mend and organise matters otherwise than has been done hitherto.'

On the 29th, the King went again to Westminster Abbey to give thanks, and on the following day to St Paul's Cathedral to attend its 800th centenary celebrations and be entertained by a series of elaborate pageants. Everywhere he received an ecstatic welcome. It was obvious to the Londoners that he had the makings of a great ruler: at the very least, he was a considerable improvement on Henry VI.

19

'A Person Well Worthy To Be King'

Unlike Henry VI, Edward looked every inch a king. Sir Thomas More called him 'princely to behold, of body mighty, strong and clean made'. Polydore Vergil, who, like More, never saw him but relied on descriptions given by those who had, described him as 'very tall of personage, exceeding the stature almost of all others, of comely visage, pleasant look, [and] broad breasted'. In 1789, when Edward's skeleton was found by workmen repaving the choir in St George's Chapel, Windsor, it was discovered to be over 6'3" long, and still had wisps of golden-brown hair adhering to the skull.

Commines remembered Edward in youth as 'the handsomest prince my eyes ever beheld'. In November 1461 the Speaker of the Commons, Sir James Strangeways, addressing the King in Parliament, referred to 'the beauty of personage that it hath pleased Almighty God to send you'. Edward was aware of the effect that his good looks had on people, and enjoyed showing off, wearing magnificent and daringly cut clothes that revealed his fine, well-proportioned physique to onlookers. By the standards of his day he was very clean, having his head, legs and feet washed every Saturday night, and sometimes more often. But he loved food and drink to excess, and in later years would even take an emetic so as to be able to gorge once more. Predictably, he steadily gained weight over the years, but as a young man in his twenties he was lean, energetic and very active. The head and shoulders portrait of him in the Royal Collection is a copy by a Flemish artist of an original believed to have been painted before 1472, and shows a strongly built man with a marked resemblance to Henry VIII, Edward's grandson. An inferior version of this portrait is in the National Portrait Gallery.

In 1461 Coppini described Edward as 'young, prudent and magnanimous'. He had courage, determination and resourcefulness, which he used to his own advantage, and was pragmatic, generous, witty and ruthless when the occasion demanded it. However, Commines, who met the King several times, concluded that he was 'not a man of any great management or foresight, but he was of invincible courage'. Mancini states that, like many big men, Edward was gentle and cheerful by nature; he was normally tolerant, easy-going and pleasure-loving, but when his anger was aroused he could be terrifying.

Vergil describes Edward as being of 'sharp wit, of passing retentive memory, diligent in doing his affairs, ready in perils, bountiful to his friends. Humanity was bred in him abundantly, but he would use himself more familiarly among private persons than the honour of his majesty required.' The common touch came naturally to him. 'He was easy of access to his friends,' wrote Mancini, and had a genial greeting for everyone. If someone showed that he was nervous, the King would place a kindly, reassuring hand on his shoulder, thus putting him at ease. He was well-skilled in the art of courtesy, and if he thought strangers were trying to have a close look at him, he would call them to his side. On a personal level he enjoyed great popularity.

In adversity, More says, Edward was 'nothing abashed'; in times of peace he showed himself 'just and merciful'. He was pious in the conventional sense, and, although intelligent, he was no intellectual, yet he did enjoy collecting books, which he took with him whenever he travelled and later, when the collection became too unwieldy to transport, deposited at Windsor, where they became the basis for the Royal Library which exists to this day. Although he personally had a preference for illuminated manuscripts, he became a patron of William Caxton, the first English printer. The King was fluent in Latin and French, and wrote a fine italic hand, rare in a mediaeval English sovereign. He was fascinated by the contemporary science of alchemy, by which it was believed that base metal could be turned into gold.

In his tastes Edward followed the dictates of the court of Burgundy, which at that time led the rest of Europe in style, culture, manners and etiquette. He spent lavishly on clothing, jewels and plate, but was unable to exercise a great deal of patronage of the arts or carry out his cherished hopes of rebuilding or extending the royal palaces until later in his reign. Today, St George's Chapel, Windsor, and the great hall at Eltham Palace in Kent bear witness to the largely vanished splendours of his reign.

Now that he was established on the throne, Edward gave himself up to the pursuit of pleasure. He was extravagant by nature, dissolute, and loved luxury too much for his own good. Commines says 'he was accustomed to more luxuries and pleasures than any prince of his day'. He was a good dancer, excelled at sports, and preferred to indulge in his pleasures than attend to matters of state. Almost the only person he went in awe of was his formidable mother who, according to the Paston Letters, could 'rule the King as she pleases'.

Edward's chief vice was his sensuality, and his debaucheries were soon notorious. 'He thought of nothing but upon women,' wrote a disapproving Commines, 'and on that more than reason would; and on hunting, and on the comfort of his person.' Mancini found him

> licentious in the extreme. Moreover, it was said that he had been most insolent to numerous women after he had seduced them, for as soon as he had satisfied his lust he abandoned the ladies, much against their will, to the other courtiers. He pursued with no discrimination the married and unmarried, the noble and lowly. However, he took none by force. He overcame all by money and promises, and, having conquered them, he dismissed them. He had many promoters and companions of his vices.

More wrote: 'He was of youth greatly given to fleshly wantonness, for no woman was there anywhere whom he set his eye upon but he would importunately pursue his appetite and have her.' Croyland, along with many of Edward's contemporaries, felt that the King 'indulged his passions and desires too intemperately'. Later it would be said that his sexual excesses in youth had permanently undermined his health and constitution. However, few of his intrigues lasted for long and none of his mistresses was allowed to interfere in politics. The names of only two are known: Elizabeth Lucy, a married woman who had an affair with Edward early in his reign and bore him a son, Arthur Plantagenet, and possibly a daughter too; and Elizabeth Shore, commonly miscalled Jane, who was the only one he is said to have loved, and who remained by his side through the latter years of his life.

For all his love of pleasure, Edward was an exceptionally able and talented warrior and general. At nineteen, he was already the veteran of several important battles and the victor of two decisive ones. In the field he was 'manly, vigorous and valiant'; Vergil says he was 'earnest and horrible to the enemy, and fortunate in all his wars'. Commines remarked, much later, that he had fought many battles but never lost one. He apparently found being in the midst of a mêlée exhilarating, even though he hated war for its own sake and tried to avoid it whenever possible. He abandoned conscription for periods longer than forty days, and restricted it to campaigns affecting the defence of the realm only. Unlike his predecessors, he had no continental ambitions: 'He was not suited to endure all the toil necessary for a king of England to make conquest in France.'

As often as possible Edward emphasised his royal status by wearing his crown in public, bestowing higher payments on those persons who were healed by his touch (touching for the King's Evil being a routine duty of monarchy that was believed to effect a cure for the distressing skin disease scrofula), and frequently presiding from the marble throne over the Court of King's Bench at Westminster to ensure that justice was being administered fairly. He loved the trappings of monarchy, the display, the ceremonial and the adulation.

As king, Edward excelled Henry VI in nearly every way, especially as a statesman and a general. He was a firm and resolute ruler, shrewd and astute, and had real ability and business acumen, as well as the willingness to apply himself. He was eventually successful in his attempts to restore the authority of the monarchy and make it into an institution that inspired respect and awe. More, who describes Edward as a great king, says he endeared himself to his subjects by small acts of consideration which made more impression on them than grand gestures would have done. More gives an example of this, relating how on one occasion the King invited the Lord Mayor and aldermen of London to Windsor 'for none other errand but to have them hunt and be merry with him'. He was undoubtedly popular with the people: 'To plaintiffs and those who complained of injustice he lent a willing ear,' wrote Mancini. 'Charges against himself he contented with an excuse, if he did not remove the cause. He was more favourable than other princes to foreigners.' He was also unusually tolerant of heresy – only one Lollard was burned at the stake during his reign.

Edward was an able and energetic administrator, always busy and always accessible to his subjects. It was said of him that he knew the names and fortunes of all men of note in the country, and he personally involved himself in many aspects of government, especially where law enforcement was involved. This is attested to by the unprecedented number of letters and warrants issued under the signet seal, which was kept by the King's secretary.

Edward's court was patterned on that of Philip of Burgundy. 'In those days,' remembered Croyland, 'you would have seen a royal court worthy of a leading kingdom, full of riches and men from every nation.' Such magnificence had not been seen at court since the time of Richard II. Scholars and men of learning were warmly welcomed. Elaborate codes of courtesy and etiquette were followed slavishly, these being considered the outward manifestations of an ordered society. So intricate were these rituals that a stream of books on manners appeared at this time. The number of steps one took to greet one's guests was determined by one's rank. According precedence was a refined art, and social inferiors were expected to refuse precedence a stated number of times, according to rank, before gracefully giving in. Pages and sons of the nobility were forbidden to drink wine while still chewing food, lean over the table, pick their noses, teeth or nails during meals, place dirty utensils on the cloth or eat with their knives.

During Edward's reign *The Black Book of the Household* was drawn up, in which were enshrined the rights and duties of all members of the royal household and the details of ceremonial to be observed at court. This was the result of the King's determination to impose economies and curb wastefulness. The money thus saved was spent on the trappings of majesty, so that both his own subjects and foreign visitors might be impressed by the magnificence of the King. Although splendid and in some ways extravagant, the court of Edward IV was thus more economically organised than those of his predecessors.

As time went by, Edward improved and beautified many of his palaces, notably Greenwich, Westminster, Windsor and Eltham. He spent lavishly on 'chambers of pleasaunce' hung with rich and vivid tapestries. One of his favourite residences was the Tower of London, where the splendid royal apartments were protected by great fortifications and were convenient for the city of London. Here Edward spent more time than any sovereign before him.

In all his palaces the King's apartments – his 'House of Magnificence' – consisted of three chambers: an outer or audience chamber, where he received ambassadors or visitors; an inner or privy chamber, for private business; and a bedchamber. Edward was attended in these chambers by some 400 men under the control of the Lord Chamberlain, Sir William Hastings. The most important members in this hierarchy were the Knights of the Body, who looked after the King's personal needs. Then came his knights, squires and gentlemen ushers, whose duty was to ensure that protocol was continually observed, followed by servers, yeomen, messengers, torch bearers, grooms of the chamber, and pages, who were usually the sons of lords, sent to court to complete their education and knightly training as well as performing menial services for the King, such as clearing up after the many dogs in the household.

The King's apartments, known as the Chamber, were the scene of royal ceremonial and display, political intrigue and much jostling for power by nobles competing for the monarch's patronage. Under the Lord Chamberlain the most important officers of the Chamber were the King's secretary, chaplain, almoner and ushers, all of whom could become quite influential through their daily dealings with the sovereign. It was compulsory for every male member of the King's household above the rank of gentleman to wear a gold collar of suns and white roses in honour of the House of York.

Each morning Edward rose at dawn and heard mass before breaking his fast on cold meat and ale. He was dressed by his squires, who slept in his bedchamber on truckle or pallet beds. Twenty squires and a gentleman usher served him at meals, which were conducted with great ceremony, 2000 people eating each day at the King's expense. A server stood at hand with basin and towel so that Edward could wash his hands after a meal, and a 'Doctor of Physic' was always in attendance to advise him 'which diet is best', although one suspects that his advice was not always heeded. The royal chefs were experts in the culinary arts, serving not only traditional dishes but also foreign and exotic ones. As the King ate, thirteen minstrels played for him in a gallery above the hall.

At night Edward slept in a tester bed which had been made up according to an elaborate ritual involving two squires, two grooms, a yeoman and a gentleman usher, who spread upon it fustian upper sheets of bleached linen, a bolster and an ermine counterpane, then sprinkled it with holy water.

In the summer Edward loved nothing better than to go hunting at Windsor. Here were served ceremonial picnics, with tables laid under the trees in the great park laden with platters of roasted meats and artistic sugar confections called 'subtleties'. The King would flirt with the ladies of his court in silken pavilions, or sail along the Thames in a gilded barge to the sound of music, laughter and conversation. Commines remarked sourly that Edward had 'wholly given himself to dances, hunting, hawking and banqueting', while monastic chroniclers were scandalised by the dress of the courtiers, in particular the short-skirted doublets of the men, which were worn over tight hose and revealed 'shameful privy members'. The extravagant headdresses of the noble ladies, steeple-shaped hennins and precarious affairs of wire and gauze known as 'butterflies', also drew adverse comments from the moralists, who saw in them the lure of the Devil.

Hospitality at court was lavish. In 1466 the Queen of Bohemia's brother, the Lord of Rozmital, was a guest of King Edward, and was as impressed with the banquet of fifty courses that was served in his honour as he was with the courtesy and decorum of the courtiers. A member of his train, Gabriel Tetzel, who wrote an account of the visit, was himself overwhelmed by the magnificence and splendour of the Yorkist court and the astonishing reverence shown to the King by his relatives and nobles. He pronounced it 'the most splendid court that one can find in all Christendom'.

After Towton, Edward IV found it relatively easy to establish himself as king, even though he still faced opposition and potential rebellion from Lancastrian supporters and even, later on, from discontented Yorkists, who felt that he had failed to live up to his promises. To survive he knew he had to eliminate the Lancastrian threat, both at home and abroad, and adopt a general policy of conciliation towards his subjects, particularly the more influential ones.

The most important challenge facing him was political reconstruction, a task that would take several years. His chief aims were to re-establish the authority of the Crown, restore law and order, win the support of his subjects, and unite the nation under a strong and stable government, thus laying down firm foundations for his dynasty. He wished to gain favour with the prosperous and influential merchant classes, especially in London, and one of the first things he did was to ban the import of inferior goods in order to protect the interests of English industry. Another priority was to secure the goodwill of other European nations, especially France and Burgundy, and so avoid the expense of war.

During the first decade of his reign the King was preoccupied with reasserting the royal authority, and several reforms had to wait. However, within this period English trade began to recover, and the Crown became more respected. Edward was not able to eliminate factions at court; indeed, by favouring the Nevilles he seemed to be encouraging them. However, unlike Henry VI, he exercised a tight rein on patronage.

Edward began restoring law and order at local level by replacing corrupt sheriffs with men of greater integrity, and corrupt officials by professionally qualified ones. In 1464 he accompanied his justices on a tour of duty in the west of England, where he intended to punish 'risers against the peace', desiring to be seen to be personally enforcing his laws. He took measures against the rigging of elections of members of Parliament by insisting that only those qualified to vote be allowed to do so, and preventing them from being intimidated by local lords and their retainers. These measures were only partly successful, as Edward did not always dare to alienate the magnates who had benefited from corrupt practices. He enjoyed greater success in his attempts to prevent piracy; gradually the seas became safe again, which pleased the merchants greatly. Contemporary sources show that under Edward's rule there was an overall improvement in law and order generally.

Finally – and this was an urgent necessity – the King had to overhaul the royal finances. He began by passing several Acts of Resumption revoking grants and pensions made by Henry VI, though never without lists of exemptions in order to preserve his policy of conciliation. This, naturally, caused some hardship, but Edward had decided on his priorities. He then purged the royal household of numerous Lancastrian officials, replacing them with men of his own affinity. He even tried to close Eton College, but Bishop Wayneflete persuaded him not to.

At the beginning of Edward's reign the Crown's annual expenditure was £50,000. The royal income barely covered that, and the King was sometimes unable to cover his costs. Later in 1461 he gained possession of the estates of Henry VI, including the income from the duchy of Lancaster, which, together with the income from his own Yorkist inheritance and from a great number of confiscated Lancastrian properties, brought him an additional income of around £30,000 a year. Much of this, however, was swallowed up in 1461 by grants and rewards to his loyal supporters, and until 1465 Edward had to live carefully. In that year Parliament granted him the revenues from customs duties at English ports for life, which brought him an extra £25,000 a year, a figure that would later increase as the trade depression lifted.

Edward IV had some talent for business and finance, and could also be ruthless. As his position became more secure, he demanded of his wealthier subjects forced loans known as 'benevolences', and even outright gifts. These were, needless to say, unpopular measures, but their end result was that the Crown, for the first time in decades, became solvent, an extraordinary achievement in the Middle Ages.

One of the King's priorities in his early years on the throne was to repay the debts owed by the Crown to London merchants and Italian banks. Henry VI's reputation for not repaying loans had resulted in him being unable to obtain any further credit. Edward IV had no intention of allowing the same thing to happen again, and by the end of his reign had repaid debts totalling £97,000. To do this, he had tightened controls on royal expenditure, streamlined the administration of the Crown's finances, and made corrupt practices difficult. He appointed professional receivers and surveyors to manage the Crown's estates, abandoning the inefficient and unwieldy system by which they had been administered under his predecessor. Estate officials were made accountable to the Chamber, the financial department of the royal household, instead of to the Exchequer, which meant there was less delay before the King received the revenues due to him, while discrepancies could be spotted early. It was not long before the Chamber replaced the Exchequer as the chief financial department of state.

In 1467 the King promised in Parliament to 'live of his own' without borrowing, and not to levy burdensome taxes unless it was for 'great and urgent causes', such as the defence of the realm. During the 1460s Parliament voted the King a total of £93,000, and most of this was spent on putting down rebellions. From 1463 Edward became heavily involved in the wool trade for his own profit, exporting thousands of sacks of wool and woollen cloth; over the years the venture proved highly successful and enabled him to pay off his debts and also provide employment for many people.

Mancini commented that, 'though not rapacious of other men's goods, [Edward] was yet so eager for money that in pursuing it he acquired a reputation for avarice. By appealing to causes, either true or at least with some semblance of truth, he did not appear to extort but almost to beg for subsidies.' Between 1461 and 1463, however, the political situation was such that he was obliged to make many financial demands of his subjects, and this did not endear him to them.

Next to the King, the greatest man in England was Richard Neville, Earl of Warwick, Edward's mainstay and foremost supporter. Warwick virtually controlled the government for the first three years of the reign, carried along on a tide of public popularity. He was so well loved that, according to an agent of the King of France, whenever he showed himself in public, accompanied by his customary train of 600 liveried retainers, crowds would run to greet him, crying, 'Warwick! Warwick!' 'It seems to the people that God has descended from the skies.' No one – especially the Earl himself – doubted that the King was indebted to Warwick for his crown. In Europe it was openly said that he reigned 'by virtue of the Earl of Warwick', while the Scots perceived Warwick as 'the conductor of the realm', Warwick and the King were allied not only by kinship, friendship, affinity and a debt of gratitude, but also because their association benefited the interests of both: Warwick did not render his services for entirely selfless motives, while the King needed his support. Many magnates, outwardly subservient to the new regime, were of doubtful loyalty, lukewarm at best, or pragmatic opportunists. Warwick in contrast had proved himself to be a loyal friend to Edward and his father in prosperity as in adversity, and at thirty-two, the Earl was thirteen years older than the King, and far more experienced in politics. It was easy, at first, for him to assert himself, and while he was using his considerable talents and energy to maintain Edward on the throne, Edward naturally felt no resentment. He made Warwick his chief adviser and allowed him to control foreign policy, giving him also complete responsibility for military affairs and the defence of the kingdom. For the present, he was content to let the Earl share the burdens of state while he enjoyed the more frivolous aspects of kingship.

'Warwick seems to me everything in this kingdom,' commented the Milanese ambassador, but although Edward IV relied on the Earl in many ways, he would not be ruled by him. This was not apparent to everyone, even Warwick himself, who certainly overestimated his influence over the King, nor was it obvious to most foreign observers, who tended to exaggerate his role. One citizen of Calais wrote to the King of France, 'They tell me that they have but two rulers in England: Monsieur de Warwick, and another whose name I have forgotten.' The Earl, observed Commines, 'could almost be called the King's father as a result of the service and education he has given him'. Prospero di Camulio had already foreseen discord between the King and his cousin, but few others had such insight.

Warwick was regarded by his contemporaries as 'the most courageous and manliest knight living'. 'Of knighthood he was the lodestar, born of a stock that shall ever be true.' His income at this time was £3900 a year, far exceeding that of any other magnate. His principal seats were at Sheriff Hutton Castle and Middleham Castle, where he maintained the greatest private household of the age, with 20,000 retainers. He also kept a lavish establishment in London, where generous hospitality was dispensed to visitors. He always appeared in public splendidly attired, and his genial manner and unfailing politeness never failed to impress those who had dealings with him.

Yet for all his wealth Warwick had no son to succeed him. His brilliant marriage had produced only two daughters, Isabel, now ten, and Anne, five. These girls would one day inherit all Warwick's riches and were therefore the greatest heiresses in England. Well-born husbands must be found for them, and Warwick was beginning now to consider potential candidates.

Warwick worked hard to restore the authority of the Crown, but, while he entertained no secret designs on the throne itself, he wanted – and needed – to wield power. He saw himself not simply as a member of the aristocracy, but as a man set apart, destined to rule by his gifts and talents. Yet he was more interested in self-aggrandisement and dabbling in international politics than in reforming the government at home or the royal finances, both of which the King regarded as vitally important. Warwick's own priority was to establish the Nevilles as the leading power in the realm and thus dominate the magnates. His fellow peers, however, were understandably jealous of his power and wealth, and reluctant to offer him their friendship and support. He had already alienated Sir William Herbert by his ambitious designs in Wales, and made enemies of several other nobles, among them Lord Audley and Humphrey Stafford. Yet his influence with the King was such that no one dared criticise him.

Edward was grateful to Warwick for many things, but he intended that there should be only one ruler in England: himself. How that would ride with Warwick's own ambitions in the long term remained to be seen.

One government body that needed reform was the Council. Lord Chief Justice Fortescue described at this time how he believed it should be done. No longer should that august body be dominated by 'the great princes and the greatest lords in the land, which lords had many matters of their own to be traded in the Council, [so that] they attended but little to the King's matters'. Instead, the Council should in future consist of a dozen 'spiritual men and twelve temporal men, of the wisest and best disposed men that can be found in all the parts of this land'. In other words, it was to be staffed, not by an aristocracy, but by a meritocracy, and its members would swear to serve no one but the King and would in return be assured of a permanent seat on the Council.

Edward IV followed Fortescue's precepts to some extent, coming to rely on a select group of about twelve trusted individuals and giving them wide responsibilities and influence as his lieutenants in different parts of the kingdom, thereby satisfying their ambitions for power. These councillors were largely highly qualified men who owed their promotion and advancement to the King and had been long-standing supporters of the House of York. Not all were magnates: some were gentlemen, canon lawyers or public servants. Hitherto, high-ranking clergy had made up the greater part of the Council; under Edward IV it became more of a secular institution.

Prominent among these councillors was Sir William Hastings, a close friend and confidant of the King, who was entrusted with control of the area around Leicester – previously Lancastrian in sympathy – where he ruled with unprecedented authority. Sir William Herbert was appointed governor of south Wales, where his word was law; the Nevilles' chief sphere of authority was in the north of England, along the border Marches (there were Nevilles on the Council throughout the 1460s – in fact, they dominated it); while Norfolk and Suffolk controlled East Anglia, and the new Earl of Devon and Humphrey Stafford the West Country. Other members of the Council included Henry Bourchier, Sir John Howard and John Tiptoft, Earl of Worcester.

Tiptoft remains one of the most enigmatic and repellent figures of the age. He was the son of Sir John Tiptoft, member of Parliament for Huntingdon and a descendant of an old Norman family. The elder Tiptoft had been Keeper of the Wardrobe and Treasurer of England under Henry IV, and had sent his son to be educated at Balliol College, Oxford. In 1443, when his father died, Tiptoft inherited his estate and left university. Six years later he married Warwick's sister, Cecily Neville, and became Earl of Worcester in right of his wife. His connection with Warwick led to his joining the latter's affinity, which helped to earn him advancement under Edward IV.

Tiptoft had served as Treasurer of England for three years under Henry VI, and in 1457 had made a pilgrimage to the Holy Land before spending two years at Padua in Italy, studying Roman law, Greek, Latin and the humanist culture of the Renaissance. After this, he rapidly acquired renown as an outstanding Latin scholar, being indeed the foremost scholar among the English nobility and one of the earliest English humanists. He translated Cicero, and his works were later some of the first to be printed by William Caxton. He also amassed a valuable collection of manuscripts, it being said abroad that he had robbed Italy to adorn England. Tiptoft certainly modelled himself on the princes of Italy, and followed many of the precepts of current Italian statecraft that would appear in Machiavelli's *The Prince*. He was a vigorous supporter of Edward IV, who was impressed by him and appointed him Constable of England; thereafter the Earl used his many talents and abilities in helping to crush Lancastrian resistance to Yorkist rule.

There was another side to Tiptoft. This ostentatiously pious and flamboyant man with the cold, protruding eyes could be ruthless and sadistic. 'The Earl of Worcester was known to be cruel and merciless,' records the Great Chronicle of London. In 1467 he 'put to death two sons of the Earl of Desmond, who were so tender of age that one of them, who had a boil on his neck, said to the executioner that was going to chop off his head, "Gentle godfather, beware of the sore on my neck."' Tiptoft seems also to have taken pleasure in devising novel methods of execution, some of which he imported from abroad, and 'for these reasons, and other similar cruelties, he was much hated by the common people and reputed in some cases even worse than he deserved'. Many complained that his judgements were based on the laws of Padua and not of England.

Edward IV's attitude towards his magnates, even such as Tiptoft, was tolerant and conciliatory. He realised that to stay in power he had to cultivate a wide base of support among the aristocracy and reward those who had supported him. He did his best to woo recalcitrant nobles by judicious patronage and promises of advancement. Some he won over; others remained loyal to Henry VI; a few cared only for their own profit and interests, and took what was offered without much commitment. In order to bolster support among the lords, Edward created or revived more than thirty-five peerages during the early years of his reign. He did not promote 'new men' with roots in the mercantile class to the peerage; although he valued their talents and services he endowed them 'with wealth, not dignity'. Thus they were not a threat to the magnates, whose wealth and influence the King could not afford to ignore.

He was careful to ward off rivalry between Yorkist nobles who were vying with each other for the prizes of high office. When important matters, such as foreign policy, rebellions or war, were being discussed in Council, the King always summoned and consulted his magnates. He made it clear that he relied on them at all times to uphold his authority, his peace and his justice in their own localities; in return, they could rely on him to be a generous patron.

The influential Londoners had long since given their allegiance to the Yorkist cause, and the King was sensitive to their needs and interests, always trying to formulate his policies to their advantage. His mercantile enterprises enabled a sense of affinity to develop between him and the London merchants, and many were honoured with his friendship. Under his rule, despite the unpopular forced loans which were demanded of them from time to time, and the liberties taken by the King with their wives and daughters, they prospered, and gave thanks for his virtues.

20

Fugitives

Once Berwick was theirs, the Scots saw no further advantage to be gained from the Lancastrian exiles, and lost interest in their cause. Mary of Gueldres was finding it expensive to support them, and by the summer of 1461 it was obvious to Queen Margaret that the faction-ridden Scottish court was unlikely to offer her any financial aid. All she could expect was the goodwill of individuals such as the Earl of Angus, who offered her men in return for the promise of a dukedom in England. Her best hope now, she realised, lay in appealing to Charles VII of France for assistance.

In July, the Queen dispatched Somerset and two other envoys, Lord Hungerford and Sir Robert Whittingham, to the French court to ask for men, ships and a loan of 20,000 crowns. She also employed Pierre de Brézé to request a further loan of 80,000 crowns and another fleet to enable the Lancastrians to conquer the Channel Islands and so make a bridgehead to England. 'If the Queen's intentions were discovered,' wrote Brézé, 'her friends would unite with her enemies to kill her.' Charles agreed that Brézé could assemble ships and men for the projected invasion, and with French help the Lancastrians did occupy Jersey that year, though it was later recaptured by the Yorkists.

By invoking foreign aid from England's traditional enemies, although it was indeed the only realistic option open to her, Margaret made the Lancastrian cause doubly unpopular in England and provided the Yorkists with splendid propaganda material. Her actions changed the course of the Wars of the Roses, which as a result now became dependent upon the tortuous diplomacy and shifting alliances of late fifteenth-century European politics. Her involvement of foreign princes in the conflict gave them the opportunity to subvert the common weal of England by playing off one faction against the other there and inciting rebellion.

Before Somerset, Hungerford and Whittingham could gain an audience, Charles VII died on 22 July and was succeeded by his son Louis XI. This was seemingly bad news for the Queen, because Louis hated his mother's family, the House of Anjou, and manifested this almost at once by placing Hungerford and Whittingham under house arrest at Dieppe, while Somerset found himself a prisoner in the Castle of Arques.

Louis had hitherto been friendly towards the Yorkists, and news of his accession was greeted with some relief at Edward IV's court as fears of a French invasion receded. But this euphoria was short-lived. During the 1460s international politics were dominated by the rivalry between France and its vassal state, Burgundy; both France and Burgundy wanted the friendship of England, but France, although more powerful, was England's traditional enemy, while the Low Countries, ruled by Burgundy, were the chief market for English wool.

Louis's main ambition was to conquer the duchy of Burgundy, as well as that of Brittany, and absorb them into the kingdom of France. He both resented and feared the power of Burgundy, and was therefore determined to prevent Edward IV from forming a defensive alliance with Duke Philip. Louis would, with reason, come to be known as the 'Universal Spider', because his web of political intrigue encompassed the whole of Europe, and his portraits show a man of uninspiring appearance, with an over-long, hooked nose, a mouth on which sat an expression of perpetual disdain, a double chin, and heavy-lidded, wary eyes.

Edward IV was in a strong position, and knew it. He was a bachelor, free to make a marriage alliance with either France or Burgundy. It was now a question of waiting to see who could offer the most advantageous terms.

On 30 August, Lord Hungerford wrote to Queen Margaret from Dieppe, sending three copies of his letter by different routes, informing her that he and Whittingham had been summoned to see King Louis. 'Madam, fear not, but be of good comfort,' he wrote, 'and beware ye venture not your person by sea till ye have other word from us.' Yet, to their surprise, the envoys found Louis prepared to be very friendly towards them and their mistress, the reason being that it now suited his purpose to see England divided by civil war. He had decided on an aggressive policy against Burgundy and did not want Edward IV to unite with Philip against him. He therefore told Hungerford and Whittingham that he would support the Queen in her attempts to subvert the north of England. This was good news indeed, for the King of France was a powerful ally. From now on Margaret's chief desire would be to meet with him and conclude a formal Franco-Lancastrian alliance.

Meanwhile, King Edward's spies had intercepted one of Hungerford's letters, which proved to him that Margaret was intriguing with the French. From this time onwards he and his government would live with the ever-present fear of invasion. Believing that this would centre on the north, the King sent Warwick to capture the great Northumbrian stronghold of Alnwick, seat of the Earl of Northumberland who had fallen at Towton and would soon be posthumously attainted. Northumberland's younger brother, Sir Ralph Percy, had submitted to Edward and was now entrusted with the safe-keeping of the defensive royal castle of Dunstanburgh on the Northumbrian coast. In September, Warwick took not only Alnwick Castle but also Bamburgh Castle. The chief strongholds of Northumbria were now in Yorkist hands.

King Edward entrusted the task of crushing the rebellious Lancastrians in Wales to his lieutenants Lord Ferrers and Sir William Herbert, the latter of whom had been created Lord Herbert of Raglan, Chepstow and Gower in July. Their first objective was to take Pembroke Castle, which surrendered on 30 September. When Herbert took possession he found four-year-old Henry Tudor living in the castle with his mother and her second husband, Henry Stafford. Herbert bought Henry's wardship for £1000 and removed him from his mother's care and into his own household. The boy spent much of the next nine years at the luxuriously appointed Raglan Castle where Herbert, although a rough and often violent man, proved a surprisingly good guardian, providing the boy with an excellent education and planning to marry him to his daughter, Maud Herbert.

By 4 October only two Welsh castles remained in enemy hands – Carreg Cennen in Dyfed, which fell to the Yorkists in 1462, and the mighty fortress of Harlech.

It was Edward IV's intention that Herbert should replace Jasper Tudor, who had now fled via Ireland to Scotland, as the King's representative in south Wales. This was no easy job, for there were many who lamented the departure of Jasper and resented the presence of Herbert. Moreover, during the campaign Herbert had again fallen out with Warwick, this time over who should have possession of the lordship of Newport, a dispute which rapidly turned into a major and long-lasting feud fuelled by Warwick's jealousy of Herbert's status in Wales. Warwick had long cherished dreams of building a power base in the principality, and now Herbert stood in his way.

The first Parliament of Edward's reign met in November in the Painted Chamber of the Palace of Westminster. Addressing the Speaker the King proclaimed his 'right and title unto the Crown', and thanked Almighty God that his house was restored to it, promising to be 'as good and gracious a sovereign lord as ever was any of my noble progenitors'. On 1 November, he created his brother Richard Duke of Gloucester and sent the boy to live in Warwick's household at Middleham to be educated with the sons of other peers, as befitted his rank. On the same day Edward raised Lord Fauconberg to be Earl of Kent.

Both King and Parliament were anxious to re-establish the moral, political and legal authority of Parliament, and there was a high turnout of magnates. The Lord Chancellor announced that the practices of livery and maintenance* would be banned by law from now on. On the King's command, a comprehensive programme of legal reform was to be launched. To enable the authorities to restore law and order, all subjects were urged to bring murderers and thieves to justice, while those who had been pardoned of earlier crimes would face the severest penalties if they re-offended. Commissioners were sent into all parts of the realm to ensure that the law was being enforced fairly, and, predictably, this resulted in the courts convicting a record number of offenders. Justice was truly being seen to be done.

On 4 November, Acts of Attainder were passed against 150 Lancastrians, including 'the usurper' Henry VI, Margaret, 'late called Queen of England', Edward, who is referred to as her son, not Henry's, Somerset, Exeter, Devon, Wiltshire, Northumberland, Fortescue, Beaumont, Roos, Clifford, Hungerford, Welles, Neville, Dacre and Trollope. Many of these were dead and beyond human retribution, in which case their relatives would suffer confiscation of all their property, but all were thus declared traitors to their liege lord Edward IV. The confiscation of so much Lancastrian property meant that Edward could reward his supporters well, and there followed a large-scale redistribution of lands, titles, offices and estates among the Yorkist hierarchy. The duchy of Lancaster was

---

* The practice whereby great lords would enter into contracts with men who were willing to fight for them and wear their livery in return for a pension, or wage, known as 'maintenance'.

also declared forfeit to the Crown, in whose hands it has remained ever since, and all true subjects were forbidden, on pain of death, to communicate with the former king and queen.

Lord Clifford's widow, Margaret Bromflete, went in great fear that the King's vengeance would extend to her seven-year-old son, Henry, the dispossessed heir. Fortunately, one of her former nursery maids at Skipton Castle had recently married a shepherd and gone to live at Londesbrough, where Lady Clifford's family had an estate, and this woman now agreed to take Henry into her home and bring him up as her own. When the King's officers came to Skipton, Lady Clifford told them that she had sent the boy and his younger brother to the safety of the Low Countries, where they were being educated. Her story was believed, but she was nevertheless evicted from Skipton and went to live with her father at Londesbrough, where she at least had the consolation of being able to see her son.

Another boy who was deprived of his title by Parliament was Henry Tudor, whose earldom of Richmond was given to the King's brother Clarence. As for the attainted Duke of Exeter, he had gone into exile on the Continent, where Commines saw him 'walking barefooted, begging his livelihood from house to house'.

Other Lancastrian supporters chose to remain in England and work for the restoration of Henry VI. Early in 1462, John de Vere, 12th Earl of Oxford, whose line could be traced back to the time of the Conqueror, was in communication with the exiled royal family in Scotland. Oxford was one of the Queen's chief agents in England and the head of a group of conspirators who were planning a Lancastrian invasion and the overthrow of Edward IV. Unfortunately for the Earl his courier was a Yorkist double-agent, who took his letters straight to the King. They revealed that Oxford, having learned that Edward was planning to march north to deal with the Lancastrian rebels, intended to follow him with a bigger force, pretending he had come to offer assistance, although, when the time was ripe, he would attack and kill him. Somerset, then in Bruges, would return to England, while Henry VI would lead an army of Scots over the border and Jasper Tudor would invade the south coast from Brittany.

On 23 February Oxford was tried by Tiptoft and convicted of treason, along with his son Aubrey and other conspirators, including Sir Thomas Tuddenham: all were sentenced to death. Oxford's sufferings were intense: he was disembowelled, then castrated, and finally, still conscious, burned alive. Edward IV permitted his second son, John, to inherit his father's earldom, and married him to Warwick's sister, Margaret Neville, to keep him loyal, but despite this John de Vere remained true to his father's ideals and stayed a staunch Lancastrian to the end of his days.

Queen Margaret was preparing to visit Louis XI, and her expectations of him were high, especially after she learned that he had been actively involved in Oxford's conspiracy. She was appalled, therefore, to learn from her agents in France that Somerset had been boasting to Louis about the mutual love between himself and the Queen. When Somerset returned to Scotland, Margaret's displeasure was all too evident and relations between them were strained for a time. She was also disappointed that none of her envoys had managed to obtain anything other than verbal support from Louis. Nevertheless Edward IV believed that Somerset's arrival in Scotland presaged a Lancastrian invasion, and had decided to take preventive action by putting diplomatic pressure on Mary of Gueldres to abandon the exiles. He even offered her marriage, though Mary was non-committal and the plan was dropped.

Margaret knew she must meet Louis face to face and solicit his help, and early in April 1462 she embarked for France at Kirkcudbright in a French ship, taking with her the Prince and Sir John Fortescue. On Good Friday, 16 April, they landed in Brittany, where the Queen was warmly welcomed by Duke Francis II, who presented her with a gift of 12,000 crowns. Awaiting her also was Jasper Tudor, who had learned of her coming and ridden to join her. The Duke told her that King Louis was away in the south of France, so she travelled on to Angers without delay. Here she was reunited with her father, King René. Both were impoverished, and René had to borrow 8000 florins to finance 'the great and sumptuous expense of her coming'. Nor was he able to offer his daughter any help, for all of his slender resources were being eaten up by a costly and unnecessary war with Aragon. At the end of two weeks, Margaret bade him farewell, and set off to meet King Louis.

In May, to show Mary of Gueldres that Edward meant business, Warwick led an army across the border and seized a Scottish castle. The ploy worked. Later that month, Mary met the Earl at Carlisle and signed a truce to last until 24 August. Warwick believed this might lead to a more permanent peace that would effectively close Scotland to the Lancastrians.

Queen Margaret, after trailing the French court for several weeks, finally caught up with it at Amboise. When she was admitted to the King's presence, she stunned everyone present by prostrating herself at Louis's feet and making an emotional plea that he should help her husband regain his throne. Louis appeared unmoved. By a show of lack of interest, he meant to force the Queen to an arrangement favourable to himself. 'I assure you,' he wrote to one of his ministers, 'I foresee good winnings.'

After his mother, Queen Marie, and King René had put pressure on him, Louis granted Margaret another interview and told her that if she would agree to surrender Calais to him he would lend her 20,000 francs with which to finance an invasion of England. But Margaret at first demurred, saying that she dared not alienate the English further by surrendering Calais. Louis conceded the point, and in June, as a favour to the Queen, he released Pierre de Brézé from the prison where he had been confined for some minor offence. On the 13th Louis saw Margaret again and offered her, in return for Calais, 2000 men under Brézé, 20,000 francs in ready cash, and the authority to muster men in Normandy. Margaret capitulated. On 28 June, on Henry VI's behalf, she signed a treaty of peace with France, providing for a hundred-year truce and barring all Englishmen from entering France unless they were certified true subjects of King Henry. Both countries compacted not to enter into alliances with each other's enemies or rebellious subjects. On the same day Louis handed over the promised 20,000 francs, and Margaret undertook to surrender Calais within a year or pay him the sum of 40,000 francs.

After the treaty was signed, the Queen went to Rouen to recruit men, while Louis sent his ships to harry the English coast. Brézé had already raised a force of between 800 and 2000 soldiers and mercenaries. When news of the agreement between Louis and Margaret filtered through to England, she was called a traitor for offering to hand Calais back to the French, and King Edward dispatched seventy ships to harry the French coast and intercept any fleet that might be sailing thence to Scotland or England. In July, he appointed Fauconberg, his most distinguished veteran, Admiral of England.

In October 1462, in anticipation of a Lancastrian invasion from France, Sir Richard Tunstall, a champion of the Queen, successfully plotted to wrest Bamburgh Castle from its constable, his brother William, and installed a Lancastrian garrison. On the 19th, Queen Margaret, Prince Edward, Pierre de Brézé and 2000 men sailed from Honfleur in Normandy in a dozen ships and made for the coast of Northumberland. The Yorkist garrison at Tynemouth prevented them from landing and fired cannon at them. Their ships were then scattered in a violent storm and some were lost. When the sea was calm again they sailed further up the coast and landed near Alnwick, where they received a warning that Warwick was approaching with an army of 40,000 men. This was enough to make most of the mercenaries abandon the Queen and flee to the ships for safety, leaving Margaret, Brézé and the Prince standing disconsolately on the shore watching their fleet retreating out to sea. Eventually they found a fisherman who agreed to take them further along the coast, but another storm blew up and his boat broke up on the rocks at Bamburgh while such provisions, baggage and weapons as they had with them were washed overboard and they themselves barely escaped with their lives.

The Queen expected loyal Lancastrians to rally to her at Bamburgh, but those who might have joined her were dismayed to find she had brought barely a soldier with her and deemed it safer to remain neutral. Undaunted, the Queen reinforced Tunstall's garrison at Bamburgh with French troops who had sailed up the coast and rejoined her, marched on to Dunstanburgh Castle and took it, and went from there to Alnwick Castle, to which her remaining soldiers laid siege. Lacking provisions, it capitulated almost at once, and soon afterwards, Warkworth Castle also fell to the Lancastrians. With these strongholds in her hands, the Queen was now in virtual possession of Northumberland, but still very few Englishmen joined her cause, and many of the locals resented the French garrisons. Margaret ordered that each castle be stocked with sufficient provisions to withstand a siege, then travelled north to Berwick, where she found Henry VI, Somerset, Exeter, Pembroke, Roos, Hungerford and Morton waiting for her.

Mary of Gueldres was not pleased to be asked for yet more aid and gave only a pittance to help finance this latest venture. Leaving the Prince at Berwick, the King and Queen then set out to invade England, accompanied only by their retinue and Margaret's 800 remaining men.

On 30 October news of the invasion reached London by fast courier. This new threat stretched the King's resources, and he was obliged to levy heavy taxes and borrow money from London merchants in order to meet the costs of raising an army. He then sent out commissioners to the south and west to array men, arranged for shipments of provisions to be sent to Newcastle, and Warwick was dispatched north with orders to lay siege to Berwick. Early in November King Edward marched his army north to confront the invaders; with him marched thirty-one peers – a record for the period – including some who had recently transferred their allegiance to the Yorkists.

News that Edward was coming at the head of an army was soon conveyed to Queen Margaret. She now placed Somerset in command of the garrison at Bamburgh Castle, supported by Roos, Pembroke and Sir Ralph Percy, who had recently turned traitor to the King. Her army, meanwhile, was causing havoc, her soldiers descending on the priories at Hexham and Durham and demanding funds for her use. When Edward IV arrived in Durham he was confronted by an angry prior demanding repayment of 400 marks which the Queen had forced him to lend her, while the Prior of Hexham was writing to anyone who might be sympathetic, including Warwick's sister, complaining about the money the Queen had made him give her 'through dread and fear'.

On 13 November, having received reports of the size of the Yorkist host, and knowing her small force was nowhere near equal to it, Margaret 'brake her field and fled' with Henry VI, Pierre de Brézé and over 400 soldiers from Bamburgh in a small caravel, with as much luggage as it would hold, hoping that a French ship would rescue them. As they neared Holy Island, wrote a London chronicler, 'There came upon them such a tempest that she was fain to leave the caravel and take a fisher's boat, and so went a-land to Berwick, and the said caravel and goods were drowned.' Four hundred of her men were stranded on Holy Island, and were obliged to surrender to two local Yorkists, when some were taken prisoner and others, not so lucky, were put to the sword as an example to others. When Edward learned of Margaret's flight, he decided to pursue her, but before he could do so he was struck down by a virulent attack of measles and confined to bed at Durham.

Warwick had meanwhile captured Warkworth Castle and made it his headquarters. He now laid siege to Bamburgh Castle, which occupied a wonderful strategic position, standing sentinel over the rocky Northumbrian coast. The Lancastrian garrison under Somerset held out for as long as possible, while Warwick sent messages promising Somerset a generous pension if he would surrender. In return, Somerset demanded that Sir Ralph Percy be granted custody of Bamburgh after he handed it over, that the lords with him would be restored to their estates and the lives of the garrison would be spared. Warwick agreed to these demands, and on Christmas Eve Somerset gave up the keys of the castle to him. Inside, Warwick found Margaret's provisions and personal effects, which he sent to King Edward. Somerset now formally pledged his allegiance to Edward IV, and rode off to assist Warwick at the siege of Alnwick, Warwick having sent a force to reduce that castle and another to Dunstanburgh.

Edward had for some time cherished notions of winning over Somerset, and had therefore been prepared to be more than conciliatory, knowing that the defection of one of their staunchest adherents would be a sickening blow to his enemies. Somerset's desertion of the Lancastrians may have been prompted by the desire for personal gain or by rivalry with Brézé for the Queen's favour; certainly relations between himself and Margaret had been strained of late.

Conducting a siege in midwinter posed almost as many problems for the besiegers as for the besieged. Food was in short supply and weather conditions were miserable. At Alnwick, according to the chronicler Warkworth, the soldiers were soon complaining that 'they had [to] lie there so long and were grieved with cold and rain, so that they had no courage to fight'. Nevertheless, by the feast of the Epiphany, 6 January 1463, Alnwick and Dunstanburgh had surrendered to the Yorkists, and Pembroke, unwilling to reach any compromise with Edward IV, returned to Scotland.

The surrender of these Northumbrian castles effectively ended the campaign, and the King withdrew his army south, leaving Warwick to guard the border, a task he undertook with commendable energy and efficiency. 'King Edward now possessed the whole of England, except a castle in north Wales called Harlech,' observed Warkworth.

With Margaret in Scotland, the King now decided to prevent her from obtaining any further support from the French by sending an embassy to negotiate a treaty of friendship, or a truce at the least, with Louis XI. When the Queen heard of his intention, she made it her aim to sabotage any attempt by Edward to win Louis over and to persuade the French king to provide further aid for her own cause.

After the Northumbrian castles had fallen, Margaret's French and Scottish mercenaries had followed her north to Scotland, where they regrouped, and just before Lent 1463, with the Queen and Brézé at their head, they marched across the River Tweed into Northumberland. Sir Ralph Percy, the untrustworthy captain of Bamburgh, allowed the Queen's French mercenaries into the castle, and thereby enabled the Lancastrians to take it for Henry VI. Percy was also captain of Dunstanburgh Castle, and as soon as the garrison saw the Queen approaching it also surrendered, while on 1 May, thanks to the treachery of Sir Ralph Grey, Alnwick Castle opened its gates to the invaders. Later that month Margaret, Henry VI and Brézé took up residence in Bamburgh, making it their headquarters. With control of the Northumbrian fortresses restored to her, Margaret was now nominally in command of much of the north, though the local population were less than enthusiastic in their support. They were sickened by constant strife and internecine warfare, and the benefits of two years of Edward's rule were beginning to manifest themselves. In London, however, the government and citizens were horrified at the swift success of the Lancastrian invasion, and the King sent Warwick north again, commanding that 'the great rebellious Harry and Margaret should not pass away by water'. On 1 June Warwick's brother Montague was made Warden of the Eastern March of the border.

Meanwhile Parliament, at the King's wish, had reversed the attainder on Somerset, restoring his titles and estates to him. Edward himself was making a point of cultivating Somerset's friendship and accorded him a place of honour at court, hunting and feasting with him and taking him with him on his travels around the kingdom. 'The King made much of him, insomuch that he lodged with the King in his own bed many nights', and tournaments were held in his honour. For a time it seemed as if Edward had succeeded in making the Duke forget those whom he had betrayed.

Early in June, suspecting that Louis XI was going over to the Yorkists, Margaret of Anjou appealed to Philip of Burgundy for aid; she had learned that a peace conference between England, France and Burgundy was due to take place on 24 June at St Omer, and was worried in case Philip signed a truce or alliance with England and France that would leave her politically isolated and without the support of a European ally. On the day the conference began, Philip sent her a token gift of 1000 crowns, which greatly encouraged her; she did not realise, however, that it was a sop to keep her quiet and – hopefully – away from St Omer.

During the conference Edward IV and Louis XI, through their envoys, concluded a truce and agreed that they would not succour each other's enemies, which effectively closed France to the Lancastrian exiles. Margaret was now desperate to cross the Channel and see Philip face to face, to pre-empt him from entering into any agreement with France or England. Although they had never been friends, Philip now represented her last hope.

Warwick was hoping to consolidate the new amity between Edward and Louis by negotiating his master's marriage to a French princess. Louis's own daughter was too young, and he offered instead Bona of Savoy, sister of his queen, Charlotte, while Philip, fearing that such an alliance posed a threat to Burgundy, countered the offer by offering Edward one of his nieces. Edward did not respond to either, though he was inclined towards friendship with France.

In June, Lord Montague repelled a Lancastrian attack on Newcastle, and ships from France, laden with supplies for the

Queen, were intercepted by sailors loyal to the King. This was a blow to Margaret as Louis was not now likely to replace what had been lost. At that time the Lancastrians were besieging Norham Castle, which stood on the banks of the Tweed and was owned by the Bishop of Durham. They were assisted by the Scots, who stood to gain more advantage from the capture of the castle than the Lancastrians, but the Queen wanted Scottish aid and had no choice but to be accommodating. The siege lasted eighteen days until Warwick arrived and, with the help of Montague and a force of local people, put both Scots and Lancastrians to flight.

The Queen and her party, hotly pursued by their enemies, fell back on Bamburgh. During their flight, one of the most famous and romanticised episodes of the Wars of the Roses took place. Many modern historians dismiss it as mere legend, but the fact remains that the chronicler Georges Chastellain heard it from the Queen herself later in the year.

On the road, the Queen and her son were separated from the rest; suddenly, a gang of robbers sprang from nearby bushes, seized her baggage, pulled off her jewellery, then dragged her with brutal violence and menacing threats before their leader. He grabbed her by her robe, wielding a drawn sword in readiness to cut her throat, threatening her with indignities and tortures, whereupon she threw herself on her knees and, with clasped hands, wept and cried for mercy, imploring him to have pity on her and not to mangle or disfigure her body and so prevent it from being recognised after death. For, she said, 'I am the daughter and wife of a king, and was in past time recognised by yourselves as your queen. Wherefore if you now stain your hands with my blood, your cruelty will be held in abhorrence by all men in all ages.'

Her words wrought a curious change in the man. Perhaps he had been a Lancastrian soldier and had once fought for her. Now he fell on his knees before her and swore to die rather than harm or forsake her or the Prince. He told her he was known as Black Jack, and led them by a secret route to a cave beside a stream in Deepden Woods, which is still to be seen and still known as the 'Queen's Cave'. Here they sheltered for two days until Brézé and his squire, Barville, who had been searching for the Queen and Prince, found them. After bidding farewell to Black Jack and pardoning him for the offences he had committed, the Queen and Brézé rode to Carlisle and thence across the Scottish border to Kirkcudbright.

While she was there, an English spy called Cork devised a plan to kidnap her and take her to Edward IV. He paid his men well, and one night they laid hands on Brézé and Barville and forced them into a small rowing boat, where they were bound and gagged. After that, it was an easy matter to capture the unguarded Queen and her son, drag them on board and put to sea. There they remained all night, but in the light of dawn the Queen recognised Brézé and surreptitiously helped him to loosen his bonds. Freed, he was able to knock Cork senseless and seize the oars. For some hours the boat was tossed in the choppy waters of the Solway Firth before being beached at Kirkcudbright Bay, a wild and desolate place. Brézé carried the Queen ashore and laid her down on the sand to recuperate, while Barville joined them with the Prince. When they had recovered they all walked to a nearby hamlet and begged shelter. Brézé sent Barville to Edinburgh – a hundred miles away – to enlist the help of Queen Mary. He came back with a message that Mary would see Margaret, but only in private, and that the betrothal between the Prince and Margaret Stewart had been broken at Burgundy's request. Perplexed and angry, Margaret made her own way to Edinburgh, but could not prevail upon the embarrassed Scottish government to change its mind. All the Regent would do was help her return to her friends in Northumberland.

Margaret was now in desperate straits, being so poor that she was obliged to borrow a groat from a Scottish archer to make an offering on the feast day of her patron saint, St Margaret. As she made her way back with Brézé towards Bamburgh, she met up with her husband and son, but their food supplies quickly ran out and, according to Chastellain, they 'were reduced to such abject misery and destitution that for five days they had but one herring between the three and not more bread than would have sufficed a day's nourishment'.

Meanwhile the activities of the Lancastrians in the north had rebounded on Somerset, who had in no way been involved. There were many at court who resented his appointment as captain of the garrison at Newcastle, and who could not forget the support given to the Lancastrians by himself and his family, and in late July the King sent him away from court for his own safety; the Duke appears to have gone to one of the royal castles in Wales.

Margaret of Anjou was now determined to make a personal plea to Burgundy for help, especially after July 1463, when she learned that Warwick was marching north with a great host, and knew she had no hope of holding out against him. After bidding farewell to Henry VI at Bamburgh, promising that she would be back in the spring with a new army, the Queen sailed with Brézé, Exeter, Fortescue, Morton and 200 men in four fishing vessels, while Henry then made his way to Berwick.

On 31 July, after enduring violent gales lasting twelve hours, the Queen's vessels were obliged to put in at Sluys in Flanders because they were too damaged to sail further. Margaret was destitute, having no money, no royal robes, and no possessions of value – they had been sold to finance her military ventures. All she had to wear was the short red gown that she stood up in, cut to the knee like a peasant woman's. Her retinue was reduced to just seven women attired as poorly as their mistress. She was totally dependent on Brézé for money and food, even though he himself was in extreme poverty, having spent all he had – 50,000 crowns – on serving her.

Margaret was trusting in an out-of-date safe-conduct issued by Philip years before to guarantee her safe passage through his territories, yet her welcome in Sluys was frosty. The people were loyal to their duke and they remembered that this woman had been his mortal enemy in the days of her prosperity, and made many 'savage comments' on her misfortunes. It was, wrote Chastellain, 'a piteous thing truly to see, this high princess so cast down and laid low in much great danger, dying of hunger and hardship because she was forced to throw herself on the mercy of the one in all the world most set against her'. Yet, despite her lack of resources and the hostility of the Flemings, the Queen was resolved to see Philip and sabotage the peace conference at St Omer. She was full of hope that her plight would move Philip to succour her,

As soon as she came on shore, Margaret sent a messenger to the Duke to request an audience, saying she came 'in humility and poverty to seek of his greatness a refuge for herself and her child, which she trusted he was too proud to deny her'. Philip was sympathetic, but he was also anxious to conclude a treaty of friendship with Edward IV and so preserve the trade links between England and Burgundy, and did not want the Lancastrian queen embarrassing him in front of the English envoys. He therefore played for time, pleading sickness, while hoping that she would go away, then sent to say he had gone on pilgrimage to Our Lady of Boulogne and, as English-owned Calais was nearby, it was too dangerous for her to join him. Margaret told his messenger, 'I will go in quest of him, whether it imperil me or not. Were my cousin of Burgundy to go to the end of the world, I would follow him.'

The messenger hurried back to Philip and told him that nothing on earth could deflect the Queen from her purpose and 'see him she would'. Philip said he would see her if he had to, at Boulogne – no doubt he hoped that the English might capture her on the way. Then his chivalry and good manners prevailed and he sent a message informing Margaret that he would meet her at St Pol. By the time he got there the English ambassadors would have departed.

When the meeting took place, previous differences were glossed over by a veneer of courtesy. The Duke told the Queen that she was welcome in Burgundy and that he was sorry for her misfortunes, but he did not commit himself further than to say that in his dealings with Edward IV he would have an eye to her interests. After he left St Pol he sent Margaret 2000 gold crowns and a diamond ring, a hundred crowns for Brézé and a hundred crowns each for the Queen's ladies. In September he sent his sister, the Duchess of Bourbon, and her daughter, who was married to Margaret's brother John of Calabria, to be companions for the Queen. A warm friendship sprang up between the two women, and Margaret told the Duchess that no parallel to her adventures could be found in books, recounting in detail the sufferings she had endured. The Duchess observed that, if a book were to be written on the troubles of royal ladies, Margaret would be found to excel them all in calamity.

In September Margaret went to Bruges, where she was royally entertained by Philip's son Charles, Count of Charolais. At a banquet given in her honour, the Queen, whose royal dignity and manners had not been impaired by her penury, indicated that Charolais should use the fingerbowl before herself and the Prince. But he, following the example of his father, who always insisted on paying due reverence to crowned heads, absolutely refused to come forward, saying that the son of a duke ought not to wash with the son of a king. The affair almost provoked a diplomatic incident. The Burgundian court, where great attention was paid to matters of etiquette, was a-buzz with consternation in case some offence had been given, and messengers were even sent to the Duke to ask his advice on the question of precedence. He agreed that Charles had acted properly and preserved the honour of Burgundy.

Margaret met the chronicler Georges Chastellain in Bruges and at his request recounted her adventures, which he related in detail in his chronicle. His imagination was stirred by her beauty and her misfortunes, and he was grieved to hear her say that she had several times thought of killing herself, 'but happily the fear of God, and His restraining grace, had preserved her from so deadly a sin'.

Enriched with a gift of 12,000 crowns from Philip, Margaret rode on to Nancy to see her father, King René. Realising the hopelessness of her cause and knowing that it would be dangerous for her to return to Scotland, he persuaded her to remain in France for the present, and lent her his castle of Koeur-la-Petite in the duchy of Bar. Here she set up a small court of exiles, who included Sir John

Fortescue, Dr John Morton, Sir Robert Whittingham, and George Ashby, her clerk of the signet. René allocated her 6000 crowns a year, but this did not cover her expenses and for most of her exile she lived on or near the breadline. This drove her to pay long visits to various relatives, including her grandmother, Yolande of Aragon, her brother, John of Calabria, and her aunt, the Dowager Queen Marie of France at Amboise. From time to time she went to Paris to try to revive King Louis's interest in her cause, but in vain. She also tried to enlist the support of the Emperor Frederick III, the King of Portugal and Charles of Charolais, but met with no better success.

All her hopes for the future rested on her ten-year-old son. She was now able to devote some time to his education, and appointed Fortescue his chief tutor. Fortescue wrote a treatise on the laws of England – *De Laudibus legum Angliae* – for the boy, and schooled him well, probably with the help of George Ashby. Edward flourished under his guidance and doubtless benefited from this more settled existence. His mother taught him courtesy and social skills, and he received the customary military training considered mandatory for a boy of his rank from the men of her household.

Early in December 1463, King Edward's prolonged negotiations with the Scots bore fruit in the form of a truce, one of the conditions of which was that James III undertook not to give any further help to the Lancastrians. This caused the Scots no heart-searching, for they believed by now that Henry VI's cause was irrevocably lost. On 8 December, Henry VI crossed the border with his small court and again took up residence at Bamburgh Castle, where for the next few months he would rule what remained of his kingdom – the Northumbrian castles.

For some time Somerset had suffered mounting frustration at King Edward's failure to pay him the pension promised a year earlier. He may also have felt guilty about abandoning Henry VI. In December 1463 he finally deserted Edward IV, riding from Wales to Newcastle, having sent ahead to instruct his men there to open the gates. In an inn near Durham he was recognised and, being awakened in the dead of night by footsteps outside his room, he was obliged to escape via the window wearing only his shirt and no shoes. Meanwhile, the Yorkist garrison at Newcastle had learned of his coming and put his retainers to flight. The Duke was therefore obliged to leave England and make his way to Margaret of Anjou's court at Bar, where he begged her forgiveness for his disloyalty and the Queen, glad to have him at her side once more, readily made her peace with him.

Edward IV was bitterly hurt by Somerset's defection, especially after he had shown the Duke such friendship. Worse still, Somerset's desertion heralded a new Lancastrian conspiracy against the King, for in Wales, Pembroke was doing his best to rouse the people in support of Henry VI, and during the early months of 1464 the deposed king's supporters were very active in the north. Somerset and Sir Ralph Percy were stirring the commons to rebellion, and a raiding party from Alnwick ventured into Yorkist territory and seized Skipton Castle in Yorkshire. Henry VI rode south as far as Lancashire to raise support, and before long the Lancastrians had sufficient strength to launch successful raids against the castles at Bywell, Langley and Hexham. There were minor risings in support of Henry VI in East Anglia, Gloucestershire, Cheshire, Lancashire, Staffordshire and Wales, but all were suppressed by King Edward with ruthless thoroughness. Sir William Tailboys was found hiding in a coalmine near Newcastle with 3000 marks, which had been destined as pay for Lancastrian troops, but were now seized by Lord Montague's men and distributed among them.

Queen Margaret was at this time trying to interest the Duke of Brittany in supporting the Lancastrian cause. Pembroke persuaded him to give ships and men for an invasion of Wales, and was allowed to gather his fleet at St Malo, whence he sailed in March, under the command of Alain de la Motte, Vice-Admiral of Brittany. But news of the suppression of the Lancastrian risings in England made Pembroke turn back, and the projected invasion of Wales never took place.

Nevertheless, information wrung out of captured Lancastrian agents convinced the government that something important was afoot. On 1 April the renowned Humphrey Neville of Brancepeth, ignoring his pardon from King Edward, rode to Bamburgh and offered Henry VI his sword. Despite the setbacks he had received in recent weeks, Henry was in an optimistic mood, believing that his restoration was imminent.

Warwick had advised King Edward that the only way to establish order in the north was to convert the truce with the Scots into a permanent peace. The Scots were willing to parley, and in April the King sent Montague north to escort their envoys to York. But Somerset, Roos, Hungerford, Humphrey Neville, Sir Ralph Grey and Sir Ralph Percy set a trap for him, concealing eight men with spears and bows in a wood near Newcastle to prevent him from reaching the envoys at Norham. Montague had been warned and neatly avoided the ambush, pressing on only to find Somerset and his companions with 500 men-at-arms confronting him on Hedgeley

Moor between Morpeth and Wooler on 25 April. A brief but fierce battle took place. Roos and Hungerford, realising that their side was losing, withdrew from the mêlée, but Sir Ralph Percy fought on to the end, when he was mortally wounded and died in the field alongside most of his men. His death was a serious blow to the Lancastrian cause: many north countrymen had supported it out of loyalty to him.

The battle ended with Montague scattering Somerset's army. Afterwards, he rode on to Norham, collected the Scottish envoys and escorted them to York, where a fifteen-year truce was agreed upon. Somerset and his remaining companions had meanwhile rejoined Henry VI in Tynedale, where they sat fast and planned their next strategy.

21

'Now Take Heed
What Love May Do'

Edward IV had other preoccupations at this time. He had fallen in love with a most unlikely – and unsuitable – partner. Elizabeth Wydville, the eldest daughter of Earl Rivers, was twenty-seven; she was four years Edward's senior and a widow. Her husband, Sir John Grey of Groby, had been killed fighting for the Lancastrians at St Albans, leaving her with two small sons, Thomas and Richard. The elder boy had inherited the manor of Bradgate in Leicestershire from his father, and there Elizabeth had been living.

Elizabeth had once been one of Queen Margaret's ladies-in-waiting, which firmly placed her in the wrong camp to start with. She was of medium height, with a good figure, and she was beautiful, having long gilt-blonde hair and an alluring smile. Edward was oblivious to the fact that she was also calculating, ambitious, devious, greedy, ruthless and arrogant.

By 1464, his subjects were concerned that he had been 'so long without any wife, and were afeared that he had not been chaste in his living', according to 'Gregory'. He had not been chaste, but this was one woman who was not prepared to fall into bed with him and then be discarded. Whatever ruses he employed, she foiled them all and held out for marriage. Yet she was a commoner, and no king of England had married a common subject since before 1066.

Before long, Edward became obsessed with Elizabeth's cool beauty. Many lurid tales were told of his courtship, even one that, as he tried to rape her, she seized a dagger and made as if to kill herself, crying that she knew herself unworthy to be a queen but valued her honour more than her life. 'Now take heed what love may do,' wrote 'Gregory', 'for love will not cast no fault nor peril in nothing.' Edward's proposal of marriage was a triumph for the ambitious Elizabeth, for love rarely figured in the unions of kings. Mancini observed that in his choice of wife the King was 'governed by lust'. His decision to marry this commoner from a Lancastrian family was an impulsive one and was unlikely to have resulted from a plan to build up a new faction at court to counterbalance the power of the Nevilles. That came later.

The Wydvilles were an old Northamptonshire family, said to be descended from a Norman called William de Wydville, and Elizabeth's father and grandfather had been loyal servants of successive Lancastrian kings. Lord Rivers had started his career as a country squire, but had improved his social standing and caused a tremendous scandal by marrying Bedford's widow, Jacquetta of Luxembourg. After their marriage they became known as the handsomest couple in England and produced fourteen children. In the reign of Henry VI Rivers had allied himself with Suffolk and the Beauforts, and he also had connections with the influential Bourchier and Ferrers families. The family seat was at Grafton in Northamptonshire.

Rivers and his eldest son Anthony were cultivated men of many talents and were respected abroad as knights of valour, Anthony especially excelling as a jouster. Mancini describes Anthony as 'a kind, serious and just man. Whatever his prosperity he injured nobody, though benefiting many.' Pious and even ascetic, he loved learning, and his treatise *The Dictes and Sayings of the Philosophers* was the first book to be printed by William Caxton.

For all this, Elizabeth was not a suitable bride for a king whose marriage was a matter of national importance, and in choosing her Edward IV showed appalling political judgement and irresponsibility. By marrying her he gained no financial or political advantage, and threw away the chance of making an advantageous foreign alliance. That he was aware of the unsuitability of the match is proved by the fact that he arranged for his wedding to take place in the strictest secrecy.

At the end of April 1464 the King was riding north to deal with the Lancastrian rebels. On the way he stopped at Stony Stratford, near Northampton, where he ordered the sheriffs of sixteen counties to have all men between sixteen and sixty 'defensibly arrayed' and ready to join him at a moment's notice. Then, before dawn on 1 May, he rode secretly to Grafton, pretending he was going hunting. There, early in the morning, he was married to Elizabeth Wydville in a small chapel called the Hermitage, tucked away in the nearby woods. Recent excavations there have revealed tiles bearing white roses and the heraldic shield of the Wydvilles. The only witnesses were the unknown priest, Elizabeth's mother, the Duchess of

Bedford, two gentlemen, and a young man who helped the priest to sing. After the ceremony Edward and his bride went to bed to consummate their marriage, but then he had to return to Stony Stratford. That night he came back again, and his new wife was secretly smuggled into his bedchamber by her mother. He stayed for four days, ostensibly receiving routine hospitality from Lord Rivers and the Duchess, although at night, again with Jacquetta's connivance, Elizabeth came to his bed. Before long, this idyll had to end, and by 10 May Edward had ridden to meet his forces at Leicester.

In the three weeks since his defeat at Hedgeley Moor, Somerset had regrouped his army and recruited more men in the north. He then marched south, determined to restore Henry VI, who was then staying at Bywell Castle. But Montague, who was marching to meet this new threat, had at least twice and possibly as many as eight times more men – Warkworth claims he had 10,000, although modern historians estimate perhaps 4000 to the Lancastrians' 500 – and was ably supported by Lords Greystoke and Willoughby.

The two armies came face to face on 15 May at Hexham, south of the River Tyne. Somerset's men encamped in a large meadow enclosed on three sides by a river and steep, wooded hillsides. The Duke believed this to be a good defensive position, but in fact it was to prove a deadly bottleneck, as Montague's men, coming upon them suddenly, blocked the only exit and charged headlong into the meadow. Somerset's army panicked at the sight, and fell into disarray. Many scrambled up the hillsides and fled into the woods; they later had no choice but to surrender. Those who stood their ground and stayed to confront the enemy were cut down mercilessly or taken prisoner. Somerset himself was captured, and his army annihilated, thus effectively crushing Lancastrian resistance in the north for good.

The Yorkists spent the next few days hunting down the Lancastrian lords who had fled the field. Immediately after the battle, in accordance with the King's wishes, Montague ordered the execution of Somerset and other captured peers. The Duke was beheaded and his remains interred in Hexham Abbey. He had never married, and left only a bastard son, Charles Somerset, who became the ancestor of the dukes of Beaufort. Somerset's brother, 25-year-old Edmund Beaufort, styled himself Duke of Somerset after the Duke's death, but was not formally confirmed in the title and spent the next few years in Burgundy, fighting as a mercenary for Duke Philip.

On 17 May Roos, Hungerford and three others were beheaded at Newcastle. The next day Montague rode south to Middleham Castle, where he ordered the executions of Sir Philip Wentworth and three Lancastrian squires. Sir Thomas Finderne and Sir Edmund Fish met the same fate in York, while others captured at Hexham were tried and convicted of treason in a court presided over by the Constable of England, the sadistic John Tiptoft. All were put to death, and Sir William Tailboys followed them to the scaffold a few weeks later.

Henry VI had narrowly avoided being captured by the Yorkists after Hexham. Enemy soldiers were already on their way to Bywell Castle when a messenger brought news of the Lancastrian defeat, and the King made such a precipitate departure that he left behind his helmet, surmounted with a crown, his sword, his cap of estate, armour and other valuables. One chronicler observed with irony that 'King Henry was the best horseman of the day, for he fled so fast that no one could overtake him.'

Thereafter he remained a fugitive for over a year, hiding in safe houses in Lancashire, Yorkshire and the Lake District. It is impossible to make a chronology of his movements, for few are known – unlike his wife's, his adventures are poorly documented. His only companion was his chamberlain, Sir Richard Tunstall. At one time, they disguised themselves as monks and stayed in a monastery in Yorkshire, and they are also said to have hidden at Bolton Hall near Sawley in the West Riding, where a well is named after them, and it is claimed Henry left behind a boot, a glove and a spoon, which are now in the Liverpool Museum; however, since none of these predates the sixteenth century, the tale of his lodging there may be spurious.

In gratitude for his services, Edward gave Montague the earldom of Northumberland and granted him most of the ancestral lands of the Percies. Alnwick Castle, however, was still occupied by the Lancastrians, but on 23 June Warwick appeared before it with an army and demanded its surrender. The garrison agreed, on condition their lives were spared, and Alnwick fell to the Nevilles.

The capitulation of Dunstanburgh and Norham followed in late May, then there remained only Bamburgh, in which Sir Ralph Grey, Humphrey Neville of Brancepeth and others had barricaded themselves after Hexham. Warwick's army arrived there on 25 May and sent Chester Herald to proclaim a free pardon for the garrison if it surrendered. Grey was exempt from this, however, because he had turned his coat too often. King Edward did not want the castle damaged by artillery, and Warwick warned Grey that every shot fired by his great iron guns, 'Newcastle' and 'London', that caused such damage, would be paid for by the head of one of the defenders. Grey still refused to open the gates, so Warwick resorted to bombarding the castle with his own guns. Great chunks of masonry crashed into the sea below, while shot from a brass cannon called 'Dijon' demolished Grey's room and he was knocked unconscious by falling stonework and left by his men for dead. Very soon the walls were breached and the victorious Yorkists surged in and occupied the castle. Neville and the garrison were allowed to go free, but Grey, in a daze, was taken prisoner and brought south to stand trial before the notorious Tiptoft, who had him beheaded.

The fall of Bamburgh deprived the Lancastrians of their last power base in the north. There now remained just one bastion of enemy resistance and that was Harlech Castle in Wales, which had been providing safe asylum for Lancastrian refugees since 1461. 'This castle is so strong that men said that it was impossible to get it,' wrote 'Gregory'. In the autumn of 1464 Edward IV appointed Lord Herbert constable of Harlech Castle, charging him to take it for the Yorkists and allocating him funds of £2000 for the purpose. Herbert began a prolonged siege, but still the enemy remained unharmed behind Harlech's forbidding walls, confident that Pembroke would come to their relief. This part of north-west Wales had remained largely Lancastrian in sympathy, and Pembroke was a local hero. In their songs the bards anticipated his return, when he would restore Henry VI and trounce the Yorkists. In fact, Pembroke was in the north of England and would soon go abroad to canvass the support of the princes of Europe. Nevertheless, Herbert was going to have a long wait.

The cost of suppressing Lancastrian resistance had been exorbitantly high and Edward's subjects were deeply resentful of the heavy taxation he had imposed upon them, and unhappy when he debased the coinage, believing it would cause 'great harm to the common people'. The promised golden age had still to arrive.

For almost a year now Warwick had been negotiating with Louis XI for the marriage of King Edward to Bona of Savoy. Warwick believed that a firm alliance between England and France, sealed by a royal marriage, was the only way to prevent the slippery King of France from a future show of friendship towards the Lancastrians, while Louis, for his part, wanted to consolidate the truce of St Omer with such an alliance. Warwick was due to go to St Omer in October for another peace conference, and hoped to conclude the negotiations then.

Burgundy naturally did not wish such an alliance to take place; he wanted Edward to join in a defensive compact with himself against France which would also boost trade between the duchy and England. Edward by now was inclined to favour Burgundy, but just then he was doing his best to negotiate the lifting of Burgundian restrictions on English imports and wished to play for time. Knowing that his marriage was a powerful bargaining counter, he had prevaricated for months, but of late, of course, there had been another, compelling reason for stalling. He knew, however, that his secret could not remain a secret for much longer.

During the summer of 1464 Edward's envoy, Lord Wenlock, had visited Louis at Hesdin and been presented to a splendidly attired Bona, with whom he was very impressed. Louis offered Wenlock a huge reward if he could persuade Edward to agree to the marriage, and Warwick added his own pleas, having no desire for an alliance with Burgundy, who had shown no inclination to honour and reward him as Louis had. Warwick was, in truth, in thrall to Louis, who had flattered and beguiled him, calling him 'cousin' and promising to make him a sovereign prince with his own European duchy.

On 4 September, a great council of the magnates assembled at Reading. Warwick spent the next few days putting tremendous pressure on the King to conclude the marriage alliance with France, and Edward knew he could prevaricate no longer. On 14 September he dropped his bombshell in the council, announcing that he was in fact married and had been for four months. The magnates, stunned and horrified to learn the identity of their new queen, did not attempt to hide their disapproval, telling the King candidly 'that she was not his match, however good and fair she might be, and he must know well that she was no wife for a prince such as himself'. Most peers regarded the Wydvilles as upstarts and viewed with distaste the prospect of their inevitable promotion.

The marriage caused not only scandal but political disruption. 'Not only did he alienate the nobles,' wrote Mancini, 'but he offended most bitterly' his mother and brothers, and Clarence 'vented his wrath conspicuously by his bitter and public denunciation of Elizabeth's obscure family'. Some nobles said they 'would not stoop to show regal honour in accordance with her exalted rank', and many members of the King's household were 'bitterly offended' by his choice of bride. Die-hard Yorkists were angered that he had married a woman whose father, brother and husband had fought for Henry VI. Above all, the magnates, and Warwick in particular, were furious that Edward had taken such a momentous step without consulting them, and were angry at having been presented with a *fait accompli*. Louis XI, on being informed of the marriage, expressed the hope that Warwick would mount a rebellion against Edward. In fact, the long-term effect of the marriage would be to create a fatal disunity among the Yorkists, which would have serious consequences for the dynasty.

Even before he learned of the King's marriage, Warwick had been growing dissatisfied. He had power and enormous wealth, yet the King cramped his style by obstinately, and to an increasing degree, asserting his own will in matters of state. Warwick had been frustrated in his attempts to extend his landed interests into Wales, and had expended a great deal of time and energy on negotiations for the marriage with Bona of Savoy. Now he had been made to look a fool. What alienated him most was Edward's failure to take him into his confidence.

As soon as he found out what Edward had done, Warwick wrote to several of his friends abroad. Only one letter survives, to King Louis, telling him that the Earl and the King were on bad terms, having almost certainly had some heated confrontation. But Louis soon heard that the rift had been patched over. However angry Warwick might have been, he still had hopes of concluding a treaty of friendship between Edward and Louis.

After Warwick had made his peace with Edward and their former amity was restored, at least on the surface, his position seemed unaltered. He was still the King's chief counsellor and the most powerful man in the kingdom. But Edward's marriage was symptomatic of his determination to act independently of Warwick and form his own policies. As the years passed and the Wydvilles rose to eminence, they could only be Warwick's rivals, and his authority gradually declined, forcing him to pay lip service to policies he deplored. Wrote Warkworth: 'The rift between them grew greater and greater.' The chief reason for Warwick's alienation was not so much the Wydville marriage but disagreement over foreign policy. He still had high personal hopes of King Louis, but Edward was unwavering in his determination to befriend Burgundy, and therefore Warwick's ambitions were constantly thwarted.

For the moment, however, he swallowed his gall and pretended that all was as it had been. On Michaelmas Day Elizabeth Wydville was escorted into Reading Abbey by Clarence and Warwick and presented to the magnates and the people as their sovereign lady and queen. The assembly knelt and honoured her, and a week of celebrations followed.

The new queen was aware of what people thought of her and was careful to insist on the most elaborate ceremonial whenever she appeared in public to emphasise her royal status. Even her brother Anthony had to kneel when addressing her. Like her husband, she followed the courtly fashions set by Burgundy, yet her household was not so extravagantly wasteful as Margaret of Anjou's and was better administered. Her jointure of 4000 marks a year was less than that allocated to Margaret, but she lived within her means. Edward gave her Greenwich Palace, which had formerly belonged to Margaret, and a London house called Ormond's Inn in Knightrider Street, just beyond the city walls at Smithfield. In 1465, the King ordered that her predecessor's arms be removed from Queen's College. Cambridge, and replaced by his wife's.

Elizabeth knew well how to manipulate her husband, and used her considerable influence over him to obtain favours and promotion for her family and friends, much to the disgust of the older nobility. Important posts in the Queen's household were filled by her Wydville and Bourchier relatives. Mancini says 'she attracted to her party many strangers and introduced them to court, so that they alone should manage the private business of the Crown, give or sell offices, and finally rule the King himself. The Wydvilles, a grasping, rapacious clan, quickly became a power in the land, but they were also a liability. Their influence at court was soon immense, 'to the exaltation of the Queen', but also to 'the displeasure of the whole realm'. Mancini says that the Wydvilles were 'certainly detested by the nobles because they were advanced beyond those who excelled them in breeding and wisdom'. Above all, this new faction was actively hostile to the Nevilles, whose power over the King they resented. Warwick himself was determined never to play a subordinate role to the Wydvilles, while they naturally came in time to oppose the French alliance so desired by Warwick, and supported the King's attempts to forge a friendship with Burgundy. This led inevitably to a rift between Edward and Warwick, whose friendship never recovered from the blow dealt it by the King's ill-advised marriage. Wydville opposition on matters of foreign policy threatened Warwick's personal ambitions, which were closely linked with the successful outcome of negotiations for a French alliance, and created dangerous tensions at court. The resurgence of rival factions there boded ill for the future of the House of York.

To the 'secret displeasure' of Warwick and other magnates, Edward advanced the Wydvilles by lucrative promotions and advantageous marriages. Overnight Lord Rivers found himself one of the most important men at court. His heir, Anthony, was already provided for by virtue of his marriage to the heiress of the late Lord Scales, whose title Anthony now bore. The younger sons, Lionel and Edward, were made Bishop of Salisbury and Admiral of the Fleet respectively. The first of the Wydville marriage alliances was made in September 1464, when the Queen's sister Margaret was betrothed to Thomas, Lord Maltravers, son and heir of the Earl of Arundel, and in January 1465, Elizabeth's nineteen-year-old brother John made a 'diabolical marriage' with the Dowager Duchess of Norfolk, 'a slip of a girl' of sixty-seven. Around February 1466, the King arranged for Katherine Wydville, the Queen's sister, to marry the Lancastrian Henry Stafford, Duke of Buckingham, whose wardship had been given to the Queen. Young Buckingham, still a minor, 'scorned to wed' the girl 'on account of her humble origins', but had no choice in the matter.

Other marriages of the Queen's sisters followed. Anne married William, Viscount Bourchier, the King's cousin; Eleanor married Lord Grey de Ruthin, whose father had recently been created Earl of Kent in place of the deceased Fauconberg; Mary married William, son and heir of Lord Herbert, the King bestowing upon the bridegroom the barony of Dunster, which Warwick himself had claimed as heir to the Montagues; Jacquetta married Lord Strange, and Martha married Sir John Bromley.

In the spring of 1466, Edward created his wife's father Earl Rivers and made him Treasurer of England, thereby offending Warwick, whose uncle, Lord Mountjoy, had been dismissed from the post to make way for Rivers. Matters were made worse in October that year, when the Queen's son, Thomas Grey, was married to Anne Holland, daughter of the Duke of Exeter by the King's sister, Anne Plantagenet. This marriage infuriated Warwick more than any of the others, because the King had paid the Duchess of Exeter, 4000 marks to break a previous alliance between Anne and the son of Warwick's brother, Northumberland. It seemed that the Queen had deliberately set out to slight Warwick.

Most nobles dared not risk the King's displeasure by refusing to allow the Wydvilles to mate with their children; indeed, they were obliged to turn down all other offers. This meant that most of the eligible heirs to the peerage were removed from the marriage market, and this angered Warwick because he had two daughters as yet unspoken for. It may have been to mollify Warwick that the King promoted his brother George Neville to the archbishopric of York in September 1464.

One thing that the King could not bestow on the Wydvilles was popularity, which they never acquired. The mass advancement of the Queen's family drew adverse comment everywhere. Not only the nobles complained but also the common people, whose sense of fitness was outraged. Even Edward's court jester dared to joke, in his presence, that 'the Rivers run so high that it is impossible to get through them!'

With the King married, Warwick could no longer consolidate the proposed French alliance with a marriage treaty. But Louis did not let that prevent him from continuing to negotiate with Warwick to bring their two countries closer together. Edward had recently made friendly approaches to Burgundy and Brittany, with regard to forming alliances with them, and Louis had no intention of letting that happen. Warwick continued to put pressure on Edward to agree to what both he and Louis wanted, while Edward refused to commit himself.

The teeth of the Lancastrians might have been drawn, but there were still those who cherished hopes of a restoration. Late in 1464 the Earl of Ormonde went to Portugal to see if the King of Portugal, a descendant of John of Gaunt, would be interested in helping Henry VI. Soon Ormonde was writing to Queen Margaret at Bar to say that the King had told him he would be pleased to assist, but these proved to be empty words. Fortescue wrote back to the Earl that they were all 'in great poverty, but yet the Queen sustaineth us in meat and drink, so we beeth not in extreme necessity'. King René's subjects in Bar constantly urged him to give more succour to his daughter, and ballads were written about her plight, but René was too impoverished himself to offer Margaret more than he had already assigned to her.

She still had friends in England, and had been gratified to hear from them of Warwick's displeasure at King Edward's marriage. At the same time, her contacts at the French court, less well informed, told her that war between Edward and Warwick was imminent. Delighted with this apparent turn of events, Margaret again appealed to Louis for aid to recover her husband's kingdom. 'Look how proudly she writes!' commented Louis, amused at the imperious tone of her letter. But he would not help her; he even took Brézé from her, summoning him to do military service in the war against Burgundy. Margaret never saw Brézé again, for in 1465 he was killed at the Battle of Montlhery and she lost her finest champion.

On Whitsunday 1465, Elizabeth Wydville was crowned by Archbishop Bourchier in Westminster Abbey amidst lavish celebrations. Warwick was not present, having been sent on an embassy to Burgundy. Thanks to Edward's procrastination and determination to befriend Philip, his hopes of a French alliance were fading fast, and by the end of that year, England's relations with France would be very strained indeed.

By July 1465, Henry VI had spent a year moving from safe house to safe house in the north, relying on the loyalty of Lancastrian partisans for shelter and protection from the Yorkist agents who were looking for him. In that month, he and the faithful Tunstall, who had been joined by Thomas Manning, formerly Keeper of the Signet Seal, were guests of Sir Richard Tempest at Waddington Hall in Lancashire, not far from the Yorkshire border. Tempest considered himself honoured to be able to shelter the man he regarded as his rightful sovereign, but his brother John, who lived nearby and often visited, was not at all sympathetic to the Lancastrian cause, and so it was decided that the King's true identity should remain a secret. This would be easily accomplished, as John Tempest had never seen the King. But another guest in the house, a 'black monk of Abingdon', had, and he had no compunction about doing what he felt was his duty. He went to John Tempest's house and told him that his brother's guest was in fact Henry VI.

John was at first unsure as to what he should do. He had no wish to lead an armed raid on his brother's house, yet as a loyal subject of Edward IV he could not let Henry slip through his fingers. At length, on 13 July, he took with him two neighbours, Thomas Talbot and his cousin John, and with a handful of men rode to Waddington Hall, where the family and their guests were at dinner. John challenged Henry VI to reveal his true identity, and made as if he would drag him from his seat, but Tunstall jumped up, unsheathed his sword, and sprang to Henry's defence. A brief but violent struggle followed in which Tunstall broke John Tempest's arm. Tunstall then grabbed Henry by the hand and slashed his way through John's men-at-arms, aiming to escape from the house into nearby Clitherow Forest. But no sooner had he and the King reached the trees than John's men had mounted their waiting horses and were riding them down. The King, Tunstall, Manning and others who had followed them ran on into the forest and downhill to the River Ribble, but at four o'clock that afternoon were all caught by their pursuers just as they were attempting to ford it near Bungerly Hippingstones.*

Edward IV was at Canterbury with the Queen when, on 18 July, he was informed by a monk – the 'black monk of Abingdon' perhaps

---

* Now called Brungerly.

– of Henry's capture. At once he had the news proclaimed and ordered that a service of thanksgiving be held in the cathedral.

Henry was brought south under guard and delivered at Islington to Warwick, who was waiting to escort him into London. On the 24th, the deposed King rode into the capital on a small horse, without spurs, with his legs ignominiously bound with leather thongs to his stirrups, a rope round his body lashing him to the saddle, and a straw hat on his head. As he rode through the streets, along Cheapside and Cornhill, then through Newgate, crowds gathered to see him, shouting derisory remarks and even pelting him with rubbish and stones. One shouted obscenities about Queen Margaret, accusing her of being 'shameless with her body'. At length, the mournful procession arrived at the Tower, where Henry was to be confined.

Loyal Yorkists, such as Robert Ratcliffe, were appointed his gaolers and were allocated £3 a week for his maintenance. At all times there were two squires and two yeomen of the Crown and their men guarding him. Lancastrian chroniclers allege that Henry was not well treated during his imprisonment, but although he may not have been kept very clean or allowed many changes of clothing, his keepers were fairly accommodating, treating him with respect and allowing him certain comforts, such as the services of a chaplain who came to say the holy offices each day for him and permitting him to receive visitors: Warkworth says that 'anybody was allowed to come and speak to him'. Yet this brought its own disadvantages. One visitor, whose name is not recorded, attacked Henry with a dagger and wounded him in the neck. Predictably, Henry forgave him, although he did administer a mild reproof, telling him he did 'foully to smite a king anointed so'. Another tactless visitor asked the prisoner how he could justify having ruled as a usurper for so long, but Henry stood up for his cause, and told him, 'My help cometh of God, who preserveth them that are true at heart.'

Yet despite these comforts and privileges – King Edward even sent him wine from his own cellar – Henry seems to have withdrawn into himself during his imprisonment. He spent much of his time reading or at prayer, but there were occasions when he was forced to face the reality of his defeat and imprisonment and would gasp with shame, or burst into tears and lament his lot, asking what sin he had committed to deserve to be thus locked up. Generally, however, he bore his confinement with fortitude and patience.

The news of her husband's capture came as a blow to Queen Margaret and ruined her hopes of a Lancastrian restoration, for even if she persuaded Louis XI or Duke Philip to finance an invasion force, Edward held Henry hostage for her good behaviour in a virtually impregnable prison, and she could not risk his life.

On 28 September 1465 George Neville was enthroned as Archbishop of York, but the failure of the King and Queen to attend the ceremony gave rise to speculation about a fresh rift between Edward and Warwick. By January 1466 Warwick was growing desperate about his future relations with King Louis. Edward could not be made to see sense about a French alliance and was moving ever closer to Burgundy; Philip's ambassadors had recently arrived to discuss a marriage between Edward's sister, Margaret of York, and Philip's heir, Charles, Count of Charolais. Warwick knew that Louis would soon hear of this, if he had not already done so, and he wanted the French king to think that his influence with Edward was such that he could turn him away from Burgundy and persuade him to restore friendly relations with France. He therefore forged a letter from Edward to Louis, promising that England had no intention of invading France or hindering him in any way from suppressing rebellion in the duchy of Normandy, which Louis had just wrested from his brother – something that Edward, just then, would never have agreed to. In fact, sending such a letter was an act of treason, but Warwick was beyond caring; he knew also that Edward's negotiations with Burgundy were not so far advanced that war against France was an imminent possibility.

Unaware of Warwick's duplicity, Edward went to his castle of Fotheringhay, where, on 30 January, he, his heavily pregnant queen, his mother, and a large gathering of relatives and friends, gathered in the collegiate church for the solemn reinterment of the bodies of the Duke of York and the Earl of Rutland, which had lain for five years in humble graves at Pontefract and had now been brought in a long and stately procession from Yorkshire. Both were laid to rest in the choir, near the tomb of Edward, Duke of York, who had fallen at Agincourt. In 1495, Duchess Cecily, at her own request, was buried beside her husband, and a century later Elizabeth I commissioned and paid for a classically inspired monument to York's memory which may still be seen today.

Afterwards, the King and Queen returned to Westminster, where Elizabeth retired to her chamber to await the birth of her first child. Edward was hoping that it would be a son, to ensure the continuance of his dynasty and the succession, and his wife's physician, Dr Domenico Serigo, had assured him that it would be a boy. Men, even doctors, were by custom forbidden to enter the Queen's apartments during her confinement, but Dr Serigo was determined to be the first to tell the King that he had a son and so hopefully gain a reward. He haunted the corridors leading to the Queen's rooms and eventually, on 11 February 1466, managed to gain entry to the antechamber to the room where Elizabeth was in labour. When he heard the cry of a newborn baby he called out to ask 'what the Queen had', at which one of her ladies called back, 'Whatsoever the Queen's Grace hath here within, sure it is that a fool standeth there without!' The baby was a girl, and the doctor made a hasty departure without seeing the King.

Edward rewarded his wife with a jewelled ornament costing £125 to mark the birth of 'our most dear daughter', who was christened Elizabeth by the Archbishop of Canterbury. Warwick was chosen as godfather, and the baby's grandmothers, the Duchesses of York and Bedford, were her godmothers.

Queen Elizabeth was afterwards churched at a dignified service in Westminster Abbey, to which she was escorted by two dukes and attended by her mother and sixty ladies of high rank. Afterwards she hosted a sumptuous banquet in the palace. Leo, Lord of Rozmital, the Queen of Bohemia's brother, was a guest, and dined at the King's table with Warwick, who represented his sovereign, custom decreeing that it was not proper for the King to attend his wife's churching. There were so many guests that the feast was laid out in four great chambers. Warwick escorted Rozmital through each of these, pausing to see his reaction to such magnificence. His guest's attendants, including the diarist Gabriel Tetzel, were allowed to stand in the corner of the Queen's room and watch her eat.

This was the most luxurious of the chambers, hung with colourful tapestries. Elizabeth sat alone at the high table in a golden chair throughout the banquet, which lasted three hours, during which time neither she nor her guests spoke a single word and her ladies-in-waiting, all of noble birth, were obliged to remain on their knees before her. Even her mother had to kneel when she wished to address the Queen. After the banquet there was dancing, as Elizabeth looked on. The courtly reverence paid to her, observed Tetzel, 'was such as I have never seen anywhere'. The day ended with a performance of the King's choristers, who sang beautifully: the Yorkist court was renowned for its music.

To foreign visitors, Warwick appeared as powerful as ever. They were amazed at his wealth and influence, and even more at his lavish and now legendary hospitality. Acting as host to the Lord of Rozmital and his suite, he served them a banquet with sixty courses.

On 15 April, the Earl, on Edward's orders, was in Calais to meet Charolais and discuss the proposed Burgundian alliance. Warwick did not trouble to hide his hostility to the plan and made it clear that he was determined to conclude an alliance with France come what may. The meeting was hardly a success.

Soon afterwards Warwick and Louis met at Calais and signed a two-year truce, under which Louis again promised not to support Margaret of Anjou, and Edward undertook not to help Burgundy or Brittany against the French. Louis also agreed to find a French husband for Margaret of York and provide her with a dowry. Edward had allowed the truce as a sop to Warwick, but had no intention of keeping to its terms and, indeed, broke them shortly afterwards by sending a safe-conduct to Francis II of Brittany's envoys, enabling them to come to England. Edward was determined to assert his own authority in this matter: the English might resent Burgundy, but they loathed the French, having never forgiven or forgotten the humiliations they had suffered at their hands at the end of the Hundred Years War.

In October 1466, Edward IV and Philip of Burgundy reached a private agreement that they would sign a treaty of friendship. The terms remained to be negotiated. Queen Margaret, learning that an Anglo-Burgundian alliance was imminent, and knowing how hard Warwick had worked for a French alliance, deduced how disillusioned and frustrated the Earl must feel. She knew that Louis too had wanted friendship with the English. If Warwick could be persuaded to abandon his Yorkist affinities and throw in his lot with the Lancastrians, then Louis might consider funding a Lancastrian invasion of England, for he had great respect for Warwick, and the Earl had the ability to make a success of the venture.

Swallowing her pride, for Warwick had been among the worst of her enemies, Margaret sent a messenger secretly into England to sound him out. But, near Harlech, the man was apprehended by Herbert's men, who searched him and found the Queen's letter. He was then sent to London under armed escort, where, under torture, he revealed that the Queen had indeed sought a *rapprochement* with Warwick. Edward himself questioned Warwick about it, but the latter denied that he had ever had any dealings with 'the foreign woman'.

Margaret's hopes were thus disappointed, but she knew it would not be long now before her son was able to take up the banner of Lancaster on his own behalf: certainly he was eager to do so, taking after his mother rather than his father. He had grown up surrounded by intrigue and the horrors of war, and had been exposed to Margaret's prejudices from an early age. The Milanese ambassador in France reported that the Prince, 'though only thirteen years of age, talks of nothing else but cutting off heads or making war, as if he had everything in his hands or was the god of battle'. In a few more years, when this boy came to maturity, Edward IV would not sit safely on his throne, but Margaret would seemingly have to rest content until then.

Early in 1467, thwarted of various marriage alliances he had been considering for his daughters, Warwick hit upon one that would outshine them all. As the greatest heiresses in England Isabel and Anne must make brilliant marriages: who better to mate with them, then, than the King's two brothers, Clarence and Gloucester? Clarence could have Isabel and Gloucester Anne.

It was true that Burgundy had already offered Clarence the hand of his granddaughter, Charolais's heiress, Mary, but Edward IV was not enthusiastic because Mary would one day inherit Burgundy and her husband would become its sovereign duke. Edward did not want his brother gaining such power on the Continent, nor did he want him embroiled in European politics, fearing that it would bode ill for England. The truth was that Edward did not trust Clarence.

George Plantagenet was now seventeen, a tall, blond, handsome youth who carried himself like the king he wished to be. He could be witty and charming when he chose, but was of weak character, unstable, impressionable, changeable and easily led. His jealousy of his brother had long been apparent, and was now eating into him like a cancer, for he was intensely ambitious. Although he had been generously endowed by Edward with lands, especially in the West Country, and had a great household of his own staffed by 300 servants and maintained at a cost of £4000 a year, he was dissatisfied, for it was power that he craved, and Edward had so far denied him that, being aware of his weaknesses.

When Warwick put it to him that he should marry Isabel, Clarence was quick to realise the benefits of such a union. But he was unable to keep the plan a secret, as Warwick had enjoined, and soon, word reached the King of the matter and caused him to be greatly perturbed. He did not want his brothers allied by marriage to Warwick, nor did he want them squabbling over Warwick's inheritance in the event of the Earl's death. It was true that these marriages would bring that inheritance to the House of York, but that might also mean Warwick intriguing against him in order to make one of his daughters queen, or inciting his brothers to treason.

Edward summoned Clarence and Gloucester and demanded to know the truth. Clarence said he knew nothing about such a marriage, although he thought 'it would not be a bad match'. At this, the King 'waxed wrath' and sent them from his presence, firmly forbidding Clarence even to contemplate a union with Warwick's daughter. Warwick had more than enough power as it was, without extending his influence through marriage with the royal house. Besides, Edward saw this as a plot to counterbalance the power of the Wydvilles.

As a result of Edward's actions, there was 'secret displeasure' between him and Warwick, and the King suspected that the Earl and Clarence might defy him and go ahead with the marriage anyway. He therefore instructed his agents in Rome to do all in their power to prevent the Pope from issuing a dispensation for it, the parties being within the forbidden degrees of affinity.

In June 1467, Philip of Burgundy's natural son, Antoine, Bastard of Burgundy, arrived in England, ostensibly to meet Anthony Wydville, Lord Scales, in the lists – for both were renowned throughout Europe as unparalleled jousters – but also to discuss the proposed Anglo-Burgundian alliance with the King. One of the chief topics for discussion was the marriage between Charolais and Margaret of York. 'If this takes place,' commented the Milanese ambassador to France, 'they [the French] have talked of treating with the Earl of Warwick to restore King Henry in England, and the ambassador of the old Queen of England is already here.'

An English alliance with Burgundy would of course release Louis from his undertaking not to aid the Lancastrians, and he himself was well aware that a Lancastrian invasion would prevent Edward from joining Burgundy in a war against France. He was still toying with the idea of approaching Warwick when, in February 1467, Margaret of Anjou's brother, John of Calabria, begged him not to do so, saying that Warwick had always been her enemy and the cause of Henry VI's fall from power. 'His Majesty would do better to help his sister to recover her kingdom than to favour the Earl of Warwick.' Louis asked what security the Lancastrians could give: would they offer the Prince as hostage? But neither Calabria nor Margaret was prepared to agree to such terms. Louis ignored Calabria's advice and continued to scheme to bring Warwick and Margaret together. The major obstacle to this was obviously going to be persuading both parties to be reconciled. Margaret had regretted her earlier abortive approach to Warwick because she could not rid herself of her bitter memories of the Earl, and had reverted to her former opinion that he was her husband's arch-enemy and a traitor of the worst kind. Warwick, in turn, was known to hold Margaret responsible for the deaths of his father, brother, uncle and cousin. It was not going to be easy bringing them together, especially since Margaret was now declaring that she wanted nothing to do with Warwick. Louis, however, was not a man to give up easily.

On 3 June, Archbishop Neville, the Lord Chancellor, did not appear in Parliament, and sent his servant to say he was ill. The 'illness' seems to have stemmed from his displeasure at the warm welcome and lavish entertainments laid on for the Bastard of Burgundy. Edward did not trust George Neville, and with good reason, for he had just discovered that the Archbishop – without asking his permission, as was customary – was working on the Pope with a view to obtaining a cardinal's hat for himself and a dispensation for his niece Isabel to marry Clarence, in spite of Edward's embargo on the match. On the 8th, therefore, the King removed Neville from the post of Chancellor and replaced him with Robert Stillington, Bishop of Bath and Wells. There is no doubt that he did this to show the Nevilles that he was capable of curbing their power and ambitions.

A week later Philip of Burgundy, who had been ailing for some time, died, and was succeeded by his son, who became known as Charles the Bold. News of the Duke's death prompted the precipitate departure from England of the Bastard of Burgundy and all his suite. Soon afterwards, a French embassy arrived in London and was accorded a warm reception by the King. Edward was keeping his options open, just in case the new Duke of Burgundy did not agree to favourable enough terms for the proposed treaty. However, despite being handsomely entertained by the King at Windsor, the French envoys left without having extracted from him any more than a vague promise to dispatch an embassy to France at some time in the future.

Thanks to Edward's diplomacy, the terms of the proposed alliance with Burgundy were so advantageous to England that even Warwick had no choice but to agree to it. Privately, however, he was still calculating, even now, how best to sabotage the alliance and persuade Edward to turn to Louis instead for friendship; in June he had met with the French king at Rouen to discuss how best to do this, but on his return he found his brother dismissed from the chancellorship and the King cold in his manner towards himself and his family.

Warwick burned with resentment. Warkworth says he 'took on as many knights, squires and gentlemen as he could to swell his forces, [while] the King did all he could to reduce the Earl's power. They were brought together several times, but they never again found pleasure in each other's company.' On one occasion, when Warwick went to the King at Westminster to ask if he would receive Louis's envoys to discuss an alliance, Edward refused to acknowledge his presence; instead, he gazed around the room. Warwick stalked out, hot with anger. The next day he brought the ambassadors with him into the King's presence, the Queen and her kinsfolk being there. Again, Edward ignored Warwick, and the Frenchmen were much offended. As they left with Warwick in his barge, the Earl cried in agitation, 'Have you not seen what traitors there are about the King's person?' One of the envoys tried to calm him down, saying, 'My lord, I pray you grow not hot, for some day you shall be avenged.' Warwick retorted, 'Know that those very traitors were the men that had my brother displaced from the office of Chancellor!' It was obvious to him that the Wydvilles now had the upper hand and that Edward was siding with them against him. Croyland states that he had continued to show himself friendly to the Queen and her kindred until he found that, contrary to his wishes, they were using their utmost endeavours to promote the Burgundian alliance, which was concluded in November that year. Desired not only by the King and the Wydvilles, but also by the London merchants who would profit by it, the alliance was in the interests of the nation's prosperity and appealed to patriotic sentiment, which was against an alliance with France.

Warwick felt he had no choice now but to throw in his lot with Louis. If Louis could offer him more than Edward he would take it, for he was not prepared to play a subordinate role to the Wydvilles and from now on would rarely attend the court if the Queen's kindred were there. 'From this moment the feud betwixt these rival families was settled, deadly and never terminated until it had completed the ruin of all parties.'

22

Secret Negotiations

In 1467 Queen Elizabeth bore another daughter, Mary, who was sent to Greenwich Palace to be brought up with her sister Elizabeth under the care of a governess, Margaret, Lady Berners. In October, the Queen was assigned £400 a year for the maintenance of her daughters.

The King kept Christmas at Coventry, where it was noted that the Duke of Clarence 'behaved in a friendly way'. Soon after Epiphany, 'by means of secret friends', Archbishop Neville persuaded Warwick to attend a council at Coventry, where he and the King were ostensibly reconciled. But nothing had changed. Negotiations between England and Burgundy were now moving towards a successful conclusion, and in February 1468 Edward and Charles signed the treaty providing for the latter's marriage to Margaret of York. The treaty dashed the hopes of Louis XI and Warwick, and Warwick did all he could to undermine it. He again urged Edward to abandon Burgundy, even now, and when Edward made it clear that that was out of the question, he set his retainers to incite the London artisans, warning them they would not profit by the alliance. Many believed the Earl's propaganda, and some went so far as to plan an attack on Flemish merchants living in Southwark. However, as soon as they boarded their boats to cross the river, the city authorities, who had been warned that trouble was likely, prevented them from going any further. A bloodbath, however, had only narrowly been averted. Undeterred, in the spring Edward IV concluded an alliance with Brittany, another thorn in Louis's side.

Even now, Lancastrian supporters were still working secretly to restore Henry VI, despite the harsh penalties lying in wait for those who were caught. At Whitsuntide, according to William Worcester, 'a certain Cornelius, a shoemaker serving Robert Whittingham, who was with Queen Margaret, was captured [while] secretly bringing divers letters into England from Queen Margaret's party, [and] was tortured until he confessed. He then accused many of the receipt of letters from Queen Margaret.' Another Lancastrian agent, one Hawkins, was also tortured. The two men were then tried by Chief Justice Markham, a just and fair man who refused to admit the Crown's evidence as it had been obtained under torture; Lord Rivers suggested to the King that Markham be removed from his office, to which Edward agreed. The unfortunate Cornelius was again put to the question, having his flesh torn from his body with red-hot pincers, but died without having disclosed any further names of those with whom the Queen had corresponded.

Between June and November 1468, the government acted to hunt out all those suspected of being Lancastrian adherents, and many arrests were made. Several lords whose families had supported Henry VI came under suspicion, and in the autumn Devon's brother Henry Courtenay was apprehended, along with Thomas, son of Lord Hungerford, and John de Vere, Earl of Oxford. All were suspected of organising a new conspiracy to restore Henry VI, but as there was very little evidence to go on Oxford was soon released while the rest were detained.

In 1468 there occurred the fall of Sir Thomas Cook, which illustrated just how powerful the Wydvilles had become. Cook was a rich London merchant and former Lord Mayor, an articulate and clever man who was respected by his colleagues and favoured by the King. Margaret of Anjou had once tried to borrow money from him, and he had refused her. Nevertheless, the Wydvilles suspected him of harbouring Lancastrian sympathies; the agent Hawkins had spoken his name under torture, claiming that he had tried to borrow money on Margaret's behalf from him; Cook had again refused to lend any, but that did not save him from the Wydvilles' wrath, nor the trap they set for him.

Cook had in his house a beautiful tapestry, much admired by the Duchess of Bedford, mother of the Queen. The Duchess demanded that Cook sell it to her at a price far less than the £800 he had paid for it, and he refused. The Wydvilles retaliated by accusing him of secretly working for the Lancastrians, reiterating what Hawkins had said, and Rivers sent his retainers to sack Cook's houses in London and in the country. Then, in his capacity as Constable of England, he convicted Cook of misprision of treason for not having disclosed his dealings with Queen Margaret's agent, and fined him the huge sum of £8000, which effectively ruined him. Queen Elizabeth, determined to take her cut, claimed an ancient privilege called

Queen's Gold, which entitled her to claim a further sum, in this case 800 marks, from the convicted man's estate. After this harsh treatment Cook did defect to the Lancastrians, but he never again prospered and died a relatively poor man.

On 3 July 1468 Margaret of York was married to Charles the Bold at Damme in Flanders. 'At this marriage the Earl of Warwick conceived great indignation,' wrote Croyland, 'it being much against his will that the views of Burgundy should in any way be promoted by means of an alliance with England. The fact is that he pursued that man [Burgundy] with a most deadly hatred.' Five days after the wedding the self-styled Duke of Somerset, who had been a fugitive in Bruges, left the city before the new duchess arrived and travelled to Queen Margaret at Bar.

Louis XI, meanwhile, was determined to undermine Edward's new alliance by aiding the Lancastrians, and had provided Pembroke with money, ships and men. Early in July the Earl landed in Wales in the Dyfi estuary near Harlech and marched east, inciting rebellion against the Yorkists. This prompted Lord Herbert to launch a new onslaught on Harlech Castle, which he had been besieging for four years without success. Herbert raised a force of 7-10,000 men on the Welsh border, then split them into two divisions, attacking Harlech by a pincer movement from both east and south. Pembroke, meanwhile, was sweeping all before him and holding many sessions of assizes, all in Henry VI's name. News of his astonishing success spread rapidly to France, and Queen Margaret prepared to go to Paris to ask Louis to send reinforcements to aid him. Her elation was premature. On 14 August, after making only token resistance, Harlech surrendered, and the last bastion of the Lancastrians fell into Yorkist hands. When they entered the fortress, Herbert's men found many incriminating letters from the Queen, which were at once dispatched to King Edward.

Pembroke was devastated by the fall of Harlech. He marched on Denbigh, burned the town and occupied the castle, but was pursued and driven out by Herbert and his brother Sir Richard. He was then obliged to dismiss his men and go into hiding, disguising himself as a peasant with a bale of straw on his back. Thus he made his way to the coast, where he boarded a ship bound for Brittany; the crew was inexperienced and he was obliged to steer the ship himself and navigate it as well. On 8 September, to complete Jasper Tudor's humiliation, his earldom of Pembroke was bestowed on Herbert by a grateful Edward IV as a reward for taking Harlech.

Tudor was not alone in being angered by Herbert's promotion, however: Warwick resented the new Earl's prominence at court and was jealous of the high favour shown him by the King. His links with the Wydvilles were already enough to damn him in Warwick's eyes, but so also were his plans to take possession of lands confiscated from the Percies and Tudors, and now held by Warwick and Clarence, in order to provide handsome dowries for his daughters and so increase his influence by allying himself to other great magnates. Warwick feared very much that Edward would agree to Herbert's schemes, given the bad feeling between himself and the King and the Wydvilles' apparent determination to slight him. Thus the rivalry between Warwick and Herbert grew daily, and may possibly have been the final straw that prompted Warwick's defection from the Yorkist cause.

Between autumn 1468 and spring 1469, according to the Great Chronicle of London, 'many rumoured tales ran in the city of conflict atween the Earl of Warwick and the Queen's blood, the which Earl was ever had in great favour of the commons of this land,' who were also hostile to the Wydvilles and frequently complained about 'the great rule which the Lord Rivers and his blood bare that time within the realm'. Warwick made no secret of his grievances, complaining that the King 'resolutely maketh more honourable account of new upstart gentlemen than of the ancient houses of nobility'.

Warwick was still in touch with King Louis through his agent, William Moneypenny, but he was alarmed by Edward's growing hostility to France, which had recently prompted Parliament to vote £62,000 for an invasion of that country. This was the last thing Warwick wanted, and all his hopes now rested on Louis. He must have been aware that Louis was intriguing to reconcile him to Margaret of Anjou, and was probably considering whether or not to throw in his lot with the Lancastrians. What he really wanted, however, was to be in control of King Edward and rule through him: he would need to be desperate before he agreed to ally himself with Margaret.

Warwick was also renewing his efforts to obtain a papal dispensation for Isabel's marriage to Clarence, but came up against a reluctant Pope, who had already assured Edward IV's envoys that such a dispensation would not be granted. Undeterred, Warwick began to negotiate a price.

Warwick had given up much of his life and much of his wealth to supporting the House of York, and his father and brother had died for it. Yet the Burgundian alliance, the King's ban on Isabel's marriage to Clarence, the promotion of the Wydvilles, Herbert's supremacy in Wales, the demotion of George Neville and Edward's relegation of Warwick to a subordinate role had all combined to change Warwick's loyalty into hatred, and his alienation from Edward was now complete. According to Croyland, it was the alliance with Burgundy which rankled most.

Warwick now spent most of his time sulking on his estates in the north, and refused to obey two summons to court. The King, alarmed, spent £2000 on strengthening England's defences. Then Archbishop Neville stepped in again and persuaded Warwick that he should make his peace with the Wydvilles. A superficial ceremony of reconciliation between Warwick and the King and Warwick and Rivers followed, but it changed nothing. However, while he was at court, Warwick discovered that Clarence was also highly dissatisfied with his lot, being jealous of his brother and frustrated because Edward would not allow him any position of power. Both men were angry with the King for forbidding the marriage with Isabel, and Clarence also hated the Wydvilles, believing that it was they who were preventing him from enjoying his supposed 'rights' as the King's brother.

Clarence fell prey to Warwick's charisma, and throughout that winter and spring they laid their plans to fuel the people's hatred of the Wydvilles and to undermine Edward's authority, though, unlike Warwick, Clarence's aim was not to control the King but to depose him and set himself up in his place. There is no proof that Warwick and Clarence incited the minor riots and disturbances that took place in the north of England at this time, but Warwick's ally in Redesdale, Sir John Conyers, was certainly ready to take up arms on the Earl's behalf. Warwick, however, preferred to wait until he was in a position to ensure the success of any uprising against the King. 'Go home,' he told Conyers, 'it is not yet time to be stirring.'

At the beginning of Edward IV's reign, his subjects had looked forward to prosperity and peace; instead, they had witnessed – and paid for – 'one battle after another and much trouble and great loss of goods among the common people'. The dominance of the Nevilles and the resurgence of factions at court had helped to convince Edward's subjects that he, like Henry VI, was unable to control his magnates. Some had never been won over, being jealous of the power enjoyed by Warwick and the Nevilles, or resentful of the men of better brains but lesser degree whom the King favoured.

The country at large was still subject to disorder and lawlessness, two problems that Edward had as yet been unable to tackle effectively. In many areas travel was dangerous and few people dared venture out at night. The late 1460s saw an alarming decline in law and order, due largely to the corrupt practices of the Yorkist magnates in their own territory; feuds between these peers inevitably led to outbreaks of violence. Discontent was especially rife in the north, where it was exacerbated by disaffected magnates such as Warwick. This posed as serious a threat to Edward IV as had the Lancastrian rebellions of the early 1460s. Lancastrian chroniclers claim that by 1469 the people of England had become disillusioned with Yorkist rule because Edward had not been able to fulfil the promises made at his accession, having been too preoccupied with foreign policy and crushing Lancastrian resistance. Warkworth says that the fifteenth taxation granted by Parliament in 1469 'annoyed the people' because the King had promised not to tax them too heavily, and they had already been overburdened with taxes to pay for military campaigns.

There is no evidence that the King himself was unpopular; the fact remained, however, that Warwick was more popular than the King and had now set about exploiting that popularity and fuelling public discontent to further his own interests. Hitherto Edward had depended on the Nevilles to hold the north safely for him, but Warwick's disaffection undermined this security. It was easy for the Earl to resurrect the slumbering grievances of the northerners, and not long before the north became a hotbed of anti-Yorkist feeling, so much so that England seemed to be on the brink of another civil war.

Edward's position might have been more secure had he had a son to succeed him, but in March 1469 the Queen gave birth to yet another daughter, Cecily. Although the infant was 'very handsome' and her arrival 'rejoiced the King and all the nobles exceedingly', they would have preferred a son. The King's lack of a male heir was becoming a matter of concern to everyone.

Government agents were still seeking out and arresting Lancastrian activists who were working on behalf of Margaret of Anjou, conveying letters and co-ordinating plans for a future Lancastrian invasion. Those who were taken were tortured in order to make them reveal the names of other traitors. Some accused seemingly reputable merchants and citizens, and more arrests and executions followed. In January 1469 Henry Courtenay and Thomas Hungerford were tried and found guilty of treason, and suffered the full horrors of a traitor's death. Sir Richard Roos, who had been imprisoned at Windsor since his arrest after Towton in 1461, risked his life by sending a poem, written in double acrostic anagrams, to the Earl of Oxford. The poem contained a coded appeal to all supporters of Henry VI to rise and support Warwick against Edward

IV, and Oxford disseminated the message among his contacts. It was now only a matter of time before Edward's enemies united in opposition against him.

By the spring of 1469 Warwick was secretly in league with Louis XI, who had promised to give him the principalities of Holland and Zeeland if he could bring about the overthrow of King Edward. Warwick may not have intended to go so far, but he was certainly scheming actively to curb Edward and set himself up as the power behind the throne. Clarence, however, enthusiastically supported Louis's plan, for his main objective was the throne, and at this time he was attempting to undermine Edward's position by spreading an unfounded rumour that the King was not the son of Richard, Duke of York, but the bastard son of Duchess Cecily by an archer of Calais called Blaybourne. This tale quickly gained currency in Europe, where it was gleefully repeated by both Louis XI and Charles of Burgundy, and it would be used again in 1483 in England by the Duke of Gloucester to suit his own purposes. Neither Clarence nor, later, Gloucester, scrupled to cast such a slur on their mother's honour, and she, outraged, emphatically denied the story.

In the spring of 1469, Warwick and his wife and daughters returned to Calais for a time, so that Warwick could fulfil his duties as Captain. The northerners, their prejudices, grievances and fears heightened by the Earl's inflammatory propaganda, were now restive and complaining that they were sorely oppressed by high taxes, for which they blamed the Wydvilles. There was unrest throughout the region, and that spring several unco-ordinated risings took place. Warwick, from his base at Calais, had been in touch by letter and through his agents with disaffected northern lords and gentry, and had masterminded a full-scale revolt against the King, which would be led by Sir John Conyers, Warwick's cousin by marriage and one of his most loyal adherents. The plan was that Conyers and Warwick's relatives – including Archbishop Neville – and their allies would raise their tenantry and affinities to crush the Wydvilles, restore Neville influence at court, and seize control of the King. Around 28 May they answered the call to arms, rioting and inciting the people to rebellion

At the same time another revolt broke out in the East Riding of Yorkshire. This was led by the mysterious 'Robin of Holderness', whose identity has never been discovered. It was an entirely separate movement from that led by Conyers, its objective being the restoration of Henry Percy to the earldom of Northumberland. Its leaders were therefore no friends to the Nevilles, and Warwick's brother, John Neville, who held the earldom, marched into Yorkshire with an armed force and made the rebels disperse.

News of the northern uprisings had not reached the King when he set out on 1 June on a pilgrimage through East Anglia to the shrine of Our Lady of Walsingham, accompanied by Gloucester, Scales and Sir John Wydville, but it must have caught up with him soon afterwards. Yet for more than two weeks he did nothing. Only on the 18th did he finally bestir himself to devise a strategy for dealing with the rebels and begin recruiting men.

Warwick, meanwhile, had returned to England and on 28 June issued a summons to his 'servants and well-wishers' to arm themselves and march with him against the northern rebels, as the King had commanded. In fact, Warwick intended to join those same rebels, but his recruits knew nothing of this. The King, however, was suspicious, and issued an order prohibiting his subjects from forming assemblies unless he himself authorised them to do so.

At the end of June Edward arrived at Croyland Abbey in Lincolnshire, where he stayed a night, and then proceeded by boat along the River Nene to Fotheringhay Castle. He stayed there a week with the Queen, and on 5 July marched to Stamford while Elizabeth returned to London. At Stamford the King wrote to the mayors of various towns, commanding them to furnish him with contingents of soldiers arrayed for war. Five days later, from Newark, he was issuing similar letters, couched in more urgent tones, ordering the levies to muster there. However, says Croyland, 'the common people came to him more slowly than he had anticipated', and there were barely enough of them: judging by alarming reports he had received from the north, he had one man to every three rebels. Knowing he could not hope to prevail, he reluctantly marched his army south to Nottingham, there to summon and await reinforcements from the west.

Warwick had now managed to purchase a dispensation from the Pope for the marriage of Isabel to Clarence, and this arrived in early July. Armed with it, the Earl left England on 4 July and sailed to Calais with Clarence, Archbishop Neville and the Earl of Oxford. He was planning a coup that would entail the renewal of civil war in England. The Duchess of York had found out what was going on and had travelled to Canterbury to try to dissuade Clarence from playing any part in it, but to no avail. Clarence had too much to gain to back out now.

When he and Warwick arrived in Calais they were 'solemnly received and joyously entertained' by the Countess of Warwick and her two daughters. On 11 July, Clarence and Isabel were married at the Church of Our Lady in the castle of Calais, with Archbishop Neville officiating. Waurin says there were 'very few guests and the celebrations only lasted two days, for Clarence was married on a Tuesday, and on the following Sunday he returned to England'. The marriage served to bind the Duke more closely to Warwick and identify him with the Earl's interests.

In the second week of July, records Warkworth, Sir John Conyers marched south through Yorkshire, leading 'many knights, squires and commons, numbering 20,000 men in all'. Conyers 'called himself Robin of Redesdale', a persona based on Robin Hood, the people's hero. Croyland claims that the rebel army was 60,000 strong: it was certainly impressive, because reports of its advance caused panic in the south,

The rebels were to join up with Warwick's affinity in the Midlands, and the leaders were careful throughout to avoid any attack on the King himself, skirting Nottingham on their way. Edward was slow to react to this new threat, and wasted much valuable time in summoning Warwick from Calais to assist him and then, when Warwick failed to obey, waiting for Herbert of Pembroke to arrive. Herbert was bringing with him 43,000 Welshmen, and in the west Humphrey Stafford, Earl of Devon, had mustered 7000 archers. In the meantime, the King had ordered the Wydvilles to seek refuge in castles in East Anglia and Wales, but Rivers and his son Sir John Wydville, who had been lodging in Herbert's castle at Chepstow, joined Edward on his march north to intercept the rebels. In Yorkshire, Northumberland forced Redesdale's men to disperse, but they merely crossed the border into Lancashire and regrouped.

From Calais, on 12 July, Warwick issued a manifesto proclaiming that he and Archbishop Neville had been urged by the King's true subjects to save his Grace from the 'deceivable and covetous rule and guiding of certain seditious persons'. He then went on to list all-too-familiar grievances, such as 'lack of governance', 'great impositions and inordinate charges' and the corruption of justice. He promised the people that he would petition the King to remove his evil counsellors, the Wydvilles and Pembroke, cut taxation, and pay heed in future to the true lords of his blood – in other words, Warwick and Clarence. If the King did not meet these demands, he would deserve the same fate as Edward II, Richard II and Henry VI – deposition. The manifesto ended with a plea for armed support from all true subjects of the King and a promise that Warwick would be in Canterbury in three days. Already, his agents were in Kent enlisting men.

On 16 July, later than planned, Warwick and Archbishop Neville returned to England unopposed and received a heartening welcome in Kent. At Canterbury crowds of armed men flocked to join them, and the common people hailed Warwick as their deliverer. On the 18th he left Canterbury and marched on London at the head of a now substantial army; two days later the Lord Mayor permitted him to march through the city on his way north, in the belief that the Earl was taking reinforcements to the King. Crowds cheered him as he went.

Pembroke, meanwhile, was hastening to join the King with his Welsh reinforcements, having joined up with Devon and his force. But on the evening of the 24th, when they came to Banbury, the two earls quarrelled over who should have the best lodgings at the inn. Pembroke, as the senior commander, insisted that he should occupy them, but Devon, who had arrived first, protested that they had earlier agreed to take lodgings on a first come, first served basis. Pembroke peremptorily ordered Devon out of the rooms, and Devon, put out because he had just seduced the innkeeper's daughter, marched off in a rage with all his men.

The next morning, Pembroke rode back to where his army was encamped by Edgecote Hill, six miles north-east of Banbury. The camp was on the western bank of a tributary of the River Cherwell, in the valley of Danes Moor. The next day, long before he had expected to do so, Pembroke sighted Robin of Redesdale's northern army, which caught him unprepared for battle. Even though Devon and his archers had now rejoined him, his army was still considerably smaller than that of the rebels, who were drawn up in battle order on Blackbird Hill, to the north-east of Danes Moor.

The Battle of Edgecote began at dawn on 26 July 1469, when both sides advanced to a crossing place on the river and tried to take it, Pembroke going ahead with a troop of horsemen and defending himself manfully against a savage northern onslaught. Despite the odds, he managed to secure the crossing and hold on to it, while the northern army withdrew to await reinforcements from Warwick. While they were waiting, they regrouped into battle order. Pembroke, meanwhile, had been joined by Sir William Parr and Sir Geoffrey Gate with fresh troops, but was still outnumbered.

Then there appeared in the distance a force of 15,000 men of Kent and soldiers of the Calais garrison, who had been sent ahead by Warwick; at the sight, Devon and his archers fled, believing that this was Warwick's entire army. After Devon had withdrawn, Pembroke found it impossible to maintain a continuous battle line, but he nevertheless led a ferocious charge and forced the rebels to fall back.

His brother, Sir Richard Herbert, fought heroically, twice crossing the enemy line, swinging his poleaxe, 'without any mortal wound returned'. Victory was almost within the Yorkists' grasp when a second force of 500 rebel reinforcements came thundering downhill behind them: it was Warwick's advance guard, and its banners bore his device of the bear and ragged staff. This was enough to strike terror into the hearts of Pembroke's Welshmen, who fled the field in disarray, many wading across the river. Casualties were high on both sides, but Pembroke's Welshmen suffered the worst losses, with 2-4000 men dead.

The rebels – and the Nevilles – had scored a resounding victory. Pembroke was taken prisoner along with his brother, the craven Devon fled into Somerset, and Rivers and Sir John Wydville went into hiding, knowing that Warwick would try to hunt them down.

After the battle, the Herbert brothers were brought before Warwick and Clarence at their headquarters at Northampton, where Warwick had no compunction in condemning them as traitors and ordering their executions. There was no legal justification for his action, since neither Herbert nor his confederates had committed treason against their lawful sovereign, nor were they guilty of any crime. Nevertheless, both were beheaded on 27 July. Herbert's wife had once promised him that if anything should happen to him she would take a vow of perpetual widowed chastity. Before he was led out to die, he wrote her a last letter: 'Pray for me, and take the said order that ye promised me, as ye had in my life my heart and love.'

People were shocked at Herbert's execution: he had been one of the chief mainstays of Edward IV's throne. His death meant that the earldom of Pembroke was once more vacant and that Jasper Tudor would almost certainly try to reclaim it. It also meant that nothing now stood between Warwick and his ambitions in Wales.

The loss of his powerful guardian left young Henry Tudor without a protector, but the widowed Countess of Pembroke took him to live with her at Weobley in Herefordshire. His mother, Margaret Beaufort, tried at this time to regain custody of him, but without success.

After Edgecote, Conyers and his northerners returned home; there is no record of Conyers receiving any reward for the sterling service he had done Warwick, yet he remained loyal to the Earl. On 17 August, the fugitive Earl of Devon was captured by the common people of Somerset at Bridgewater, where, says Hall, he was 'cut shorter by the head'.

Meanwhile, on the 29th the King had decided it was unsafe to remain at Nottingham waiting for Pembroke, and had ridden south. At the village of Olney, near Coventry, he learned of the Earl's crushing defeat at Edgecote, news which prompted many of the nobles with him to desert, leaving him isolated and vulnerable. He now had no choice but to dismiss those lords who were still in attendance, and leave himself at the mercy of his enemies. Only Gloucester and Hastings remained with him.

Archbishop Neville soon found out that the King was at Olney 'and that all the men he had raised had fled from him, so, on the advice of the Earl of Warwick, he went with a few horsemen' to seize him. At midnight, the King was awoken by the sound of many horses' hooves and men shouting outside his window. Looking out, he saw in the street below a troop of soldiers wearing Warwick's livery. Then there was a sharp knock on the door. The King's attendants opened it to reveal Archbishop Neville, fully armed, standing in the antechamber. The Archbishop offered a courteous greeting to the King and bade him dress at once. Edward refused, saying he was tired and had not had sufficient rest. But the Archbishop was firm – this was no social call. 'Sire,' he said, 'you must rise and come to see my brother of Warwick, nor do I think that you can refuse.' Edward meekly did as he was told, as Gloucester and Hastings, roused from sleep, looked on helplessly. Presently the King was ready, and rode with the Archbishop and his soldiers to confront a triumphant Warwick and Clarence. The Nevilles were now in control.

On 2 August, Edward was brought before Warwick and Clarence at Coventry. He greeted them amiably and made no protest at their treatment of him. For Warwick, the capture of the King was in some respects an anti-climax. Now that he had him, what was he to do with him? He himself had no royal authority, he and Clarence were not in a strong enough position to indict and execute Edward without fear of reprisals, nor had they gathered enough support to depose him and set Clarence on the throne in his place. In fact, by deferring to Edward as king while holding him in captivity they had placed themselves in an invidious position, for it was no light matter to imprison one's anointed sovereign. Moreover, without the King at the helm much of the business of government must be held in suspension.

Warwick and Clarence tried to resolve their dilemma by placing Edward in honourable confinement in Warwick Castle and attempting to rule England in his name. Warwick, using the Great Seal, issued writs summoning Parliament to meet at York on 22 September, since some cloak of legality had to be given to the present regime. But the King's subjects remained staunchly loyal to him, and the magnates were determined to curb Warwick's power rather than help extend it. Without their support, the Earl found that ruling England was impossible. Unlike the King, he had no means of dispensing patronage with which to buy noble loyalties, and even his Neville kinsfolk were pointing out the dangers inherent in what he had done. There was a general feeling that, this time, Warwick had gone too far.

Edward, meanwhile, cheerfully acted like a well-behaved puppet, doing as he was told, signing everything that Warwick put before him, and comporting himself with unfailing courtesy and good humour. He was well aware that Warwick could not hope to maintain the status quo, but enough of a realist to know that no one would attempt to liberate him at present. Nevertheless, Warwick was nervous that a rescue attempt might be made, and had the King moved at the dead of night to Middleham Castle in Yorkshire.

Queen Elizabeth had been lodging in the royal apartments of the Tower of London when Edward IV was taken into captivity, and Warwick allowed her to remain there, insisting only that she kept 'scant state'. But he was determined to have his revenge on the other Wydvilles. One of his agents tracked down and apprehended Lord Rivers and Sir John Wydville in the Forest of Dean, and brought them to Coventry, where they were condemned to death on the orders of Warwick and Clarence. Both were beheaded on 12 August at Gosford Green outside the city walls. Rivers's body was carried to Kent and buried in All Saints' Church in Maidstone, where an indent remains to show where his brass lay. His son Anthony now became Earl Rivers, and his office of Treasurer of England was given to a former Lancastrian, Sir John Langstrother. When Queen Elizabeth learned the fate of her father and brother, she vowed vengeance on those who had perpetrated the deed.

Warwick's hatred of the Wydvilles extended also to Rivers's widow, the Duchess of Bedford. Shortly after the Earl's execution, she was arrested on a charge of witchcraft. Two men had been paid by Warwick to give evidence that she had made obscene leaden images of Edward IV and Elizabeth Wydville and had practised her black arts upon them to bring about her daughter's marriage to the King. It was also alleged that she had cast another image to bring about Warwick's death. The Duchess, mindful of the fate of Eleanor Cobham thirty years earlier, immediately wrote to the Lord Mayor of London soliciting his protection. The mayor forwarded the letter to Clarence, but then remembered how the Duchess had tried to save London from the savagery of Margaret of Anjou's northern army in

1461, and forcefully interceded on her behalf with the Council. Further investigation proved that the evidence against her was deeply suspect. Witnesses had been bribed to make them testify against her, but when it came to it and they would not take the oath in court, the prosecution's case collapsed and the Duchess was freed. In February 1470 she was officially declared innocent of all the charges by Edward IV.

By the end of August 1469 Warwick's authority was crumbling and the government beginning to descend into anarchy. Many lords were taking advantage of Edward's captivity to settle old feuds or pervert justice in their localities. The people were angry with Warwick for imprisoning the King and were attributing all their ills to this. In London angry mobs were gathering, threatening violence, while Clarence and Archbishop Neville vainly strove to maintain a semblance of normality at Westminster. Warwick himself issued several proclamations in the King's name demanding civil obedience, but the people ignored them. The situation was getting out of control, and Warwick was obliged to issue a further writ cancelling the Parliament at York.

At that moment, Humphrey Neville of Brancepeth, who had been in hiding near Derwentwater since Hexham, raised Henry VI's standard and incited his northern compatriots to rebellion. He had a strong following and large numbers of men came in at his summons. Warwick rode north with an army to suppress the rising, but was unable to do so, for his men threatened to desert unless they were assured of Edward IV's health and safety. Nor would the magnates support Warwick, though they would undoubtedly obey a summons from the King. Warwick therefore had no choice but to invoke Edward's authority, and Archbishop Neville asked Edward if, in return for a degree of liberty, he would support Warwick against the rebels. The King, who had been kept secretly informed by his own supporters and Burgundian agents as to what was happening, declared himself willing to co-operate, telling the Archbishop that he harboured no ill-will against the Nevilles. He was then taken to York, where his entry to the city was marked by fanfares and ceremony, while crowds turned out to cheer him, and lords thronged round him, eager to renew their vows of homage. When, at Warwick's request, the King summoned his lieges to arms such was his authority that there was an enthusiastic response. The royal army, commanded by Warwick, then marched north and crushed Humphrey Neville's rebellion almost effortlessly. Neville himself was captured by Warwick and brought back to York where, on 29 September, he was beheaded in the presence of the King.

Warwick had no choice but to keep his promise and allow Edward more freedom. It was clear to both him and to Clarence that their victory had been a hollow one that had gained them precisely nothing. Now they had to retrieve the situation without bringing down charges of treason upon their heads. In fact, there was no way of holding Edward. The King had secretly summoned his loyal lords and supporters – Gloucester, Hastings, Buckingham, Essex, Arundel, Northumberland (who had not supported his brother's rebellion), Howard, Dynham and Mountjoy – who all rode at speed to join him. Early in October, with Warwick's blessing, Edward rode out of York to Pontefract and freedom.

Surrounded now by his loyal lords, the King informed Warwick that he was returning to London. He arrived in triumph in his capital, followed by 1000 mounted men, and received a tumultuous reception from the citizens, being formally welcomed back by the Lord Mayor and aldermen in their scarlet robes and 200 prominent citizens clad in blue. Archbishop Neville and the Earl of Oxford had been waiting at the Archbishop's residence called The More in Hertfordshire to follow the King into London and so present themselves as his loyal supporters, but he forbade them to approach the city.

Edward immediately set to work to re-establish his authority, adopting a conciliatory policy that would, he hoped, persuade those who had deserted him to return to their allegiance. Although Warkworth says that once in London he 'did as he liked', the King had to tread carefully, and once he was settled at Westminster he wisely referred to Warwick and Clarence in courteous and forgiving terms, never once showing any mark of disfavour towards them.

Herbert's death had left a vacuum in Wales, of which Lancastrian sympathisers in the south of the principality had been quick to take advantage, stirring up rebellion, seizing royal castles, and using them as a base from which to terrorise the local population. In December the King acted to remedy this situation, granting his brother, Gloucester, then only seventeen, full powers to secure the castles that had fallen to the Welsh rebels, a task which the young Duke fulfilled with commendable efficiency.

Warwick and Clarence remained in the north for at least a month after Edward left for London. Then the King summoned them to a meeting of a great council in the capital, which was intended to be a forum in which all grievances could be aired, discussed and, it was hoped, redressed. When Warwick and Clarence arrived at Westminster in December, the King staged a very public ceremony of reconciliation, doing his best to convince everyone that he harboured no ill-feelings towards his brother and cousin. John Paston reported that he had 'good language of the lords of Clarence and Warwick, saying they be his best friends; but his household men have other language, so what shall hastily fall I cannot say'. Soon afterwards Warwick and Clarence returned north, where they remained for the rest of the winter. Presently, the King issued full and unconditional pardons to those who had been involved in the previous summer's rebellion. Nevertheless, Warwick's wings had been well and truly clipped, and he must have realised with dismay that his influence in government was now less than it had ever been and was diminishing daily. Edward might present a smiling face, but he would never again trust Warwick, still less be controlled by him.

Louis XI had been quick to take advantage of the political confusion in England, and had made public his intention of allying himself to the House of Lancaster. In December, in response to his invitation, Margaret left Bar and travelled to Tours to see him. At the French court she had an emotional reunion with her father, and Louis himself extended a warm welcome to her, assuring her that the restoration of Henry VI would be one of his prime concerns.

News of events in France prompted unfounded rumours in England that the Queen was at Harfleur with an invasion fleet, ready to set sail. In fact, she was still at Tours, discussing strategies with Louis and her relatives. Soon, she was writing to her supporters in England that they should hold themselves in readiness to rise against the Yorkists, for the time was fast approaching when King Henry would come into his own again.

23

The Queen and M. de Warwick

By February 1470 it was clear to Warwick that the King would do nothing to redress his grievances, and the Earl was growing desperate. Again, he began to intrigue with Clarence, both of them resolving that this time they would not be satisfied with anything less than the deposition of the King and the elevation of Clarence to the throne. Warwick must have realised that Clarence was unstable and could not be counted upon to restore him to his former power, but the only alternative was Henry VI, and Warwick still had no wish to ally himself with Margaret of Anjou, even if she were willing: she was even less likely to allow him to enjoy his former dominance at court once her husband had been restored.

Warwick's strategy would be to instigate a rebellion against the King. Then, while Edward was preoccupied with suppressing it, he would enlist the help of King Louis to depose him. He hoped the rebellion would lead to an armed confrontation in which the King would be defeated and easily overthrown, or even killed.

No sooner was the plan conceived than Warwick began to put it into action, using all the resources at his disposal – wealth, territorial influence and the weight of his formidable personality. Again, he used the old tactic of exploiting the grievances of the commons to effect a popular rising, targeting the lower orders and the gentry, who had always supported him, rather than the nobility, who had not. Predictably, it was the commons who responded to his propaganda.

By late February, as Edward IV worked conscientiously to re-establish himself, Warwick and Clarence had become involved with certain disaffected gentlemen of Lincolnshire and Yorkshire, men of Lancastrian sympathies who heartily resented the Yorkist king and his onerous taxes. The chief of these was Robert, Lord Welles and

Willoughby. Warwick did not find it difficult to encourage these men and their tenants to rise on the basis of their local grievances and with the aim of restoring Henry VI to the throne, nor did Welles and other leaders have any trouble in getting others to join them.

However, early in March the King summoned Lord Welles, his brother-in-law, Thomas de la Lande, and Sir Thomas Dymoke to London to receive pardons for their part in the previous uprising. Fearing Edward's displeasure, they all obeyed his summons. In the meantime, Clarence arranged that Sir Robert Welles, the son of Lord Welles, should lead the rebels in his father's absence, then himself rode to London, saying that he would speak in Lord Welles's favour and prevent the King from marching north to confront Sir Robert. Yet when Clarence arrived in London on 4 March he did neither of these things.

On that day Sir Robert Welles arranged for a summons to arms, signed by Warwick and Clarence, to be posted on church doors in the county of Lincoln. All able-bodied men were commanded to attend Sir Robert, fully armed, on Ranby Hawe, seven miles north of Horncastle, on 7 March in order to resist the King who, it was alleged, would be coming north to punish the commons for their involvement in riots the previous year.

As soon as Lord Welles had departed for London, a Yorkist knight, Sir Thomas Burgh, had destroyed his house and taken all his goods and livestock. This incensed Lancastrian sympathisers in the region, and 30,000 of them answered Sir Robert's summons, crying, 'King Henry!' and shouting derision at King Edward. At the same time, Sir John Conyers, Lord Scrope of Bolton and Lord FitzWalter were orchestrating a rising in Yorkshire, ostensibly in protest at the King's failure to restore Henry Percy to the earldom of Northumberland.

On 6 March the King left London and went to Waltham Abbey in Essex, where the next day he was informed of Sir Robert's proclamation and told that a great army was assembling in Lincolnshire for the purpose of restoring Henry VI. Edward summoned his captains and told them to begin recruiting, then he sent for Lord Welles and Dymoke to join him. He did not send for Clarence because he had not yet learned that the Duke was one of the prime movers in the rebellion.

On the 8th the King arrived at Royston, whence he issued commissions of array to Clarence and Warwick, who had both written to offer their help in suppressing the revolt. The next day Edward was in Huntingdon, raising an army which was to muster at Grantham on the 12th. Clearly, he was expecting a French invasion:

'We be ascertained', he wrote, 'that our rebels and outward enemies intend in haste to arrive in this our realm.' Then he rode towards Lincolnshire, ordering Lord Welles to write to his son and his tenants saying that they should surrender to the King as their sovereign lord, or else the King had vowed that Welles should lose his head.

With the King on the march, displaying no trace of the lethargy that had proved so damaging before Edgecote, very few people joined the rebels; even supporters of Warwick and Clarence refrained. On the 11th the King came to Fotheringhay, whence he issued more commissions of array, commanding that his lieges rendezvous at Stamford. Soon afterwards his scouts reported that the rebels had passed Grantham and were forty miles off, moving towards Leicester where Warwick had promised to meet them with 20,000 men. The Earl would then wait with them in the hope that the King would move north, in which case the Yorkshire rebels would advance on him, while Warwick and Sir Robert would close in from behind in a pincer movement, thus blocking Edward's retreat south.

The King had no intention of moving any further north. Instead, at dawn on the 12th he led his own force to join up with the greater one awaiting him at Stamford. Here he learned that Sir Robert's army was five miles west of the town, at Empingham in Rutland, and ordered his vanguard to advance on them, taking their artillery.

Just then, a messenger arrived with a letter from Warwick and Clarence, promising that they would bring reinforcements and join the King at Leicester that evening. This was obviously a trap: the reinforcements were for Sir Robert, and Edward resolved to march west to do battle with Welles at once. Before he went, however, in order to forestall any desertions, his lords advised him to show the world what happened to those who committed treason against their king. Edward ordered that Lord Welles be summarily decapitated, which was done before the incredulous eyes of the waiting soldiers. Then a herald was dispatched to Sir Robert Welles to inform him of his father's execution and offer him the King's mercy if he would submit. Sir Robert, horrified at the news, refused.

The King's army confronted the rebels in a field at Empingham and struck so swiftly that Warwick and Clarence had no time to bring reinforcements. Edward had with him an impressive array of artillery, and when he used the full force of it upon the rebels, the casualties were such that the peasants in Sir Robert's army panicked and fled. Some left the field in such haste that they threw off their surcoats as they ran, which led to the battle being named 'Losecoat Field'. The rebels had had no chance against the King's seasoned and well-armed troops and the magnates' experienced retainers. Although many of the rebels were wearing Clarence's livery, some were so bewildered that they were uncertain as to whom they were fighting for, and in the heat of the battle cried, 'King Henry!' instead of 'Warwick!' or 'Clarence!' Waurin says that most of the fleeing men would have been slaughtered in the rout had not the King ordered his men to stop the pursuit. Sir Robert Welles, Sir Thomas de la Lande and other rebel captains were captured. Meanwhile, among the corpses that littered the battlefield was found one that was identified as a servant of Clarence, and on the body were discovered letters from the Duke and Warwick confirming their part in the rebellion.

Later that day Edward rode in triumph back to Stamford. His victory ensured that he remained in control of London, East Anglia and the East Midlands, while in Yorkshire Sir John Conyers's uprising had collapsed in the wake of the royal victory. On 13 March, prompted by his knowledge of Warwick's true intentions, the King issued a proclamation forbidding any of his lieges to array their men.

When he arrived in Grantham the next day, the captured rebel leaders were brought before him and publicly confessed their faults. They also revealed that Warwick and Clarence had initiated the rising and promised to aid them against him. Sir Robert Welles kept repeating that they had told him several times that they meant to make Clarence king. All three were condemned to be beheaded: de la Lande and Dymoke were executed on the 15th at Grantham, Welles on the 19th at Doncaster. The King ordered an official account of the rebellion and a transcript of Sir Robert's confession to be distributed and read throughout his kingdom.

On 13 March the King issued an urgent summons to Warwick and Clarence to present themselves before him 'in humble wise' with only a few retainers to answer grave charges of treason. Warwick and Clarence ignored his summons and, having recruited more men at Coventry, marched north via Burton-on-Trent, Derby and Chesterfield, which they reached on the 18th, intending to orchestrate another rebellion. As they rode, they sent ahead messengers with proclamations demanding that the men of Yorkshire rise in arms and join them on pain of death.

The King, too, rode north, having sent a further abortive summons to Warwick and Clarence from Newark. In Doncaster, he received a message from them demanding his assurance of their safety should they come into his presence; angrily, he refused to give it. Two days later, he drew up his army in battle order; according to the Paston Letters, 'it was said that there were never seen in England

so many goodly men, and so well arrayed'. The royal army marched
south towards Chesterfield, then discovered that Warwick had sent
his scouts ahead to secure lodgings for the night at Rotherham, so the
King advanced there, only to find the place deserted. He guessed that
the Earl had deliberately lured him there, and later discovered that
Yorkshire rebels under Sir John Conyers and Lord Scrope had
planned an ambush in the vicinity, but had not arrived in time.
Warwick, meanwhile, had swung west towards Manchester, hoping
to enlist the aid of Lord Stanley and his Lancashire levies and so
march with them to join the Yorkshire rebels. Stanley, however,
refused to commit himself.

Warwick was in favour of turning back at night and marching east
to confront the King in battle, but the Earl of Shrewsbury, one of his
captains, suddenly deserted with a large force, and left the Earl with
no alternative but flight. Shrewsbury's reinforcements joined
Edward, who temporarily abandoned his pursuit of Warwick and
Clarence and rode into York to 'refresh and victual' his men and
receive the submission of Scrope and other rebels, who all confirmed
that Warwick and Clarence had been behind the northern rebellions.

Edward was worried that the powerful John Neville, Earl of
Northumberland, who had hitherto remained loyal, would desert
him for his brother, Warwick, and on 25 March he deprived him of
the earldom of Northumberland and restored it to young Henry
Percy, whose father had fallen at Towton. This found favour with
the people of the north, and was plainly intended to counterbalance
the power of the Nevilles, who were the Percies' greatest rivals in the
region. The King created John Neville Marquess of Montague to
compensate him for the loss of the earldom, but failed to endow him
with any lands, leaving him unable to support the dignities of his
new rank. Angrily he complained that Edward had given him 'a
magpie's nest', and even the creation of his son George as Duke of
Bedford did not mollify him.

Edward had made a grave misjudgement, but matters were
seemingly put right when he offered the hand of his eldest daughter,
Elizabeth of York, for Bedford, knowing that if anything should
happen to him Montague would then ensure that Elizabeth's right to
succeed him would be upheld. The King was determined at all costs
to prevent Clarence and Warwick's daughter Isabel from being
crowned, and knew he could rely not just on Montague's loyalty but
also on his self-interest, for what man could resist the prospect of his
son becoming a king?

On 24 March, the King issued a proclamation denouncing both
Warwick and Clarence as traitors and 'great rebels' and putting a

price on their heads. He then issued a further summons ordering them to appear before him by 28 March at the latest or be dealt with as traitors. On the 27th he left York with his host to hunt them down, marching south via Nottingham and Coventry.

Warwick knew he was in too weak a position to oppose the King. He and Clarence rode hastily to Warwick Castle, collected the Countess of Warwick and her daughter Anne and left, making as much speed as they could for the south. On 18 March, Isabel of Clarence had gone to Exeter and lodged in the bishop's palace, and Warwick planned that they should join her there and then flee to Calais, which he hoped would have remained loyal to him, and where he might be able to raise support. First, however, they went to Southampton, where one of Warwick's great ships, the *Trinity*, was expected to dock shortly. However, the King had anticipated their arrival, and had sent ahead Lords Rivers and Howard, who captured not only the *Trinity* but also every other ship owned by Warwick that was in port, along with all their crews. Warwick and Clarence were forced to continue on to Exeter by land, where they were reunited with the Duchess Isabel, then nine months pregnant, commandeered a ship and on 3 April put to sea.

On 14 April the King came from Wells to Exeter to find his quarry were beyond his reach. Baulked of bringing them to justice, Edward marched east along the coast to Southampton, where he commanded Tiptoft to sit in judgement on the men who had been captured in Warwick's ships. Twenty gentlemen and yeomen were hanged, drawn and quartered, but what appalled the watching crowds was that, after they were dead, on Tiptoft's orders their corpses were beheaded and the naked torsoes hung up by the legs. Stakes, sharpened at both ends, were forced between their buttocks, the heads being impaled on the protruding ends. Warkworth says that 'for ever afterwards the Earl of Worcester was greatly hated by [the people] for the irregular and unlawful manner of execution he had inflicted upon his captives'.

Meanwhile, Warwick had appeared before Calais, which was under the command of Lord Wenlock. Twelve hours before Warwick's arrival, Wenlock had received orders from Edward IV not to allow 'the great rebel' to land, and instead of according Warwick the welcome he had expected, fired guns on him. The Earl had always looked upon Wenlock as his most trustworthy lieutenant, and his apparent disaffection was a severe blow.

For a time Warwick's ship remained at anchor before Calais; then, on 16 April, Isabel went into labour. Despite Warwick's entreaties,

Wenlock would still not let them land, and even when her pains grew severe and there were obstetrical complications he remained obdurate. Although personally sympathetic to the Duchess's plight, Wenlock's loyalty to the King prevented him from disobeying Edward's orders, though he did contrive to send Warwick two flagons of wine for his daughter and a secret message to say that, if the Earl and his party were to sail around the coast, land in Normandy and then obtain aid from Louis XI, he, Wenlock, and the Calais garrison would support him.

Fortunately for Isabel, her mother was a skilled enough midwife to assist her during a very difficult delivery, but she could not save her baby. The sex of the child is still subject to dispute: it was either an unnamed, stillborn son, or a daughter named Anne who died immediately after birth. The tiny corpse was taken ashore at Calais and buried there, and Warwick then sailed on towards Honfleur, harrying and capturing Breton and Burgundian merchant ships as he went.

Warwick's timely arrival in France gave Louis the opportunity to put into action the plans he had long been devising. Warwick and Clarence anchored off Honfleur on 1 May, and were formally welcomed by the Admiral of France and the Archbishop of Narbonne, as Louis's representatives. They had been commanded by the French king to tell Warwick that he would do everything in his power to help him recover England, either by arranging an alliance with the Lancastrians, or by any other means that Warwick might suggest. Either would suit Louis's purpose of driving a wedge between England and Burgundy, but he wanted the decision to attempt a Lancastrian restoration to be Warwick's.

Warwick responded, asking for an audience, but before the King would grant one, he insisted that the captured Burgundian ships must be secreted away where they could not cause him any embarrassment. Burgundian spies had soon apprised Duke Charles of their capture, and he warned the French king that he intended to launch an attack on Warwick and Clarence as soon as he could find them, whether it was on land or sea. If Louis aided them, he would be breaking the terms of the Treaty of St Omer.

Louis was still hoping to bring about a reconciliation and alliance between Warwick and Margaret of Anjou that would lead to the restoration of Henry VI to the English throne. He invited both Queen Margaret and Warwick to visit him at Angers, although initially Warwick declined to accept. The Milanese ambassador to France reported: 'The Earl of Warwick does not want to be here when the Queen arrives, but wishes to allow His Majesty to shape matters a little with her and move her to agree to an alliance between the Prince, her son, and a daughter of Warwick.' After some persuasion, however, Warwick agreed to meet Louis, who promised to see him separately and to act as mediator.

On 8 June, Louis received Warwick first, at Amboise on the Loire, Clarence being present at the audience. Warwick knew he was in a desperate situation, and had by now persuaded himself that the only way out was to abandon his plan to put Clarence on the throne and ally himself to the Lancastrians. He therefore indicated that he was willing to link his fortunes with those of Henry VI and Margaret of Anjou, and was ready to fight for them, while Louis told him he would press Queen Margaret to pardon him and guarantee him a prominent role in the government of England, should their plans come to fruition. Louis could be very persuasive, and Warwick allowed himself to be convinced. The French king promised a fleet of ships, men and money for the recovery of England, if, as soon as victory was his, Warwick would undertake to bind England in a treaty of peace with France and aid Louis in his proposed offensive against Burgundy. Warwick was happy to go along with this, particularly when Louis suggested that the alliance with Margaret be sealed by the marriage of Edward of Lancaster to Anne Neville.

Louis had made it clear to Warwick that he thought Clarence was unreliable and that his own plan to restore Henry VI stood a better chance of success than Warwick's original scheme to place Clarence on the throne. Clarence was not a fool, and very quickly realised that he was to play no part at all in the French plan save that of supporting Warwick, and that his father-in-law was less interested in making him king than in serving his own interests.

At about this time, Louis wrote to Margaret, proposing that she sign a thirty-year truce between France and the House of Lancaster in return for his promise to help Henry VI recover his kingdom. Margaret readily agreed, and as a compliment to his new allies Louis chose Prince Edward as godfather to the son that Queen Charlotte bore him at the end of the month. Meanwhile, in England, Edward IV was raising men for the defence of the south against a possible invasion by Warwick and Clarence.

Soon after meeting Warwick, Louis received Queen Margaret at Amboise, and wasted no time in coming straight to the point: with his help the Lancastrians had a good chance of overthrowing Edward IV, but this could only be achieved with the assistance of Warwick, and he asked the Queen seriously to consider allying herself with the Earl since he was the only man who could win England for her.

Margaret was shocked, then horrified, then furious. When she

could speak, she produced a whole tirade of arguments as to why
such an alliance was impossible. Louis waited until the storm had
passed and heard her out patiently, then told her bluntly that her
arguments might be valid but, if she was to regain her husband's
throne for him, she should put her personal feelings aside and adopt a
pragmatic attitude. If she could not do this, then he could not
support her. According to a report in the Harleian MSS, 'the Queen
was right difficult', saying that 'King Henry, she and her son had
certain friends which they might lose by this mean, and that might
do them more harm than the [good] that the Earl might bring.
Wherefore she besought the King that it would please him to leave
off.' Warwick, she cried,

> had pierced her heart with wounds that could never be healed;
> they would bleed till the Day of Judgement, when she would
> appeal to the justice of God for vengeance against him. His pride
> and insolence had first broken the peace of England and stirred
> up those fatal wars which had desolated the realm. Through
> him, she and her son had been attainted, proscribed and driven
> out to beg their bread in foreign lands, and not only had he
> injured her as a queen, but he had dared to defame her
> reputation as a woman by divers false and malicious slanders, as
> if she had been false to her royal lord the King – which things
> she could never forgive.

Louis persevered, and Fortescue added his own pleas, perceiving
that this alliance was the only way of restoring Henry VI. The
Milanese ambassador reported that 'His Majesty has spent and still
spends every day in long discussions with the Queen to induce her to
make the alliance with Warwick and to let the Prince go with the Earl
to the enterprise of England. Up to the present the Queen has shown
herself very hard and difficult.' Eventually, though, she allowed
Louis to overrule her objections and consented to grant Warwick
an audience, saying she would let him have her final decision after
the interview. She would not agree in any case to the Prince
accompanying Warwick, despite Louis's arguments that his presence
would inspire the people of England to rise in favour of Lancaster.
She feared to expose her son to the risks that such an expedition must
necessarily attract, though Louis was relentless in insisting that there
was no question but that the boy should go. Again, Margaret said
she would defer any decision on the matter until she had seen
Warwick.

On 15 July, the court moved to Angers, where the Countess of

Warwick and her daughter Anne were formally presented to Queen Margaret. It cannot have been a comfortable meeting, given Margaret's hostility towards Warwick. Worse was to follow, for later that day Louis told her that the Earl was ready to agree to a marriage between Anne and Prince Edward. At this, Margaret exploded. 'What!' she cried. 'Will he indeed give his daughter to my son, whom he has so often branded as the offspring of adultery or fraud?' And she 'would not in any wise consent thereunto', alleging she would gain more advantages by marrying Edward to Edward IV's heiress, Elizabeth of York – through such an alliance, the House of Lancaster would regain the throne on Edward's death providing he had no son to succeed him. And she produced for Louis to see a letter she had received from England the previous week, offering the hand of the Princess Elizabeth for Prince Edward.

Louis reported all that Margaret had said to Warwick so that he could marshal his arguments, and on the evening of the 22nd the Earl was at last ushered by the King into the frigid presence of the Queen, and abased himself on his knees, 'addressing her in the most moving words he could devise', according to Chastellain, 'begging forgiveness for all the wrongs he had done her, and humbly beseeching her to pardon and restore him to her favour'. The Harleian MSS account reports him conceding 'that by his conduct King Henry and she were put out of the realm of England', but excused this by saying he had believed they 'had enterprised the destruction of him and his friends in body and in goods, which he had never deserved. He told her he had been the means of upsetting King Edward and unsettling his realm' and promised that he would in future 'be as much his foe as he had formerly been his friend and maker'. He now offered himself as a true friend and subject of King Henry.

The Queen, however, 'scarcely vouchsafed him any answer, and kept him on his knees a full quarter of an hour'. Seeing that matters were not going as he had planned, King Louis stepped in and offered personally to guarantee the Earl's fidelity. Margaret demanded that Warwick publicly withdraw his slanderous remarks concerning the paternity of her son, which he assured her he would do, not only in France, but also in England when he had conquered it for her. At length, after much persuasion, the Queen pardoned Warwick.

Louis then brought in the Earl of Oxford, who received a much warmer reception. Margaret forgave him also, saying that his pardon was easy to purchase, for she knew well that he and his friends had suffered much for King Henry's quarrels.

The next three days found Louis, Margaret and Warwick busily negotiating the terms of their alliance. After prolonged discussions, the Queen finally agreed to the marriage of Prince Edward and Anne Neville, although she said she would not allow it to take place until after Warwick had proved his loyalty by taking the field against King Edward, and it should not be consummated until England was mostly conquered. The Prince must therefore remain in France while the Earl invaded England.

Louis promised for his part to provide money, soldiers and a fleet of ships. All the parties were aware that Henry VI would never be fit to rule England again, so Margaret agreed that, when he 'took joyful possession of England again', Warwick would be named Regent and Governor of England. Should Henry die before the Prince attained his majority, Warwick would become his guardian. And if the Prince should die without heirs, 'then the kingdom should pass to Clarence and his heirs for ever more'.

It was also agreed that Exeter, Somerset 'and all the knights, squires and others who had been exiled or dishonoured in the cause of King Henry, should come back to England and retake possession of their property'. Finally, England would join France in an offensive alliance against Burgundy.

The accord between Warwick and Margaret of Anjou astonished observers in Europe. Commines observed that Margaret had consistently condemned Warwick as the man who had worked to dethrone and imprison Henry VI, and was now marrying her only son to 'the daughter of him that did it!'

On 25 July 1470 Prince Edward was betrothed to Anne Neville in Angers Cathedral. 'Today,' observed King Louis, 'we have made the marriage of the Queen of England and the Earl of Warwick.' The ceremony took place in the presence of the King of France, King René, Queen Margaret, the Duchess of Clarence and the Earl and Countess of Warwick.

Nothing is recorded of the feelings of the young couple concerned. The chronicler John Rous describes Anne Neville as 'seemly, amiable and beauteous, right virtuous and full gracious', but these were the routine courtly compliments to be expected of one who had great respect for her family. Queen Margaret had no doubt been the bogey of Anne's childhood, and yet now she was being made to do all reverence to this formidable woman who was her future mother-in-law, and who had made it quite clear that she did not want Anne for her son but had only agreed to their marriage as a means of restoring the House of Lancaster to the English throne. Nor was the sixteen-year-old Prince the most prepossessing of bridegrooms, having a notorious penchant for war and violence, and carrying on his shoulders all the grudges of his mother and her desire for revenge on their enemies.

They could not as yet be married because they were cousins in the fourth degree, both being great-grandchildren of John of Gaunt, and a dispensation from the Pope had to be applied for. It was vital that the Pope be made to see the urgency of the matter, but to speed up the process took money. Louis had therefore procured a loan from a merchant in Tours to pay whatever bribes were needful, then dispatched his envoys to the Vatican. After the betrothal ceremony Anne was committed to the safe-keeping of Queen Margaret.

Clarence, meanwhile, had refused to attend the betrothal and was sulking in Normandy. His plan had been to supplant Edward IV himself, but Warwick had abandoned him without a qualm and was now promoting the claims of Lancaster. All he could offer Clarence was a vague promise that if Prince Edward and Anne Neville had no children he would be heir to the throne. And it was for this that Clarence had betrayed his brother, slandered his mother and risked his life and his fortune.

Margaret had kept her part of the bargain, now it was up to Warwick to fulfil his. On 30 July, in Angers Cathedral, the Earl publicly swore an oath on a fragment of the True Cross to keep faith with King Henry, Queen Margaret and Prince Edward and to uphold the right of the House of Lancaster to the throne of England. Margaret, in turn, swore to treat the Earl as a true and faithful subject and never to reproach him for his past deeds.

It had been agreed by the allies that Warwick and Jasper Tudor, who had recently arrived in France, would lead the invasion force, and that Margaret and her son would follow them to England when it was safe to do so. Warwick would sail to the south-east coast, while Jasper would lead an assault on Wales, where he could count on the support of many loyal Lancastrians. Warwick had already sent word of his coming to his affinity in Yorkshire and they were arming themselves, while Queen Margaret wrote to her supporters in England, bidding them be ready to rise when Warwick came.

On the 31st, Margaret, the Prince and Anne Neville left Angers for Amboise, and a day or so later Warwick set off for the coast to prepare for the invasion. Queen Margaret soon joined him at Harfleur in Normandy to help him recruit men. Already, his invasion was expected in England, for on 5 August the Paston Letters record rumours 'that Clarence and Warwick will essay to land every day, as folks fear'.

Clarence had swallowed his grievances for the time being and rejoined Warwick, and together they produced a manifesto which was addressed to the 'worshipful, discreet and true commons of England', and dispatched across the Channel and posted in various towns on church doors and on London Bridge and buildings in Cheapside. The manifesto referred in harsh terms to Edward IV's misrule and the oppression and injustice that had resulted from it, and ended with a promise from Warwick that he would 'redeem for ever the said realm from thralldom of all outward nations and make it as free within itself as ever it was heretofore'.

Clarence was especially active in arranging for this and other propaganda material to be displayed in London, and he also went to Calais to rally the garrison. Commines says that, while he was there, a mysterious Englishwoman 'of few words' arrived, and told Lord Wenlock that she was a friend of the Duchess Isabel, on her way to comfort her for the loss of her child. He did not believe her, and when pressed she revealed that she had come to negotiate a peace between Edward IV and Warwick, showing Wenlock papers to prove this. Wenlock, no doubt hoping that this time of conflicting loyalties would soon be ended, allowed the woman to go free.

She went straight to Clarence, saying that she had come from England to serve his wife as a waiting woman and would be grateful for a private interview. When they were closeted alone together, the woman – who was undoubtedly a female undercover agent working for the Yorkists – produced a letter from Edward IV to Clarence promising the Duke that, if he forsook Warwick and returned to England, the King would forgive him and restore him to his former position at court. Clarence was heartened by his brother's message and seriously tempted to accept his offer, but in the end he decided that he had more to hope for from Warwick than Edward at the moment. Nevertheless, he was careful to keep his options open, and sent the woman back with a promise to Edward that he would join him as soon as the opportunity presented itself. According to Commines, the female agent, whose name has never been discovered and who disappears from the records at this point, was 'the only contriver of the enterprise whereby the Earl of Warwick and his whole faction were utterly destroyed'. From this, we may deduce that she played a greater role behind the scenes than is anywhere recorded in the surviving sources.

By the second week of August, the Milanese ambassador was reporting that Warwick's embarkation for England was expected at any time. Charles of Burgundy had been deeply concerned about the Earl's presence in France and had made strong representations to Louis about harbouring English traitors, even threatening war if Louis did not expel them. When Louis ignored this, Charles sent a fleet of ships to blockade the mouth of the Seine, so that Warwick's invasion force could not sail. The presence of these Burgundian ships delayed his departure for many days, and since Louis had not been over-generous with money, the Earl found it difficult to provide food and stores for his men during this period. He was also anxious to see his daughter married to Prince Edward before he left for England, but when the dispensation did not arrive in time he had to content himself with Louis's promise that Anne would be treated as if she were royalty and married as soon as it came.

Although Edward IV had been informed by his ambassadors and spies of events in France, he seems to have underestimated the danger. Commines scathingly accuses him of being more preoccupied with hunting than with preparing to resist an invasion. He 'was not so much concerned about the invasion of the Earl of Warwick as the Duke of Burgundy was, for [Burgundy] knew [of] the movements in England in favour of the Earl of Warwick and had often warned King Edward of them, but he had no fear. It seems to me folly not to fear one's enemy, seeing the resources that he had.'

At the beginning of August, Lord FitzHugh, Warwick's brother-in-law and a member of his northern affinity, staged a sham rebellion in Yorkshire. As a trick to lure the King away from London it worked, and by 5 August Edward was summoning his levies. Before he left the capital he installed Queen Elizabeth, who was again pregnant, in the Tower of London, where she occupied luxuriously appointed chambers which she now had specially prepared for her confinement. She also arranged for the royal apartments to be 'well-victualled and fortified', and the King stored there extra ammunition and several large cannon from Bristol.

By the middle of August Edward was in Yorkshire, marching from York to Ripon. His government had not been popular in recent months and he found his subjects less enthusiastic than on former occasions. Nevertheless, he did manage to recruit over 3000 men, who were augmented by another 3000 horse brought by Sir William Hastings, while news came that Lord Montague had gathered 6000 men and was also preparing to join the King. On 7 September, Edward was in York, issuing signet letters to his lieges, commanding them to attend him to vanquish the traitors in his realm. Yet there was now no one to vanquish, for, at news of the King's advance, Lord FitzHugh had fled north to seek asylum in Scotland.

The real danger was approaching from the south, for across the Channel a violent storm had dispersed the Burgundian blockade of ships, and now there was nothing to prevent Warwick from launching an invasion.

24

The Readeption of Henry VI

On 9 September, Warwick and Clarence and a fleet of sixty ships carrying their invasion force sailed from La Hogue in Normandy. Their company included Jasper Tudor, the Earl of Oxford and Thomas Neville, Bastard of Fauconberg. Edward IV, learning that Warwick had been preparing for an invasion, had sent a royal fleet to prevent him from landing, but a storm had scattered it, leaving the coast unguarded. On the 13th, when Edward was still in Yorkshire, the Earl's fleet arrived in the West Country, putting in at Dartmouth and Plymouth.

Warwick was still very popular in England. Commines says that, although it was late in the campaigning season, he 'found infinite numbers to take his part'. As he marched towards Exeter, he 'gathered a great people', according to Warkworth, and in Plymouth his supporters proclaimed Henry VI king. In Exeter, Warwick issued a proclamation declaring that his invasion was authorised 'by the assent of the most noble princess, Margaret, Queen of England, and the right high and mighty Prince Edward'. It was signed by Warwick, Clarence, Jasper Tudor and Oxford, and called upon all true subjects of Henry VI, 'the very true and undoubted King of England', to take up arms against the usurper Edward, whose misgovernment was dwelt upon in some detail. The proclamation also prohibited members of the invasion force from pillage and rape. No one wanted a repeat of the atrocities of 1461.

Jasper Tudor set off for Wales to recruit more men there, while Warwick marched northwards, hoping to link up with his supporters from Kent and the north. From all over England Lancastrian supporters came rallying to his banners, and many men deserted King Edward's army so that they could join Warwick, 'in such sort that every day his force increased'. His objective now was to hunt down the King, confront him and, he hoped, defeat him in battle. At first he made for Nottingham, having received reports that Edward had been recruiting there. By the time he reached Coventry, he himself was in command of an army variously estimated as 30,000 or 60,000 strong. Presently, he was joined by Shrewsbury and Lord Stanley.

London had been plunged into a turmoil at the news of Warwick's invasion. At the end of September his Kentishmen marched on the capital and rioted against the Flemish and Dutch weavers living in Southwark, causing extensive damage to their homes. The Lord Chancellor, Bishop Stillington, had fled into sanctuary, and when Warwick learned of this he reappointed his brother, Archbishop Neville, as Chancellor in his place.

On 29 September, Edward IV learned of Warwick's advance and also that Montague was coming with a large force to help his sovereign deal with the rebels. The King therefore galloped south to meet him. At Doncaster, says Commines, 'the King lodged (as himself told) in a strong house into which no man could enter but by a drawbridge. His army lay in villages round about. But as he sat at dinner, his serjeant of the minstrels came running in and brought news that the Marquess of Montague and certain others were mounted on horseback and had caused all their men to cry. "God save King Henry!"' At first Edward did not believe this, but he did send messengers to find out the truth, 'and armed himself, and set men at the barriers of his lodging to defend it'. He then donned armour as did his companions Hastings and Rivers 'and divers other knights and esquires'.

Montague, says Warkworth, 'hated the King and intended to capture him, so when he came within a mile of King Edward he told his people that he would side with Warwick. Immediately, however, one of the men went from this gathering to inform King Edward about it, and told him to stay away, because he was not strong enough to take on Lord Montague.' Montague's desertion was a terrible blow to the King, for Edward had relied on him to hold the north secure while he moved south to deal with Warwick, who was now at Coventry.

By now, Edward's men were deserting in large numbers, and his force had been reduced to a mere 2000 soldiers. In alarm, he realised that his authority was rapidly crumbling and that he had no choice but to take flight. Accompanied by Hastings, Gloucester, Rivers and those troops who remained loyal, the King sped east across Lincolnshire, narrowly avoiding being drowned in the Wash, and at ten o'clock at night on Sunday, 30 September, came to the port of

King's Lynn in Norfolk, intending to leave England and seek asylum with his ally, Charles of Burgundy. Fortunately, says Commines, 'God so provided for the King' that he found two Dutch hulks, 'freighted with merchandise' and bound for Holland, lying at anchor. The ships' masters were willing to take Edward and his party of 7-800 persons, and at eight in the morning of 2 October, they put to sea. 'The King had not one penny on him' and no change of clothing, so he 'gave the master of the ship for his passage a goodly gown furred with martens, promising one day to do him a good turn. As touching his train, never so poor a company was seen.' Presently, the ships docked at Alkmaar in Holland, which was in Burgundian territory.

Meanwhile, Duke Charles had sent Commines to Calais to ensure that Lord Wenlock and his garrison remained loyal to Edward IV. Wenlock, however, had long been displaying outward loyalty to King Edward while secretly negotiating with his enemies. Commines perceived this and went to Boulogne to warn the Duke. While they were there, news arrived of Edward's defeat; one report, which Charles believed, even said he had been killed. The Duke sent Commines back to Calais to obtain further information and do all he could to preserve the English alliance, but when he got there Commines found Wenlock and the garrison all wearing Warwick's emblem of the bear and ragged staff. Worse still, when he returned to his lodgings, he saw that the doors were covered in graffiti, white crosses and verses lauding Louis's pact with Warwick. Commines saw Wenlock at once, but while Wenlock agreed to continue to support the Burgundian alliance, he said he would only do so with Henry VI as king, not Edward IV.

On 1 October news of King Edward's flight from Yorkshire was cried in London. Queen Elizabeth was eight months pregnant and, feeling that it was no longer safe for her to remain in the Tower, that night, with her children and her mother, sought sanctuary in Westminster Abbey. When she arrived, 'in great penury and forsaken of all friends', Abbot Thomas Milling received her kindly and, rather than lodging her with the common rabble in the cruciform bulk of the sanctuary building, placed at her disposal the three best rooms in his own house within the abbey precincts.

No sooner had the Queen arrived than she received word that Warwick's advance company had entered London unopposed. Elizabeth at once sent the abbot to the Lord Mayor and aldermen, asking them to take command of the Tower of London and secure the city against the men of Kent and the rest of Warwick's approaching army. The mayor, however, knew that it would be folly to resist such a large force, and that he and his fellows would be better advised to come to terms with Warwick, then entreat him to spare the city from the more violent members of his affinity.

Warwick sent his representative, Sir Geoffrey Gate, ahead into London to receive its submission and liberate Henry VI. Gate was unpopular with the citizens because he had incited the Kentishmen to riot, and there was much murmuring against him. Nevertheless, on the 3rd the Constable of the Tower surrendered the fortress to Gate and the Lord Mayor, which placed Gate in control of the person of Henry VI. Acting on Warwick's instructions, Gate sent the Bishop of Winchester to liberate the King. Henry emerged 'as a man amazed, utterly dulled with troubles and adversities'. According to Warkworth he 'was not worshipfully arrayed as a prince, and not so cleanly kept as should seem such a prince'. Gate arranged for him to be moved to the royal apartments in the Tower and lodged in the sumptuous rooms prepared for Queen Elizabeth's confinement.

On the 5th Archbishop Neville marched into London at the head of a strong force and took control of the Tower. The next day, Warwick and Clarence, accompanied by Shrewsbury, Stanley and the main body of their army, rode in triumphal procession into the City and made straight for the Tower, where they knelt before Henry VI and greeted him as their 'lawful king'. Their arrival prompted many Yorkist knights and squires, as well as some members of the Council, to seek refuge in various sanctuaries, just as a similar number of Lancastrian and Neville sympathisers were emerging from them. One was Thomas Howard, treasurer of Edward IV's household, who, after an abortive attempt to flee abroad to join his master, took sanctuary at Colchester.

Warwick ordered that the King be 'new arrayed' in a robe of blue velvet, then he and the lords escorted him in procession into London, passing along Cheapside to the Bishop of London's palace by St Paul's Cathedral, where he was to lodge temporarily. Here, they sat him on a throne and placed the crown on his head. Warwick paid Henry 'great reverence', says Warkworth, 'and so he was restored to the crown again, whereof all his good lovers were full glad'. But it was noted that the restored King sat on his throne as limp and helpless as a sack of wool. 'He was a mere shadow and pretence', a puppet worked by Warwick – who, as the King's Lieutenant, was now the real ruler of England – and Clarence. Henry, states the Great Chronicle of London, did not rejoice in his restoration, 'but merely thanked God and gave all his mind to serve and please Him, and feared little or nothing of the pomp and vanity of the world'. He appeared, says Commines, 'mute as a crowned calf', and must have been quite bewildered by this new turn of events. His mind, never very acute or stable before his captivity, had become duller as a result of it. During the months to come, 'what was done in his name was done without his will and knowledge'. However, he was by no means deranged, and was quite capable of issuing a pardon to the man who had stabbed him in the Tower during his imprisonment.

That same day, Edward IV's ignominious flight from England was announced to the people from Paul's Cross and he was declared deposed. From then on, all letters, writs and other records showed Henry VI's regnal year in the following style: 'In the 49th year of the reign of Henry VI and the first of his readeption to royal power.' Thus historians refer to the period of Henry's restoration as 'the Readeption'.

The new Lancastrians were soon saying that the troubles of Henry's previous reign were the fault of 'the mischievous people that were about the King', whose greed had undermined his royal prestige and the prosperity and well-being of the realm. It was these 'false lords', and not Henry himself, who had been to blame for the loss of England's possessions in France. Now there was to be a new order, and the first sign of this was when the chief officers of Edward IV's household were required to resign their posts, which were then filled with men of impeccable Lancastrian backgrounds.

By 11 October King Edward had safely arrived at The Hague. He then travelled to St Pol, where he spent several days in the company of Charles of Burgundy. Edward pressed the Duke to help him regain his kingdom, but Charles was not yet prepared to commit himself. He was waiting to see whether or not Warwick would keep his promise and ally himself to Louis XI, and wished to do nothing that might provoke the Earl's hostility towards Burgundy. Edward had to resign himself to waiting, and travelled to Bruges, where he took up residence in the palace of the Lord of Gruthuyse, Governor of Holland. Commines says Gruthuyse 'dealt very honourably' with Edward and his companions, 'for he gave them much apparel among them' and accorded them the respect due to visiting royalty.

In Paris, meanwhile, Louis XI had learned of Henry VI's restoration and ordered that a *Te Deum* be sung in Notre Dame and that the event be marked by a three-day holiday and festival. He then told the chief dignitaries of the city to prepare an honourable welcome for Queen Margaret, the Prince of Wales and the Countess of Warwick and her daughters, who would be arriving in Paris very soon, *en route* for England.

On the 13th, Warwick had King Henry attired in his crown and in

King Edward's robes of state and paraded him through the streets of London to St Paul's Cathedral, himself bearing the King's train. Crowds flocked to see the spectacle and 'all the people rejoiced with clapping of hands and cried, "God save King Henry!"' After a service in which the King gave thanks to God for his restoration, he took up residence in the Palace of Westminster.

Later that day, John Tiptoft, Earl of Worcester, was arraigned in Westminster Hall and found guilty of treason. Although Warwick's policy towards the Yorkist nobility was to be of necessity conciliatory, he had had no compunction about apprehending the much hated Tiptoft. After Edward IV's flight, the Earl had taken refuge in a forest in Huntingdonshire, where he was found hiding at the top of a tree, and thence brought to London. The Earl of Oxford, who presided over the court and whose father and elder brother had been condemned to death in 1462 by the man people were now calling 'the Butcher of England', found Tiptoft guilty of all charges and sentenced him 'to go on foot to Tower Hill to have his head cut off', a remarkably lenient sentence in the circumstances.

At three o'clock that afternoon, the sheriffs of London received their prisoner at Temple Bar, intending to have him executed that evening. But the crowds were enormous; some had just come to 'gawp and gaze' at Tiptoft, while others were baying for his blood and would have lynched him had he not been protected by a heavily armed band of guards. It was nearly night by the time that the procession had forced its way as far as the Fleet Bridge, so the sheriffs asked the warden of the Fleet if they could borrow his prison and locked Tiptoft up there until morning. The next day they managed to escort him to Tower Hill. He showed no emotion on the scaffold and ignored the taunts and curses of the watching crowd, only unbending to speak to an Italian friar, who reproached him for his cruelty, to which he replied loftily that he had governed his deeds for the good of the state. He then requested the executioner to sever his head in three strokes in honour of the Holy Trinity. Thus died the only member of the Yorkist nobility to be executed by the readeption government. On 20 October, John Langstrother, Prior of the Hospital of the Knights of St John, was appointed Treasurer of England in his place.

In October, Jasper Tudor arrived in Hereford, where his nephew Henry Tudor was living with Lady Herbert's niece and her husband, Sir Richard Corbet. Corbet handed over the boy, now thirteen, to his uncle, who took him to London to be presented to Henry VI. Polydore Vergil asserts that at their meeting the King, indicating young Henry Tudor, said to Jasper, 'This truly is he unto whom both we and our adversaries must yield and give over the dominion.' Yet it is highly unlikely that Henry VI would have said such a thing, for at that time the hopes of the Lancastrian dynasty were centred on the Prince of Wales. If he died, the throne would pass to Clarence, and even then there were others who might contest his claim, such as the descendants of the Dukes of Somerset and Exeter. No one then would have envisaged that Henry Tudor would one day become King Henry VII and found one of the most successful dynasties to rule in England. Vergil was the official historian to Henry VII, and this tale was no doubt invented to flatter his master, who claimed to be the heir to Lancaster.

Jasper was now styling himself Earl of Pembroke, even though the attainder against him had not been reversed. He also tried to have the earldom of Richmond restored to Henry Tudor, but was unsuccessful because it was still held by Clarence.

After his presentation at court, young Henry visited his mother and her husband Henry Stafford at Woking, before rejoining Jasper on 12 November and returning to Wales. This would be the last time he saw Margaret Beaufort for over fourteen years, and their next meeting would take place in very different circumstances, for he would then be king.

By November 1470, says Rous, Warwick 'had all England at his leading and was feared and respected through many lands'. Not only was he the King's Lieutenant but he had also resumed his offices of Great Chamberlain of England and Captain of Calais. Clarence had been appointed Lieutenant of Ireland, and the composition of the Council was still much as it had been under Edward IV, being largely made up of men of ability rather than of rank. Clarence, who had been excluded from the Council by Edward IV, now had a place on it, although Montague did not, having been sent north to carry out his duties as Warden of the East Marches. Nor were Shrewsbury, Oxford, Stanley, Devon or Pembroke given seats; Warwick preferred them to exert their influence in their own territories. The self-styled Dukes of Exeter and Somerset were still in Burgundy, supported by pensions from Duke Charles, but their presence was an embarrassment to him since Edward IV had become a guest in his duchy, and he was fervently hoping that the exiles would soon go home now that it was safe to do so.

Warwick's situation, however, was not as strong as it seemed. Many die-hard Lancastrians still distrusted him and refused to co-operate with him, regarding him as a traitor who had brought about the ruin of the House of Lancaster. Nor could the Earl count upon the loyalties of those Yorkists who had previously supported him in his efforts to regain power and curb the influence of the Wydvilles, for many felt he had gone much too far in deposing King Edward. In fact, the only persons on whom he could rely were his Neville adherents and those Lancastrian nobles who had benefited from the readeption and were safeguarding their own interests. The rest of the nobility merely paid lip-service to Warwick's government.

It was only among the commons that Warwick was popular. The middle classes in London resented his deputy, Sir Geoffrey Gate, who appeared to be encouraging vandalism among his soldiers in the city, and were alarmed by the falling off of trade with Burgundy which had resulted from Warwick's friendship with France. Some London merchants were complaining vigorously to the Council about Edward IV's precipitate flight and demanding repayment of loans they had made him.

The Earl could not be confident that Margaret of Anjou would allow him to remain in power once she returned to England, especially as the Prince, who was now seventeen, was older than Henry VI had been when he attained his majority. The future did not seem as secure as it had in France: Warwick realised that the success of his regime and the fulfilment of his ambitions depended on co-operation between himself, the unstable and increasingly dissatisfied Clarence, and the Lancastrian and Yorkist magnates, and that the prospect of that was remote.

When Henry VI was informed that Queen Elizabeth was about to bear a child in sanctuary, he sent Lady Scrope to wait on her and act as midwife. He also authorised a London butcher, John Gould, to supply her household with half a beef and two muttons a week. Yet although the King had shown kindness to her and Warwick had left her in peace, Elizabeth chose to remain in sanctuary, 'in great trouble and heaviness'. On 2 November, in the Abbot's House, she gave birth to her first son by the King, a healthy boy whom she named Edward after his father. The infant was nursed by Old Mother Cobb, the resident sanctuary midwife, and baptised by the sub-prior in the Abbot's House 'with no more ceremony than if he had been a poor man's son', according to Sir Thomas More. The abbot and prior stood as godfathers and Lady Scrope as godmother, and four-year-old Princess Elizabeth held the chrysom.

Warwick was well aware that the birth of a Yorkist heir might prove a focus for rebellion, and would certainly inspire King Edward to greater efforts to recover his kingdom. He decided therefore that now was the time for Queen Margaret to bring the Prince of Wales and his future bride to England, reasoning that the presence of a prince nearly grown to manhood would have more popular appeal than that of one in swaddling bands. Having persuaded Henry VI to agree with him, Warwick wrote to Queen Margaret, urging her to return to England at once.

Throughout September and October, Queen Margaret, Prince Edward and the Countess of Warwick and her daughters had remained at the French court at King Louis's expense. During that period, Jean Briconnet, Louis's receiver of finances, paid out 2550 livres for their maintenance. After they had returned from a short visit to King René in early November, Briconnet paid a further 2831 livres for the purchase of silverware for them and 1000 livres 'for their pleasures'. Margaret was wary of returning to England, believing that it was still an unsafe place for the precious heir to Lancaster. Nevertheless, she was inclined to agree with Warwick that the birth of a son to Elizabeth Wydville posed a threat to the security of the restored dynasty, and reluctantly began making plans to leave France.

On 26 November, the readeption Parliament met at Westminster. Henry VI presided in person over this assembly, which confirmed his right to be King of England and vested the succession in the Prince of Wales and his heirs and, failing them, the Duke of Clarence and his heirs. At the opening session, Archbishop Neville, as Chancellor, preached a sermon on the text 'Return, O backsliding children, saith the Lord'.

The Parliament roll for this assembly no longer survives, yet its business is recorded in other contemporary documents. The Great Chronicle of London states that 'King Edward was disinherited with all his children, and proclaimed throughout the city as usurper of the crown. Gloucester, his younger brother, was pronounced a traitor, and both were attainted.' The attainders passed since 1461 on Lancastrian nobles were reversed. Jasper Tudor was formally restored to the earldom of Pembroke and was given back his property as well as being handsomely rewarded by the King with other estates, including the substantial lands formerly owned by Lord Herbert in South Wales and the Welsh Marches. Other Lancastrian nobles who were restored 'in blood' to their inheritance included Exeter, Somerset and Ormonde. Parliament recognised Warwick as Lieutenant and Protector of the Realm and the King, with Clarence as his associate, and dismantled much of the machinery of Yorkist government. Lord Montague received a royal pardon for his earlier loyalty to Edward IV after protesting that it was prompted by fear.

Clarence had gained very little so far from supporting the readeption of Henry VI; no doubt he had believed he would enjoy more political power with Warwick holding the reins of government, but there had been little sign of that as yet. Nor did he have much hope of ever succeeding to the throne. Now he also stood to lose some of his estates as a result of the reversal of attainders on Lancastrian peers, and while Warwick had promised to compensate him for their loss, Clarence was realist enough to wonder whether the Earl would be able to keep that promise.

On 3 December, in a great assembly at Tours, Louis XI formally repudiated his treaty of friendship with Burgundy, denouncing it as void by virtue of Charles's alliance with Edward IV. This hostile move heralded the commencement of war between Louis and his powerful vassal, which was what Louis had been intending all along. His aim now was to crush Burgundy with England's help, and he wasted no time in ordering his armies to advance into Burgundian territory. Only then did he send his ambassador to discuss what form England's aid would take, thus presenting Warwick with a *fait accompli*.

Before the French ambassadors embarked for England, they had an audience with the Prince of Wales, who agreed to affix his seal to an indenture whereby he agreed to make war on Burgundy until every last part of the Duke's territories were conquered, and to persuade his father the King to ratify this undertaking.

Once in England, the ambassadors began pressing Warwick to fulfil his part of the agreement with Louis, offering him Burgundy's counties of Holland and Zeeland as bait; Louis knew that Warwick wanted a principality of his own so desperately that, against this, the objections of others could not prevail. Both the ambassadors and the Earl, though, had great difficulty in persuading the English magnates and merchants that an alliance with France would be more advantageous than the one Edward IV had already made with Burgundy. No ships were leaving the Port of London or docking there, and English goods could not be exported abroad. The last thing the London merchants wanted at this time was an alliance with France. Nor did the common people, for the treaty with Burgundy had brought new prosperity to England and provided her with a lucrative market for her goods. They saw no reason to jeopardise it. If, then, Warwick was determined to honour his agreement with

Louis he would have to dissociate himself from the interests of the English people.

Until now, Charles the Bold had shown himself cordial to the restored Henry VI, but news of Louis's repudiation of their alliance made him reconsider his position and wonder if it would be more profitable to support the Yorkists, who had always shown themselves friendly towards him.

The Pope had still not granted a dispensation for the marriage of Prince Edward and Anne Neville; Louis's patience had long since been exhausted, and in desperation he had sent the Grand Vicar of Bayeux to procure one from the Eastern Orthodox Patriarch of Jerusalem. This arrived early in December, at which time the King moved to Amboise where the wedding would take place. On 13 December, the Prince was married to Anne Neville by the Grand Vicar of Bayeux in a sumptuous ceremony in the palace chapel which was attended by a host of members of the royal houses of France and Anjou, as well as the Duke of Clarence.

There is good reason to believe that Queen Margaret had forbidden her son to consummate the marriage. Should Warwick be toppled – and his position in England was by no means secure – Anne Neville would no longer be a fit wife for the heir to Lancaster, and if the union had not been consummated an annulment could easily be obtained, leaving the Prince free to marry a more suitable bride. In 1472, Anne was described by Croyland as a 'maiden' or 'damsel', terms normally used to describe an unmarried virgin.

Reports received by King Louis from his ambassadors in London had convinced him and Queen Margaret that it was now safe for her to return to England. On the day after the wedding, the Queen, the Prince and Princess of Wales and the Countess of Warwick left Amboise on the first stage of their journey home, being escorted by a guard of honour formed by the Counts of Eu, Vendôme, Dunois and Châtillon. Shortly afterwards they made a ceremonial entry into Paris, being received outside the city gates by the chief officers of the university, the Parliament and the Châtelet, as well as the civic authorities, all wearing their finest robes. These gentlemen conducted the Queen and her party into a city made festive with tapestries and gaily coloured painted cloths hung from windows and balconies, and with streets thronged with cheering citizens. At the same time, in England, King Henry was instructing his Exchequer to pay £2000 to enable Warwick to cross to France with an army of ships and men 'for the bringing home of our most dear and entirely beloved wife, the Queen, and our son, the Prince'.

Margaret remained in Paris over Christmas, and was preparing to leave for England when she learned that, on 5 January 1471, Charles of Burgundy and Edward IV had had a meeting near St Omer. This unnerved her somewhat, yet she was reassured by reports sent to King Louis by the French ambassadors in London that the political situation there was stable and that it would be quite safe for her and her son to return. The Queen therefore left Paris and travelled to Rouen to await the arrival of Warwick, who was to escort her to England.

Warwick never came. Most of his annual income, which cannot have exceeded £15,000, had been spent in financing his large retinue, his military operations of the previous autumn, and the maintenance of his estates. Short of funds, he had spent the money granted for his journey on other, more pressing, things, and could not now afford to go to France to collect the Queen. Not knowing of this, Margaret refused to consider leaving until Warwick had actually arrived at a French port. While she waited at Rouen, the Earl waited for her at Dover, confident that she would have sailed without him. Soon, though, pressing matters of state obliged him to return to London.

At last Margaret was forced to accept that Warwick was not coming, and went to Dieppe, intending to embark for England without further delay. Even though the masters of her ships warned her that the weather was not favourable, she refused to listen. Three times her fleet put to sea, and each time it was hurled back upon the coast of Normandy, driven by rough winds and storm-tossed waves. Some ships were badly damaged and had to be repaired, and the more superstitious among the Queen's men said that the tempest had been conjured up by sorcerers employed by the Yorkists; others perceived the hand of God at work. There was to be no break in the weather for some time, and she had no choice but to wait, fuming in frustration at the interminable delay.

Back in England, Warwick was desperately trying to consolidate his position. He was concerned about the loyalty of the King's subjects in the counties of Gloucester and Hereford, and granted Pembroke – who was already responsible for keeping the peace in south Wales and the Marcher lordships – wide military and administrative powers in the Severn Valley. At the same time, Clarence, still outwardly loyal to Warwick but perhaps working for his own ends, was planting his spies in the houses of several noblemen suspected of secret sympathies with Edward IV, among them Northumberland, Shrewsbury and Stanley. Unbeknown to the lords in question, the spies were to monitor all conversations and comings and goings, in order to detect any weakening in their loyalty to the government.

The Duke placed two spies in each household, so that one would always be there while the other was reporting back to him.

Early in February, Parliament considered Warwick's demand that England be joined in an offensive alliance with France against Burgundy in fulfilment of his promise to Louis XI. The Lords and Commons debated the matter, but would agree only to a ten-year truce, not a formal alliance. Nor, knowing the temper of the people, would they sanction a declaration of war on Burgundy.

Warwick, however, told Louis's envoys that England would help their master and that he had already begun recruiting an army and would send it to France as soon as possible. On 12 February, on his instructions, the garrison at Calais prepared to attack Burgundy's lands in northern France, and the next day, Warwick himself wrote to Louis:

> I pray Almighty God to give you the victory. In the matter of beginning the war at Calais, I have sent instructions to start it, and have today had certain news that the garrison of Calais has already begun and has advanced from Ardres and has killed two of the garrison at Gravelines. As soon as I possibly can I will come to you to serve you against this accursed Burgundian without any default, please God. Your very humble servant, R. Warrewyk.

The London merchants were furious when Warwick dragged England into a war against Burgundy without Parliament's consent, knowing that this would be potentially highly injurious to the city's economic prosperity, and they refused to lend any more money to the readeption government. As for Charles the Bold, the actions of the Calais garrison drove him straight into an alliance with Edward IV, knowing it was now vital to his interests to see the House of York restored to the English throne. The deposition of Henry VI would deprive Louis XI of his principal ally, and so remove the threat of war from Burgundy. With this in mind, Charles agreed to help Edward IV recover his kingdom and gave him 50,000 crowns. Burgundy's assistance made a Yorkist invasion a realistic possibility.

When Charles made his decision to support the Yorkists, the self-styled Dukes of Exeter and Somerset, who were still refugees at his court because they did not trust Warwick, begged the Duke not to do anything that would prejudice Henry VI's tenure of the throne. Charles suggested that they might like to return to England and take up arms against Warwick in the cause of Lancaster, since this, in his view, could only benefit King Edward. Exeter and Somerset returned to England, where they found public opinion united against the French alliance. By his pursuit of it, Warwick had effectively alienated much of the Lancastrian establishment, and Somerset and Exeter had no difficulty in enlisting support for a renewal of the alliance with Burgundy.

They had hoped that this would leave Edward IV in political isolation, but, with the help of his sister, the Duchess of Burgundy, Edward was already pushing ahead with his plans, and by late February had raised an army of 1000-1500 Englishmen and 300 Flemish mercenaries armed with handguns, according to Warkworth. One London chronicler, however, stated he had 500 Englishmen and 500 Flemings. He had also obtained, through the good offices of the Hanseatic League, a fleet of ships which awaited the order to depart in Flushing harbour. Now Edward, like Queen Margaret in Dieppe, was obliged to wait for a break in the weather.

25

'The Perfect Victory'

In England, Edward's invasion had been expected for some time, and contingency plans to deal with it had been made back in January, when commissions of array were sent to Wales and the Marches. In the north, Montague was mustering an army at Pontefract; Oxford was guarding the coast of East Anglia, Pembroke was preparing to defend Wales, Clarence was in Bristol, guarding the West Country, and the Bastard of Fauconberg had been placed in command of the royal fleet, which was stationed on alert in the English Channel.

Yet, despite these defence strategies, Warwick's authority was crumbling, especially in London, where his retainers were now regarded as little better than hooligans – men who 'would have been right glad of a common robbery'. He had alienated not only the middle and lower classes, but also the lords, who increasingly resented his self-aggrandisement. Neither Lancastrians nor Yorkists trusted him, and his legendary popularity was fast fading. Neville supremacy in the north had declined since Percy's restoration to the earldom of Northumberland and the removal of Montague from that sphere of influence. It was Percy who now held sway in the north, particularly in Yorkshire, and Warwick knew for a certainty that Percy would not support him. Nor did the Queen's imminent return bode well for the future prosperity of Warwick, or of England for that matter, for it was unlikely that Margaret and the Earl would remain in concord for long.

On 2 March, King Edward boarded his flagship, the *Anthony*, at Flushing, 'with the intention to re-enter and recover his realm', but before his fleet of thirty-six ships could sail the wind turned against him. He would not go back on land, and was obliged to remain in the harbour for nine days until the 11th, when good weather returned and the ships were able to head straight for the Norfolk coast. On the evening of Tuesday, 12 March, they appeared before Cromer, but since Oxford's men were waiting for them there, it was impossible to land. Edward decided instead to sail north for the Humber estuary, and his fleet cast anchor late that night. Clarence, anticipating that his brother might land in the north, had already planted spies in Yorkshire in order to discover Edward's movements.

While at sea, the King's ships were caught in a violent storm and separated. There was no sign of the others when, on the 14th, Edward landed at Ravenspur in Yorkshire – at the same spot where Henry of Bolingbroke had landed seventy-two years earlier – a long way from the south where most of his support was concentrated. As the King and his party were mustering their men on the beach, they saw the glint of the sun on steel on a hill in the distance and, thinking it was the enemy, seized their weapons. The 'hostile' force turned out to be Gloucester and his men, whose ship had landed five miles along the coast. Later, Rivers and his troops joined the King at Ravenspur, having landed fourteen miles away at Paull.

To cover his traces and show his men that he had no intention of retreating, Edward ordered his ship to be burned. Yet his presence in the vicinity could not be concealed, and before long 'all the country of Holderness' – 6-7000 men in all – was rising in arms against him, led by a local vicar, a captain called John Westerdale, and one Martin of the Sea. However, none of these men demonstrated any real qualities of leadership, and their movement therefore lacked cohesion and direction. The King had no difficulty in convincing the leaders that he had come to claim only his duchy of York, after which they let him continue on his way.

Edward rode to Hull, but its gates remained firmly closed to him. At Beverley, however, the citizens were more hospitable and received him in friendly fashion. After a brief sojourn there, the King drew up his army into marching order, raised his banners aloft, and made for York. He met with no opposition, but then neither did he attract much support, for few people believed he stood much chance of victory. According to the *Historie of the Arrivall of King Edward IV in England*, the official account of his enterprise, he himself was well aware that he was 'had in great suspicion and hatred' by some of the magnates, and knew that the recovery of his kingdom was a dangerous gamble.

On 19 March, Oxford, then at Bury St Edmunds, received 'credible tidings' of Edward's invasion, and issued an urgent summons to the men of the region to array themselves and attend him. Warwick responded to the news of Edward's coming with a summons to all loyal Englishmen to take up arms, but some Lancastrian nobles – notably Shrewsbury, Stanley, Somerset, Exeter and Pembroke – disobeyed it, preferring to await Queen Margaret's arrival. Nevertheless, Warwick managed to raise a sizeable army: the *Arrivall* claimed that, 'where he could not raise the people with goodwill, he straitly charged them to come forth on pain of death'. Parliament granted the Prince of Wales the power to array men for the defence of the realm, and commissions were sent out in his name, threatening those who did not comply with the penalties meted out to traitors.

That Warwick was now a desperate man is evident from a postscript he appended in his own hand to a letter he sent to Sir Henry Vernon, the only surviving one of many that he dispatched at this time to his friends and supporters: 'Henry, I pray you, fail not now, as ever I may do for you.' Vernon, like many others, paid no heed to the summons: he received several from both Warwick and Clarence and ignored them all.

Warwick marched north, leaving Archbishop Neville responsible for the safe-keeping of King Henry and the capital. Clarence was already active in Bristol and Wells, recruiting men, and soon had a force of 4000 soldiers. Montague as yet lacked sufficient numbers to attack Edward's force in the north.

When the King arrived before York, the city magistrates at first refused him entry. But he again requested admission, saying he was a simple duke, come only to claim the duchy of York, his rightful inheritance. The city fathers would not argue with that, and reasoned that admitting a duke did not constitute an act of treason. They were further convinced of Edward's good intentions when, says Warkworth, 'afore all the people, he cried, "À King Harry! À King Harry!"', and stuck an ostrich feather, the badge of the Prince of Wales, in his hat. On 18 March he was allowed to ride into York with a few companions, leaving his army encamped outside the city walls. Within the city, he swore a solemn oath before the citizens that he had no intention of reclaiming the throne.

Edward waited now to see if Northumberland would join him, but the Earl 'sat still' on his northern estates with a strong force of retainers, who would not fight for the King but heeded their master's injunction to let him pass unmolested. Edward also learned that Montague was waiting for him at Pontefract, but of military movements further south he as yet knew nothing.

While Edward was in York, Warwick and his army had marched on Coventry to join up with Oxford and Clarence. Oxford was already bringing 4000 men of East Anglia up the Fosse Way towards Newark, and Clarence was marching his army north from the southwest. The combined strength of Edward's enemies was a formidable challenge to his military abilities, but he was more than equal to it. He left York on 19 March and moved to Tadcaster. The next day, he suddenly swung west, to avoid Pontefract, and began recruiting men in his former lordships of Sandal and Wakefield. Montague, surprisingly, made no move to block Edward's progress after he had given him the slip.

From Wakefield, Edward marched via Doncaster to Nottingham, where he abandoned his pretence of having come only to claim the duchy of York and issued proclamations using the royal style. The townsfolk, seeing him astride his horse, smiling, confident and radiantly handsome, came swarming to his standard. He was now approaching the territory of his Yorkist supporters, and many knights and magnates came to him with their retainers, among them Sir William Parr and Sir James Harington with 600 men, Sir William Stanley, brother of Lord Stanley, and Sir William Norris. It was at this point that Edward discovered the full extent of the forces ranged against him, and from Nottingham, he sent his scourers into the surrounding countryside to learn more of his enemies' movements. Thus he found out that Oxford had occupied Newark, and decided to attack it, sending aforeriders to demand its surrender. Oxford was alarmed by their sudden appearance and – believing his troops would be no match for Edward's mercenaries – promptly evacuated the town, many of his men deserting at this point. A jubilant Edward, with an army now numbering over 2000 and swelling all the time, next advanced to Leicester, where he was joined by nearly 3000 of Hastings's men, and so on towards Coventry.

When Warwick learned of Oxford's retreat, he withdrew his army of 6–7000 men inside the walls of Coventry, to await the arrival of Oxford and Clarence with reinforcements. In a letter written on the 25th he observed that Edward's force was still small, thanks to the reluctance of men to rally to his cause, and he was confident of beating it. Warwick, however, was in for a shock.

All this time, Queen Margaret had continued to delay her departure from France, having received alarming reports that Edward IV was planning to invade England. King Louis told her that, when his ambassadors returned from England, she could use their ships, but she was too fearful and declined the offer. Shortly afterwards, Sir John Langstrother sailed his own ship over to France to collect her, and on 24 March, with grave misgivings, the Queen left Harfleur, accompanied by the Prince and Princess of Wales, Fortescue, Wenlock, Morton and 3000 knights and squires of France. The Countess of Warwick was in a different ship and this landed ahead of the Queen's fleet at Portsmouth. Knowing that Margaret was making for the south-west coast, the Countess took passage on another ship bound for Weymouth. Once the ship was at sea, however, a fierce storm blew up and tossed it back to Southampton. As the turbulent weather showed no sign of abating, the Countess decided to travel overland to join the Queen.

On the 29th, King Edward arrived at Coventry, arguably one of the best-fortified towns in England. He stood before the walls and shouted out his defiance of Warwick, calling upon him either to come forth in peace and receive a pardon or to come out and fight. Warwick, looking out upon Edward's sizeable host, was well aware that if he responded to Edward's challenge to sally forth and decide their quarrel by recourse to arms the day might well go against him. Moreover, many men in his army were averse to confronting the King in the field since he had never yet lost a battle.

For three days running Edward sent heralds bearing formal challenges to Warwick, but received no reply. Accepting that the Earl was not going to come forth, he withdrew and marched to the town of Warwick, where he seized and occupied the Earl's castle. From here, he had himself formally proclaimed king once more. While he was at Warwick, he received reports that Oxford, Exeter and Montague were marching to join up with Warwick at Coventry. Edward quickly dispatched a force of men to intercept Oxford at Leicester, where they defeated the Earl on 3 April. Clarence, however, failed to join Warwick and instead proclaimed his intention of returning to his allegiance to his brother.

Hoping to score a decisive victory, the King marched back to Coventry, drew his army up in battle order before the walls, and issued a further challenge to Warwick, which the Earl declined to accept. At this, Edward abandoned his attempts to lure Warwick out of Coventry, 'not thinking it behoveful to assail nor to tarry for the assieging thereof, as well for the avoidance of great slaughter that should thereby ensue, and for that it was thought more expedient to them to draw towards London', according to the *Arrivall*. He now withdrew three miles off and set up camp on the road to Banbury to await the arrival of Clarence and his men.

Both Burgundy and the Duchess of York had put pressure on Clarence to make peace with Edward IV, and the young Duke of Gloucester was also instrumental in bringing about their reconciliation. On the night of 2 April he had paid a secret visit to Clarence, who was then encamped near Banbury, and persuaded him to return to his allegiance. Clarence, however, needed little persuading. His patience had run out when on 23 March Warwick had forced him to surrender some of his property to Queen Margaret and Prince Edward, 'notwithstanding the agreements made between the Queen, Prince, himself and Warwick, that he should retain all his possessions until duly recompensed'. Clearly, he could expect very little from his father-in-law. He was also aware that Warwick's position was growing extremely precarious and that it would be wise to dissociate himself from him; if he delayed much longer in making his peace with Edward, it might be too late.

On 3 April, Clarence led his army of 12,000 men into the King's camp at Banbury and knelt in submission. Edward forgave him and promised to restore all his estates, at which there 'was right kind and loving language betwixt them'. At Clarence's suggestion, the royal brothers then rode to Warwick, where they issued a final challenge to the Earl, who was still at Coventry. Warwick, appalled by Clarence's defection and the size of the forces ranged against him, had not the nerve to accept it. He was still looking for the arrival of fresh reinforcements and would not consider confronting Edward until these had come.

While the King's host was at Warwick, Queen Margaret's supporters were preparing for her coming. Somerset, his brother, John Beaufort, Marquess of Dorset, and Thomas Courtenay, Earl of Devon, having learned in London that the Queen was sailing for the West Country, left the capital and rode west, trying as they went to recruit as many men as possible to receive Margaret when she disembarked.

Both Edward and Warwick now knew that whoever could secure London stood a good chance of gaining a decisive victory, and the race for the capital began. Early in April, the King was in Northampton, where he was well received. He then took the quickest route to London, always keeping an experienced band of spearmen and archers as a rearguard to counter, if need be, any attack made from behind by Warwick's men.

Edward left Northampton on the 5th. Warwick was still in Coventry on that day, but he soon realised that the King 'would do much to be received in London, and, not knowing whether he would be or not, he issued out of Coventry with a great force and made his way through Northampton' two days after Edward had left it. 'The Earl thought he had the advantage of the King in one of two ways: either the city [London] would keep the King out or, if he were let in, he would there be keeping the solemnity of Easter, so that the Earl could suddenly come upon him, take him, and destroy him by surprise.'

On Palm Sunday, 6 April 1471, Edward came to Daventry, and attended a service there in the parish church. Within the church was a statue of St Anne, whom the King especially venerated. The statue, however, was boarded up because at that time all holy images in English churches were hidden from view from Ash Wednesday to Easter Sunday; yet when the King genuflected at the Rood, the boards surrounding St Anne crashed to the floor. This was seen as miraculous evidence of the saint having the King under her special protection.

As Edward neared London, his army growing all the time, Lord Howard emerged from sanctuary at Colchester and hurried with his retainers to join him. Warwick, whose scouts kept him apprised of the King's movements, sent letters to the city authorities, ordering them to resist Edward and refuse to receive him. He also wrote to his brother Archbishop Neville, 'desiring him to do all he could to provoke the city against Edward and keep him out for two or three days, promising that he would then not fail to come up with great forces from behind, intending utterly to destroy Edward and his men'. The Archbishop summoned to St Paul's such lords as were known to be loyal to Henry VI and Warwick, 'with as many of their armed men and servants as they could muster', and some 6–7000 gathered there. He then had King Henry mount a horse and ride from St Paul's down Cheapside and round to Walbrook, then back to St Paul's and to his lodging in the adjacent bishop's palace, 'supposing that when he showed Henry the Londoners would be encouraged to stand by them and come on to their side'. Yet Henry VI and his escort were hardly a sight to inspire confidence – the latter few and armed to the teeth, the former wearing his old blue gown that had seen better days, 'as though he had no more to change with', slouched on his horse, and regarding the citizens with sad, tired eyes. It was said that their progress through London was 'more like a play than a showing of a prince to win men's hearts, for by this means he lost many and won none, or right few'.

From Dunstable, on 9 April, according to the *Arrivall*, King Edward sent 'very comfortable messages to his queen, his true lords and his servants and supporters in London'. 'Wherefore,' continues the *Arrivall*, 'they considered as secretly as possible how he might be received and welcomed there.' On the 10th, Edward advanced to St Albans.

That day, according to the *Arrivall*, 'the rulers of the city were in council, and had set men at all the gates and wards'. Then, seeing that the power of Henry VI and his adherents 'was so feeble', they 'could find no courage' to support them. 'Rather the opposite obtained, as they well saw that Henry's forces could not resist the King, who was approaching the city, being at St Albans that night. Thus the mayor and the aldermen determined to keep the city for the King, to open it to him at his coming, so they sent to him that they would be guided at his pleasure.' As many of the Lancastrian lords had by now left London to go to greet Queen Margaret in the West Country, there remained no one powerful enough to hold London against Edward, nor to resist the Lord Mayor's decision to open the gates to him.

Archbishop Neville, fearful for his own skin, also sent a message to the King, 'desiring to be admitted to his good grace and promising in return to give [him] great pleasure for his well-being and security'. Edward 'for his own good reasons agreed to take the Archbishop into his good grace, and the Archbishop, assured of this, was very well pleased and truly acquitted himself of his promise', undertaking to deliver Henry VI into Edward's hands. 'That night, the Tower of London was taken for the King, whereby he had a clear entry into the city.'

On the 11th, Warwick learned that Louis XI had signed a three-month truce with Burgundy, having by now realised that Warwick would not be honouring his part of their agreement and knowing that he himself could not fight Burgundy without England's support. The truce was a wait-and-see ploy, designed to last until Louis knew the outcome of Warwick's struggle with Edward IV. Warwick realised that he could expect no further aid from Louis, that he was now on his own, and that confrontation with Edward was imminent.

Late in the morning of the same day, the Lord Mayor and aldermen of London dismissed the city militia, saying they could go home for dinner. At noon King Edward and his brothers marched into the city, which joyfully opened its gates to him as the lawful sovereign of England. The mayor and chief citizens welcomed him warmly and the crowds lining the streets yelled their appreciation. Commines says that there were three reasons for their enthusiasm: the birth of a male heir to the King, the prospect of the wealthier citizens being paid back the loans they had made to him, and the delight of 'the ladies of quality and rich citizens' wives, with whom he had formerly intrigued', who had 'forced their husbands to declare themselves on his side'.

The King went immediately to St Paul's Cathedral to hear the Archbishop of Canterbury give thanks for his restoration to the throne and declare King Henry deposed. Then he entered the bishop's palace where Archbishop Neville presented him to Henry VI. Henry embraced him, saying, 'My cousin of York, you are very welcome. I know that in your hands my life will not be in danger.' Edward received him into custody and ordered his immediate transfer to the Tower, commanding also that a number of Yorkist prisoners incarcerated there be set at liberty without delay. He had already sent a deputation to Westminster Abbey to escort the Queen and her children from sanctuary to the Palace of Westminster. The King then went himself to Westminster Abbey, where Archbishop Bourchier set the crown on his head to demonstrate to the people that he was formally restored to the throne, after which Edward knelt to give thanks to God, St Peter and St Edward the Confessor.

Giving orders that his army of 7000 men be deployed in manning the city's defences and holding it against Warwick, whom he knew to be in pursuit, Edward went in procession to the Palace of Westminster, where Queen Elizabeth and their children awaited him. The sight of his little daughters and his wife holding his first-born son, now five months old, moved the King to tears. He kissed the children 'full tenderly' and took the Prince in his arms, expressing his 'greatest joy' and 'his heart's singular comfort and gladness', referring to the infant as 'God's precious sending and gift, and our most desired treasure'. Having embraced and comforted his wife, he escorted his family to 'the lodging of my lady his mother' at Baynard's Castle, where they heard Mass and stayed the night.

On the morning of the 12th, Edward took counsel with his brothers and the great magnates before attending a solemn service in his mother's private chapel to mark Good Friday. When it ended, he installed the Queen, the royal children, the Duchess of York and the Archbishop of Canterbury in the Tower of London for their safety. He had spent as much time in London as he dared, long enough for his captains to recruit and muster more reinforcements, and the time had now come to face Warwick. The *Arrivall* states that the King 'took pains to encounter him before he came near to the city and as far from it as possible'. On the afternoon of the 13th, taking King Henry with him, he led his army ten miles north to Barnet, where his advance guard met the advance guard of Warwick's host and, after a skirmish, chased them out of the town for a distance of half a mile. Edward, when he arrived and was told what had happened, forbade his men to remain in Barnet 'but had them all to the field with him, and drew towards his enemies outside the town'.

Earlier that day, Warwick had moved his army through St Albans to Barnet, arriving, like the King, after dark. Both armies spent some considerable time searching for advantageous positions, and Warwick finally drew up his men on a 400-foot ridge concealed 'under a hedge side' and running south from Hadley Green to the village of Barnet. Edward 'could not see very well where his enemies lay, and he camped with all his host before them, much nearer than he supposed'. By a stroke of fortune, the King's right wing overlapped Warwick's left wing, and Warwick's right wing overlapped Edward's left. This meant that Warwick's cannon, which he had positioned on the far right, were pointed at no one. The *Arrivall* states that the Earl's soldiers 'shot guns almost all night, thinking thereby to do great damage to the King and his host. But it so happened that they always overshot the King's army and did them no harm, because the King's host lay much nearer than they thought.' Edward refused to allow his men to fire their cannon in retaliation because Warwick would then know his position and would redirect his guns towards the Yorkist army.

All sources agree that Warwick had the larger army, and Warkworth says Edward knew he was outnumbered. Warkworth estimated Warwick's force at 20,000, while the *Arrivall* claimed he had 30,000 men. Most sources agree that the King had between 9000 and 10,000 men. The King himself commanded the Yorkist centre, Gloucester the right wing and Hastings the left. Montague, who had joined up with Warwick on the road south, led the Lancastrian centre, which straddled the road from St Albans to Barnet; Exeter commanded the left wing, which was drawn up on soft, marshy ground and consisted partly of cavalry, while Oxford commanded the right wing, which was stationed to the west of the road behind a hedge. Warwick placed himself in command of the reserve, which was well-armed with the newly invented handguns, and was drawn up where the present monument to the battle – erected in 1740 – stands on Hadley Green, north of Barnet. Both armies consisted mainly of foot soldiers, and both had guns and ordnance, although Warwick was better provided with the latter. Henry VI was held in custody behind the lines with the Yorkist reserve.

That evening, as the armies prepared to do battle, the fleet carrying Queen Margaret and her company landed at Weymouth in Dorset. The Queen had endured the most appalling voyage, having been at sea for twenty days 'for lack of good winds and because of great tempests at sea'. Nevertheless, she remained undaunted, hoping to raise the south-west to the cause of Lancaster. This was no vain hope, for many of her chief adherents held lands and exercised political influence in the region, among them Somerset, Exeter, Devon, and Clarence, of whose defection she knew nothing.

What Margaret did not realise was that the readeption government was already thoroughly discredited as a result of Warwick's unpopular foreign policy, and that she had arrived weeks too late to undo the damage. Nor did she know that Henry VI had again been overthrown by Edward IV. 'I trow', wrote a Paston correspondent, on learning of the Queen's arrival, 'that tomorrow, or else the next day, King Edward will depart from hence to her-ward to drive her out again.'

Early the next morning, which was Easter Sunday, between four and five o'clock, the King, knowing that day was approaching and, says the *Arrivall*, 'notwithstanding that there was a dense mist which prevented them from seeing each other', fell on his knees before his alerted army and 'committed his cause to Almighty God'. He then 'advanced banners, blew the trumpets and set upon [the enemy], at first with shot; very soon they joined and came to hand strokes, wherein his enemies manfully and courageously received them. With the faithful and mighty assistance of his supporters, who did not desert him and were as devoted to him as they possibly could be, King Edward vigorously, manfully and valiantly assailed his enemies in the centre and strongest part of their army, and with great violence.'

The King 'beat and bore down' all before him that stood in his way, 'so that nothing might stand in the sight of him and the well-assured fellowship that attended truly upon him'. Soon, both sides sent in their reserves to reinforce the embattled centres. The two left wings gave way early on, but because of the mist neither Edward nor Warwick was aware that this had happened, each believing his own side to be winning. Oxford chased the Yorkist left wing for several miles through and beyond Barnet, while Gloucester charged through a deep depression called Dead Man's Bottom into the centre of the confused Lancastrian left wing, where King Edward, leading the Yorkist centre, was already using his battle axe to deadly effect. As Exeter wheeled round to join Warwick for an assault on Gloucester, Montague swung round also.

Meanwhile, some of Oxford's men had disappeared during the pursuit of the Yorkists; others took the opportunity to do a little pillaging in Barnet, and the Earl had a great deal of difficulty in getting them back into line. He then rode back to the battlefield, he and his men wearing the blazing star badge of the de Veres. In the dark and mist, Montague's soldiers, who saw them coming first, mistook it for the King's 'Sun in Splendour' badge, and fired several volleys of arrows, at which Oxford and his force of 800 men fled from the field, crying 'Treason! Treason!' The word 'treason' spread like wildfire through the Lancastrian centre and shattered morale, and it was clearly this that turned the tide of the battle. Men panicked and began to run away from the fighting. Even when Montague's men realised what had happened, they thought that Oxford and his troops had gone over to the Yorkists and pursued and fell on them in anger. Some cried that Warwick was planning to halt the battle and come to terms with the King, which many regarded as a betrayal. There was chaos in the Lancastrian ranks, and the King took full advantage of it, leading in his reserve to attack Warwick's centre. A furious mêlée ensued, which broke the Lancastrian line. Montague was killed, possibly by one of Oxford's men.

Hard-pressed in the thick of the mêlée, Warwick tried to rally his men to fill in the gap left by Montague, but failed. The panic manifested by his soldiers was infectious, and he could not prevent the increasing surge of terrified men from fleeing the battle. In desperation, he dismounted and, gathering his best knights together, cried, 'If we withstand this one charge, the field will be ours!' As the Yorkist cavalry came up at full speed, the Earl wielded his sword to great effect and fought bravely, as did his household knights and retainers, but most of them were cut down by mounted Yorkist knights in armour, who galloped on, leaving behind them a scene of carnage.

Warwick, realising at this point that the day was lost, decided on flight, and made his way on foot towards Wrotham Wood where his horse was tethered. The King, knowing that victory was his, had sent a messenger cantering across the field to shout out the order that Warwick's life was to be spared, but a group of Yorkist soldiers, who had seen the Earl making his escape, either ignored the order or did not hear it, for they bore down on him and killed him, stripping his body of its armour and leaving it lying there naked. As news of his death spread, the remnants of his army lost heart and fled.

There were heavy casualties on both sides. The King, unusually, had not instructed his men to spare the common foot soldiers, and at least 1000 Lancastrians lay dead on the field. Yorkist losses amounted to about 500, among them many of Edward's most faithful adherents – Lord Cromwell, Lord Say, Lord Berners' son Humphrey Bourchier, Sir John Paston and many members of the Yorkist royal household. Thomas Howard was 'sore hurt', while on the Lancastrian side Exeter was 'greatly despoiled and wounded', according to Warkworth, and left for dead on the field. Only later did he manage to make his escape. Oxford and a small band of retainers likewise fled, taking refuge in Scotland.

John Paston, whose father had died in the battle fighting for the Yorkists, had himself fought for Warwick and fled wounded from the field with the rest of the Earl's army. He now went into hiding, desperate with anxiety as to what might happen to him, and praying that the King would proclaim a general pardon. Edward was markedly lenient with men of the gentry class who had fought for the enemy, being concerned only to bring the magnates to justice, but John Paston did not know that. For two weeks he lay low until his money ran out. Unable to obtain credit, he wrote to his mother asking for help to pay for 'leech craft and physic and rewards to them that have kept me and conducted me to London, and hath cost me since Easter Day more than £5, and now I have neither meat, drink, clothes, leechcraft nor money'. John Paston did in the end secure a royal pardon, as did his younger brother who had also fought for Warwick.

The battle lasted between two and three hours and was over by eight o'clock – before the morning mist had lifted. Superstitious persons in the Lancastrian ranks believed that Edward had instructed a friar to conjure up the mist by sorcery in order to confuse them. The King now allowed his men some time to rest and refresh themselves, then he ordered them to seize possession of Warwick's guns, gathered his forces together and began the march back to London.

While the battle was raging, men had come running into the capital crying that the King and his brothers had been routed by Warwick and slaughtered. No one knew if this was true or not until the King's messenger came riding at speed into the city and galloped through the streets, triumphantly waving one of Edward's gauntlets as a sure token of his victory before taking it to the Queen. That afternoon the King himself entered London, accompanied by Clarence and Gloucester and attended by a great retinue of magnates. He was welcomed, says the *Arrivall*, 'with much joy and gladness'. By evening Henry VI was again a prisoner in the Tower, where four days later he was joined by the perfidious Archbishop Neville. The Archbishop, however, had the King's 'promise of safety'.

The bodies of Warwick and Montague were brought back to London by ten o'clock on Easter Monday morning and displayed naked, except for loincloths, in a single open coffin at St Paul's Cathedral, where they remained for three days, 'so that the people should not be abused by feigned and seditious tales' claiming that Warwick yet lived, which were even now being circulated by his adherents. The bodies were then taken to the Augustinian abbey at Bisham in Berkshire, which had been founded in the fourteenth century by William de Montacute, Earl of Salisbury, as a sepulchre for his descendants. Here, next to four of the earls of Salisbury, Warwick and Montague were buried. Their graves have long since disappeared. Bisham Abbey was dissolved during the Reformation and its site is now occupied by a modern leisure centre.

Despite the rejoicing in London, however, Edward IV knew that the struggle was not yet over, and that he must recruit more men, for there yet remained to be dealt with the threat posed by Queen Margaret and Prince Edward of Lancaster in the West.

26

To Tewkesbury and the Tower

Anne, Countess of Warwick, had been travelling towards Dorset, hoping to meet up with Queen Margaret and her troops. On the way, however, she received reports of the Battle of Barnet, and then came the grievous news of her husband's death. Fearing that King Edward's vengeance would fall upon her, the Countess fled through the New Forest and sought sanctuary in the Cistercian abbey at Beaulieu. Here she would remain for more than a year, until Gloucester, who had prevailed upon the King to declare her legally dead and settle upon him half her lands, took her to live with him – as a prisoner, according to John Rous – in his household at Middleham,

On Easter Monday, Queen Margaret and her company rode to the Benedictine abbey at Cerne in Dorset, where they would stay for the next ten days. Abbot Roger Beyminster extended a warm welcome to the Queen and lodged her in the abbey guest house, the remains of which may still be seen today. Soon, Margaret was joined by Pembroke, Devon and the Beaufort brothers, Somerset and his younger brother, Sir John, who broke the news of Warwick's defeat and death at Barnet. The shock caused her to collapse in a faint. Edward Hall records that when she recovered her senses and could speak she 'reviled the calamitous times in which she lived and reproached herself for all her painful labours, now turned to her own misery, and declared she desired rather to die than live longer in this state of infelicity'. Her chief concern now was the Prince's safety, and she 'passionately implored' the lords to do all in their power to ensure it. In her opinion, no good could come of a further armed confrontation with King Edward, and therefore it would be best if she and the Prince returned to France, 'there to tarry until it pleased God to send her better luck'. However, the lords prevailed upon her to remain and pursue her chosen course. Warwick's defeat had indeed been a setback, but they were confident that there remained many Englishmen who were ready and eager to fight for Lancaster. If she were wise, she would recruit those men and force a final trial of strength with King Edward.

When Margaret was calmer she may have reflected that Warwick's death was not such a tragedy after all. They had at best been reluctant allies, forced out of necessity to the pact between them, and now, if her army triumphed, the House of Lancaster would be able to reign unhampered by the problem of Warwick.

According to the Tudor chronicler Edward Hall, the Lancastrian lords told Margaret that 'they had already a good puissance in the field and trusted, with the encouragement of her presence and that of the Prince, soon to draw all the northern and western counties to the banner of the red rose'. The Queen and Prince sent out summonses to their supporters, and during the next few days more Lancastrian peers and their companies arrived at Cerne, their appearance reviving Margaret's spirits. Soon she had recovered her former energy and began to feel more optimistic about the outcome of her enterprise. And still they kept coming, men from Dorset, Somerset and Wiltshire, to join her ever-increasing army.

Somerset, Sir John Beaufort, Devon, Wenlock and Langstrother now held a council of war, in which they debated whether the Queen's army should travel speedily up the west coast, perhaps through Bristol, Gloucester and Chester, and thus reach those parts of Lancashire where they could raise a large force of archers. They were certain that in that region, more than anywhere, the lords and commons would support them. Jasper Tudor was dispatched at once to Wales to recruit an army there, and the final plan was that the Queen would march west and link up with him on her way north.

King Edward was in London when, on 16 April 1471, he received news of the Queen's landing. Croyland says he was 'worn down by many different blows' and had had little time in which to 'refresh himself. No sooner was he done with one battle in the east than he was faced with another in the western part of England, and had to prepare himself to fight at full strength.' He had dismissed his army after Barnet and now had to send 'to all parts to get him fresh men'. He issued a proclamation against the Queen and her supporters, reminding the people that God had vindicated his right to the throne by giving him the victory at Barnet and 'in divers battles against our great adversary Harry and his adherents'. Speed, he realised, was crucial to his success on this occasion, and, having ordered that workmen be recruited to service and repair the royal ordnance, he went to Windsor to gather an army with Hastings's help.

On the 23rd, Edward celebrated the Feast of St George with his Knights of the Garter at Windsor Castle, and the next day led his host of more than 3000 foot soldiers west in pursuit of Queen Margaret, hoping to overtake her before she crossed the River Severn and linked up with Jasper Tudor in Wales, which his intelligence sources had advised him was her objective.

Margaret intended to cross the Severn at Gloucester, and although she and her captains took precautions to conceal their movements, Edward's scouts managed to shadow them for most of the time. To put her pursuers off the scent, her own scouts were ordered to move east, as if the army behind them intended to march on London. At first, the King was taken in by this ruse, but his outriders soon discovered the Queen's true intention. Thereafter, the Lancastrians 'knew well that the King ever approached towards them, near and near, ever ready, in good array', and this made them panicky and all the more eager to press on towards Wales. Nevertheless, their ranks were still swelled daily, for, says Croyland, 'there were many in the west who favoured King Henry's cause'. Edward IV, marching at great speed, drove his soldiers on mercilessly, not even allowing them time to stop and eat or forage for food.

From Cerne, the Queen moved west to Exeter, where her appearance, and that of the Prince, inspired the 'whole might' of Devon and Cornwall to come flocking to them. Then it was on to Taunton, Glastonbury and Wells, where the Lancastrian army arrived on 27 April and sacked the bishop's palace. Here, the lords advised the Queen to pause awhile, to allow more men to muster. Although she was anxious to press on, she agreed, saying, 'I pray God speed us well.' On that day, the King reached Abingdon, where he received certain intelligence that the Queen was at Wells.

On the 29th, Edward arrived at Cirencester, where he learned that Margaret was on her way north to Bath, thirty miles south-west of his position. Other reports said she would be advancing on Cirencester on 1 May. At this, the King ordered all his men out of the town and set up camp that night three miles away, drawing his troops up in battle order. However, the next day there were no further reports of the enemy moving towards Cirencester, so Edward moved south along the road to Malmesbury, hoping to intercept them there. The Queen, however, was in Bath on 30 April. Edward, learning of his mistake, went after her there, but when he arrived on 1 May was told that she had gone west to Bristol and was planning to meet him in the field at nearby Chipping Sodbury.

Margaret did indeed arrive at Bristol on 1 May, and received a warm welcome there, being presented with ordnance, provisions and money by the citizens. She 'took new courage' at this, but was later disappointed to learn that her captains had not recruited as many men as they had hoped in the city.

After leaving Bristol, Margaret rested a while at Berkeley Castle, scene of the murder of Edward II in 1327. She had left her vanguard at Chipping Sodbury to put the King off her trail, and when, on the 2nd, Edward sent his advance riders there, the two sides engaged in a skirmish, with the Lancastrians managing to capture a number of the Yorkist quartermasters before they withdrew. That afternoon, Edward himself arrived in Chipping Sodbury, and spent the night there, camped in the open 'on a great and fair large plain called a wold', thinking that the Lancastrian army was nearby. His scouts, however, found no trace of it.

Back in London, the court anxiously awaited news. 'We have such different reports', wrote the Milanese ambassador to King Louis, 'that I cannot possibly find out the truth.'

On the evening of the 2nd, the Queen left Berkeley Castle and marched through the night to Gloucester, where she planned to cross the Severn. Once she had joined forces with Jasper Tudor, Edward would stand little chance of prevailing against their combined strength. By 3.00 am the next day, the King had received reliable reports that the Lancastrian army had evaded him once more and was moving towards Gloucester. Determined to overtake it before it could cross the river, he at once dispatched a letter to Sir Richard Beauchamp, governor of Gloucester, commanding him to close his gates to the Lancastrians pending the King's arrival. The royal messenger circumvented the Queen's army by taking a different route, and reached the city first. Edward, meanwhile, had drawn up his army in battle array and begun a thirty-mile march through the Cotswolds to Cheltenham, leaving at dawn.

At ten o'clock in the morning the Queen and her army reached Gloucester and demanded admission, but the gates remained closed. Beauchamp told her that he and the citizens were bound by their oath of loyalty to the King to oppose her passage. She therefore had no alternative but to cross the River Portway and make for Tewkesbury, ten miles to the north. 'All that day was ever the King's host within five or six miles of his enemies; he in the plain country, and they amongst woods, [he] having always good espialls upon them,' says the *Arrivall*. However, Edward's food supplies were dwindling fast, and his men were on short rations. It was very warm, and they were obliged to drink from a brook that was polluted with mire from the carts that had passed by it. Fortunately, their quarry was almost within reach.

At four o'clock in the afternoon of 3 May, Margaret's great army tramped into Tewkesbury; here they could cross the Severn and pass into Wales. However, having marched for a night and a day, they were 'right weary, for by that time they had travelled thirty-six long miles in a foul country, all in lanes and stony ways, betwixt woods, without any good refreshing'. Some of the Queen's soldiers, overcome by heat and exhaustion, had collapsed on the march and been left to fend for themselves. Margaret herself was too exhausted to go any further, and it was decided that everyone should rest for the night and take the field on the morrow. The Queen, the Princess of Wales, the Countess of Devon, Katherine Vaux and other ladies-in-waiting all retired for the night to nearby Glupshill Manor, a house built in 1430 in the shadow of Glupshill Castle, an old Norman motte-and-bailey fortress whose mound may still be seen today.

King Edward had arrived in Cheltenham late that afternoon, to be informed that the Lancastrians were making for Tewkesbury. He ordered his men to rest for a while and 'a little comforted himself and his people with such meat and drink as he had carried with him'. Then, in the early evening, he pressed on to Tredington, three miles from Tewkesbury, where he set up camp for the night. Like the Lancastrians, his men were so 'footsore and thirsty' that they could have marched no further.

At dawn the next day the Lancastrian army began preparing for the battle that would surely take place very soon. Somerset, as commander-in-chief, drew up his men in battle array in a strong position on a hill rising out of a field at the southern end of Tewkesbury, with the town and abbey at their backs, although his captains and the Queen expressed concern that 'afore them, and on every hand of them, were foul lanes and deep dykes, and many hedges with hills and valleys, a right evil place to approach', which is still today known as Margaret's Camp.

Later that morning, the King's army caught up with the Lancastrians at Tewkesbury, crossing the Swillgate Brook and passing Stonehouse Farm, then taking up battle stations 4–600 yards south of the enemy.

Meanwhile, the Queen and the Prince of Wales had mounted their horses and were riding through the Lancastrian ranks, speaking words of encouragement to their soldiers and promising them fame, glory and great rewards if they fought well. The Queen then left the field and returned to Glupshill Manor, leaving Somerset in command. The Prince, seeing active service for the first time, was to lead the centre, under the tutelage of Wenlock, a seasoned soldier but hardly a wise choice for he had twice changed sides in recent years. Somerset chose to lead the right wing, and gave Devon command of the left. On the Yorkist side, the King commanded the centre, Gloucester the left wing and Hastings the right. Thomas Grey, Marquess of Dorset, Elizabeth Wydville's son by her first husband, was to lead the rearguard.

The Lancastrian army numbered around 5-6000 men, the Yorkists around 3500-5000. The King, however, had more noble support than Somerset, and consequently more professional troops with better arms and equipment; nor had his men suffered loss of morale through being hunted down over a number of days.

Somerset's plan was that Wenlock should attack the Yorkists from the front while he bore down on them from the right side, but it was the King who opened hostilities, leading his army with some difficulty up the hill where the Lancastrians were positioned, and then ordering Gloucester to commence the assault. The Duke led his men across what the *Arrivall* describes as an 'evil place' thick with 'so many hedges and trees that it was right hard to approach them near and come to hands'. For an hour, his soldiers, armed with the cannon captured after Barnet and traditional English longbows, inflicted many casualties, loosing upon the enemy 'right a-sharp shower' of arrows, so that it appeared that the Yorkists already had the advantage. Then Gloucester gave the order to sound the retreat, an old ruse intended to provoke the enemy into leaving a good defensive position. Somerset fell into the trap, leading his men in a headlong charge down the hill, shouting at Wenlock and Prince Edward to follow him, and crashing full tilt into the Yorkist left flank.

Because he feared an ambush by Lancastrian cavalry hidden in the trees, the King had prudently detailed 2-300 spearmen to deploy themselves in a wood or park a quarter of a mile to the right of the Lancastrian position, there to await orders. At this point their captain, on learning of Somerset's collision with Gloucester's men, entered the battle on his own initiative, attacking Somerset from the rear while the Duke and his men were engaged in heavy fighting with Gloucester's left wing, which had fallen upon them savagely with axes and swords, and the Yorkist centre under King Edward.

Somerset was now surrounded on every side, yet he and his men at first fought furiously. Wenlock, however, made Prince Edward hold back the Lancastrian centre, refusing to let it advance to Somerset's aid. As a result, the Duke's men were cut to pieces, which caused his remaining soldiers to panic and begin to flee. At that point, the battle was lost. When Somerset returned to the Lancastrian lines with the remnants of his force and realised that Wenlock had not lifted a finger to help him, he publicly branded him a traitor to his face; then, before Wenlock had a chance to answer, the Duke split his head open with his battle mace. This left the inexperienced Prince Edward in sole command of the Lancastrian centre and vulnerable to a Yorkist charge.

Seizing his advantage, Gloucester led his men in a vicious onslaught on the Lancastrian centre. Prince Edward resisted valiantly, but his line broke and his men scrambled off in a full-scale retreat. King Edward now surged forward to fill in the gap left by Somerset, and there followed a desperate rout in which the Lancastrians fled the field, hotly pursued by Yorkists out for their blood. Many were cut down as they ran, while others sought refuge in Tewkesbury Abbey, little realising that it did not enjoy the privilege of sanctuary. Hundreds tried to escape by crossing the River Severn, but perished there by drowning or at the hands of their pursuers. A good many more were trapped and slaughtered near the abbey mill, but the worst carnage was to be seen on the battlefield, which is still called the 'Bloody Meadow' and was then rough pasture.

During the rout, bands of Yorkist soldiers forced their way into Tewkesbury Abbey and ran riot through its sacred buildings, looting and vandalising as they went. Anyone who stood in their way was dealt with viciously, and Lancastrian soldiers who had sought refuge were savagely dispatched, their blood desecrating the sanctified ground. In the sacristy today is a wooden door completely covered with plates of armour stripped from Lancastrian casualties or prisoners. In places, the armour is perforated with gunshot or arrow holes.

King Edward had won what Croyland calls 'a famous victory', having at last inflicted a devastating and final defeat on the Lancastrians, 2000 of whom were killed in the battle. Among the dead were Somerset's younger brother, Sir John Beaufort, who was buried in Tewkesbury Abbey, Sir Walter Courtenay, Sir William Vaux, Sir Robert Whittingham, Sir William Roos and Sir Edmund Hampden, all stalwart supporters of the Queen. The chief Yorkist casualty was the King's cousin, Humphrey Bourchier, son of York's sister Isabella. Yet by far the most important casualty of all was Prince Edward of Lancaster.

Commines and most other contemporary writers state that the Prince 'died in the field', and on 6 May Clarence reported that he 'had been slain in plain battle'. The *Arrivall*, the official Yorkist account of the battle, says that the Prince 'was taken fleeing to the townwards and slain in the field', crying 'for succour to his brother-in-law, Clarence'.

But Croyland, writing in 1486 after Edward IV and his brothers were dead, states rather ambiguously that the Prince died 'either on the field, or after the battle, by the avenging hands of certain persons'. The sixteenth-century historians Vergil, More and Hall all implicate Gloucester in his death, stating that the Prince was taken during the rout and brought before King Edward when the battle had ended. The King received him graciously and asked him to explain why he had taken up arms against him. The young man retorted defiantly, 'I came to recover my father's heritage. My father has been miserably oppressed, and the crown usurped.' This made Edward angry, and with 'a look of indignation' he slapped the Prince across the mouth with his gauntlet. At that moment Clarence, Gloucester and Hastings raised their swords and cut him down.

This tale may not have been an invention. In the confusion following the battle, it would not have been difficult to make it appear that the Prince had fallen in the field. Tudor chroniclers were happy to slander Gloucester – later the notorious Richard III – but had no reason to defame without due cause Edward IV or Lord Hastings, who was usually depicted by them as a noble hero. If the motive behind the tale was to discredit Gloucester, why not allege that he alone had murdered the Prince? But Edward IV had many sound reasons for wanting the young man dead, and when the opportunity presented itself would doubtless have been happy for his closest supporters to take advantage of it. Indeed, the murder may even have been premeditated and planned. Clarence's use of the words 'plain battle' may have been significantly over-emphatic, and Croyland was certainly hinting that there was more to the Prince's death than contemporary reports had made clear.

With Prince Edward died the hopes of the House of Lancaster. His remains were 'homely interred with the other simple corpses in the church of the monastery of the black monks in Tewkesbury' with only 'maimed rites'. A modern diamond of brass beneath the church tower and a vaulted roof emblazoned with gilded suns in splendour (placed there to commemorate the Yorkist victory) marks his resting place, and bears the Latin inscription:

> Here lies Edward, Prince of Wales,
> cruelly slain while a youth.
> Anno Domini 1471.
> Alas, the savagery of men,

Thou art the sole light of thy mother,
the last hope of thy race.

While the Battle of Tewkesbury raged, Queen Margaret and Anne Neville had remained with the other ladies in their party at Glupshill Manor, anxiously awaiting news. When a messenger brought them the dreadful tidings of the Lancastrian defeat, the Queen determined on flight, but was so overcome by the realisation of the disaster that had overtaken her and anxiety as to the fate of her son, of whom there was no news as yet, that she fainted and had to be carried out by her ladies to a waiting litter. She and her party then travelled to a house called Payne's Place in the village of Bushley, where a loyal family was willing to hide them for the night.

After the battle, Somerset and other Lancastrian leaders, including Sir John Langstrother, Sir Humphrey Audley, Sir John Fortescue and Dr John Morton, had sought sanctuary in Tewkesbury Abbey. Notwithstanding this, they were dragged out by the King's men. Some were killed on the spot, others were left to await judgement, and the rest, including Fortescue and Morton, remained prisoners for a time.

On 6th May Somerset and twelve others were brought before a military tribunal presided over by Gloucester as Constable of England, and condemned to immediate execution as traitors and rebels. That same day, Somerset was beheaded in the market place at Tewkesbury and buried in the abbey there. He was the last direct male descendant of the Beauforts, and on his death, Margaret Beaufort became the senior representative of her house. The other twelve leaders also suffered that day in the same manner, 'at the King's will'. Edward pardoned all the common soldiers who had fought against him.

The Battle of Tewkesbury effectively ended Lancastrian resistance for good, and was the last battle of the wars between Lancaster and York. When it ended, Henry VI was a prisoner, his only son was dead, his wife was in hiding, and the last male heir of the Beauforts – whom Henry might conceivably have chosen to succeed him – had perished. No one yet regarded Henry Tudor, a fourteen-year-old fugitive, as the hope of the House of Lancaster, which now lacked a male heir. The Lancastrian heir-general was Alfonso V, King of Portugal, a descendant of John of Gaunt, and no one in England was going to rise in his favour. Even Margaret Beaufort had abandoned the Lancastrian cause and declared her loyalty to Edward IV. 'In every part of England', says the *Arrivall*, 'it appeared to every man that the said party was extinct and repressed for ever, without any hope of again quickening.'

On 5 May, as the King rode in triumph to Worcester, he had been informed that Queen Margaret could not be found and had probably fled after the battle. In fact, Margaret and Anne Neville had left Payne's Place and made their way in secret to a fourteenth-century moated and fortified manor house called Birtsmorton Court, a fine building enclosing a courtyard and boasting a handsome hall. The Queen was accommodated in a chamber which still exists, but evidently did not feel it was safe to remain there, for she soon removed herself and her party five miles north-west to Little Malvern Priory in Worcestershire, 'a poor religious place' founded in 1171 and situated in woodland beneath Hereford Beacon.

Meanwhile, the King had been receiving reports of rebellions brewing in the north and in Wales, and, having dismissed the soldiers who had fought for him at Tewkesbury, began to recruit a new army. Jasper Tudor had been at Chepstow with Henry Tudor when he learned of the Lancastrian defeat, and was now doing his best to maintain his hold over south Wales. On Edward's orders, Roger Vaughan of Tretower tried to trap him there, but was unsuccessful, and it was Jasper who managed to capture Vaughan and have him beheaded. Some said that this was in revenge for Vaughan having urged Edward to order the execution of Jasper's father, Owen Tudor, in 1461. Afterwards, Jasper fled west to Pembroke Castle, where he was besieged by a Yorkist partisan called Morgan Thomas. He was rescued a week later, however, by a loyal supporter and friend, David Thomas.

By 14 May, the King received word that the Earl of Northumberland, now returned to his allegiance, had snuffed out the northern rebellion before it gathered momentum.

King Louis's worst fears were confirmed on 1 June, when he received credible tidings of Edward's victory. Charles the Bold, however, was delighted by the news, and hastened to dispatch his envoys to offer his congratulations and remind Edward of the enmity of Louis, urging him to set about re-conquering England's lost lands in France and assuring him of Burgundy's assistance in that venture.

For the present, however, the King had more pressing matters to occupy him. On 7 May Queen Margaret and Anne Neville had been discovered by Sir William Stanley and his men at Little Malvern Priory and taken into custody. It was Stanley who informed the Queen, none too gently, of her son's death. Margaret collapsed on hearing this bitter news, and had to be dragged almost senseless from the priory by Sir William's soldiers. On the 11th, both she and Anne

Neville were brought before the King at Coventry. Margaret was in a state of great distress, calling down curses on Edward's head and screaming abuse at him, so that for a time he seriously considered ordering her execution. But then he relented: knights did not behave thus to women, and this woman was distracted by grief and the burden of failure. He would be lenient with her. When she had calmed down, he informed her she would be dealt with honourably and with respect, to which she replied, with commendable meekness, that she placed herself 'at his commandment'. On the 14th Edward left Coventry for London with Margaret of Anjou in his train, having consigned Anne Neville to the custody of her brother-in-law, the Duke of Clarence, who arranged for her to enter his household, where she would come under the care of her elder sister, the Duchess Isabel. Her name does not appear among those of the prisoners who rode with Edward to London.

While these events were taking place, says Croyland, 'the frenzy of the King's enemies was in no way quelled, particularly in Kent, and their numbers increased in spite of the fact that King Edward's double victory seemed to all a clear sign of the justice of his cause. Incited by the few men who remained of those who had been with the Earl of Warwick, as well as by the Calais regulars, sailors and pirates, such men assembled under the command of Thomas, Bastard of Fauconberg.' Fauconberg was Warwick's cousin and had managed to retain control of the Earl's ships. On hearing of Warwick's death at Barnet, he had landed in Kent and begun to incite rebellion, calling himself 'captain and leader of our liege lord Henry's people in Kent'.

Men came flocking to him 'from the furthest corners of Kent', ready to march on London. Sir Geoffrey Gate, who had taken asylum in Calais, sent Fauconberg 300 soldiers, while the mayor of Canterbury joined him with 200 citizens. 'In Essex,' records the Great Chronicle of London, 'the faint husbands cast from them their sharp scythes and armed them with their wives' smocks, cheese cloths and old sheets, and weaponed them with heavy and great clubs and long pitchforks and staves, and so in all haste sped them towards London, and so joined unto the Kentishmen.' Many, says the *Arrivall*, 'would right fain have still been at home and not to have run into the danger of such rebellion'.

The rebels travelled to the capital by road and by boat along the Thames, 'surveying all the ways in and out of London, to discover what forces would be necessary and how they might enter to pillage that most wealthy of cities'. On 8 May, Fauconberg, from his base at

Sittingbourne, demanded that the Lord Mayor of London open the city gates to him, but the Londoners had already learned of the King's victory at Tewkesbury and were not going to be bullied. When Edward IV heard of Fauconberg's rising, he sent commissions of array out to many shires and within days 'there came to him men to the number of 30,000', according to Warkworth.

On the 13th, the Bastard appeared before London on the Surrey shore of the Thames and announced his intention of taking the city and freeing Henry VI from the Tower. But God, says Croyland, 'gave stout hearts to the people of London that they might stand firm in the battle'. The Lord Mayor and aldermen refused him entry, saying they were holding the capital for King Edward. Fauconberg then marched his men to Kingston and crossed the Thames there, intending to lead an assault on Westminster, but when he received reports that the King's army would soon be at his back, he retreated to Southwark, near to where his ships were moored. He then lined his guns up along the shore and fired upon the Tower, where Queen Elizabeth and her children were in residence and 'all likely to stand in the greatest jeopardy that ever there was'. Elizabeth's brother, Lord Rivers, was in command of the Tower, and ably defended the city against its attackers, ordering an intense bombardment of Fauconberg's position by the cannon on the Tower walls and beating off the rebel assault.

The following day, Fauconberg made a futile attempt to fire London Bridge, but was driven back by cannonfire. Meanwhile, 3000 of his men had burst into the city through St Katherine's Docks and were rampaging through the streets, firing guns and arrows indiscriminately, pillaging, and setting fire to Aldgate and Bishopsgate. At that point the Earl of Essex arrived to reinforce the city levies and sent them against the rebels, just as Rivers was sallying forth from the Tower with 4500 men. Fierce fighting ensued, and many of Fauconberg's men were killed. Gradually the rebels were forced back to the banks of the Thames, and from there they were pursued to their ships, although not before they had impudently led away fifty of Butcher Gould's oxen – destined to feed the Queen's household – from their grazing place by the Tower.

On the 15th the rebels retreated quietly enough to Blackheath, where they regrouped. However, at news that the King was advancing at the head of 30,000 men, all their courage melted away, and they decided that they should disperse. The Duke of Gloucester, riding ahead of the King's main force, received Fauconberg's submission. Nothing now stood in the way of Edward's triumphal return to London.

On Tuesday 21 May, the King was formally welcomed by the Lord Mayor and the city fathers at Islington and then, accompanied by a larger retinue than was usual, which included almost the entire peerage of England, he rode into the capital, says Croyland, 'ordering his standards to be unfurled and borne before him. Many who saw this were surprised and amazed, for no enemy remained to be dealt with, but this prudent prince was familiar with the untrustworthy ways of the people of Kent and resolved not to lay down his arms until he had punished those rebellious men, which he did soon after.' He also knighted those who had distinguished themselves in the defence of London.

Praise of the King 'sounded through all lands' and the Londoners were enthusiastic in their acclaim of his triumph, cheering exuberantly and crying out blessings upon him. He had emerged victorious after a brilliant campaign, during the course of which he had eliminated most of his enemies. His success had not only been due to his speed, tenacity and daring, but also to his outstanding abilities as a general and his deployment of men of calibre in positions of command.

But if there was triumph in London that day, there was also the manifestation of tragedy, for ahead of the King in the procession was borne a litter in which sat Margaret of Anjou, exposed to the derision and taunts of the crowds and tasting the bitter dregs of humiliation and grief. As she passed, bystanders flung mud and stones at her and yelled abuse.

Henry VI was still in the Tower, but Fauconberg, by rising in the name of Lancaster, had virtually signed his death warrant. With Prince Edward dead, Edward IV no doubt felt that there was every justification for removing the deposed King. While Henry lived, there would always be further military confrontations involving pointless loss of life and consumption of the Crown's revenues, and with these demands on his purse and his energies, Edward IV could not hope to make progress with his programme of reconstruction. There was no point in allowing civil war to continue unchecked. Therefore Henry must die.

'And in the same night that King Edward came to London,' wrote Warkworth, whose account is contemporary, 'King Henry, being in ward in prison in the Tower of London, was put to death, between eleven and twelve of the clock, being then at the Tower the Duke of Gloucester.' Tradition has it that Henry's murderer came upon him as he knelt at prayer in a deep niche in the eastern wall of his chamber in the Wakefield Tower, a room in which the crown jewels were later displayed.

The official account of his death in the *Arrivall* states that Henry reacted to news of the death of his son, the capture of his wife and the bitter certainty that his cause was 'utterly despaired of' with 'so great despite, ire and indignation that, of pure displeasure and melancholy he died'. Few were deceived by this. The Milanese ambassador in Paris soon heard that King Edward had 'caused King Henry to be secretly assassinated in the Tower. He has, in short, chosen to crush the seed'. Commines had reason to believe that it was Gloucester who 'killed poor King Henry with his own hand, or else caused him to be killed in his presence', while Vergil states that by the time of Henry VII it was generally believed that 'Gloucester killed him with a sword'. Whatever Richard of Gloucester's involvement – and it seems probable, from Warkworth's significant mention of him, that his purpose at the Tower that night was to see that the act of regicide was carried out – the order for the murder of Henry VI can only have come from King Edward. Gloucester would not have acted alone in such a matter.

For murder it most certainly was. Henry VI died of the effects of a severe blow to the head. In 1911, when his body was exhumed and examined, his skeleton was found to be in pieces, and the bones of the skull were 'much broken', according to the report in *Archaeologia*. Moreover, 'to one of the pieces of skull there was still attached some of the hair, which was brown in colour, save in one place, where it was much darker and apparently matted with blood'. Croyland was in no doubt as to the cause of death.

> I shall pass over the discovery of the lifeless body of King Henry in the Tower of London. May God have mercy upon, and grant sufficient time for repentance to him, whoever he may be, who dared to lay sacriligeous hands on the Lord's Anointed! Let the doer merit the title of tyrant, and the victim be called a glorious martyr.

On 22 May, says Warkworth, the late King's corpse was laid in a coffin and carried through the streets of London to St Paul's where it lay in state for several days. 'And his face was open that every man might see him, and in his lying he bled on the pavement there; and afterwards at the Black Friars was brought, and there he bled new and fresh.' The people murmured at this, and the Great Chronicle reports that 'the common fame then went that the Duke of Gloucester was not all guiltless' of Henry's death.

The chroniclers do not record where Margaret of Anjou spent the night of the 21st. However, on the following day she was certainly imprisoned in the Tower. Her reaction to the news of her husband's death is not recorded either, but she did make a determined attempt to gain custody of his body, which was denied her. Before long, she received a letter from her grief-stricken father, King René: 'My child, may God help thee with His counsels! For rarely is the aid of man tendered in such reverse of fortune.' René himself had recently suffered a triple bereavement – his son, John of Calabria, his bastard daughter Blanche and his son-in-law Ferry de Vaudemont had all died within weeks of each other the previous year. 'When you can spare a thought from your own sufferings,' he wrote to Margaret, 'think of mine. They are great, my daughter, yet would I console thee.'

Henry VI's funeral service was conducted at the monastery of the Black Friars, after which his body was carried in a barge 'suitably equipped with lamps fifteen miles up the Thames' to Chertsey Abbey in Surrey where it was 'honourably interred' in the Lady Chapel.

'There is many a great sore, many a perilous wound left unhealed,' records the Parliament Roll of 1474, three years after the wars between Lancaster and York had ended. Croyland states that 'this unhappy plague of division' had spread 'not only among princes and people, but even in every society, whether chapter, college or convent'. Many lords came out of the conflict facing financial ruin. 'The slaughter of men was immense, for besides the dukes, earls, barons and distinguished warriors who were cruelly slain, multitudes almost innumerable of the common people died of their wounds. Such was the state of the kingdom.'

The Wars of the Roses did not in fact bring about the destruction of most of the mediaeval aristocracy, as this lament would seem to imply. Although thirty-eight peers perished, only seven noble families, not counting the royal houses, became extinct. And while the conflict undoubtedly led to the aggrandisement of some already 'over-mighty' subjects, other members of the aristocracy refused to become involved in it at all. Certainly the effect of the wars was to narrow the gap between the King and the magnates and gradually erode the royal authority, while the slaughter of so many lords and knights also signalled an end to the age of chivalry.

Tudor historians were fond of reminding their readers of the horrors of the Wars of the Roses, recounting how the realm had been plunged into a vicious civil war over a disputed crown that lasted more than thirty years. They spared no efforts to portray this as a grim period of violence, political anarchy and social decay. Edward Hall posed the rhetorical question, 'What misery, what murder, and what execrable plagues this famous region hath suffered by the division and dissension of the renowned Houses of Lancaster and York, my wit cannot comprehend nor my tongue declare. For what noble man, what gentleman of any ancient stock or progeny, whose lineage hath not been infected and plagued by this unnatural division?' The Elizabethan antiquarian, John Stow, referred to the Wars of the Roses as 'all that heaving in and hurling out', while Shakespeare wrote a cycle of plays about them, saying famously:

> England hath long been mad and scarred herself,
> The brother blindly shed the brother's blood,
> The father rashly slaughtered his own son,
> The son, compelled, been butcher to the sire:
> All this divided York and Lancaster.

Croyland, writing in 1486, viewed the Wars of the Roses primarily as a dynastic struggle that had its origins in York's assertion of his claim to the throne. This became the accepted Tudor view, and proves that the tradition had a very early source. Polydore Vergil, Henry VII's official historian, traced the origins of the conflict to the usurpation of Henry IV, but this was too simplistic a view and did not take account of the political decline of the 1440s and 1450s. Vergil had no difficulty in believing that God had visited the sins of Henry IV upon his descendant, Henry VI, yet he did not explain how this was to be reconciled with the triumphant career of Henry V.

Tudor historians were adepts at rewriting history. The dynasty they served had brought peace, firm government and prosperity to England, but its monarchs were still usurpers. A striking contrast had to be drawn, therefore, between the peaceful England of Tudor times and the political anarchy it had suffered under the later Plantagenets, the implication being that if Henry VII had not become king in 1485, the civil wars would probably have dragged on for much longer. More importantly, the subjects of the Tudor kings had to be reminded of what might happen if the crown came into dispute again.

There is certainly no doubt that violence and lawlessness flourished during the Wars of the Roses. Soldiers brutalised in the French wars behaved with a ferocity which their commanding officers were powerless to control, while some magnates were little better than sadistic ruffians. Thousands of men died horribly in battle, or were mercilessly butchered while trying to escape. Murder was often committed with impunity both on and off the battlefield.

Yet the wars were by no means continuous, as we have seen, nor did England experience many of the usual horrors of civil war, like those suffered in fifteenth-century France or seventeenth-century Britain. There were, at most, thirteen weeks of fighting in the thirty-two years covered by both of the Wars of the Roses, while the total amount of time spent campaigning amounted to approximately one year. The problems of keeping an army fed and watered meant that individual campaigns lasted for a matter of days or weeks, not months. Some of the battles were very short, and none lasted longer than a day. Most took place in open countryside and hardly affected life in the towns and villages. The conflict had very little effect upon the population at large, except on the rare occasions when a battle resulted in great loss of life that devastated a whole local community, as happened at Towton in 1461. This was why the behaviour of the Scots and men of the north on the Queen's march south that year provoked such outrage. Relatively few civilians suffered attack or privation, and – with the exception of Stamford, St Albans and Ludlow – no town suffered a siege or a sacking. Nor did the castles, halls and manors of the aristocracy suffer greatly. Only the great defensive castles of the north became targets for military action.

The accounts of foreign visitors to England give the impression that the country appeared settled and prosperous in the second half of the fifteenth century, not torn by war. The architecture of the period reflects a trend of growing prosperity rather than a need to build defensively. Fortifications were no longer added as a matter of course to castles and manor houses, and moats and crenellations had become merely ornamental. Neither does the literature of the age reflect a preoccupation with the evils of civil war. This was because most of the population did not regard the Wars of the Roses as a civil war as such, but as a dispute between noble factions. Few English people really cared who sat on the throne, so long as he was able to govern effectively and maintain justice. The leaders of the political factions therefore used propaganda to sway public opinion, which was very fickle, and did their best to canvass the support of other magnates who, left to themselves, would have remained strictly neutral. In fact, the majority of peers, both spiritual and temporal, managed to avoid committing themselves wholeheartedly to either party, while some tended to wait and see which way a battle was going, and only went in to assist the winning side. Self-interest usually governed political loyalties.

Henry VI's reign had been one of the most catastrophic in England's history, yet after his death his reputation grew steadily. Tales of his piety and holy life spread rapidly, and were just as rapidly embellished. Within weeks of his death, pilgrims were hastening from all over the kingdom to pray at his tomb, many from the north of England where Lancastrian sympathies were still strong. It was said in those parts that Henry had died a martyr. Soon he was venerated as a saint, and 155 miracles were said to have taken place at his tomb, most of them cures for the sick. Croyland says that 'the miracles which God worked in response to the prayers of those devoutly seeking his intercession are witness to his blameless life, the extent of his love for God and the Church, of his patience in adversity and his other outstanding virtues'. People forgot that Henry had failed them in nearly every way that mattered – as king, as warlord, and as the fount of justice – and remembered only his virtuous life and the fact that he had bequeathed to them two enduring monuments to his piety and love of learning – Eton College and King's College, Cambridge.

In 1484, Richard III, apparently with the aim of making reparation for Henry's murder, ordered his reburial to the south of the high altar in St George's Chapel, Windsor. Rous says that when the King's body was exhumed after lying for thirteen years at Chertsey it was found to be virtually incorrupt. The face was skeletal and sweet-smelling – 'certainly not from spices, since he was buried by his enemies and tormentors' – a sure sign of sanctity. The body was reverently laid to rest in a vault beneath a plain stone slab near the tomb of Henry's great adversary, Edward IV. In recognition of the common people's devotion to 'Saint' Henry, King Richard ordered that his armour, robes and other possessions be displayed near the tomb as relics; Stow records that his crimson velvet cap was considered an effective cure for headaches. An iron alms box bearing a gothic 'H' was set up for pilgrims, and still remains in place today.

By Tudor times, Henry VI's saintly reputation had grown immensely, and people forgot that he had been a weak king who was responsible for decades of misrule and the loss of England's possessions in France. John Blacman's memoir was written in this climate, and for centuries was accepted as a reliable account of Henry's life. Only recently has its veracity been called into question. It was in fact written to support Henry VII's campaign to have his uncle formally canonised; it would have been beneficial to the image of the new dynasty to have a Lancastrian saint among its forbears, but despite strenuous efforts on the part of Henry Tudor, the campaign was unsuccessful. In England, however, up until the

Reformation, people continued to venerate Henry VI. As his cult spread, the room in the Tower in which he had met his end was converted into a shrine, and was also visited by pilgrims. The shrine was dismantled by Henry VIII's commissioners in the 1530s, but ever since then, each year on the night of 21 May, the governors of Eton College have placed a sheaf of lilies and red roses on the traditional site of Henry's murder.

Margaret of Anjou did not remain long in the Tower. Elizabeth Wydville pleaded with her husband to mitigate the severity of the former queen's imprisonment, and Edward IV, who could never resist his wife's importunings, soon ordered Margaret's removal to the more congenial surroundings of Windsor Castle, where she remained under house arrest until 8 July 1471, when she moved to Wallingford Castle. This was an act of kindness on Edward's part, for Wallingford was near Ewelme, the Oxfordshire home of Alice Chaucer, Duchess of Suffolk, one of Margaret's closest friends. Alice was appointed by the King to be her guardian and was paid five marks a week for her expenses.

In 1476, after the Duchess's death, Margaret was ransomed by Louis XI and returned to France, where she was maintained by her father. After René's death in 1480, she lived in very reduced circumstances, subsisting on a meagre pension provided by King Louis. She died in great poverty after a short unspecified illness on 25 August 1482 and was buried in Angers Cathedral.

Anne Neville became, in 1472, the wife of Richard, Duke of Gloucester, to whom she bore one son, Edward of Middleham, who died in childhood. Two years after Richard became King, Anne herself died, possibly of tuberculosis or cancer, in 1485, at the age of twenty-nine.

George, Duke of Clarence was executed for treason in 1478; he died privately, in the Tower of London, probably – at his own request – by drowning in a butt of Malmsey wine. His wife, Isabel, had died in childbed in 1476.

After learning of Henry VI's murder, Jasper Tudor fled to Henry Tudor in France, to begin fourteen years of exile. After Henry became King in 1485, Jasper was created Duke of Bedford and married Katherine Wydville, dying in 1495.

Sir John Fortescue was pardoned after he had written a treatise upholding Edward IV's claim to the throne and abjuring his former writings; he was made a member of Edward's Council and died around 1477-9. King Edward also pardoned Dr John Morton, the

Earl of Ormonde, Sir Richard Tunstall, young Lord Clifford and Sir Henry Vernon.

From 1471 to 1483 Edward IV ruled England firmly and well, unchallenged by any. In 1473, the birth of another son, Richard, to Elizabeth Wydville made the House of York seem almost invincible. But when Edward died suddenly, in 1483, and his twelve-year-old son Edward V succeeded him, a power struggle erupted between the Duke of Gloucester, whom Edward had designated Protector of England, and the Wydville faction. Gloucester emerged the victor from this, imprisoned the boy king, deposed him, and had himself crowned Richard III, all within three months. He then almost certainly arranged for young Edward and his brother to be murdered in the Tower of London. This made him so unpopular that within two years both he and the House of York had been overthrown by Henry Tudor, who became King Henry VII after winning the Battle of Bosworth in 1485.

'Time has his revolutions,' wrote a seventeenth-century Lord Chief Justice, Sir Ranulph Crew,

> there must be a period and an end to all temporal things, *finis rerum*, an end of names and dignities and whatsoever is of this earth. Where is Bohun? Where is Mowbray? Where is Mortimer? Nay, which is more and most of all, where is Plantagenet? They are entombed in the urns and sepulchres of mortality.

Simplified Genealogical Tables

I Lancaster and York

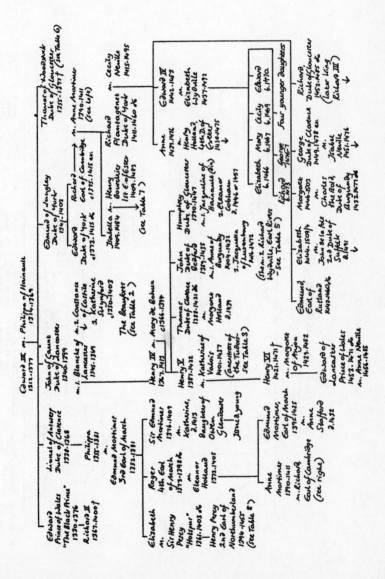

2 The Beauforts

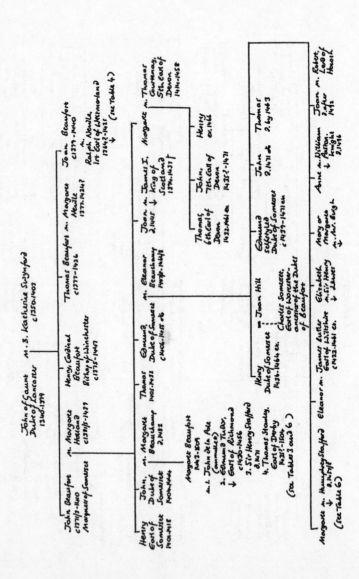

Henry V 1387-1422   1. m.   Katherine of Valois 1401-1437   m. (1)   (2) 2. Owen Tudor c.1400-1461 ex.

Edmund Tudor Earl of Richmond c.1430-1456   m.   Margaret Beaufort (see Table 2) 1443-1509

Henry Tudor Earl of Richmond 1457-1509 became King Henry VII in 1485; the first Sovereign of the House of Tudor

Jasper Tudor Earl of Pembroke, later Duke of Bedford c.1431-1495

Helen/Ellen m. William Godwin of London →

m. Katherine Wydeville 2. by 1513 (see Table 5)

Owen Thomas Tudor 1432-1502 a monk at Westminster Abbey under the name Edward Bridgewater

Unnamed daughter, became a nun.

Margate or Katherine b.v.2.1477

4 The Nevilles

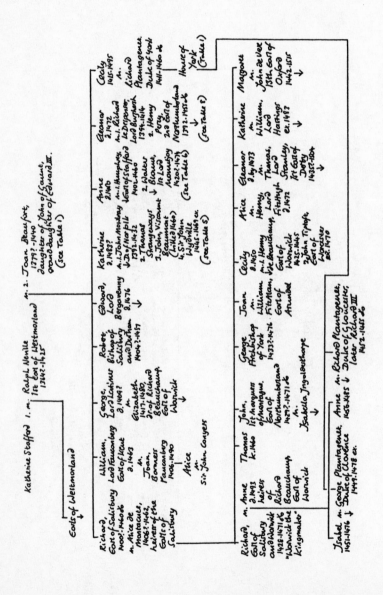

5   The Wydvilles

John of Lancaster, Duke of Bedford 1389-1435   1. m.   Jacquetta of Luxembourg 1416?-1472, daughter of Pier of Luxembourg, Count of St. Pol.   m. 2.   Richard Wydville, 1st Earl Rivers 1405?-1469 ex.

Elizabeth 1437?-1492 m. 1. Sir John Grey 2. Edward IV (see Table 1)

Anne 1438?-1489 m. 1. William, Viscount Bourchier (see Table 7) 2. Sir Edward Wingfield 3. George Grey, Earl of Kent

Margaret 1439?-1490? m. Thomas Maltravers, Earl of Arundel 1450?-1524

Anthony, 2nd Earl Rivers 1440?-1483 ex. m. 1. Elizabeth Bonser Scales 1436?-1473 2. Mary FitzLewis

Thomas, Marquess of Dorset c1455-1501 m. 1. Anne Holland c1455-1475 2. Cecilia, Baroness Bonville d.1529

Richard, a knight 1462?-1483 ex.

Mary 1438?-by 1481 m. William Herbert, Earl of Pembroke and Huntingdon (c.1461)

Jacquetta 1444?-1509 m. John, Lord Strange of Knockin d.1479

John, a knight ex. 1469

Katherine Neville 2. aft 1487, Dowager Duchess of Norfolk

Lionel, Bishop of Salisbury 1446?-1484

Edward, a knight d.1488

Richard, 3rd Earl Rivers d.1491

John, and Lewis d. young

Eleanor m. Anthony, Lord Grey de Ruthin d.1490

Martha m. Sir John Bromley

Katherine m. 1. Henry Stafford, 2nd Duke of Buckingham 1455? ex. m.1483 2. Jasper Tudor, Duke of Bedford 1431?-1495 (d. by 1513)

(see Tables 6 and 3)

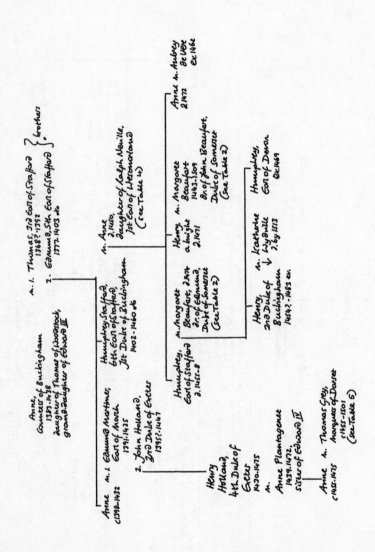

7 *The Bourchiers*

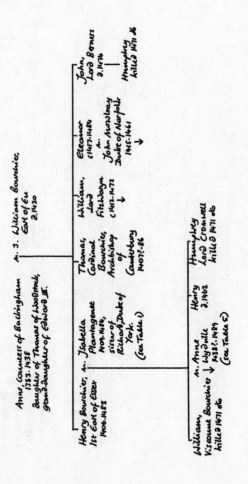

8 *The Percies and the Cliffords*

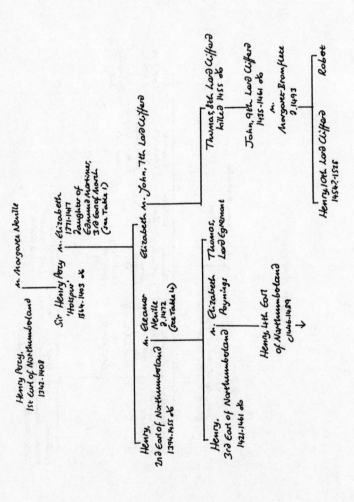

Henry Percy,
1st Earl of Northumberland
1342-1408
m. Margare Neville

Sir Henry Percy
'Hotspur',
1364-1403 ✗
m. Elizabeth
1371-1447
daughter of
Edmund Mortimer,
3rd Earl of March
(see Table 1)

Henry,
2nd Earl of Northumberland
1394-1455 ✗
m. Eleanor
Neville
d. 1472
(see Table 4)

Elizabeth m. John, 7th Lord Clifford

Henry,
3rd Earl of Northumberland
1421-1461 ✗
m. Elizabeth
Poynings

Thomas,
Lord Egremont

Henry, 4th Earl
of Northumberland
c.1446-1489
→

Thomas, 8th Lord Clifford
killed 1455 ✗

John, 9th Lord Clifford
1435-1461 ✗
m.
Margaret Bromflete
d. 1493

Henry, 10th Lord Clifford
1454-1526

Robert

Bibliography

Primary Sources

Adam of Usk: *Cronicon Adae de Usk* (ed. E. M. Thompson, London, 1904)

Archaeologia, or Miscellaneous Tracts relating to Antiquity (102 vols., Society of Antiquaries, 1777-1969)

Basin, Thomas: *Histoire de Charles VII* (ed. C. Samaran, Paris, 1964-5)

Basin, Thomas: *Histoire de Louis XI* (ed. C. Samaran and M. C. Garand, Paris, 1963-6)

Basin, Thomas: *Histoires des Règnes de Charles VII et de Louis XI* (ed. J. Quicherat, Paris, 1855-9)

Benet, John: *John Benet's Chronicle for the Years 1400 to 1462* (ed. G. L. Harriss and M. A. Harriss, *Camden Miscellany*. vol. XXIV, London, 1972)

Blacman, John: *Henry the Sixth: A Reprint of John Blacman's Memoir* (ed. M. R. James, Cambridge, 1919)

The Brut, or the Chronicles of England (ed. F. Brie, Early English Texts Society, 1906-8)

Calendar of Charter Rolls, Vol. VI, 1427-1516 (HMSO, 1927)

Calendar of Close Rolls, 1454-61, 1461-68, 1468-76 (HMSO, 1954)

Calendar of Documents relating to Scotland, Vol. IV 1357-1509 (ed. J. Bain, London, 1888)

Calendar of Patent Rolls, Henry VI and Edward IV (HMSO, London, 1949-67)

Calendar of Signet Letters, Henry IV and Henry V (HMSO, London, 1978)

Calendar of State Papers and Manuscripts existing in the Archives and

Collections of Milan, Vol. I 1388-1618 (ed. A. B. Hinds, London, 1913)

Calendar of State Papers and Manuscripts relating to English Affairs existing in the Archives and Collections of Venice, Vol. I 1202-1509 (ed. R. Brown, London, 1864)

Capgrave, John: *The Book of the Illustrious Henries* (ed. F. C. Hingeston, London, 1858)

The Cely Papers (ed. Henry Elliot Malden, Camden Society, 1900)

Chastellain, Georges: *Chronicles of the Dukes of Burgundy* (in *Oeuvres*, vols. IV and V, ed. K. de Lettenhove, Brussels, 1864)

The Chronicle of Bermondsey, 1042-1442 (in *Annales Monastici*, 5 vols., ed. H. R. Luard, Rolls Series, 1864-9)

A Chronicle of London from 1089 to 1483 (ed. H. Nicolas and E. Tyrell, London, 1827)

The Chronicle of the Rebellion in Lincolnshire, 1470 (ed. J. G. Nichols, Camden Miscellany, 1847)

Chronicles of London (ed. C. L. Kingsford, Oxford, 1905; reprinted Alan Sutton, 1977)

Chronicles of the White Rose of York (ed. J. A. Giles, 1845)

Chronique de la Traïson et Mort de Richard Deux, Roy Dengleterre (ed. and trans. B. Williams, English Historical Society, 1847)

Chronique du Religieux de Saint-Denys, 1380-1422 (6 vols., ed. and trans. F. Bellaguet, Paris, 1839-52)

Clerq, Jacques du: *Mémoires sur le Règne de Philippe le Bon, Duc de Bourgogne* (4 vols., ed. M. le Baron de Reiffenberg, Brussels, 1836)

A Collection of Ordinances and Regulations for the Government of the Royal Household made in divers reigns from King Edward III to King William and Queen Mary (Society of Antiquaries, 1790)

A Collection of Wills of the Kings and Queens of England from William the Conqueror to Henry VII (ed. J. Nichols, Society of Antiquaries, 1780)

Commines, Philippe de: *Mémoires* (3 vols., ed. J. L. A. Calmette and G. Durville, Paris, 1824-5; ed. and trans. M. Jones, Penguin Classics, London, 1972)

The Cotton Manuscripts in the British Library

The Coventry Leet Book (ed. M. D. Harris in four parts, Early English Texts Society, Original Series, 1907-13)

Creton, Jean: *Histoire du Roy d'Angleterre, Richard* (manuscript in the Bibliothèque Nationale Paris, ed. and trans. J. Webb in *Archaeologia*, XX, 1824)

The Croyland Chronicle Continuation, 1459-1486 (ed. N. Prona and J. Cox, Alan Sutton, 1986)

Dépêches des ambassadeurs Milanais en France sous Louis XI et François Sforza (4 vols., ed. B. de Mandrot, Paris, 1916-19)

The Dieulacres Chronicle (in *The Deposition of Richard II* by M. V. Clarke and V. H. Galbraith, Bulletin of the John Rylands Library, XIV, 1930; reprinted in M. V. Clarke, *Fourteenth Century Studies*, Oxford, 1939)

England under the Yorkists (ed. I. D. Thornley, 1920)

An English Chronicle of the Reigns of Richard II, Henry IV, Henry V and Henry VI (ed. J. S. Davies, Camden Society, 1856)

English Historical Documents, Vol. 5 1327-1485 (ed. A. R. Myers, Eyre and Spottiswoode, 1969)

English Historical Literature in the Fifteenth Century (ed. C. L. Kingsford, Oxford, 1913: reprinted New York, 1962)

Fabyan, Robert: *The Concordance of Histories: The New Chronicles of England and France* (ed. H. Ellis, London, 1811)

Foedera, Conventiones, Litterae, etc., 1101-1654, Vols. I-XV (20 vols., compiled by Thomas Rymer, London, 1704-35)

Fortescue, Sir John: *The Governance of England* (ed. C. Plummer, Oxford, 1885)

Fortescue, Sir John: *De Laudibus Legum Angliae* (trans. F. Grigor, London, 1917)

Gesta Henrici Quinti: The Deeds of Henry the Fifth (trans. and ed. F. Taylor and J. S. Roskell, Oxford, 1975)

The Great Chronicle of London (ed. A. H. Thomas and I. D. Thornley, Guildhall Library, London, 1938, privately printed)

'Gregory's Chronicle': The Historical Collections of a Citizen of London in the Fifteenth Century (ed. James Gairdner, Camden Society, 1876)

Hall, Edward: *The Union of the Two Noble and Illustre Families of Lancaster and York* (ed. H. Ellis, London, 1809; facsimile edition of the original published 1970)

Hardying, John: *Chronicle* (ed. H. Ellis, London, 1812, and ed. C. L. Kingsford in *English Historical Review*, XXVII, 1912)

The Harleian Manuscripts in the British Library

Historiae Croylandensis Continuario (in *Rerum Anglicarum Scriptores Veterum, Vol. I*, ed W. Fulman, Oxford, 1684)

Historiae Vitae et Regni Ricardi Secundi (ed. G. B. Snow, University of Pennsylvania, 1977)

Historie of the Arrivall of King Edward IV in England and the final Recoverye of his Kingdomes from Henry VI, A.D. 1471 (ed. J. Bruce, Camden Society, 1838)

The Household of Edward IV (ed. A. R. Myers. 1959)

Illustrated Letters of the Paston Family (ed. Roger Virgoe, Macmillan, 1989)

Ingulph's Chronicle of the Abbey of Croyland (trans. and ed. H. T. Riley, Bohn's Antiquarian Library, London, 1854)

Juvénal des Ursins, Jean: *Écrits politiques* (ed. P. S. Lewis, Paris, 1978)

Juvénal des Ursins, Jean: *Histoire de Charles VI* (ed. J. A. C. Buchon, Paris, 1836)

Knyghthode and Bataile (ed. R. Dyboski and Z. M. Arend, Early English Texts Society, 1935)

The Legeaud Manuscripts in the Bibliothèque Nationale, Paris

Letters and Papers illustrative of the Wars of the English in France during the Reign of Henry the Sixth, King of England (2 vols., ed. J. Stevenson, Rolls Series, 1861-81)

Letters of Margaret of Anjou (ed. Cecil Monroe, Camden Society, 1863)

Lettres de Louis XI, Roi de France (11 vols., ed. J. Vaesen and others, Paris, 1883-1909)

Lettres des Rois, Reines et autres Personnages des Cours de France et d'Angleterre (ed. J. Champollion-Figeac, Paris, 1839-47)

A London Chronicle of 1460 (ed. G. Baskerville, *English Historical Review*, XXVIII, 1913)

Mancini, Dominic: *De Occupatione Regni Anglie per Riccardum Tercium* (trans. and ed. C. A. J. Armstrong, 2nd edition, Oxford, 1969)

Marche, Olivier de la: *Mémoires d'Olivier de la Marche* (ed. H. Beaune and J. Arbaumont, Paris, 1883)

Memorials of Henry the Fifth (ed. C. A. Cole, Rolls Series, 1858)

Molinet, Jean: *Chroniques de Jean Molinet, 1474-1506* (3 vols., ed. G. Doutrepont and O. Jodogne, Académie Royale Belgique, Brussels, 1935-7)

Monstrelet, Enguerrand de: *Chroniques d'Enguerran de Monstrelet* (ed. L. Douet d'Arcq, Paris, 1857-62)

Narratives of the Expulsion of the English from Normandy, 1449-1450 (ed. J. Stevenson, London, 1863)

Original Letters Illustrative of English History (11 vols., ed. Sir Henry Ellis, London, 1824-46)

Pageant of the Birth, Life and Death of Richard Beauchamp, Earl of Warwick, K. G., 1389-1439 (ed. Viscount Dillon and W. H. St John Hope, London, 1914)

The Paston Letters, 1422-1509 (3 vols., ed. J. Gairdner, Edinburgh, 1910)

Paston Letters and Papers of the Fifteenth Century (2 vols., ed. N. Davis, Oxford, 1971-6)

The Plumpton Correspondence (ed. T. Stapleton, Camden Society, 1839)

Political Poems and Songs relating to English History, from the Accession of Edward III to that of Richard III (2 vols., ed. T. Wright, Rolls Series, 1852)

The Priory of Hexham, Vol. I (Surtees Society, 1864)

Proceedings and Ordinances of the Privy Council of England, Vol. VI (ed. Sir H. Nicolas, London, 1837)

Records of the Borough of Nottingham, Vols. II and III (London, 1883-5)

A Relation of the Island of England (ed. C. A. Sneyd, Camden Society, 1847)

Rotuli Parliamentorum (The Rolls of Parliament) (7 vols., ed. J. Strachey and others, Record Commissioners, 1767-83)

Rous, John: *Historiae Regum Angliae* (ed. T. Hearne, Oxford, 1716)

Rous, John: *The Rous Roll* (ed. C. Ross and W. Courthope, Alan Sutton, 1980)

Roye, Jean de: *Journal de Jean de Roye connu sous le nom de Chronique Scandaleuse, 1460-1483* (2 vols., ed. B. de Mandrot, Paris, 1894-6)

Shillingford, John: *Letters and Papers of John Shillingford* (ed. S. A. Moore, Camden Society, 1871)

Six Town Chronicles of England (ed. R. Flenley, Oxford, 1911)

Stone, John: *Chronicle* (ed. W. G. Searle, Cambridge Antiquarian Society, 1902)

The Stonor Letters and Papers (2 vols., ed. C. L. Kingsford, Camden Society, 1919)

Stow, John: *A Survey of London* (2 vols., ed. C. L. Kingsford, Oxford, 1908, and H. B. Wheatley, Dent, 1987)

Strecche, John: *The Chronicle of John Strecche for the Reign of Henry V, 1414-22* (ed. F. Taylor, Manchester, 1932)

Thomas of Elmham (Pseudo-Elmham): *Vita et Gesta Henrici Quinti* (ed. T. Hearne, Oxford, 1727)

Three Chronicles of the Reign of Edward IV (ed. Keith Dockray, Alan Sutton, 1988)

Three Fifteenth Century Chronicles (ed. J. Gairdner, Camden Society, 1880)

Titus Livius: *The First English Life of King Henry the Fifth* (ed. C. L. Kingsford, Oxford, 1911)

Titus Livius: *Vita Henrici Quinti* (ed. T. Hearne, Oxford, 1716)

Vergil, Polydore: *The Anglica Historia of Polydore Vergil, AD 1485-1573* (trans. and ed. D. Hay, Camden Series, 1950)

Vergil, Polydore: *Three Books of Polydore Vergil's English History* (ed. H. Ellis, Camden Society, 1844)

Vita et Gesta Henrici Quinti (ed. T. Hearne, London, 1727)

Walsingham, Thomas: *Thomas Walsingham, quondam monachi S.*

Albani, Historia Anglicana (2 vols., ed. H. T. Riley, Rolls Series, 1863-4)

The Wardrobe Book of Margaret of Anjou

Warkworth, John: *A Chronicle of the First Thirteen Years of the Reign of King Edward the Fourth* (ed. J. O. Halliwell, Camden Society, 1839)

Waurin, Jean de: *Receuil des Chroniques et Anchiennes Istories de la Grant Brétagne, à present nommé Engleterre* (5 vols., ed. Sir William Hardy and E. L. C. P. Hardy, Rolls Series, 1864-91)

Weever, John: *Ancient Funeral Monuments* (London, 1631)

Whethamstead, John: *Registrum* (in *Registra quorundam Abbatum Monasterii S. Albani*, 2 vols., ed. H. T. Riley, Rolls Series, 1872-3)

Worcester, William: *The Boke of Noblesse* (ed. J. G. Nichols, Roxburgh Club, London, 1860; reprinted New York, 1972)

Worcester, William: *Itineraries* (ed. J. H. Harvey, Oxford Mediaeval Texts, Oxford, 1969)

York Civic Records, Vols. I and II (ed. Angelo Raine, Yorkshire Archaeological Society, Record Series, 1939-41)

York Records: Extracts from the Municipal Records of the City of York during the Reigns of Edward IV, Edward V and Richard III (ed. R. Davies, London, 1843)

Secondary Sources

Allen, Kenneth: *The Wars of the Roses* (Wayland, 1973)

Allmand, Christopher: *Henry V* (Methuen, 1992)

Allmand, C.: *Lancastrian Normandy, 1415-1450* (Oxford, 1983)

Armitage-Smith, Sydney: *John of Gaunt* (Constable, 1904)

Armstrong, C. A. J.: *The Inauguration Ceremonies of the Yorkist Kings and their Title to the Throne* (*Transactions of the Royal Historical Society*, 4th Series, XXX, 1948)

Armstrong, C. A. J.: *The Piety of Cecily, Duchess of York: A Study in Later Mediaeval Culture* (in *For Hilaire Belloc*, ed. D. Woodruff, 1942)

Armstrong, C. A. J.: *Politics and the Battle of St Albans, 1455* (British Institute of Historical Research, 33, 1960)

Armstrong, C. A. J.: *Some Examples of the Distribution and Speed of News in England at the Time of the Wars of the Roses* (*Mediaeval History*, 1, No. 2, 1991)

Ashdown, Dulcie M.: *Ladies in Waiting* (Arthur Barker, 1976)

Ashdown, Dulcie M.: *Princess of Wales* (John Murray, 1979)

Aylmer, G. E. and Cant, R. (eds.): *A History of York Minster* (Oxford, 1977)

Bagley, J. J.: *Margaret of Anjou* (Batsford, 1948)

Baudier, Michael: *A History of the Memorable and Extraordinary Calamities of Margaret of Anjou, Queen of England* (London, 1737)

Bellamy, J.: *Crime and Public Order in England in the Later Middle Ages* (Routledge and Kegan Paul, 1973)

Blyth, J. D.: *The Battle of Tewkesbury* (*Transactions of the Bristol and Gloucestershire Archaeological Society, LXX,* 1961)

Calmette, J. and Perinelle, G.: *Louis XI et Angleterre* (Paris, 1930)

Charlesworth, D.: *The Battle of Hexham, 1464* (*Archaeologia Aeliana,* 4th Series, 30, 1952)

Charlesworth, D.: *Northumberland in the Early Years of Edward IV* (*Archaeologia Aeliana,* 4th Series, 31, 1953)

Clarke, B.: *Mental Illness in Early Britain* (Cardiff, 1975)

Clifford, Hugh: *The House of Clifford* (Phillimore, 1987)

Clive, Mary M.: *This Sun of York: A Biography of Edward IV* (Macmillan, 1973)

Cole, Hubert: *The Wars of the Roses* (Hart-Davis Macgibbon, 1973)

The Complete Peerage of England, Scotland, Ireland, Great Britain and the United Kingdom (13 vols., ed. V. Gibbs, H. A. Doubleday, D. Warrand, Thomas, Lord Howard de Walden and G. White, St Catherine's Press, 1910-59)

Cook, David R.: *Lancastrians and Yorkists: The Wars of the Roses* (Longman, 1984)

Cust, Mrs Henry: *Gentleman Errant: Gabriel Tetzel of Nuremberg* (1909)

Davies, C. S. L.: *Peace, Print and Protestantism, 1450-1558* (Hart-Davis Macgibbon, 1976)

The Dictionary of National Biography (63 vols., ed. L. Stephen and S. Lee, 1885-1938)

Erlanger, Philippe: *Margaret of Anjou, Queen of England* (Elek Books, 1970)

Fairbairn, Neil: *A Traveller's Guide to the Battlefields of Britain* (Evans Brothers, 1983)

Falkus, Gila: *The Life and Times of Edward IV* (Weidenfeld and Nicolson, 1981)

Fowler, Kenneth: *The Age of Plantagenet and Valois* (Ferndale, 1967)

Gillingham, John: *The Wars of the Roses* (Weidenfeld and Nicolson, 1981)

Goodman, Anthony: *A Traveller's Guide to Early Mediaeval Britain* (Routledge and Kegan Paul, 1986)

Goodman, Anthony: *The Wars of the Roses* (Routledge and Kegan Paul, 1981)

Gransden, Antonia: *Historical Writing in England, c. 1307 to the Early Sixteenth Century* (Routledge and Kegan Paul, 1982)

Green, V. H. H.: *The Later Plantagenets* (Edward Arnold, 1955)

Griffiths, Ralph A. *Duke Richard of York's Intentions in 1450 and the Origins of the Wars of the Roses (Journal of Mediaeval History,* 1, 1975)

Griffiths, Ralph A.: *Local Rivalries and National Politics: The Percies, the Nevilles and the Duke of Exeter (Speculum,* 43, 1968)

Griffiths, Ralph A. and Thomas, Roger S.: *The Making of the Tudor Dynasty* (Alan Sutton, 1985)

Griffiths, Ralph A.: *The Reign of King Henry VI* (Ernest Benn, 1981)

Griffiths, Ralph A.: *The Trial of Eleanor Cobham: An Episode in the Fall of Humphrey, Duke of Gloucester* (Bulletin of the John Rylands Library, 51, 1968-9)

Hallam, Elizabeth (ed.): *The Chronicles of the Wars of the Roses* (Weidenfeld and Nicolson, 1988)

The Handbook of British Chronology (ed. F. M. Powicke and E. B. Fryde, Royal Historical Society, 1961)

Harriss, G. L.: *Cardinal Beaufort: Patriot or Usurer? (Transactions of the Royal Historical Society,* 5th Series, 20, 1970)

Harriss, G. L.: *The Struggle for Calais: An Aspect of the Rivalry between Lancaster and York (English Historical Review,* 75, 1960)

Harvey, John: *The Plantagenets* (Batsford, 1948)

Hassall, W. O.: *They Saw it Happen, 55 B.C. to 1485* (Oxford, 1957)

Hassall, W. O.: *Who's Who in History, Vol. 1: 55 B.C. to 1485* (Oxford, 1960)

Haswell, Jock: *The Ardent Queen: Margaret of Anjou and the Lancastrian Heritage* (Peter Davies, 1976)

Hebden, William: *Yorkshire Battles* (Daleman Publishing Company, 1971)

Hibbert, Christopher: *Agincourt* (Batsford, 1964)

Hibbert, Christopher: *The Court at Windsor* (Longmans, 1964)

Hicks, Michael: *False, Fleeting, Perjur'd Clarence* (Alan Sutton, 1980)

Hicks, Michael: *Warwick, the Reluctant Kingmaker (Mediaeval History,* Vol. 1, No. 2, 1991)

Hicks, Michael: *Who's Who in Late Mediaeval England* (Shepheard-Walwyn, 1991)

Hookham, Mary Anne: *The Life and Times of Margaret of Anjou* (2 vols., London, 1872)

Jacob, E. F.: *The Fifteenth Century, 1399-1485* (Oxford, 1961, 1969)

Joelson, Annette: *Heirs to the Throne: The Story of the Princes of Wales* (Heinemann, 1966)

Johnson, P. and Leslie S. (eds.): *The Miracles of King Henry VI* (Cambridge, 1923)

Johnson, P. A.: *Richard, Duke of York* (Oxford, 1988)

Jones, Michael K. and Underwood, Malcolm G.: *The King's Mother: Lady Margaret Beaufort, Countess of Richmond and Derby* (Cambridge, 1992)

Kendall, Paul Murray: *Warwick the Kingmaker* (George Allen and Unwin, 1957)

Kendall, Paul Murray: *The Yorkist Age: Daily Life during the Wars of the Roses* (George Allen and Unwin, 1962)

Kightly, Charles: *The Dukes of York and their Duchesses* (York City Council, 1987)

Kingsford, C. L.: *The Earl of Warwick at Calais, 1460* (*English Historical Review*, 37, 1922)

Kinross, John: *The Battlefields of Britain* (David and Charles, 1979)

Kirby, J. L.: *Henry IV of England* (Constable, 1970)

Lander, J. R.: *Conflict and Stability in 15th Century England* (Hutchinson, 1969)

Lander, J. R.: *Crown and Nobility, 1450-1509* (Edward Arnold, 1976)

Lander, J. R.: *Government and Community: England, 1450-1509* (Edward Arnold, 1980)

Lander, J. R.: *Henry VI and the Duke of York's Second Protectorate* (Bulletin of the John Rylands Library, XLIII, 1960)

Lander, J. R.: *The Wars of the Roses* (Secker and Warburg, 1968)

Lane, Henry Murray: *The Royal Daughters of England* (2 vols., Constable, 1910)

Levron, Jacques: *Le Bon Roi René* (Paris, 1972)

Lofts, Norah: *Queens of Britain* (Hodder and Stoughton, 1977)

Longmate, Norman: *Defending the Island* (Hutchinson, 1989)

McFarlane, K. B.: *The Nobility of Later Mediaeval England* (Oxford, 1973)

McFarlane, K. B.: *Parliament and Bastard Feudalism* (*Transactions of the Royal Historical Society*, 4th Series, 26, 1944)

McFarlane, K. B.: *The Wars of the Roses* (*Proceedings of the British Academy*, 50, 1964)

McKisack, M.: *The Fourteenth Century, 1307-1399* (Oxford, 1959)

Mathew, Gervase: *The Court of Richard II* (John Murray, 1968)

Myers, A. R.: *The Outbreak of War between England and Burgundy in February 1471* (Bulletin of the Institute of Historical Research, 23, 1960)

Neillands, Robin: *The Wars of the Roses* (Cassell, 1992)

Palmer, Alan: *Princes of Wales* (Weidenfeld and Nicolson, 1979)

Pollard, A. J.: *The Wars of the Roses* (London, 1988)

Poole, Austin Lane: *Late Mediaeval England* (2 vols., Oxford, 1958)

Prévost, Abbé: *Histoire de Marguerite d'Anjou* (2 vols., Paris, 1750)

Rawcliffe, Caroline: *The Staffords, Earls of Stafford and Dukes of Buckingham, 1394-1521* (Cambridge, 1978)

Richmond, C.: *Fauconberg's Kentish Rising of May 1471* (*English Historical Review*, 85, 1970)

Richmond, C.: *The Nobility and the Wars of the Roses, 1459-1461* (*Nottingham Mediaeval Studies*, 21, 1977)

Robson-Scott, W. D.: *German Travellers in England, 1400-1800* (1953)

Ross, Charles: *Edward IV* (Eyre Methuen, 1974)

Ross, Charles: *The Estates and Finances of Richard, Duke of York* (*Welsh History Review*, 3, 1967)

Ross, Charles (ed.): *Patronage, Pedigree and Power in Later Mediaeval England* (Alan Sutton, 1979)

Ross, Charles: *The Wars of the Roses* (London, 1976)

Rowse, A. L.: *Bosworth Field and the Wars of the Roses* (Macmillan, 1966)

Rowse, A. L.: *The Tower of London in the History of the Nation* (Weidenfeld and Nicolson, 1972)

Royal Britain (The Automobile Association, 1976)

Saltmarsh, J.: *King Henry VI and the Royal Foundations* (Cambridge, 1972)

Scofield, Cora L.: *The Capture of Lord Rivers and Sir Anthony Woodville* (*English Historical Review*, 37, 1922)

Scofield, Cora L.: *The Life and Reign of Edward IV* (London, 1923; reprinted by Frank Cass and Co. 1967)

Seward, Desmond: *Henry V as Warlord* (Sidgewick and Jackson, 1987)

The Shell Guide to England (ed. John Hadfield, Shell Marketing, 1970)

Smurthwaite, David: *The Ordnance Survey Guide to the Battlefields of Britain* (Webb and Bower, 1984)

Softly, Barbara: *The Queens of England* (David and Charles, 1976)

Somerville, R.: *History of the Duchy of Lancaster, 1265-1603* (London, 1953)

Staley, Edgcumbe: *King René d'Anjou and his Seven Queens* (London, 1912)

Storey, R. L.: *The End of the House of Lancaster* (Barnes Rockliffe, 1966; reprinted Alan Sutton, 1986)

Storey, R. L.: *The Wardens of the Marches of England towards Scotland, 1377-1489* (*English Historical Review*, 72, 1957)

Strickland, Agnes: *Lives of the Queens of England, Vol. II* (London, 1885)

Tuck, A.: *Crown and Nobility, 1272-1462* (Oxford, 1985)

Vickers, K. H.: *Humphrey, Duke of Gloucester* (London, 1907)

Virgoe, R.: *The Death of William de la Pole, Duke of Suffolk* (Bulletin of the John Rylands Library, 47, 1965)

Williams, E. C.: *My Lord of Bedford, 1389-1435* (London, 1963)

Wolffe, B. P.: *Henry VI* (Eyre Methuen, 1981)

Index

York, archbishops of (see Tideman
of Winchcombe, John Kempe)
York, dukes of (see Edmund of
Langley, Edward of Aumale,
Richard, Henry)

York, Royal House of 18, 24, 28,
42, 49, 132, 138, 196–7, 276, 285,
297, 302, 345, 416, 420
Young, Thomas 162–3

© Koo Stark

About the Author

ALISON WEIR is the author of *Britain's Royal Families: The Complete Genealogy, The Six Wives of Henry VIII, The Princes in the Tower, The Children of Henry VIII, The Life of Elizabeth I,* and *Eleanor of Aquitaine.* She lives outside London with her husband and two children.